THE OTTOMAN ARMY, 1914–1918

Utah Series in Turkish and Islamic Studies
M. Hakan Yavuz, series editor

Debating Moderate Islam: The Geopolitics of Islam and the West
Edited by M. A. Muqtedar Khan

The Armenian Massacres in Ottoman Turkey: A Disputed Genocide
Guenter Lewy

The Armenian Rebellion at Van
Justin McCarthy, Esat Arslan, Cemalettin Taşkiran, and Ömer Turan

Autobiographies of Orhan Pamuk: The Writer in His Novels
Michael McGaha

The Ottoman Army, 1914–1918: Disease and Death on the Battlefield
Hikmet Özdemir
Translated by Saban Kardaş

The Emergence of a New Turkey: Democracy and the AK Parti
Edited by M. Hakan Yavuz

THE OTTOMAN ARMY
1914–1918

DISEASE & DEATH ON THE BATTLEFIELD

HİKMET ÖZDEMİR
TRANSLATED BY SABAN KARDAŞ

*Utah Series in Turkish
and Islamic Studies*

THE UNIVERSITY OF UTAH PRESS
Salt Lake City

© 2008 by The University of Utah Press. All rights reserved.

Utah Series in Turkish and Islamic Studies
M. Hakan Yavuz, series editor

Material in this book was originally published in Turkish in *Salgın Hastalıklardan Ölümler, 1914–1918*. Ankara: Türk tarih Kurumu, 2005.

 The Defiance House Man colophon is a registered trademark of the University of Utah Press. It is based upon a four-foot-tall, Ancient Puebloan pictograph (late PIII) near Glen Canyon, Utah.

12 11 10 09 08   1 2 3 4 5

LIBRARY OF CONGRESS CATALOGING-IN-PUBLICATION DATA

Özdemir, Hikmet, 1950–
  The Ottoman army, 1914–1918 : disease and death on the battlefield / Hikmet Özdemir.
      p. cm.
  Includes bibliographical references and index.
  ISBN 978-0-87480-923-7 (pbk. : alk. paper) 1. World War, 1914–1918—Health aspects—Turkey. 2. World War, 1914–1918—Medical care—Turkey. 3. Soldiers—Health and hygiene—Turkey—History—20th century. 4. Turkey. Ordu—Medical care—History. 5. Public health—Turkey—History—20th century. 6. Epidemics—Turkey—History. 7. Communicable diseases—Turkey—History. I. Title.
  D629.T9O928 2008
  940.4'7520956—dc22   2008000551

Printed and bound by Sheridan Books, Inc., Ann Arbor, Michigan.

Interior printed on recycled paper with 50% post-consumer content.

To Birsen and Manas

Table of Contents

List of Figures and Tables viii

List of Abbreviations xi

Pronunciation Guide xii

Acknowledgments xiii

1. Introduction 1
2. Between Two Fires 10
3. Under the Crescent 28
4. Epidemic Disaster 50
5. Ordeal with Diseases 68
6. Unburied Corpses 106
7. Unexpected Results 134
8. Unarmed Warriors 165
9. Epilogue 186

Appendix 1 205

Appendix 2 217

Notes 233

Bibliography 257

Index 267

Figures and Tables

FIGURES

3.1 Major Railways in the Ottoman Empire During World War I   29

TABLES

1.1. Casualties occurring in some wars before 1914   5
2.1. Casualties in the Crimean War (1854–1856)   13
2.2. Cholera epidemic 1910–1913   19
2.3. Çatalca Army Medical Inspectorate's hospital records   21
3.1. Casualties of the Fifth Expeditionary Force that occurred during its journey to the front (1915)   37
4.1. Casualties of Sarıkamış disaster   52
4.2. Red Cross hospital admissions records   55
4.3. Death causes of the Ottoman medical officers (1914–1918)   57
4.4. The months of deaths of the Ottoman medical officers   58
5.1. Number of sick in a British brigade   72
5.2. The numbers of ill and wounded treated in hospitals in Akbaş and Akdere   74
5.3. Deaths from dysentery in the 3rd Army   80
5.4. Deaths from tetanus in the 3rd Army   81
5.5. Deaths from erysipelas in the 3rd Army   81
5.6. Laboratories in the army stations in Mosul, Kirkuk, Shikrat, and Nusaybin (1917–1918)   90

FIGURES AND TABLES   ix

5.7. Deaths from influenza in some countries   93

5.8. Deaths as found in the records of İzmir municipality   95

5.9. Data relevant to various diseases encountered in Aydın Province (March 1919)   97

5.10. The epidemics and deaths in Turkey   103

6.1. French, German, Belgian and American death ratios   107

6.2. Total war casualties according to Cruttwell   108

6.3. Total war casualties according to Colonel Butler   111

6.4. Austro-Hungarian casualties (1914–1918)   112

6.5. French casualties (1914–1918)   112

6.6. British army hospital admissions (in November 1916)   116

6.7. Casualties suffered up to October 1917   116

6.8. German casualties according to Colonel Butler (1914–1918)   117

6.9. US Army fatalities   118

6.10. Bulgarian casualties (1914–1918)   118

6.11. Casualties of Ottoman Empire according to a British source   119

6.12. Total casualties of the Ottoman armies (1914–1918)   121

6.13. Deaths in the nine Ottoman armies   121

6.14. Distribution of deaths by various diseases   123

6.15. Ottoman military casualties according to hospital records (1914–1918)   124

6.16. Deaths in hospitals among the 1st Army units (1914–1918)   126

6.17. Deaths in hospitals among the 2nd Army units (1914–1918)   126

6.18. Deaths in hospitals among the 3rd Army units (1914–1918)   126

6.19. Deaths in hospitals among the 4th Army units (1914–1918)   127

6.20. Deaths in hospitals among the 5th Army units (1914–1918)   127

6.21. Deaths in hospitals among the 6th Army units (1914–1918)   127

6.22. Deaths in hospitals among the 7th Army units (1914–1918)   128

6.23. Deaths in hospitals (1914–1918)   129

6.24. The ill and wounded in the 3rd Army (1915–1918)   132

6.25. Admissions to hospitals from the 3rd Army   132

7.1. Deaths that occurred in the Ba'Quba Refugee Camp (September 1918–October 1919)   140

7.2. Infectious diseases and deaths recorded in Pozanti hospitals (August 1917–July 1918)   148

7.3. Deaths in the 6th Army attributed to recurrent fever   153

7.4. Deaths in Baghdad and Mosul attributed to typhoid   153

8.1. The medical officers shown according to their ranks   178

8.2. Medical officers who died from disease   180

ABBREVIATIONS

ATASE	Turkish Military Archive
AÜ	Ankara University
AÜDTCF	Faculty of Letters, Ankara University
AÜSBF	Faculty of Political Sciences, Ankara University
AÜTF	Faculty of Medicine in Ankara University
BAO	Archives of Turkish Prime Ministry (Ottoman Section)
BCA	Archives of Turkish Prime Ministry (Republican Section)
Ed.	Editor
FO	Foreign Office (UK)
GATA	Academy of Military Medicine of Gülhane
İÜ	İstanbul University
İÜCTF	Medical Faculty of Cerrahpaşa, İstanbul University
İÜTF	Medical Faculty of İstanbul University
LON	League of Nations Archive in Geneva
MB	Bulletin of Microbiology in Ankara University
ODTÜ	Middle East Technical University in Ankara
Prep.	Preparer
PTT	Turkish Post Office Administration
Pub.	Publishing House
SBE	Institute of Health Sciences
SBF	Faculty of Political Sciences
TAE	Institute of Turkology Studies
TBMM	Grand National Assembly of Turkey
TİTE	Institute of Turkish Revolution History
Trans.	Translator
TTE	Institute of Medical History
TTK	Turkish History Council
TÜBİTAK	The Scientific and Research Council of Turkey
UK	United Kingdom

PRONUNCIATION OF TURKISH NAMES

The Latin Turkish alphabet, introduced by Atatürk in 1928, is an extremely clear and consistent one.

Most of the letters sound very similar to their English equivalents, with the following exceptions:

c	j as in *join*.
ç	ch as in *church*.
b, d	as in English, but at the end of a syllable they are frequently pronounced and often written p, t (e.g., Recep/Receb, Ahmet/Ahmed). Both are correct.
ğ	soft g, lengthens the preceding vowel.
h	h is always pronounced, including at the end of syllables (e.g., Falih)
ı	somewhat like u in *stadium*.
j	stands for the English sound in *pleasure*.
ö	like French word *deux* or the German ü.
ş	sh as in *shout*.
ü	like French *lumiere*.
v	lighter than English v.

The stress on a Turkish word usually comes on the last syllable, and this is always the case with the names of people: *Kemal, Tevfik, Hasan*.

However, place names regularly have the stress on the first syllable: *Ankara, Erzurum, Elazığ*.

ACKNOWLEDGMENTS

THE FOLLOWING PEOPLE AND ORGANIZATIONS have generously contributed to the completion of the study. Hence, I would kindly like to thank each one for their invaluable help, hospitality, and encouragement. I present my special thanks to İlker Başbuğ, Aslan Güner, and Nusret Taşdeler from the Headquarters of the Turkish Armed Forces; to Ertuğrul Apakan and Ecvet Tezcan from the Turkish Ministry of Foreign Affairs; and to Baki Komsuoğlu from Kocaeli University. In addition, I am particularly grateful to Yusuf Sarınay, the general director of the State Archives of the Turkish Republic; to Neşecan Uysal, the chief librarian of the Turkish History Council; to Ahmet Tetik from the Turkish Military Archive; and to M. Rıfat Hisarcıklıoğlu, the president of the Union of Chambers and Commodity Exchanges of Turkey (TOBB). I am also very thankful to the National Archives of the United Kingdom, Lidell Hart Center for Military Archives, the Wellcome Library, and to Mehmet Ali Dikerdem in London; and to Blandine Blukacz-Louisfert and Bernhardine Pejovic from the United Nations Archives in Geneva.

None of these people, of course, bears any responsibility for my views as expressed in this volume. I accept full and exclusive responsibility for all opinions expressed throughout the work.

Finally, I cannot neglect mentioning the great patience of my wife, Birsen, and my dearest daughter, Manas, as I spent so many hours among books and files and before computer screens. Their encouragement has been invaluable.

HÖ
Ankara, January 2008

1

INTRODUCTION

> The word history carries two meanings in common parlance. It refers both to what actually happened in the past and to the representation of that past in the work of historians.
>
> —John Tosh,
> *The Pursuit of History*

WHAT KIND OF A RELATIONSHIP can be said to exist between wars and epidemics? It is widely held that epidemics have affected the outcomes of many wars, and that a significant relationship between the spread of infectious diseases and the fall of empires existed in the Old World. Because diseases are among the primary causes of death, they are considered to be one of the decisive factors shaping the course of history. Until World War II, more victims of war died of war-borne microbes than of battle wounds.[1] As a corollary, other scholars also emphasize that not only goods, ideas, and technology, but also "microorganisms causing various diseases" were in constant circulation between different communities in the Old World. The intensification of interactions across different parts of the Old World resulted in the spread of various types of diseases, which were previously confined to one or another part of Eurasia or Africa, to new regions, causing very heavy mortality among previously unexposed societies. Historical records from China and Rome, for instance, make it clear that these societies suffered from a series of plagues in the first and second centuries A.D. Many parts of the Roman Empire, indeed, began to experience depopulation, and the lack of manpower became a chronic problem for the Roman authorities from 200 A.D. on, if not before. One could, therefore, reasonably suggest that epidemic diseases resulting from increasing contacts between Eurasia and Africa played a major role in the collapse of the Roman and Han empires, along with several other factors, such as internal social tensions and barbarian attacks from without.[2]

The epidemics of infectious diseases, besides their effect on the structure of military organization, also affected the architecture of cities and castles. In the Roman Empire, the duties of the medical companies within the army included not only the treatment of wounded soldiers, but also, and more importantly, the prevention of the emergence and spread of infectious diseases. The Roman commanders were concerned more with controlling epidemics than with fighting against attacking enemy forces. Therefore, "the hospital (*valetudinarian*)" was considered an integral part of Roman castle architecture.[3] These facts led M. W. Flinn of Edinburgh University to argue that had the cross-border plague epidemics affecting several nations between the fourteenth and nineteenth centuries not occurred, European history would have taken a very different course. During this period, the plague became extremely contagious, and in some cases the fatality rate increased from 60 to 100 percent.[4]

The Peloponnesian War is the notorious example of how epidemics resulting from infectious diseases had an impact on the outcomes of major wars in ancient Greece. A terrible plague breaking out toward the end of the twenty-seven-year war between Athens and Sparta decisively determined the outcome of the war; by ravaging Athens it paved the way for the defeat of the Athenians. Even Pericles, the preeminent Athenian statesman, died of that plague.[5]

In Asia Minor, one of the most important consequences of the epidemics that took place during the Seljuk dynasty in Anatolia was the population loss caused by mass deaths. The plague epidemics no doubt dealt a serious blow to economic and commercial activities, increasing the prices of various commodities and services, hence stimulating inflation. Although the written records provide no direct relationship, it is estimated that the same epidemics account for some of the migration and mass resettlement programs, which led to social unrest and disorder. The epidemics, moreover, severely limited the maneuvering capabilities of military forces operating in the regions affected. The epidemics, ravaging both soldiers and animals, prevented countries from attaining the desired results of military campaigns, hence depriving the societies of potentially beneficial social consequences and political advantages of a military victory. In some cases, on the contrary, starvation and epidemics breaking out in the besieged cities aided the eventual capture of those cities by the enemy. In that sense, depending on the circumstances, plague epidemics acted as either facilitating or inhibiting factors for military campaigns.[6]

The fatality rates due to infectious diseases are beyond any comparison with those of other causes of death. In 1875, an average of 266.5 per 10,000 people died in Prussia; of those, an average of 26.8 people, or approximately

10 percent, died of old age. The remaining 90 percent died prematurely, one-third of whom lost their lives due to infectious diseases. In Prussia in 1912, the number of deaths per 10,000 inhabitants was 154.9, and the ratio of deaths from infectious diseases remained the same. According to other statistics, the number of inhabitants in Prussia in 1900 who died as a result of epidemics was 162,224. Of those, a total of 70,602 deaths—nearly 44 percent—were caused by tuberculosis. Another statistic regarding children shows that in 1900, an average of 471.5 out of every 10,000 children under one year of age died from infectious diseases. In other words, one in 21 children died of epidemics.[7]

According to a popular study published in 1991, throughout most of "civilized" history, peasants have been biological fodder for the great microbial communities that cities grew and nurtured. Until the 1600s, most of the world's great metropolises renewed their wealth by swallowing the sons and daughters of soil tillers. Whenever the peasants multiplied too quickly, city-states usually disposed of the surplus by declaring a war on a neighbor, or through famine or disease triggered by overpopulation. The outcome of war mostly depended on which side developed the strongest disease resistance response. The Arabs, for instance, defeated the Crusaders with malaria, while the Russians repelled Napoleon's armies with typhoid. One of the reasons why the Union Army won the American Civil War was because it outnumbered the Confederate Army in the wake of a diarrhea epidemic. Similarly, nomads, hunters, and New World aborigines lost their battles against expansionist European powers largely because of their lower levels of exposure to the germs transmitted by the European invaders. It therefore has been suggested that until this century, all wars had been fought with germs and won by farm and city people with the stronger resistance mechanisms against infection.[8]

The four-year-long Civil War cost the United States 200,000 lives out of a national population of around 32 million, according to the 1860 census. When an additional 400,000 who died in the same period as a result of diseases or other causes related to the war are added, the human toll of the Civil War amounts to around 600,000 people.[9] In another illustrative example, during the Balkan War of 1913 the Bulgarian army was forced to retreat due to the outbreak of a severe cholera epidemic. The retreating Bulgarians threw the dead bodies into the streams and wells to contaminate the drinking water, causing the Greek soldiers drinking the water to catch the same disease.[10]

Andrew Nikiforuk believes that the medical reformist Rudolf Virchow conclusively answered the question of how humans become infected. Based on his in-depth research into microorganisms, Virchow, a Prussian bacteriologist, provided a succinct definition of illness: "a life under altered conditions." By "altered conditions," he meant changes in nutritional habits, commercial activities, travel, lifestyle, clothing, weather conditions—in short, the whole environment. Virchow maintained that when living conditions are significantly altered, the relationship between human beings and microorganisms takes an unpredictable turn, in most cases leading to fatal consequences. Virchow, widely regarded as the father of modern epidemiology, first expressed these ideas based on his investigations into the typhus epidemic that swept through the poor cotton workers in Upper Silesia (a part of today's Czech Republic and Germany) in 1848. In the long report he prepared following his visit to the region, Virchow argued that severe rains, adverse living conditions, and poverty, rather than the microorganisms themselves, were the main cause of the epidemic.[11]

In another influential study, J. N. Biraben compiled a wealth of data showing how the movement of troops carried the plague across Europe during the fourteenth through seventeenth centuries.[12] Daniel Panzac presents additional data documenting the spread of plague, which further substantiate the same claim in the case of the Ottoman Empire in the eighteenth century and the beginning of the nineteenth century.[13] P. Mühlens, a German hygiene expert, in his discussion about how the health conditions of the civilian population and the army affect the outcomes of wars, reached an important conclusion: "The wars fought in the territories of the Ottoman Empire have demonstrated that maintaining hygienic standards during the war, especially in the regions with hot climate conditions, constitutes an important part of strategic war planning."[14] Cold regions, on the other hand, have their unique military conditions, which are unlike those of warmer regions. An example of the influence of colder climatic conditions can be found in earlier Turkish history. Since the earliest times of Turkish settlement in Central Asia, large-scale death of humans and animals was recorded during periods of *yutmak* (swallowing up) caused by severe winter conditions.[15]

Another way through which war amplifies the adverse effects of climatic and hygienic conditions is the need to allocate the means of transportation for military purposes, i.e., carrying soldiers and munitions. According to a British report dated 1 February 1878, many Muslim refugees traveling along the railways in an attempt to reach areas protected by the Ottoman soldiers froze to death while they were waiting at the train stations in Philippopolis and Çorlu.[16]

The frequency, prevalence, and severity of epidemics vary also according

TABLE 1.1. Casualties occurring in some wars before 1914*

ARMY	YEARS	NUMBER OF SOLDIERS	COMBAT DEATHS	DISEASE-RELATED DEATHS
Crimean War (French)	1854–56	301,000	20,000	75,000
French-Prussian War (Prussian)	1870–71	800,000	28,300	14,904
Russian-Japanese War (Japanese)	1904–05	420,000	58,887	27,158
Russian-Japanese War (Russian)	1904–05	490,000	47,608	27,830

*From *Manual of Elementary Military Hygiene*, 1912, in Butler, *Australian Army Medical Services*, 866.

to seasonal changes. Winters are marked by increases in deaths, as well as by the occurrence of certain diseases. For instance, influenza epidemics are observed during the winter and the highest numbers of patients are recorded in the winter.[17]

Typhoid epidemics of various scales ravaged armies in literally every war in history, which led many to consider it the disease of warfare conditions. During the World War I, for instance, all the armies fighting on the European front suffered greatly from typhoid epidemics. While the number of persons affected by the illness was very high in the Austrian, French, and German armies, that of the U.S. Army remained remarkably low because of the successful implementation of hygiene measures and regular vaccinations.[18] One needs to note a progressive trend, though: until 1914, the scourge of diseases on armies, hitherto the major cause of death, had been reduced significantly by the British and French armies. In the case of the British Army, the Boer War (1899–1902) was the last war in which the number of disease-related deaths exceeded that of combat related fatalities. The British Army initiated several programs to improve health conditions following the Boer War, which brought down the British Army's casualty rates to tolerable levels during World War I. As a result, the health conditions were better in the military barracks than in the urban areas. Moreover, the recruits had nutrition superior to the civilian population because they were supplied with high-quality agricultural food products. The regular physical exercises undertaken as part of military training further improved the health conditions of soldiers. The figures about fatalities suffered during World War I also demonstrate a steady decline in infant mortality and a rise in civilian life expectancy as compared to the previous century. By September 1915 the British army had one million casualties, one-third of which were considered fatal, in the battles for the Marne, Aisne, Picardy, and Champagne fronts. In the battle of Verdun (1916), the army's casualties skyrocketed: the number of dead, wounded, and missing soldiers approached five hundred thousand (the conventional death-to-wounded ratio is one to three). In the same war, the German casualties were more than four hundred thousand. On the first day of the battle of the Somme on 1 July 1916, almost twenty thousand British soldiers were killed, a number which equals the total number of combat- and disease-related casualties it had suffered in the entire Boer War.[19]

The improvements in fighting diseases did not eliminate completely the effect of epidemics on armies during World War I, though. Illustrative examples are the Balkan and Caucasus fronts. Just at the beginning of World War I, a severe typhus epidemic broke out in Serbia, claiming 100,000 lives between January and April 1915. One-fifth of the Serbian population caught the disease, and nearly a third of the doctors fighting against the epidemic fell victim to it.[20]

Soldiers captured from the enemy ranks also played an important role in spreading diseases, hence affecting the fate of war. The drastic typhus epidemic that broke out in Serbia in 1915 was in fact sparked by the arrival of the Austrian war prisoners; it later spread to Bulgaria and Romania through Serbian war prisoners captured by those countries.[21] Another major typhus epidemic recorded during the Great War affected the Russian soldiers kept in German war prisoner camps.[22] During the Turkish Liberation War, it also was observed that moving around war prisoners between different "garrisons and battalions" caused the spread of epidemics.[23]

As one war quickly followed another and armies had to fight successive enemies, a sort of chain reaction developed through which diseases spread. In the case of the Ottoman Army, Major General Dr. Ekrem Şadi identified a path by which infectious diseases were transferred from the Balkan Wars to World War I. He maintains that the soldiers discharged from the army in the aftermath of the Balkan Wars acted as carriers of infectious and parasitic diseases, causing epidemics throughout Anatolia. When the First World War started shortly thereafter, the same diseases afflicted the Ottoman armies severely, particularly the 3rd Army fighting on the Caucasus front. According to the same source, the effects of those infectious diseases causing epidemics continued to be felt throughout the Turkish National Liberation War.[24]

A severe typhus epidemic, similarly, erupted during the Russian civil war in the wake of the First World War. At the beginning of 1920, some 50,000 soldiers of the White Army died of typhus, whereas 573,000 cases of typhus were reported by the Red Army between 1918 and 1923. During the period between 1918 and 1922, the population of St. Petersburg decreased from 2 million to 700,000. Of the factors behind this drastic fall, the typhus epidemic had the largest share. Between 1918 and 1922, some 25 to 30 million cases of typhus were recorded in Russia alone. In other words, 20 to 25 percent of the total population was affected by the disease. In his address to the Seventh Soviet Congress, Lenin put it bluntly:

> We hear the cracking of a whip on us; lice and typhus are spreading through our armies. The terrible conditions existing in the regions afflicted by typhus, where people are dying in masses, where no livestock are available, and where the life has literally stopped are beyond imagination.[25]

The German influence was growing in the Sublime Porte as a result of the Ottoman-German Treaty of Alliance signed on August 2, 1914. The Ottoman Empire's decision to enter the war on the side of the Central Powers a few weeks later was taken in desperation by a small group of energetic and ambitious men. The war, however, turned out to be disastrous for Turkey as she was handicapped by her poverty, technical backwardness, and extremely inadequate communications and supply lines.[26] Exact figures are not available on the Ottoman military casualties in the war, which stems from several factors. Most importantly, much of the widespread deaths from diseases took place in regions, or at times, where and when nobody was available or in a position to count the human toll. In other cases, nobody cared to count the death toll at a time when the country was overwhelmed by the contingencies of the war.

In 1982, Sarkis Karayan published an article disputing the figures on Ottoman casualties in World War I, provided by Turkish historians and other experts on Ottoman history, such as Professor Stanford Shaw and Norman Itzkowitz. According to Karayan, in order to justify the massacre of some two million Armenians during 1915–1918, Turkish authorities and historians have repeatedly insisted over the last sixty-seven years (as of 1982) that if a few thousand Armenians died due to deportations from strategic military zones in Turkey, the number of Turks who lost their lives due to "Armenian atrocities" during the same period was between 1.5 and 3 million.[27]

Sarkis Karayan continued his argument as follows:

> The actual and direct cause of the terrible Turkish loss of life from illness, among soldiers and civilians alike, was the Union and Progress Party, the İttihad, under the autocratic rule of the Talat-Cemal-Enver triumvirate. There is general agreement among both Turkish and other historians that Turkey's entry into World War I was a disaster for Turkey, a desperate gamble taken by a small group of ambitious men.

He went on to say that

> Turkey was not ready to wage a large-scale war after her 1911 defeats in Tripoli Tania [now Libya], in Africa, and in the Balkan Wars of 1912 and 1913. The miserable state of the Ottoman army is well known to surviving Armenians who were in Turkey before and during the war.[28]

Eric Jan Zürcher's subsequent studies on the issue concluded that following the outbreak of war in 1914, the Army and Navy Headquarters of the Ottoman Empire mobilized at a very slow pace (even slower than the Russians). The fact that mobilization took place under winter conditions further augmented problems, rendering the whole process of mobilization more burdensome, especially in eastern Anatolia. The terrain and severe winter weather made warfare practically impossible, posing obstacles to the military campaigns on the Caucasian front. In fact, if Enver Pasha had not squandered the lives of 72,000 (out of 90,000) by ordering a premature attack over the mountain passes at Sarıkamış, the Ottoman army would have been at full war strength in men, weapons, and equipment by spring. As noted by Zürcher,

> the call to arms was answered relatively well, in Anatolia if not in the Arab provinces, but as in the Balkan War, the conditions in the army (payment with worthless paper money, undernourishment, lack of medical care, epidemics of typhus, cholera and dysentery, bad or non-existent clothing and shoes) were so bad, that desertions soon started to become a problem of enormous proportions. By the end of the war the number of deserters was four times that of soldiers on the front.[29]

The tragic human consequences of the war on the Ottoman Empire are not the main focus of this current study. The question this study attempts to answer is this: how many Ottoman soldiers were lost during the First World War, and by what causes?

When I commenced this study to explore these questions one very hot day in the summer of 2004 in Ankara, I didn't move into a realm of scientific inquiry already populated by established theories. I approached my research with an open mind to capture various perspectives on the issue. Although significant limitations exist on accessing relevant material, a wealth of information was available in the state archives as well as national and international libraries. I endeavored to gather a wide variety of data from as many sources as possible, most of which are surely biased in one way or another. The conclusions of my study establish unequivocally that during World War I the number of soldiers dying from infectious diseases in the Ottoman Army was far greater than that of combat-related fatalities. My findings, moreover, show that the outbreak of epidemic diseases in the Ottoman battles during World War I resulted in great losses of life not only in the Ottoman military but also among the civilian population in the region. Although further research is needed to validate these conclusions, the preliminary findings of the current study provide a very solid picture of the reasons behind the casualties suffered by the Ottoman Army during the war.

As an academic specializing in the history of Modern Turkey, I would like to end this chapter with a citation from a great historian, Professor Stanford Shaw (who passed away on 15 December 2006), which I regard as his last will and testament:

> Only when all the sources which have survived from all parties involved in the Ottoman Empire during World War I are fully available to all historians wishing to use them with an open mind and without preconceptions will we really secure as full a picture as is humanly possible of events and conditions that went on in Ottoman Empire during World War I.[30]

2

BETWEEN TWO FIRES

> During these early days of January 1878, the mortality in Erzurum was something appalling. Out of a total number of about seventeen thousand troops in the town, there were on one day no fewer than three hundred and two deaths, and the daily death rate frequently rose two hundred! The weak, emaciated survivors had hardly strength left to dig graves for their dead comrades in the hard and frozen ground. At last they gave up even the pretence of digging, and the bodies were simply carted out about a mile from the main thoroughfares of the town, and left in the snow just inside the city walls.
>
> —Charles S. Ryan,
> *Under the Red Crescent*

IT IS SUGGESTED THAT EPIDEMICS in the Ottoman Empire followed a predictable pattern as they occurred in the wake of uprisings, banditries, migrations, famines, earthquakes, fires, and floods.[1] This theory can be accepted provided that the crucial relationship between wars and the outbreak of epidemics in the Ottoman imperial domain is also recognized. This phenomenon might apply to the Ottoman Empire as it would to other countries. Another study, however, puts the emphasis on a different factor which plays a more decisive role in the occurrence of epidemics than those mentioned above. According to this study, a more accurate explanation would need to consider the territories of the Ottoman Empire as areas constantly vulnerable to epidemics. The author of this interesting thesis, French historian Daniel Panzac, in his study entitled *La peste dans l'Empire Ottoman* (*Plague in the Ottoman Empire*), demonstrates that the vast area extending between the Atlantic Ocean and the Persian Gulf shared substantial commonalities in terms of health (or, to put it better, unhealthiness) in the modern age. The same kinds of diseases affected different people living in various parts of that area, from the North Sea to the Sahara in Africa, and from Bretagne in France to Iraq. Starting from the end of the seventeenth century, however, the common destiny of these peoples slowly came to an end, to a certain extent due to different trajectories of plague in these regions. Whereas the plague disappeared from most parts of western, northern, and central Europe after 1718, it remained a threat to the societies in the Balkans, Anatolia, and the Arabian Middle East until the mid-nineteenth century.[2]

The plague even had a weakening impact on relations between the Ottoman Empire and the European powers. Disappearance of the plague from European countries complicated the nature of European-Ottoman diplomatic and commercial relations, as well as military conflicts. This situation produced a *sui generis* relationship between the two sides, giving way to new forms of cultural and scientific attitudes and exchanges affecting both parties.[3]

William Witmann, an English medical doctor, recorded in his memoirs his observations of the hygienic conditions and epidemics in the Ottoman Empire at the beginning of the nineteenth century (covering the period between 2 July 1800 and 7 March 1802). Dr. Witmann reports that about eighteen months before his visit to Çanakkale and its environs in November 1799, a plague epidemic had broken out in the region, claiming thirty to forty lives each day. Smallpox was one of several diseases Witmann documented. In another record, he estimates that in November and December 1800, between sixty and one hundred deaths occurred daily in the Ottoman garrison of Jaffa due to dysentery, tropical malaria, and plague. His notes dated 19 March 1801 are particularly illustrative of the extent of epidemic-related deaths in the Ottoman army. According to these notes, the Ottoman base in El-Arish lost half of its men due to a plague ravaging the city since 7 March. A few weeks before, fatalities from the plague amounted to six thousand.[4]

Severe epidemics affecting the soldiers transferred from Anatolia to Istanbul during the Ottoman-Russian War of 1828, causing numerous deaths, are also widely documented. An English medical doctor by the name of McFerline, who was working in Istanbul at the time, identified the disease as marsh fever (*L. grippotyphosa*).[5] Dr. Osman Şevki believed that the disease known as marsh fever was possibly the spotted fever (typhus). He also noted that marsh fever and other infectious diseases, which were widespread among the Russian soldiers, were transmitted to the Ottoman Army.[6]

THE CRIMEAN WAR

Although the estimates differ, it is not disputed that disease was a significant factor in casualties among Ottoman troops in the Crimean War. An article published in 1919 by Dr. Osman Şevki discusses the medical conditions within the Ottoman Army during that war. The article provides valuable information about the breadth of the typhus epidemic, stating that 70 percent of those infected lost their lives. According to Dr. Şevki, although numerically it was possible to fight the enemy, the army fell victim to the disease.[7] Carl Rousso, on the other hand, states that the total casualties in the Ottoman Army due to spotted fever were thirty-five thousand. Kemal Özbay reasons that a casualty figure of around eighty-five thousand is likely for the Ottoman Army, given that it did not have better sanitary conditions than its allies.[8] Ekrem Kadri Unat, however, estimates the Ottoman casualties in the Crimean War at around thirty-five thousand.[9]

It would be legitimate to say that the next stage of the Crimean War was fought in the hospitals located in Istanbul and its environs. While the number of combat deaths by 31 December 1857 was 1,200, the deaths that occurred in hospitals reached 90,000. During the Crimean War, the armies in the battlefields looked like mobile hospitals. Several times a week, large groups of soldiers, consisting of thousands of men, were transferred in boats to Istanbul to be treated in the hospitals of Kasımpaşa, Deniz (Navy), Selimiye, and Haydarpaşa, or on board the battleships anchored in the Golden Horn.[10]

It is illustrative to note that chief commanders of the British and French armies, too, died from epidemics during the Crimean War. French Commander St. Arnaud and British Commander Lord Raglan were also among those who died from disease. St. Arnaud contracted cholera when he was in Sevastopol, and died on the ship transferring him to France. Lord Raglan also died from cholera on 28 June 1855.[11] As for the soldiers, they literally perished. Despite their numerical superiority over the Russians, the allied forces suffered the first blow from the epidemics, rather than from the Russian Army. Thousands of officers and soldiers found themselves struggling against infectious diseases instead of fighting the Russians.

The Crimea came to resemble a headquarters for patients rather than a battlefield. The Selimiye Barracks, Haydarpaşa Hospital, Kavak Summer Pavilion in Selimiye, the Cavalry Barracks in Çengelköy, the British St. George Hospital, and two battleships anchored in the Golden Horn were full of patients arriving from the Crimea. The French casualties caused by typhus during the Crimean War were 90,000.[12] In the French army, the number of deaths from spotted fever was 734 in December 1854, then 1,524 in January 1855, and 3,400 in February 1855. Seventy percent of those infected by the disease lost their lives. Spotted fever took its toll among the medical doctors as well. In the French Army alone, 58 doctors died of the

TABLE 2.1. Casualties in the Crimean War (1854–1856)*

ARMIES	BRITISH	FRENCH	OTTOMAN	RUSSIAN	TOTAL
Deaths	98,100	309,400	165,000	888,000	1,460,500
CASUALTIES DUE TO OTHER REASONS					
Combat Losses	2,755	8,490	10,100	30,600	51,945
Wounded	1,847	11,750	10,800	42,000	66,397
From Disease	17,580	75,375	24,500	374,000	491,455
TOTAL (OTHER REASONS)	22,182	95,615	45,400	446,000	609,797

*From the German source titled Sanitatsbericht, in Butler, *Australian Army Medical Services*, 866.

disease within a few months.[13] In that war, the casualty rate for the British and French armies was around 30 percent, and disease-related deaths accounted for 70 percent of the total losses. The diseases causing those deaths were mainly spotted fever, typhoid, and cholera. A French doctor, who was the first to diagnose spotted fever among the patients arriving from Crimea, also differentiated spotted fever (typhus) from its rival typhoid.[14]

Because the number of deaths due to infectious diseases such as typhus, cholera, fever, and scurvy were ten times greater than the combat deaths, the French hospitals in Crimea were overwhelmed. As a result, the French had to transfer their patients to hospitals in Varna, Gallipoli, Çanakkale, and Edirne, in addition to the thirteen hospitals in Istanbul used by the allied forces.[15] The miseries of the British and French soldiers during the Crimean War aroused deep concern among European public opinion, which led to several fund-raising campaigns. Florence Nightingale utilized some of these funds to set up a medical care service in the Crimea. In 1854 she assumed the care of patients in the Selimiye Barracks, where sixty patients were dying every day. She brought hygiene and order to the wards, significantly improving the medical conditions. However, she also caught typhus in spite of her efforts in preventive care.[16]

A major cholera epidemic, which broke out in Varna on 28 June 1854 during the course of the Crimean War, killed many English and French soldiers. This epidemic is believed to have been ignited by the corpses of Russian soldiers and dead animals left behind by the retreating Russian Army. The same cholera epidemic continued severely through August 1854.[17]

Coincidently, it also is believed that the spread of syphilis throughout Turkey was facilitated by the movement of Ottoman and foreign soldiers during and after the Crimean War of 1854.[18]

OTTOMAN-RUSSIAN WAR OF 1877–1878

The epidemics caused by the movements of immigrants during the Ottoman-Russian War of 1877–1878 resulted in colossal losses of life. The exact number of soldiers and emigrants who died after their arrival in Istanbul is unknown. During that war, the hospitals in Erzurum were overcrowded, and all doctors, whether Ottoman or contracted foreigner, without exception caught infectious diseases. Half of all the doctors serving in the city, including Colonel Yusuf Ziya, the chief medical officer of the army, died. Of the military contingent defending the city, around three hundred sick soldiers per day lost their lives due to the disease. The extreme poverty of the local people, in addition, exacerbated the severity of the epidemic even further.[19]

In 1877, on another front during the Ottoman-Russian War, the Ottoman Army fighting in Plevna converted some houses into temporary hospitals, where wounded soldiers were taken for treatment. According to Osman Şevki, "dysentery swept through the population, perishing almost a hundred soldiers a day." The Grand Mosque of Plevna was also turned into a hospital, flying a Red Crescent flag on its minaret. The patients inside were struggling to keep themselves warm by burning the wooden parts of the mosque, such as the *mahfel* (screened and elevated loge in a mosque), the *mihrap* (niche in the wall indicating the direction of Mecca), and the *minber* (pulpit beside the mihrap).[20]

During the Ottoman-Russian War, the Muslim inhabitants of territories occupied by the Russian Army fled in masses to Anatolia and particularly Istanbul to seek refuge under the protection of the Ottoman Army. On their way to Anatolia, however, they not only were infected by severe diseases, but also contributed to further epidemics by transmitting the diseases en route. In 1878, the public health in Istanbul deteriorated as the diseases brought by the emigrants sparked epidemics, further augmenting the deaths among Istanbul residents.[21] To address the problem, 60,000 of the refugees were transferred to other provinces by early April 1878, of whom 18,000 died. Approximately 300 to 500 people were dying each day in Istanbul due to continual epidemics of typhoid, typhus, and pneumonia.[22] The accommodation of more than 100,000 refugees in large buildings, mainly mosques, stimulated unrest. Moreover, the sick people among the refugees, as well as the decaying corpses, acted as agents in transmitting new epidemics. With the advent of spring and warmer weather, the typhus spread further; as a result, within only a few days 22,000 patients flooded the hospitals. Especially the places like mosques became centers of epidemics such as typhus. Only in May 1878 could the disease be contained somewhat, and the weekly number of deaths due to typhus was reduced to 400.[23]

The number of immigrants who died of infectious diseases during the Ottoman-Russian War exceeds that of those killed by the Russians or the Bulgarians. Typhus, typhoid, and in some cases smallpox surfaced wherever the refugees were concentrated. Of the 45,000 refugees living in Edirne, 16,000 caught typhus, which resulted in 100 to 120 deaths a day. The hundreds of thousands of people arriving in Istanbul had to go through unimaginable misery and pain. Foreign doctors, who examined the situation upon the invitation of the Sublime Porte, reported that a total of 180,000 refugees arrived in Istanbul as of April 1878. Of those emigrants, 60,000 were transferred to other cities, and 18,000 died of several diseases. On the Anatolian side of Istanbul alone, 21 deaths were recorded daily. Of the 4,000 immigrants who were sheltered in the Saint Sophia Mosque, 25 to 30 died daily.[24]

A major problem encountered during the 1878 epidemic in Istanbul was the haphazard burial of the corpses. As an initial precaution, burials in the cemeteries of the city were prohibited. The failure to designate new cemeteries outside the city center, however, led the refugees to bury their dead in Eyüp Cemetery, which was within the city boundaries. The huge number of deaths overwhelmed the capacity of the Eyüp Cemetery in a short time, which even forced the people to reopen the graves every two to three days to bury another body. The smell coming out of the decaying corpses spread all over the neighborhood. The corpses brought to the Gümüşsuyu Cemetery close to the German Embassy were placed haphazardly in graves that were not dug deep enough or covered properly. In another case, several corpses were barged to the Haydarpaşa Quay, after having waited for burial up to three or four days, and were kept there one more day until they finally were buried in Karacaahmet Cemetery. Such practices spread microorganisms into the environment, facilitating the outbreak of further epidemics.[25]

THE OTTOMAN-GREEK WAR OF 1897

Another case illustrative of the toll of epidemics on wars is the Ottoman-Greek War of 1897. Of the 40,000 casualties the Ottoman Army suffered during the war, 28,000 died from infectious diseases, whereas only 2,000 died from combat-related wounds. A total of 35 doctors, moreover, died of spotted fever.[26] Severe epidemics ravaged throughout the war, with soldiers losing their lives due to spotted fever (typhus), dysentery, malaria, and cholera.[27] The chief medical officer of the 3rd Army Corps and his colleagues were also among those who died of spotted fever, which was not diagnosed as typhus back then.[28]

THE BALKAN WAR

Stories of the tragic impact of those epidemics can be found in the memoirs of G. v. Hochwaechter, a German major who was stationed in the Ottoman headquarters during the Balkan War. Below are some excerpts from his memoirs:

Friday, 8 November [1912]. Unfortunately a very severe cholera epidemic broke out; 400 soldiers brought here on a train were quarantined in a camp. It is hoped that the epidemic be contained.

Sunday, 10 November. Cholera epidemic spread to Yassıviran. Only today, 70 cases were diagnosed. The soldier doing the private service of Kemal Bey died in our house in miserable conditions. We found the poor man this morning lying doubled up in the stable of our house.

Monday, 11 November. The worst of all is the threat of cholera, as I had previously mentioned. The disease still continues to spread, and I was told that they had many kinds of medicines in the main depot here, but none for cholera.... Since no fresh water can be found here, soldiers are drinking water from dirty puddles. All of the men seem scrawny. Under those miserable conditions, it would be impossible for them to endure epidemics, rain, cold, and hunger any longer. The soldier in my private service was given food only yesterday since we came here....

It is 4.30 p.m. I was out a short while ago. About 2,000 soldiers arrived, all hungry, who later were given food and sent to Istanbul by train. Dozens of them were falling down on the ground. Two soldiers were lying as if they were dead between the rails. I called a doctor's attention to them; but he glanced at me indifferently and walked away. Just after a second, a third one fell down near them. At last, their friends came to their help and carried them on their backs to a wagon carrying goods. It is only a matter of time before others fall down like them. The ones who faint due to hunger are mistakenly thought to be patients of cholera, and very frequently, cholera lime is poured on them without checking to see if they are really dead or not. The lime is burning the hollow eyes of those men. Those who want to live a bit longer are looking around in horror; but only for a minute!

Tuesday, 12 November. The number of deaths from cholera and typhus is terrifying. During a one-hour journey we made a while ago, I counted sixty five people who were either dead, or were about to die.

Friday, 15 November. The sanitary conditions in the army are getting worse and worse. I saw many sick in the rear lines of the Second Army Corps, though the troops on the frontlines still seemed healthy. In Hadımköy, however, hundreds of corpses were waiting to be buried. One of every two soldiers was ill. The civilians are still fleeing. The sickest patients had flooded into a few railway cars left in Ispartakule, and they were lying in masses on the roofs of the wagons. The medical equipment and supplies are no longer sufficient.... Exciting news coming from Istanbul is spreading; but I don't know what to believe anymore. Meanwhile, it is said that because an epidemic occurred among the Bulgarians too, a truce is likely to be signed soon.

November 16, Saturday. I couldn't sleep last night; the terrible scenes I witnessed yesterday stayed in my head all-night. They were really horrible. On the right hand side of the road heading to Hadımköy is a large piece of land, on the upper side of which a few houses are built. Those houses, which used to be used as hospitals, have been empty for a long time. Although separate graves were dug in the field, all corpses were amassed together. The hardened arms and legs could not be buried properly and were visible above the ground. Most of those poor people died on their way to hospital, in the places where they had fallen down. On the other side of the road, men in white clothes were digging very large holes. At first, I thought that they were for the dead people from the area. After a while, however, I saw a large convoy of carriages bringing the dead people, who would be buried in the holes, unknown to anyone, and no tears being shed for them.

At the station, it was almost impossible to move because of the huge crowd. Thousands of people, with sunken cheeks, and red eyes fixed on a point somewhere far, were running as if they were dragged toward the two long lines of wagons. They were trying to climb onto the wagons and the roofs. Some had died on the roofs, from where their arms and legs were hanging down. Some dead bodies even were lying between the wagons. Even healthy people would definitely catch the disease in such an environment.

One could rarely see an officer or a doctor in the vicinity; possibly they fell victim to the epidemic too. In a house that used to be the Officers' Club of the High Command till four days ago, where I dined for the last time, beds are placed for severely ill officers.

Everywhere, we hear endless moaning. Vacant ground is full of vultures and dogs, fighting over the spoils they find there. The air is contaminated, and the entire field is covered with corpses. I don't think that I could bear to see these scenes anymore![29]

The 1910–1913 cholera epidemics created various dramatic scenes similar to those narrated by the German major. That epidemic, which continued throughout the Balkan Wars, annihilated large numbers of army members as well as civilians, irrespective of their religious or national identities. On another note, Ekrem Kadri Unat argued that the epidemics occurring during the Balkan Wars were continuation of the pandemic that broke out in 1899.[30] The number of deaths from cholera along the Çatalca front alone was estimated to be forty thousand in 1912.[31]

Despite the measures taken, a cholera epidemic hit Istanbul in November 1912, which prompted the Municipality of Istanbul to issue an official notification on the matter.[32] Moreover, the Council of Medical Affairs set up a ninety-bed cholera hospital in Istanbul in December 1912.[33] Medical statistics from the period of 1913–1914 demonstrate that Istanbul Municipality made the following assessment regarding the cholera epidemic:

> Based on the information obtained regarding the outbreak of the disease, it appeared that the continuation of the severe epidemic in Thrace and in the areas occupied by the armies of the Balkan states through 1912–1913 forced people to move from Tselonika and its environs to Istanbul, who brought the disease to Istanbul, and sparked an epidemic by November (as seen in the table [Table 2.2]). After September, following the dissolution of the army in Thrace, the severity of the epidemic markedly increased, as indicated in the table. Although the city was threatened by the impending epidemic caused by both the refugees, and the military operations, further escalation of the crisis was prevented by acquiring timely information about the situation, tracing the course of the disease, and quarantining and treating the patients.[34]

The situation was different on the frontlines, though. During the Balkan War, outbreaks of epidemics such as cholera, typhus, typhoid, and dysentery could not be prevented due to the lack of essential sanitary measures

TABLE 2.2. Cholera Epidemic 1910–1913

YEAR	DURATION OF DISEASE	NUMBER OF CASES
1910	4 months	1,343
1911	5 months	2,620
1912	2 months	2,529
1913	6 months	238

in the areas of military build up, on the battlefield, and during the movements of the army.[35]

Seyhülislam (the chief religious authority in the Ottoman Empire for Muslims) Cemaleddin Efendi points out that the Ottoman Army called a truce in the First Balkan War due mainly to the lack of ammunition and the cholera epidemic. "When the cholera, God willed it, grew more fatal than the war, calling a truce became necessary in order to respond to the impending threat to the government center." In fact, the Bulgarians were also in desperate need of a truce because the battlefield moved away from their headquarters; they started experiencing interruptions in the supply of ammunition and food to the frontlines due to weather conditions; they, too, suffered heavy casualties on the Çatalca front; and cholera swept through their soldiers. The commanders and representatives of both parties, therefore, agreed to come together in Bahşayiş village, near Çatalca, where they decided to call an armistice in order to start peace negotiations.[36] A. Nazlimov, who served in the Bulgarian army during the Balkan War, testifies how the Bulgarian Army was also struck by the same set of problems as the Ottoman Army. According to Nazlimov, the first case of cholera in the Bulgarian Army was encountered in the Cavalry Division around Çorlu on 28 October 1911.[37]

In Istanbul a cholera epidemic broke out in January 1911 among the reserve units returning from the autumn maneuver, carried out in Albania. Because no cases of cholera had been reported in the hometowns of the soldiers serving in these contingents until that time (all of them were coming from the provinces on the coast of the Eastern Black Sea), the epidemic was thought to have been transmitted by the soldiers from the areas of maneuver in Albania through the ports and quays of Thrace, where they stopped on their way back home.[38] In 1912, when a cholera epidemic broke out in the Ottoman contingent returning from Albania, which was sent to suppress the uprising there, the soldiers were quarantined in a military camp in Serviburun. As a protective measure, a health officer was tasked, at the quaysides in Istanbul, to spray a few drops of corrosive sublimate on the passengers getting off the steamers.[39] According to another source, the cholera epidemic, which broke out during the Balkan Wars, causing many military and civilian fatalities, originally had been carried from Egypt and Syria.[40]

In the Balkan Wars, the Ottoman Army was on the retreat from 21 October 1912 on. During that retreat, too, which took place under adverse weather conditions, a cholera epidemic broke out. The cholera epidemic, of course, brought several unexpected problems, amplifying the hardships experienced by the army. The epidemic intensified and expanded in a short time span in Hadımköy, and the entire city of Istanbul was threatened by a possible outbreak which could be sparked by the soldiers being relocated from Hadımköy to Istanbul. To avoid such a crisis, the field medical inspectorate ordered that the patients be taken off the train at Yeşilköy station, before reaching Istanbul, and be treated there. However, neither the Greek School, nor the tents set up in vacant lands, nor the houses converted into hospitals, sufficed to accommodate all of the patients in Yeşilköy. The chaotic situation in the region frightened the inhabitants of Yeşilköy, causing them to flee. During the Balkan Wars, the senior students of the Military Medical School were drafted into the army at the rank of captain. The sheds set up for the patients with epidemic diseases in Yeşilköy during the Balkan Wars were later used in the First World War.[41] After its defeat, the Ottoman Army retreated rapidly and formed a defensive line in the trenches in Çatalca. The Muslim inhabitants of the areas abandoned by the retreating Ottoman Army migrated to Anatolia under grave conditions. The majority of those who finally reached Istanbul, after a difficult journey through muddy roads and heavy winter conditions, became ill. As many as ninety large buildings and mansions were used as hospitals for the treatment and care of those migrants.[42] Following a decision of the medical department of the Ottoman Army, the soldiers infected with cholera were boarded in large mosques: 3,600 in St. Sophia Mosque, 1,200 in the Sultanahmet (Blue) Mosque, 450 in Nuruosmaniye Mosque, and 1,250 in Mahmutpaşa Mosque.[43]

The Indian Red Crescent Organization also sent a twenty-four-member delegation consisting of Indian Muslims, chaired by Dr. Ahmed Erzari who was working in Charing Cross Hospital in London. The delegation actively participated in the efforts to control the epidemics in Istanbul during the Balkan Wars.[44] In addition, the Red Crescent Organization from Egypt, and Red Cross Organizations from England, Romania, Austria-Hungary, and Germany also sent delegations in order to help the sick and wounded during the Balkan Wars.[45]

TABLE 2.3. Çatalca Army Medical Inspectorate's hospital records

REFERRED PATIENTS	CHOLERA	OTHER DISEASES	TOTAL NUMBER	NUMBER OF DEATHS
Officers	219	–	219	11
Recruits	11,443	4,336	15,779	137

The units defending the Çatalca line suffered from insufficient numbers of doctors and health officers, as well as an inadequate or nonexistent supply of medical equipment and medicine. Cholera and dysentery were rampant among the troops. In the face of those difficulties, not only appropriate treatment but also protective measures were insufficiently provided. According to the records of the army medical inspectorate in Çatalca, the situation in the hospitals within that inspectorate's area of responsibility was as follows (see Table 2.3).[46]

The observations of military doctor Abdülkadir Noyan provide a good insight into the grim state of medical facilities at a central place like Istanbul:

> The trains were halting at a point between the gramophone factory and the station. The sick were unloaded there, while the dead were simply dumped, being rolled down from the slope to the land below. We, the doctors, wearing rubber boots and black oilcloth coats, and carrying Red Crescent mark on our arms, were coming to work at dawn, staying there until late at night.
>
> In the first chaotic days, the patients had only soup, and the only available medicine was lemonade prepared with lactic acid containing labdanum. Freshly slaked lime and lime milk were used to sterilize the inner and outer surfaces of the tents. The increasing number of patients surpassed the capacity of the tents, sheds, and houses used as hospitals. The farm where tents and temporary hospitals were set up resembled the doomsday. Some of the patients transported from the Çatalca front-line died on the way; only their dead bodies made it. It was impossible to bury the dead in separate graves. Cholera victims were buried with their clothes on in the deep ditches dug on the vacant fields in the south of the record factory, close to the sea shore. The number of the cholera patients arriving in Yeşilköy was 20,000. In the course of that epidemic, a total of over 30,000 soldiers caught the disease, one third of whom died.[47]

The enemy was stopped eventually on the Çatalca front on 15–19 November 1912. Nazım Pasha reinforced the Ottoman forces in Çatalca with the divisions coming from Trabzon, Erzurum, and İzmir, which in fact contained soldiers diagnosed with cholera, who then were known as the *zuafayı askeriye* (weak soldiers of the army).[48]

An interesting witness of the Ottoman Army's struggle against cholera was Leon Trotsky, one of the future leaders of the Bolshevik Revolution in 1917, who at the time was in exile in Vienna. In the fall of 1912, Trotsky went to the Balkans as a "war correspondent" of the journal *Kievskaya Misl* (*Kiev's View*). In the reports he sent from the battlefield, Trotsky remarked that in Çatalca the Ottoman Army was fighting not only the Bulgarian Army but also the "monster of cholera."[49] In one of his articles, Leon Trotsky quotes the following words from a letter written by a clerk who was dispatched to Stip to open a branch of the National Bank in Bulgaria:

> A horrible situation! It is depressing to witness how the Ottoman civilian villagers sometimes were killed without any reason, their properties were seized, and their wives and children were left in poverty and hunger. Around 2,000 Ottoman migrants, mostly women and children, died from hunger between Radovishte and Stip. Yes, they died only from hunger.

After quoting these words from the official, Trotsky goes on to observe that

> life in a region liberated [from the Ottomans] is made up of a 70 year old elderly man, whose head lay mangled, thousands of women and children dying from hunger, revolutionary partisans degenerated into bandits, a police chief protecting burglars. One cannot expect the newly assigned administrators to act as honorably as Catos, when they find themselves in such an environment. No limitations exist on the government's arbitrary practices, and opportunities for making a quick fortune are appealing. A state official writes to one of his colleagues: "Tell N.N. that the mentioned land can be purchased at a very little cost here, and especially in Ovtse Polje." The Turks fled leaving all their lands and properties behind, and nowadays, the plundering of them has reached its highest point.[50]

Shortly after the measures implemented against cholera bore some fruits in Yeşilköy, another cholera epidemic broke out in a division dispatched from Elazığ. A sanitary cordon was placed around the site of the outbreak (the Kartal and Yakacık districts of Istanbul), and the troops from the contingent were housed in the homes nearby. The gardens of those houses were contaminated with human feces, and most of the wells also were under the threat of pollution by the groundwater. After a while, the authorities decided to relocate the infected division to Tuzla, another district of Istanbul.

According to a witness, however, "no medical means were available to combat the epidemic of cholera."[51]

In March 1913, cases of spotted fever (typhus) were encountered in the Yeşilköy Hospital of Infectious Diseases. At that time this disease was believed to be occurring sporadically in the eastern provinces. Typhus was also detected among the troops dispatched from Erzurum.[52] In May 1913, an epidemic of recurrent fever broke out in the Yeşilköy hospital. It turned out that the soldiers originating from the east brought this disease.[53] Meanwhile, a cholera epidemic broke out once more, during the army's offensive which resulted in the recapture of Edirne on 10 July 1913. About 400 patients were referred to the hospital in Dimetoca suspected of cholera; 134 of them were diagnosed with the disease. On this occasion, proper medical measures were employed to combat the epidemic. A cholera vaccine developed by Dr. Reşat Rıza and Dr. Mustafa was used. Besides the Ottoman Army, cholera was also diagnosed in the Bulgarian and Greek armies around the same time.[54] In October 1913, a cholera epidemic broke out among the Ottoman troops who were congregated in Derince upon their return from enemy captivity. Among the 6,000 soldiers gathered in the military camp, about 25 to 30 new cholera cases were emerging each day.[55] According to the statistics collected later, the total casualties of the army from cholera on the Çatalca front were 40,000.[56] Against the background of defeat in the Balkan Wars, a dysentery epidemic broke out just as the cholera epidemic was about to end. The total number of dysentery cases was about 6,000 to 7,000, 15 percent of which resulted in death.[57] Cholera also hit the Bulgarian Army during the Balkan Wars, and according to one estimate, its death toll was around 19,000.[58] When Edirne was besieged during the Second Balkan War of 1912–1913, A. Geron, who was then principal of the Jewish Girls' School in Edirne, took the following interesting notes in her diary about the hunger and epidemics reigning in the city:

> *18 December 1912.* The sanitary conditions in the city are very bad. Epidemics of scarlet fever, cholera, and dysentery have broken out. Our children are drinking water from the Arda River, which is full of corpses. This is very dangerous. I will immediately inform the School's Administrative Board about the situation and request them to take urgent measures.
>
> *January 17, 1913.* Death, exacerbated by hunger, lack of salt and wood, dysentery, and cholera, is spreading every day, causing a great concern. More people are dying due to these conditions of deprivation created by the siege than due to the bombardments.

> *March 9, 1913.* Hunger is becoming severer [sic] every day. Authorities allocate each adult individual a daily ration of bread equal to 100–150 g. The poverty is unbearable for the poor who have been unemployed for months. The ugly death is chasing the weakened and anemic organisms. Hundreds of people died of hunger. Human beings compete with animals for the fresh grass on land. Although the grass suppresses their hunger, it also irritates their stomach. Deceiving the feeling of hunger has been the only occupation of these people for months.[59]

In the aftermath of the war, when the army started discharging troops in September 1913, the 31st and 32nd divisions were ordered to move to Gelibolu. Because the troops passed through areas where the epidemic was still present, including Dimetoca, and some of them already had suffered from the disease, inevitably an epidemic broke out again in Gelibolu.[60] In March 1914, epidemics of recurrent fever and cholera were encountered in the 2nd Army Corps stationed in Edirne. Furthermore, 25 to 30 cases of spotted fever were diagnosed among the troops every day. A total of 104 soldiers died during this epidemic.[61] The epidemic also took its toll in other parts of Anatolia and advanced into the central parts of the country. In November 1914, 5 to 6 spotted fever cases per day were being detected among the inmates in the Prison of Konya. That outbreak was immediately followed by another spotted fever epidemic in Sille (a small village near Konya).[62]

Cemil Pasha, the mayor and a surgeon by profession, provides interesting observations about the Balkan War in his memoirs:

> A few days after the declaration of the war, migrants started to arrive in our city. But what an arrival! They were all in a very miserable condition. Those poor people coming to Istanbul, packed in sailboats and trains, were then finding themselves in Sirkeci, hungry and broke. Not to mention those who set off from their villages and towns on oxcarts.
>
> In the meantime, a cholera epidemic beginning among the troops in Kartal aggravated the situation. The poverty in the city reached an extreme level. The disease claimed many lives every day.
>
> It was winter. Every day thousands of people infected with cholera were abandoned in large fields—where the Gülhane Park is located today. As I was contemplating where and how to treat those poor people, suddenly the large mosques came to my mind. I called the late Ziya Pasha, the then Minister of Foundations, to request his permission to have some of the mosques placed under the authority of the Municipality immediately. Ziya Pasha, however, turned down my request on the grounds that "[he] can never

give permission for making the places of worshipping filthy." I decided to bring the matter to Sadrazam [Prime Minister] Kamil Pasha without delay. Though it is unusual to listen to the Mayor during the cabinet meetings, they let me in.

Cemil Pasha goes on to narrate the exchange between himself and Ziya Pasha. Whereas he made a case to demonstrate that the urgent health conditions in the city made it necessary to use large mosques for accommodating the people affected by the epidemic, Ziya Pasha insisted that this act would be disgraceful to these holy sites, hence not acceptable from his perspective. In the face of this opposition, Prime Minister Kamil Pasha remained hesitant, which prompted Şeyhülislam Cemaleddin Efendi to throw his weight behind Mayor Cemil Pasha by saying that he would support the idea of using not only one, but if necessary all, mosques for the treatment of patients and refugees suffering from cholera. He went on to add that he could even issue a fatwa (opinion on a matter involving the Islamic religious rules) to that end. He concluded by saying that "harboring the refugees and patients in mosques under such critical conditions is not against the Shari'a, because Islamic places of worship are at the same time Houses of God." This strong support lent by the Şeyhülislam removed the obstacles before Cemil Pasha's proposal, and the Council of Ministers unanimously decided that the mosques would be placed under the authority of the municipality to be used for the purpose of fighting the epidemic.[63]

Another witness of the chaotic conditions reigning in Istanbul, Doctor Major General Ekrem Şadi, who was a high school student then, writes that during the Balkan Wars countless people were arriving in Istanbul in a great panic.

> I saw those people in mosques [transferred from vegetable gardens]. Their cheeks were sunken. They were looking for wheat grains in the soil. Back then, we used to go to Gülhane hospital to prepare war packages (bandages, gauzes, and cotton in them) for the wounded. When we visited the operating room of the hospital in our spare time, we used to run into wounded soldiers on the stretchers, screaming.

Ekrem Şadi also recalls the following:

> In the tents set up in a disorderly manner along the banks of the Danube River, 20–25 soldiers were packed into a single tent. The ill and healthy soldiers were lumped together. In this overcrowded camping area, even the

death of a soldier could not be noticed. Whereas 50–60 of our soldiers were losing their lives per day, thanks to the preventive measures taken, later that number was reduced to 4–5 a day.[64]

WORKS ON HYGIENE AT THE BEGINNING OF THE WAR

When the First World War started in 1914, the Ottoman Empire was confronted with new problems, particularly a typhus epidemic. Throughout the war, widespread cases of typhus appeared in the center of Istanbul and in the region around Üsküdar-Galata-Eyüp. In order to combat that epidemic, which persisted due to the war conditions, an elaborate plan of action was drafted, as though the whole city was mobilized to fight against the disease. As part of the measures taken to address the crisis, first of all, soon after the commencement of World War I, all civilian doctors, pharmacists, and dentists between the ages of twenty and forty-five were drafted into the army under Law No. 1097, dated 1 August 1914.[65] Shortly before the war, in fact, during Dr. Reşat Rıza's term in office as the director of hygiene, a directive on the "Regulations on the Infectious Diseases and Epidemics," consisting of sixty-five articles, was issued on 13 April 1914.[66] The directive laid out the responsibilities of respective bodies to prepare for the city's upcoming combat against infectious diseases.[67] Under that framework, the Istanbul Commission to Combat Infectious Diseases was established. At the beginning, the commission dealt with diseases such as typhus, recurrent fever, and cholera. Later its mandate was extended to include smallpox and the plague.[68]

The following are some of the measures proposed by the plan:

- Let it be communicated to health officers working in the countryside that passengers traveling to Istanbul from the places in Anatolia or the Marmara region where typhus epidemics exist shall undergo a medical examination before boarding the trains, or sea vehicles, and it shall be deemed necessary to disinfect their belongings as much as possible.

- New recruits shall be sent to the quarantine establishment at Tuzla to be cleaned, where they shall be kept under observation for fourteen days before being dispatched to their units. In the military units, appropriate measures shall be taken to prevent infections. The soldiers, who return from leave after recovering from typhus, shall also undergo the same process.

- The servicemen with typhus, who are in hospitals, barracks, and various units, shall not be sent on leave, nor shall they be discharged.

- In the military places which are the origin of spotted fever cases, such as the Selimiye Barracks and Hospital, and Hospitals of Rami and Davutpaşa, as well as various military units where spotted fever cases are detected, urgent measures shall be taken to eliminate the micro organisms of diseases and parasites thoroughly. Those places shall be kept under strict medical control and surveillance.

- Even when all of the abovementioned measures are implemented strictly, the elimination of the disease completely would be near to impossible. When the seasonal conditions allow, the people previously residing in the designed parts of the city shall be resettled outside the city, or be placed in the tents.

- The doctors working for the Municipality's medical services shall be considered to be on emergency duty during the course of the epidemic, and they shall be compensated for the travel expenses related to their duties.

- As it would be beyond doctors' capacity to examine all the cases referred to them, a health officer shall be assigned to each of the 38 public health centers in order to carry out doctors' duties, and help the doctors.

- When the trains, irrespective of whether they are operating within the city or coming from other places, have to wait for more than an hour at a station, their wagons shall be disinfected, using 5% petroleum or phonic acid solutions, or 3% cresol solution. The furnishings, carpets, mats, and floor shall first be wetted with those solutions, and then brushed and rinsed.

- Hotelkeepers are responsible to maintain the cleanliness of hotel rooms, corridors, and bedclothes. They shall be informed that the hotels failing to do so, or are found to contain lice, fleas, or bedbugs will be closed until they are cleaned, in order to maintain the public health.

- Although the Municipality decided to subcontract the disinfection of the personal belongings and furniture of those living in hostels, bachelors' housing, and brothels step by step, those individuals are required to take utmost care to keep their bodies, clothes, and other belongings clean from lice, fleas, and bedbugs. Let them know that otherwise they shall be punished.

- The Ministry of Foundations shall be asked to ensure that naphthalene powder is sprinkled on and beneath the carpets in the mosques and other places of worshipping in order to protect them against moths.

- The Municipality shall lease five public baths in certain neighborhoods initially in order to allow the poor to bathe.[69]

3

UNDER THE CRESCENT

> In fact all corps had been reduced from the strength of divisions to that of regiments, and regiments to that of battalions or even companies. A drastic reorganization of the Third Army became essential.
>
> —W. E. D. Allen and Paul Muratoff, *Caucasian Battlefields*

The great disaster in Sarıkamış in the winter of 1914–1915 reduced the 3rd Army to a mere 12,000 men who were left unorganized and were afflicted with eruptive typhus. Their commander, Hafız Hakkı, died of this terrible sickness. These meager forces were reinforced by about 20,000 recruits, many of whom succumbed over time to typhus, malnutrition, and lack of hygiene and medical supplies. The main reason for these misfortunes was the enormous distance separating the Caucasian front from the last station of the railway, a distance of between five and six hundred kilometers comprised of trails passing through rough terrain. Moving troops by sea was considered impossible since the superior Russian fleet would be able to intercept Ottoman ships.[1]

TROOPS AND ROUTES

One question that begs an answer is this: what was the situation of the Ottoman transportation facilities in Anatolia, Syria, and Iraq during the First World War? This question is important for a proper understanding of the Ottoman Army's performance during the Great War, as the level of a country's transportation infrastructure has a direct bearing on its social, economic, military and political achievements.[2]

The Ottoman Empire was only able to operate around one hundred small trains in 1914.[3] Before the outbreak of the Great War, only the Haydarpaşa (Istanbul)-Konya segment of the Istanbul-Baghdad railroad could be completed. Later during the war it was extended further from

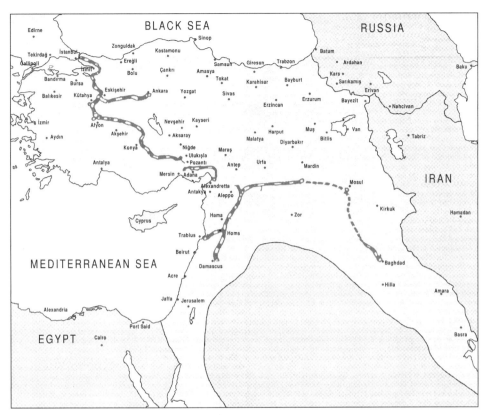

Figure 3.1. Major Railways in the Ottoman Empire during World War I.

Konya. By the end of 1914, the following lines became operational: Konya-Karapınar (291 km), Durak-Yenice, Adana-Misis-Toprakkale-Osmaniye, Carablus-Telebyaz (81 km), Baghdad-Samarra (119 km), and the Toprakkale-Osmaniye-İskenderun line.[4] By the end of 1915, only three sections remained unfinished: the 37 km from Karapınar to Durak in the Taurus; the 54 km stretch between Mamure and Islahiye in the Amanus; and the 588 km between Ras-ul-Ain and Samarra in Mesopotamia. In 1915–1916, as a result, the soldiers had to pass through the Gülek Pass in the Taurus Mountains on foot in order to reach the Syrian territories from Anatolia.[5] The war later made the Baghdad-Basra section completely out of reach for the Ottoman Army.[6] Between Ulukışla and Erzurum no railway connection was available back then. This was the grim condition of the transportation facilities available to the wartime Ottoman Army.

İ. Hakkı Bey, who was assigned as a reserve officer to the Caucasus front while he was a second-year student at Istanbul Faculty of Law, traveled to

Pozantı together with his unit by train. He relates the following about his journey:

> All troops got off the train in Pozantı. On the night of 20/21 June, we slept in the pine groves of Pozantı. Since no vehicle was available, we would have to travel on food to the plain of Adana.⁷

The journey of the First Expeditionary Force from Istanbul to Aleppo, Syria, also started from Haydarpaşa railway station on 24 December 1914. Meanwhile, because the British Navy controlling the Gulf of İskenderun had destroyed the railways and bridges with cannon fire and through the detachments landed there, the first Ottoman units dispatched to Aleppo had to walk from Toprakkale to İskenderun, while the rest marched from Osmaniye to Aleppo directly, bypassing İskenderun.⁸ When mobilization was declared in August 1914, Münim Mustafa and his friends, who were drafted into the army while studying at Istanbul Faculty of Law, were assigned to the 4th Army headquarters in Syria. In order to join their unit, they also traveled to Pozantı by train, but as no rail service was available after Pozantı, they had to pass through the Taurus Mountains on foot, and continued their way by marching along the Osmaniye-Hasanbeyli-İslahiye-Raco route. They first participated in the military campaign in the Canal region (in Suez), and later fought in Çanakkale and at the Caucasus front.⁹

The memoirs of a military doctor are of great value, in this case providing detailed information on the situation of the roads in Anatolia and Syria at the onset of the war. Abdülkadir Noyan of the Ottoman Army started his duty in Iraq as the deputy chief doctor of the 6th Army in December 1915. The route the medical captain followed to reach his place of duty, as well as the vehicles he used en route, were as follows. On his way to Baghdad, where he was assigned, he first took the train from Istanbul to Pozantı. He then traveled from Pozantı to Mosul on horseback and from there to Baghdad on *keleks* (a kind of raft mounted on animal skins filled with air).¹⁰

All Ottoman troops deployed to the Iraqi front could reach that region only after a two-month walk, which naturally had a very adverse effect on their health condition.¹¹

In an illustrative example, the contingent where Bartınlı Hamid, one of the Ottoman recruits, served moved from Viranşehir to Revandiz in fifty days in March 1915, including breaks taken along the way. In the spring of 1915, his unit engaged Russian forces in Urumiye, Iran. In the meantime, hunger and epidemics started to affect the troops. They had insufficient food and many times they went hungry for days. In addition, more than two hundred soldiers drowned in the Tigris River. The unit eventually arrived in Ahlat on 25 June 1915 to find an entirely empty town.[12]

After mobilization was declared, the 29th Division stationed in Erzincan was dispatched to Erzurum. It took ten days for the division to walk the distance of 180 km between Erzincan and Erzurum, at an average speed of 20 to 30 km per day.[13] The units subordinate to the First Expeditionary Force, which were deployed in Aleppo, set off for Erzurum on 22 January 1915. The contingent first was transported from Aleppo to Akçakale by train, and from there the soldiers had to walk.[14] As the "longest walk" in the four-year history of the Great War started there, in an unfortunate coincidence, the diseases of spotted fever, black fever, recurrent fever, and dysentery were occurring all over Anatolia, either as isolated cases, or in the form of epidemics.[15]

Dr. Abdülkadir Noyan, who had ample opportunity to observe the health conditions along the route between Istanbul and Baghdad, took the following notes in December 1915:

> My impressions about the medical conditions on the roads after Adana and Aleppo were upsetting. The migration of the Armenians from the east toward the south also took place during the same time. As far as I was informed, the epidemics of spotted fever and typhoid were advancing toward Istanbul. On the other hand, on the way from Istanbul to Aleppo and Mosul, one could easily notice the increase in the number of spotted fever cases.[16]

The "death walk" taken by the young people, who were drafted into the army to defend the homeland after the Ottoman Empire joined the war, lasted for four long years until the end of the war. These Ottoman youth, en route to battlefields, had to travel under the most arduous conditions, sometimes having to march 800 km under the desert sun. A German medical officer, Colonel Seuber, who served as the chief doctor of the Lightning Group of Armies, took the following notes between 1917 and 1918:

> A 800 km-long journey through the desert, where no railroad but one road parts of which are convenient for automobile transportation exists! What a journey! 800 kilometers with insufficient water and food supply. The German units would never endure this 800 km.-march in summer conditions. Even the winter and rainy seasons were of no help to ease the hardships.[17]

In 1918 Hamdullah Suphi visited the Syrian front together with Halide Edip upon the invitation of Cemal Pasha. Suphi reported his observations during their journey to Syria through Ulukışla, which is located at the crossroads of the military dispatch routes, in the *Türk Yurdu* magazine. He depicted the condition of the soldiers he met in Ulukışla as follows:

> I used to hear the name of Ulukışla from those who traveled between Syria or Iraq and Anatolia. We arrived there early in the morning, while one could still smell fresh morning air. On a small square on the left side of where we stopped, one could see gatherings of camels, donkeys, and people. It was noticeable at first sight that Ulukışla, located at the intersection of the roads leading to various battlefronts, was distinctively vivid, unlike other towns.
>
> As months pass by, we see younger and younger people joining those feverish activities going on behind the battlefronts for years. The youngsters from the towns, which are deserted day by day, have been flowing incessantly to Suez, Diyarbakır, Iraq, and the Caucasus. The atmosphere in this town reminds me more than anywhere else of the fellow brothers, and of those who, after resting for five to ten minutes in such destructed towns, have traveled to the farthest frontlines, with a noble hope in their hearts, many of whom have fallen to the ground, decaying in unknown places, without leaving any name or any trace behind. The overcrowded dispatch routes and the endless noise that accompanies them make one think of war more than anywhere else in Ulukışla.
>
> The carriages, horses, camels, donkeys, mules, and automobiles carrying goods are coming and going in haste on the roads. A huge mechanism, consisting of those different means of transportation, is constantly in operation to keep the war machines far away from here running. All these vehicles and animals are transporting the soldiers from Anatolia and pouring them into the deserts, to Iraq, Syria, and Diyarbakır. On the other side of the road, convoys of weak soldiers, comprising the youngsters worn-out and exhausted by war, are returning [to] their homes. These youngsters, with hollow eyes looking at the death or darkness, and with sunken cheeks, appeared unsure whether they would be able to see their distant villages again.[18]

In 1917, one year before Hamdullah Suphi and Halide Edip's journey to Syria, the German military doctor Seuber, mentioned above, had traveled to the region by train and stopped in Karapınar in the Taurus Mountains. He provides the following impressions from a doctor's point of view:

> For the time being, Karapınar serves as a crucial transfer point. Karapınar, which is very hot even in the morning, becomes like a hell during the day,

conducive to the spread of malaria. I had some time to visit the centre where the sick are gathered, and the facilities for cleaning lice, as well as other medical facilities, which were in poor conditions. Then we continued our trip through decauville railways, traveling in wagons open on all sides whose roofs are covered with tents.

All kinds of houses exist in Karapınar. The Turks, the Armenians, and the Greeks are living together in tents, underground shelters, or booths, surrounded with the germs of malaria. In contrast, above this miserable hell of malaria, on the skirts of the mountains, one could see beautiful and well-ornamented houses resided by the German engineers working in the construction of the Anatolian railways. In Karapınar, a large mass of people consisting of diverse races from Europe and Asia are working together under the German leadership for the common purpose of building a road to the south, through the Taurus Mountains.[19]

Some soldiers had to be left behind because they became ill during the longest walk "under the crescent." İ. Hakkı's unit was about to leave the district of Eloğlu (Türkoğlu), located on the plain stretching from the outskirts of the Gavur Mountains between Adana and Maraş. The onset of cholera within the unit forced them to leave the ill soldiers:

It is evening, and we are about to leave. I watched the ill to be left here: all of them were scrawny, and their cheeks were sunken. Some of them were throwing up, while some others were defecating in one corner. Some of them were bathing in a large puddle in front of the village. I shouted at them: "is it a good time to do that?" One of the soldiers replied to me: "Sir, it is cholera. They are afraid of dying without ablution."

It was a tragic scene: There was no hospital, nor anybody to look after them. We left by saying "May God protect you." I only wished the disease would not be transmitted to the villagers.[20]

Of the 10,000 troops serving in the Ottoman division that set off from Istanbul, only 4,635 could make it to Palestine. The rest either became ill or deserted. The ones who reached Palestine were ill and had lost their strength. Most of the troops in the Ottoman division did not even have blankets. As narrated by the medical officer serving in an Ottoman-German joint machine-gun company, none of the soldiers in the company were healthy as of May 1917. The most common diseases were amoebic dysentery and malaria.[21]

As of early 1917, the number of wounded continued to rise due to the ongoing battles. About eight to nine thousand ill and wounded soldiers had to be accommodated in the houses and tents in the town of Samra, on the left bank of the Tigris River. Soon after, however, the military had to withdraw from Samra, which made it necessary to move those ill and wounded servicemen across the river:

> In order to transfer the ill and wounded to Mosul, first of all they had to be moved across the river. The only means of transportation that were available in Samra were a few simple baskets covered with pitch (called a "kufe"). Each of those kufes could hold 8–10 persons. First, they were lifted up to a height of 200–250 meters, and left to the current of the river. Later, by using the oars the people inside could reach the other bank. It took more than half an hour to move a kufe from one side to the other and back.[22]

In January 1915, cognizant of the difficulties that would arise if the German Army attempted to cross the desert on foot, Liman von Sanders argued against a proposed offensive. When the headquarters in Berlin ordered the offensive anyway, the units set off for Suez under the command of Kress von Kressenstein. During the offensive in Suez, and on the return from there, the water shortage and other problems emanating from it sparked various intestinal disorders which later turned into dysentery. Von Kressenstein observed that "few of the Germans under [von Sanders'] command remained healthy enough to carry out the daily routines." Von Sanders himself lost one third of his body weight due to malnutrition.[23] According to von Sanders, malaria and dysentery in particular took a heavy toll in the hot summer months of 1918. All the mobile hospitals and convalescent-hospitals along the frontlines as well as in the interior were overcrowded.[24]

SUPPLY OF FOOD AND SHELTER FOR THE TROOPS[25]

Excluding the first three months of 1914, during the entire period of war till the declaration of the ceasefire, a total of 654,468 Ottoman troops were admitted to military hospitals and other central hospitals. The main reason causing such a large number was the chronic problem of malnutrition, which could not be eliminated despite all efforts.[26] The situation of the 3rd Army deployed on the eastern front was particularly critical. The nutrition levels for the officers and the troops were alarming; the difficulties encountered in transportation due to insufficient and primitive transportation vehicles, and the long and severe winters caused frequent interruptions in the food supply.[27]

An Ottoman officer who inspected the 4th Division of the Reserve Cavalry Army Corps during the war had the following observations fifteen years after the Great War:

> What I saw during the inspection of the 4th Division in Velibaba was deeply upsetting. The headquarters of that division was in Viranşehir, and its troops were recruited from regions with hot climates, who only had underclothes on, and instead of military greatcoats were wearing *maşlahs* (long, open-fronted cloak). They were sleeping on the ground, on earth in the narrow and dirty rooms of the miserable village, and they did not have any blankets to cover their bodies while sleeping. At a temperature 5 degrees below 0 Celsius, it was a torture to task those insufficiently clothed young village boys to guard the front door. When the whole division was on horses for inspection in the early morning, I saw their naked feet twisted on the iron stirrups because of the cold. I felt ashamed of seeing them. At the same time, I wondered how those soldiers could fight in a battle. I went to Erzurum on 1 October 1914. I told the Army Commander (Hasan İzzet Pasha) about my impressions of the general situation of the cavalry regiments, their equipment, and their combat readiness. The Army Commander replied: "In the Balkan War, our Army was well clothed and equipped, yet we were defeated. This time, let's fight without equipment."[28]

Another Ottoman officer, Colonel Sadık Sabri, in his report submitted from the 17th Division to the 9th Army Corps, which was subordinate to the 3rd Army, documents the terrible consequences of poor health conditions and disease on his unit:

> Most of the soldiers were recruited by the Recruiting Branch of the 10th Army Corps, and joined their battalions after walking for 35–40 days. Most of them are old, weak, and vulnerable to diseases. Some of them got sick and died soon after they joined their battalions. The disease is still prevalent among the survivors. You would find the medical report on the general health conditions, attached. Since no doctors and medicines were available in those units, the spread of the disease could not be prevented. That the capacity of the mobile hospital had to be increased to 790 beds is an indication of the persistence of the disease. Most of the animals are emaciated. Most of them were wounded but could not be treated since the units had no veterinarians and medicines. Obviously those wounded and emaciated animals cannot be used in any military operation. The number of mule drivers is not sufficient to carry all the loads of the units according to

current calculations. Since the Division would not be able to compensate for the required mule drivers, I have requested you to reinforce them.

More than half of the recruits are still in their civilian clothing. We sent 80 animals without packsaddles to Hamdi Village. I had 900 cartridge belts belonging to the Division picked up from Bayburt and distributed them to the soldiers. They were, however, sufficient for only half of the soldiers. The rest still doesn't have any. Nor do they have haversacks. The soldiers could carry their rations in the bags they brought from their villages; however they have no means to carry their ammunition. Furthermore, the shoes of many of the soldiers are in a very bad condition. It is obvious that the tired and weakened soldiers cannot walk as desired with those shoes.

I warned the officers several times about the need to prevent the transmission of the diseases and eradicate them. The officers, who even don't care about their own health, have difficulty in understanding the dangers of the disease. The lack of doctors and medicines, and the vulnerability of the poorly-dressed, tired, and weakened soldiers to diseases set obstacles to efforts at preventing the epidemics. The disease is spreading rapidly even among the officers; therefore the number of officers is constantly decreasing.[29]

According to Dr. Abdülkadir Noyan, the course and fatality level of a disease depends mainly on environmental conditions, nutritional intake, and clothing. Particularly in the case of amoebic dysentery and chronic enteritis, malnutrition and cold play a major role. Those diseases cause sudden deaths among people who have gone hungry for long periods. That phenomenon might explain the cases of sudden deaths observed in soldiers who came back from the desert after gathering wood, and in the patients who died shortly after they were hospitalized or while they were being examined.[30]

A Palestinian Jew of Romanian origin was among those recruited during the war and assigned to the 4th Army. As he narrates, most of the uniforms given to the soldiers were old and dirty, having been previously worn by others and probably still carrying the germs of various diseases.[31] This situation was in fact unusual, as in many places the soldiers did not even have access to such "previously used, old, dirty, and infected" uniforms. For instance, the units of the 3rd Army dispatched to their concentration region were not dressed suitably for the severe climate conditions of the East Anatolia.

According to a note sent in March 1916 from the Detached Cavalry Brigade to the Battle Group of Iraq, although they were able to send the troops to the public baths in Mosul and Baghdad, the soldiers had to wash their

TABLE 3.1. Casualties of the Fifth Expeditionary Force that occurred during its journey to the front (1915)

Ill soldiers who could travel with their units (970 foot injuries)	2,708
Ill soldiers who could not travel with their units	1,040
Desertions	1,041
Deaths (49 due to diseases, 39 freezing to death, 16 due to other reasons)	102

clothes only with water, as there was no soap available. Lice spread through the troops since they had no soap to wash their hands, let alone their bodies. The Cavalry Brigade tried to purchase some soap from Baghdad, but there was none to be had. Under those conditions, naturally, it was not possible to prevent the spread of typhus.[32]

Typhus was the most dangerous disease threatening the military forces operating in Syria and Iraq. The Ottoman soldiers who were taken prisoner by General Allenby's army were first placed in barrels filled with corrosive sublimate to prevent the introduction of the disease to the British soldiers.[33] On the other hand, epidemics and endemics of hepatitis were observed among British and French prisoners of war in the Mediterranean region during the Great War.[34]

In 1915, the units of the 5th Expeditionary Force fell victim to freezing temperatures as they were transferred from Istanbul to Erzurum, a two-month trek via the Taurus Mountains. Particularly the 40th Infantry Regiment and the Artillery Battalion of the same force, which set off from Erzurum, were caught in a snowstorm around Deveboynu, where many of the troops froze to death.[35]

The First Expeditionary Force, which conducted operations in Iran, "had to carry the ill soldiers with it while it was going to Mosul via the route of Pozantı, Aleppo and Telleübyas, since no medical facilities were available on the way past Aleppo. Some of the patients were left behind in Mosul and Erbil. When the Expeditionary Force eventually arrived in Urumiye, an epidemic of spotted fever was spreading among the migrants there."[36]

Since the winters were long, and heavy snowfalls and temperatures below −40°C were common on the Caucasus front, providing soldiers with clothes and equipment suitable for severe winter conditions was critical.[37] The troops of the 28th Division dispatched to the environs of Hasankale on 31 January, however, had no greatcoats and some of them did not even have proper clothing. The troops could hardly endure the cold temperatures, which fell to −20°C during the night. Every day three to four hundred of them were getting ill and were sent to Hasankale.[38]

Major Guze, the Commander of the 3rd Army, documents how illness acted as a major force shaping the course and outcome of the war, in his report dated 25 May 1915: "Of the soldiers dispatched from the army training grounds only few can make it to their units. Disease, and poor nutrition and housing conditions, as well as desertions decreased the number of soldiers arriving significantly."[39]

A telegram message sent by the German Consulate in Erzurum on 2 June 1915 recorded the following observations: "One third of the soldiers in the military encampment in Erzurum are ill. On the other hand, another third of the soldiers desert on the road to here."[40]

During the course of the Battle for Erzurum in 1916, Ottoman forces suffered 2,000 combat deaths, and another 2,546 were taken as prisoners. When the wounded and frozen soldiers are also added, the losses of the Ottoman Army reached 13,000. The toll of the battle on the Russian side was equally terrific: 14,000, including dead, wounded, and frozen.[41] The deciphered message which the 3rd Army Command had sent to the Supreme Command headquarters on 12 September 1915 is of historical significance as it recognized the miserable conditions of the army, which was in fact an early warning sign of the tragic end awaiting the Ottoman soldiers:

> The strength of the 3rd Army is about 160,000 men for the time being. Only parts of the troops wear uniforms, whereas the rest are still in their civilian clothes. They in fact have nothing but underclothes and shirts. Set aside the disciplinary implications of this situation, most of the troops in those clothes will soon get sick due to the severe climate conditions prevailing in this area. We resorted to every measure to find a solution to this problem; for example any fabric that could be found was used to make military clothes. Although the soldiers whose clothes seem to be relatively okay are not given new ones, the ones we would be able to tailor in these primitive ways are enough to protect only a small portion of the troops. It appears that many soldiers will become ill and eventually die during the long and severe winter. Clothes for 100,000 soldiers, as well as conical tents sufficient to hold those soldiers are badly needed. We request immediate supply of as many greatcoats, shoes, clothes, and tents as possible.[42]

Those urgent calls and warnings, however, were of no avail: there was no way to equip the entire troops of the 3rd Army with sufficient clothing. As a result, it is common to find entries similar to the one below in the journals of many military personnel: "The weather is very cold. On the night of 25/26 April [1915], eight soldiers were frozen to death."[43]

The Russian Army, on the other hand, was well supplied. Therefore, when an Ottoman soldier was able to take the clothes of a dead Russian soldier, his friends envied him:

> Russian soldiers were wearing long greatcoats covering their legs entirely, and had good clothes keeping their bodies warm. They were wearing leather boots on rainy days. Their haversacks were full of daily food rations, including even tea, and sugar. An Ottoman soldier who happens to seize them from Russian soldiers aroused intensive feelings of envy among his friends: as if he had captured a treasure from the enemy.[44]

Liman von Sanders, based on his experience on the Mesopotamian and Syrian fronts, had the following observations about the incidents of appropriating the clothes of the dead soldiers in desert conditions:

> The Ottoman soldiers did not have clothes suitable for summer conditions, and were wearing coarse woolen clothes (which could be better called as rags). Considering that more than three-fourths of the Ottoman soldiers did not have underclothes any more, it was apparent how uncomfortable it was for those soldiers to wear such thick clothes directly on their skin. Therefore, one cannot consider Ottoman soldiers' attempt to strip of the clothes of the dead British and Indian soldiers who fell in front of the Ottoman trenches after another unsuccessful attack callousness. It was the only opportunity for the Ottoman soldiers to find clothes, shoes, and underwear. The prohibitions issued against seizing the clothing of the dead bore no fruits. In such cases "the European manners" were of no use; and the Ottoman soldiers were immediately replacing the shabby clothes on their scrawny bodies with the new ones taken from the enemy.[45]

İbrahim Tali, chief doctor of the 3rd Army, after inspecting the 34th and 18th divisions in February 1915 together with the deputy chief of administration, noted the following: "We observed that the troops were living under miserable conditions in the tents, and were not provided with sufficient food. The meat given to them had a gelatinous appearance and seemed to have lost all its nutritive value."[46]

In 1916, already during the early stages of war, the Ottoman troops deployed in Palestine also were being fed insufficiently. From that year on, the bread rations of soldiers were reduced from nine hundred to five hundred grams. Sometimes they did not even receive that amount. Most of the soldiers were so weakened that they did not even have the strength to do routine training or military exercises. Many incidents of poisoning occurred as the hungry soldiers started to eat poisonous leaves and plants.[47]

By the end of October 1914, the 11th Army Corps was desperately in need of provisions. The means of transportation at the disposal of the army corps were insufficient. The governor undertook the responsibility to have the 150,000 kg of provisions carried on the backs of civilians only once. The commander of the Army Cavalry Corps in Erzurum recounts the following after the disaster in Sarıkamış:

> The people of Erzurum, with their proven love for their homeland, eagerly accepted to transport the provisions. Sacks with a capacity to carry 30 kg were prepared. Upon seeing the school children, starting to walk from the Government House in a self-sacrificing manner with the bags of flour on their backs, none of us could control their tears.
>
> According to the initial plan, the people of Erzurum would bring the flour to Nebi Han, where the residents of Hasankale would take their turn and transport it to Hasankale. The people from Erzurum fulfilled their duty completely. Because Hasankale was under-populated, however, the city could assign only 700 people a day. As a result, it took rather longer to have the flour carried from Nebi Han on by the people and the military vehicles.[48]

According to the German Major Paraguin, who was the commander of the 6th Army, out of the total strength of 3,332 the 18th Army Corps had, 1,895 remained out of service due to hunger. During an inspection he made in December 1917, Paraguin also observed that the soldiers were sent to combat missions in torn clothes, some of whom even had no boots on their feet.[49]

HYGIENE

At the outset of the war in 1914, the Ottoman Army did not have sufficient medical institutions, medicines, or medical supplies. What is more, only 37,000 beds were available in the stationary hospitals, 14,000 of which were in Istanbul.[50] As a result of the efforts of the Supreme Command headquarters, the number of doctors serving in the 3rd Army, which had a total strength of 150,000, was increased from 234 as of 5 October 1914 to 425, by recruiting the previously retired doctors and the reserve officers. The Mevkii (local) Hospital in Erzurum was requisitioned to the Fortified Base Command in Erzurum. In addition, two mobile hospitals were established in Erzurum. Of the fourteen army station command posts established at the beginning of the war, doctors could be assigned to only the ones in Erzincan, Kelkit, and Bayburt. None of the latter, however, had sufficient medical supplies and equipment. Moreover, no medical stations or rest areas could be built on the main roads which were used for the transportation of the ill, wounded, and weak soldiers as well as the soldiers temporarily sent to other places for medical reasons. Those units had no vehicles to transport the sick.[51]

German Officer Gusse, the Commander of the 3rd Army, had some interesting observations:

> Infectious diseases such as typhus, spotted fever, dysentery, and recurrent fever ravaging the army, the shooting ranges, and numerous towns throughout the country, particularly Erzurum. Although it was not clear whether the immediate cause of these diseases was the large-scale troop relocations in the ranges, or the battles against the irregulars at the border areas, it is certainly true that the outbreak of the diseases were precipitated by the lack of hygienic practice among the inhabitants of the East. In addition, that the troops had to serve for extended periods of time under adverse climate conditions made them vulnerable to those diseases. The medical measures implemented so far have not proven effective in eliminating the diseases affecting a large number of individuals.
>
> The number and capacity of hospitals were far from meeting the demand; whereas the existing hospitals were very dirty. Beds and sheets were far from sufficient, nor the number of doctors. There seemed to be no way out to improve the situation. Furthermore, the steps taken toward the amelioration of the conditions were too slow. Whatever could be found in the country were collected to this end, and new hospitals gradually were made available. The intensive efforts and utmost care put in these initiatives, and some improvements achieved increased the morale within the army. Food supplies are handled carefully and necessary precautions are taken for the treatment of the patients.
>
> Despite these advancements, great difficulties were being encountered in the transfer of the patients to the areas in the interior. No railroads or automobiles were available for that purpose. The patients had to be transported with vehicles such as horse pulled carriages, oxcarts, or packhorses, which were not suitable for their health conditions. Even those impractical transportation means were in short supply. Some patients, who in fact

should not walk, had to walk. The number of the sick was increasing everyday on the frontlines, and there was no way to avoid the enormous task of carrying them to the rear out of fire. Difficulties had increased.[52]

Colonel Ali Osman, commander of the 30th Division subordinate to the 3rd Army, submitted a report to the Command of the 10th Army Corps on 15 November 1914. The information provided in the report under the heading of "medical situation in general" and the "medical company" is striking:

> Though the medical situation was good back in Giresun, it deteriorated rapidly after coming to this cold region since it was impossible to provide food and shelter to the troops in the regular way. As a result, diseases such as diarrhea, dysentery and the common cold became widespread particularly among the troops who did not have greatcoats and shoes and still wore summer clothes. Even though previously the division had more units, the average number of patients seeing a doctor was about 250 a day. That number has now reached 550, and the average number of soldiers hospitalized per day has increased to 60. That the clothes the soldiers were supplied with were not suitable to winter conditions has been the major factor leading to the increase in the cases of disease.
>
> The most badly needed medical supplies in the Division, lately, are alcohol, quinine, and iodine, which should be sent urgently. Additionally, 1,200 bandages are needed. Previously twenty crates and two bales of medicines and medical supplies had been sent to Trabzon from Istanbul for the Division. Lack of transport prevented delivery [from Trabzon].
>
> The medical company consisted of 184 recruits; when the mule drivers, cart drivers and nurse attendants are subtracted from that number, only 32 recruits were available. As this figure was below the minimum number of recruits needed in a medical company, the musical instruments belonging to the band company of the Division were stored in a depot in Hasankale, and the officers and recruits of the band company were assigned to the medical company, where they underwent medical training.
>
> Since there was no ongoing battle, no mobile hospital was established for the Division. As new recruits arrive in Erzurum they will be used to make up for the missing staff.[53]

In the wake of the Sarıkamış disaster in late 1914, epidemics of various diseases broke out in Erzurum:

Erzurum was full of sick, wounded, weak, and deserted soldiers. Many people died on the streets, in hotels, and in stables. Cases of spotted fever and recurrent fever were at their peak levels. The Field Medical Inspector General caught spotted fever, and the Army Commander had died of the same disease. Most of the doctors were infected with the disease, and a large number of them fell victim to it. In some hospitals, all medical and administrative personnel became ill, except one or two of them. Since Erzurum could not hold the entire ill and wounded, the weak and ill soldiers were accommodated in the villages of Ilıca, Kan, and Stavuk. A great misery was prevailing in those places. It was impossible to keep track of the deaths occurring daily. The diseases were also transmitted to the local people. Every day 20–30 inhabitants were dying in Erzurum. The epidemics spread to the rear areas as well. Erzincan was also surrounded with a large wave of epidemic.[54]

Tevfik Sağlam also adds: "As of 8 March 1915 no doctor was available in Aşkale, 60% of the inhabitants had caught spotted fever, and 5–6 victims were dying of the disease every day. About 500 of those patients were sent to Erzincan."[55]

The bitter fact of the war, though, was that the ill and wounded had to be transferred to other places on foot. Transferring the ill and wounded from Erzurum to Erzincan proved troublesome. Although initially necessary precautions were taken on the road, the number of patients soon overwhelmed the existing capacity, and a "great misery" erupted. Between 14 January and 2 February 1916, a total of 11,897 sick and wounded were evacuated from Erzurum; 7,342 of them reached Tercan, 1,131 reached Aşkale, and 2,888 reached Erzincan as of 2 February. A further 4,454 ill and wounded were estimated to be en route to Tercan from Erzurum. During the course of that withdrawal, a total of 18,080 ill and wounded were evacuated from Erzurum.[56] The transfer could not be carried out as planned since it was extremely cold, and the Army could not utilize the means of transportation owned by the local people, who also were fleeing to other areas.[57]

In the winter of 1916, the Ottoman Army suffered great losses due to lack of transportation vehicles and to problems encountered in the supply of food and clothing. A report dated 24 November 1916, prepared by a division commander in the area, contained the following information:

> We suffer great losses due to the lack of food and clothes. Many of the Ottoman soldiers still are wearing thin summer clothes. They don't have

shoes and greatcoats. Most of the time, they are wrapping rags around their feet, but of course that doesn't help much. Their feet remain naked anyway. The daily food supply is only one third of the suggested daily intake. The faces of the soldiers reflect their malnutrition. Draft animals barely get any feed whereas riding animals are given daily 1 or 1.5 kg barley. Consequently, animal losses are also high, and the number of animals available for carrying loads is ever-decreasing.[58]

German Doctor Schilling, in his report dated 16 December 1916, tells of the situation in Diyarbakır as follows:

It seems that the Ottoman Army Station Command is unable to care for the numerous sick; only in Diyarbakır there are approximately 5,000 to 6,000 patients. I personally saw about 500 to 600 patients in bad conditions in Mardin, who were brought there in the empty vehicles of the German truck convoys. They seemed very dirty and helpless.[59]

Another doctor, Dr. Nikau, reported on the situation in Harput in his report dated 24 December 1916:

The patients brought here really were in a pitiable condition. Besides being very dirty and lousy, they were about to die of hunger. I could find two places to use as graveyards only with the help of the medical unit of the Army. The monthly average death toll is about 900.[60]

Liman von Sanders goes on to say that "mass deaths started to occur in the 2nd Army, and 1916 was a year of disaster on the Caucasus front."[61]

The following description is very disconcerting. As of the beginning of October 1916, the strength of one company was 6,575 men. Through October, the company suffered 51 dead, 17 of whom were in combat, and 105 injuries. Furthermore, 622 soldiers were hospitalized, whereas 422 cases of desertion were recorded. As winter approached, naturally, the conditions prevailing in the company further deteriorated. In November 1916, a total of 215 soldiers died due to exhaustion and weakness in the shooting ranges, and another 1,340 were admitted to hospitals. As a result, the strength of the company decreased markedly. Nor were the reinforcements sent there sufficient to make up for the previous losses. By January, not surprisingly, the total strength of the company was down to 3,424 men. These perilous conditions led German Officer Guhr to write that probably the patients who died during transportation to other places were "luckier" since "their pains came to an end."[62]

The Fifth Expeditionary Force gathered around Erzurum. That expeditionary force had the strength of a division, formed through the reassignment of some units of the 5th Army Corps in Istanbul. It set off from Istanbul as a well-equipped force and walked for two months. During this walk, 2 percent of the troops encountered foot disorders, and 1.5 percent had common diarrhea. Rarely, cases of dysentery were observed, and three or four soldiers drowned while crossing rivers. Around forty cases of hypothermia occurred when the force was only a few days from Erzurum, as well as when it was passing through Deveboynu after Erzurum. The Fifth Expeditionary Force established a 300-bed army station hospital in Diyarbakır, in addition to the Guraba Hospital already existing there. A doctor from the mobile forces was assigned to that hospital. As of 26 February, the new hospital had 239 patients. The Fifth Expeditionary Force established another hospital in Palu and put it under the responsibility of the municipality's doctor, where about 100 severe patients were treated. The force also assigned one doctor at another hospital it established in Kiğı, which admitted 123 patients. Although the expeditionary force was able to transport a mobile drying oven used for sterilization as far as Diyarbakır, despite various difficulties encountered on the way, it could not carry it any farther. Despite the fact that the division was walking in an orderly manner and was rather successful in observing the rules of hygiene, it could not protect itself from being contaminated in Erzurum. Because epidemics were prevalent in Erzurum, as a precaution the detachments there preferred to set up their own infirmaries for the treatment of their ill personnel. As many seriously ill patients had to be treated in the infirmaries under primitive conditions, large numbers of deaths were recorded. A mobile hospital established in Müdürke started to admit patients on 19 February. By the time it reached Erzurum's environs, the health conditions in the Fifth Expeditionary Force had deteriorated rapidly, and besides diarrhea, dysentery, and malaria, several cases of spotted fever were also encountered.[63]

Dr. Mecit, who was assigned as the chief doctor to Ağvanis Hospital in Kara Yakup Gazi, east of Suşehri, reported the following on 18 January 1917:

> There is no hospital in Ağvanis; there is only one sefalethane (dispensary/nursing home). A 500-bed hospital is oxymoron for Ağvanis since it is only a village, half of which is burned to the ground. The 49th Division occupied

the rest. The detachments deployed here are the following: the Division headquarters, a military band, workshop, depots, a medical company, an artillery regiment, an assault battalion, and a battalion of convalescence consisting of 400 men. Only the stables were left to be used as a hospital. Yesterday, I visited the wards, during the daytime. Due to the darkness, it was impossible to walk inside, or recognize the faces of patients. The thickness of walls renders it difficult to open windows. In fact some of them have openings in the ceiling. When those holes are covered, it becomes very dark inside, whereas if they are left open, snow comes inside. No glass is available here [to be used for windows]. Except for one or two wards, the patients are either lying on beds on earth, or directly on earth without any bed. Nor is there any wood to build beds. There are no trees nearby to cut down. The forest is far away and it takes hours to go there. The wards have no lighting or heating systems. The soldiers had tried to put a dome-shaped earth stove in the middle; but it could not be used since there was no flow of air inside. Everywhere is ice-cold. Two of the wards are separated from others for "hospital admissions" and "convalescence." You can also see inside the wards some bodies lying on the ground, which belong to the soldiers who died while being brought here.

To give you an idea about how crowded the wards were, the following comparison is in order. The size of a ward is 130 cubic meters and it was holding a total of 150 patients including exhausted soldiers, those discharged from the hospital and still on sick leave.

Yesterday morning, four corpses were lying in front of the quarantine ward. As the ward is very crowded, the four ill recruits brought from the detachment the previous evening could only be placed in front of the door. Until morning, however, all of them died. Yesterday, I discharged the exhausted soldiers; many of them will die in a few days. At the headquarters of the division, there is a battalion of 400 convalescent men. The soldiers of that battalion are lying on the ground, one on top of another. Yesterday, I sent 11 of those soldiers to the rear, on foot. The number of patients in the hospital is 711. Only 23 of them were sent from other detachments; the rest are from the 49th Division. Five cases of smallpox were recorded among the troops of the division. Nine patients yesterday and eight patients today died in the hospital, apart from the deaths occurring outside of the hospital.

Yesterday, 100 exhausted soldiers sent from various detachments arrived here. Since they cannot be transported to the rear areas, these exhausted soldiers constantly are being transferred from the battalion to the hospital, then from the hospital to the battalion of convalescence, and from the battalion of convalescence to the hospital again. Today, four individuals were admitted to the hospital suspected of typhus, whereas three of the previously admitted patients diagnosed for typhus died. As recurrent fever cannot be diagnosed without medical tests, previously it could not be differentiated from other diseases. As of today's morning, the microscope is operating; hence it will be possible to diagnose recurrent fever. My personal opinion is that unless a disciplined and devoted chief doctor is assigned to this division, it soon will entirely melt away. There is no army station command stationed around here. No vehicle belonging to any of the columns passes nearby. In case a hospital is established here, it will be necessary to ensure transportation to the interior on a daily basis, in order to maintain the number of personnel here. But how can it be realized under those conditions? The Suşehri Commander states in his telegram that the provisions needed for the hospital would be supplied from Suşehri, and asks the 49th Division to send animals to carry them. The Division however has to have its own provisions carried on the backs of the residents of Alakilise. Only once or twice a week, 5 to 10 animals are sent to Koyulhisar in order to deliver barley to the detachments there. The same animals also are used for transporting the exhausted soldiers from the convalescence battalion to the Mesudiye Recovery Centre.[64]

Following the withdrawal of the Russian forces in 1917, the 6th Army was now fighting against only the British army. The units of the 6th Army, however, had been completely exhausted by the war. What is more, because the tribes in the region allied with the British, food supplies could not be obtained from local sources. An epidemic of dysentery continued to inflict its harm, the victims of which filled up all the hospitals in the area including the mobile hospitals of the Army Corps.[65]

COMMANDERS ALSO DIE

In the case of the Ottoman Empire, the first death of a commander from disease during the Great War occurred on the Caucasus Front. Hafız Hakkı Pasha, commander of the Ottoman 3rd Army in Erzurum, died of typhus on 12 February 1915, shortly after he had replaced the previous commander, Hasan İzzet Pasha, on 8 January 1915. Hafız Hakkı Pasha was a young commander. The following are his words quoted from the book *Bozgun* (The Rout), which he had written after the Balkan War:

> The rout resembles a storm, or a hurricane. It breaks out suddenly, destroying and upsetting everything, and leaving ruins behind. A well-trained

soldier is no different than a well-grown crop field standing against storm. Just as the wheat ears bend down in the wind, but return to their original shapes immediately after the storm subsides, he also recovers in a short time, as if nothing had happened.[66]

The "rout," however, defined by Hafız Hakkı Pasha was nothing compared to an epidemic. Even strong and well-trained soldiers and healthy civilians were helpless against the epidemics, as was Hafız Hakkı Pasha himself, who fell victim to disease. Another commander who lost his life because of illness was the famous German field marshal Goltz who served in the Ottoman Army during the Great War. In November 1914, Marshal Goltz wrote the following in his diary: "I wish I could die in battle. Unfortunately no bullet shoots me!"[67] Marshal Goltz returned to Baghdad on 31 March 1916, on a ship full of ill and wounded. On 9 April his situation worsened and he died from typhus, "the epidemic disease of the Great War," ten days later.[68] (Although the French colonel Lamouche states that Marshal Goltz died on 6 August 1916, he is incorrect.[69]) Lieutenant Colonel von Kisling, in a letter to Major Restorf dated 16 June 1916, describes the last days of Marshal Goltz and his illness, which lasted quite a short time:

> When the Marshal came back from the headquarters on 9 April, he complained about dizziness and in the evening he had a lack of appetite. The next day, he had high fever. We brought three doctors to examine him: Dr. Haerle, Dr. Sandrok, and the Turkish doctor Abdülkadir Bey. They diagnosed the disease as spotted fever. Since his heart seemed well, we had some hope in the beginning. He recognized me when I approached him. However, on the morning of 18 April, one day before his death, his periods of unconsciousness became more frequent. He summoned me many times to his bed to work together; but soon after he started to talk, he became mentally confused. Though unconscious, he still continued to be preoccupied with the management of military matters. He was talking unconsciously about the Army food supplies, the situation in Kut al-Amarah, the next military operation, as well as Colonel Gleich and Adolf Friedrich, the Grand Duke of Mecklenburg, who had been just assigned here.
>
> He probably realized that he had come to the end of his life. On the third day of his illness, he said to me, "I am about to retreat gradually to the grand general headquarters." Another time, he said: "I know, these doctors don't want to tell me that I'm going to die soon; they act attentively. Anyway, I know it."
>
> During the first days of his illness, he was yelling at the doctors con-

stantly and complaining that they were giving him a hard time. He later became a very obedient patient and did whatever the doctors told him to do. On the morning of 18 April, I gave him the good news about the victory won by Halil Bey in Kut, which made him very happy. After that, he entered into a long lasting period of mental confusion and unconsciousness, and we lost him on the night of April 18/19.[70]

Dr. Abdülkadir Noyan, the chief doctor of the 6th Army, writes the following about the illness and death of Marshal Goltz:

I began the vaccination campaign at the army headquarters. Kazım Karabekir, our Chief Officer, as well as other staff officers, the chief doctor, and other doctors were all vaccinated. I suggested our Army Commander Marshal von der Goltz and his private doctor Oberndörfer be vaccinated too. But they refused, probably because they did not believe in the benefits of vaccination. Army Commander Marshal von der Goltz was gone for inspecting the Kut al-Amarah Front. Ten days after his return, he became ill. Together with the German Naval Doctor Lieutenant Sandrock, I tried to treat the Marshal at the Army headquarters. The course of the illness was not alarming at the beginning, but on the eleventh day, pneumonia started in both lungs, accompanied by difficulty in respiration and high fever. The next day, that brave Marshal, who was very fond of the Turks, passed away. Like everybody else, I too wept for his loss. It was not his fault to reject the vaccination against typhus; his doctor had not given him the permission to do that.[71]

Another commander who lost his life during the typhus epidemic in the Great War was the British general Maude, who died on 18 November 1917.[72]

4

EPIDEMIC DISASTER

> 7 November 1916, I set off from Silvan for Bitlis....Just as we passed over the Batman Bridge, we saw a man lying, like dead, on the road as he couldn't find any strength to walk any further due to hunger. We saw two more men lying in the same position on the road between the bridge and the resting area. We found out that they were refugees.
>
> On the road between the Batman Bridge and Silvan, and after passing over the bridge, we also saw two horses that seemed to have died a short while ago (both the people and animals are dying from hunger).
>
> —Atatürk'ün Hatıra Defteri

A POPULAR BOOK ENTITLED *Captain Selahaddin's Novel* provides valuable information about the Ottoman military losses in the Sarıkamış Mountains during the winter of 1914–1915:

> The forces of Tsarist Russia had crossed our eastern border on 1 November 1914. At the end of the battle which started in the vicinity of Hasankale (on 10 January 1915), our 3rd Army was almost completely wiped out....At that time, Enver Pasha was thirty-five years old. As a result of the offensive against the Russian forces, initiated on his orders during the coldest days of the winter, out of the total of 112,000 men serving in the Ottoman army, 53,000 froze to death, 7,000 were taken as prisoners, and 30,000 were sent to hospitals, unable to fight....Whereas on the Russian side, 10,000 soldiers got frozen to death, and 2,000 were taken as prisoners. The number of those who were either killed in fighting or became ill was 20,000.[1]

The numbers stipulated by the Russians themselves approximate those figures. The losses suffered by the Russian Caucasus Army in Sarıkamış were 29,000 dead, 20,000 of whom were killed during combat and 9,000 who froze to death. When another 2,000 to 3,000 Russians taken as prisoner by the Turks are added, the total death toll of the Russian Army reaches a figure as high as 32,000.[2] The official figures released by the Russians indicate that they captured 7,000 Turkish soldiers in the course of the fighting, and after the battle another 23,000 dead were buried. The Ottoman losses reach 60,000, when the 10,000 soldiers who died in the sector of the 11th Army Corps deployment, and the 20,000 who were frozen to death at the back of the frontlines, are also taken into consideration. As of 14 February 1915, the total strength of the army was calculated at 42,000 men. Since the army consisted of 118,000 men before the battle, the fate of the remaining 16,000 soldiers is not known. It is estimated that probably some of those soldiers joined the local militia, whereas some others spread through the villages nearby. On the other hand, according to another assessment made by the officials, "one reason behind the enormous loss of life in the war was the insufficient number of medical staff and hospitals." The clothing and food provided to the soldiers also were far from being adequate. Whereas the hospital in Erzurum had only 900 beds, at times as many as 15,000 sick and wounded gathered in that city.[3]

Marshal Fevzi Çakmak, the chief of general staff, gave the following information at a speech he made at the War College on January 22, 1935:

> Based on the figures we gathered from different documents, initially the fate of around 78,000 soldiers could not be accounted for. These recruits were thought to have been killed or captured by the enemy. Eventually, we were able to find traces of some of them in the hospital registers. In March, 38,000 men were admitted to hospitals. If we add 10,000 dead per month to that figure, as well as those who had taken refuge in the villages close-by, a total casualty toll of 50,000 men can be obtained. When we add a further 10,000 killed in the battle, 10,000 deserted from the hospital one month later, and 8,000 other deserters, which make a total of 28,000, we can account for 78,000 soldiers initially unknown. Since all of the soldiers admitted to hospitals during those days died, it would be a correct estimation to say that half of the soldiers participated in the Sarıkamış battles, i.e., 60,000, lost their lives.
>
> You can see how the lives of soldiers were wasted. When as many as 30,000 patients were admitted to hospitals per month, various epidemics, such as typhus, recurrent fever, dysentery, typhoid, and the like inevitably broke out. Under those miserable conditions, the soldiers were looking for some place to die on the roads. As we understand from the information provided in a book written by Arif Bey, Gazi Ahmet Muhtar Pasha's secretary, similar things also took place in Erzurum during the 1877–78 Russian

TABLE 4.1. Casualties of Sarıkamış disaster

UNITS	22 DECEMBER 1914	18 JANUARY 1915	CASUALTIES
9th Army Corps	36,784	–	36,784
10th Army Corps	48,943	2,200	46,743
11th Army Corps	27,019	5,200	21,816
2nd Cavalry Division	5,428	1,500	3,928
TOTAL	118,174	8,900	109,271

War. The epidemics caused the death of 30,000 soldiers back then, which was related to the fact that the villages in the area had long been suffering from epidemics of infectious diseases.

The medical infrastructure was not well organized yet. Although Erzurum needed a medical capacity for 16,000 patients, only one 900-bedded hospital was available. The dead were being piled up in the tents like heaps of wood.[4]

A study published in 1988, on the other hand, contends that the Ottoman losses in Sarıkamış amounted to 109,274 men. The findings of this study are presented in Table 4.1, prepared based on the number of troops in the units as of 22 December 1914 and 18 January 1915.

Doctor Colonel Tevfik Sağlam, who was assigned as the medical chief of the 3rd Army after the Sarıkamış disaster, makes the following assessment in his study published in 1940:

> It could be easily imagined how difficult it was to carry out medical services during the course of the arduous offensive and the tragic retreat. Though it was not possible to calculate the exact figure of our casualties, Marshal Fevzi Çakmak admits that around 60,000 soldiers died in that battle, a figure which is likely to reflect the actual death toll. In fact, numerous officers and soldiers were martyred during the long walks and battles. Many of them died from hypothermia, whereas the ones, whose hands and feet were frozen, either died or became disabled. The soldiers returning from the frontlines were completely exhausted, several of whom easily became ill and died. Under such conditions, it was only natural that the epidemics found a very suitable environment for spreading and affecting the people severely. The ill and the wounded spread over the area, and sought shelter

in different places. Whereas some others traveled long distances to reach their homes, many of whom died on the roads. Especially among those who found shelter in the villages located in the Pasinler Plain, the Tortum Valley, and the Erzurum Plain, many died, and the ill were left without proper treatment. Many villages in Hasankale, as well as on the plains of Pasinler and Erzurum were full of ill and wounded soldiers.[5]

Dr. Begfeld, the German consul in Trabzon, in his report from 2 March 1915, illustrates the effects of the Sarıkamış disaster on Trabzon. He observed: "All the hospitals in the town are full of patients with spotted typhus. That infectious disease has created a real disaster here; of the 900–1000 ill soldiers, 30–50 are dying each day."[6]

WHAT OCCURRED IN ERZURUM AND ITS ENVIRONS AT THE BEGINNING OF 1915?

During the three-month period between the start of mobilization and the declaration of war, the 3rd Army had the largest military build up in Erzurum and its vicinity. The soldiers arrived there from remote areas on foot and had close contacts with the local people in villages where they stopped over on their way. Both the soldiers and the people were lousy. The soldiers did not have a chance to bathe on the way, nor did they have any means to get rid of the lice in their contingents. Not only in large cities such as Erzurum, but also in small villages, housing conditions were extremely bad, and all these areas were overcrowded. The soldiers were mixed with the local inhabitants. As a result, right from the onset of the war, the army was regularly exposed to louse-borne diseases such as spotted fever and recurrent fever.[7]

The real disaster, though, started after Sarıkamış. In the aftermath of that dramatic offensive, which resulted in the destruction of a large part of the army, all the villages in the Pasinler Plain, Hasankale, Erzurum, and the villages in the Erzurum Plain were flooded by ill, disabled, and exhausted soldiers. The hospitals could not accommodate all the soldiers in need of treatment. In most hospitals, almost all doctors and administrative personnel caught spotted fever. Süleyman Numan Pasha, the field medical inspector general, also became ill with spotted fever. The disease turned into an epidemic among the people, causing twenty to thirty deaths daily in Erzurum. In February, the situation deteriorated even further. The soldiers sent to their homes on sick leave, as well as those who deserted from the army, acted as agents for transmitting the infection to the interior. Another epidemic broke out in Erzincan, overwhelming the capacity of the hospitals.

The epidemic ravaged the main line where the army stations were located (extending to Ulukışla), as well as along the roads connecting Erzurum-Kiği-Palu-Maden-Diyarbakır and Erzurum-Erzincan-Harput-Diyarbakır, including the villages close by. At the beginning of March, the epidemic started to ease after taking a heavy toll at the battlefront. The epidemic, however, still persisted very severely among the labor battalions, the gendarmerie, and the warehouse personnel, as well as among the people living in the region.[8]

The contagious diseases, such as typhus, spotted fever, and dysentery, caused a second disaster for the 3rd Army after the one inflicted in Sarıkamış. Because the disease was transmitted to the animals, too, most of the time it was not possible to transport patients from the battlefront to even the closest hospital. Thousands of ill soldiers had to walk to hospitals. The number of hospitals and medical personnel were far from meeting the demand anyway. On some occasions, 15,000 patients had to wait for treatment at Erzurum's only hospital which in fact had only a capacity for 900 patients. There was no way to implement effective methods of disinfection for most of the soldiers stationed in the trenches on the high mountains covered with snow. Not only the soldiers, but also the officers in contact with the soldiers, were infected by the disease. Two of the three German doctors serving in Erzincan had to be sent back to Germany since they became ill with typhus, whereas the third died of typhus in Erzincan.[9]

Doctors Colley and Zlosisti, who were among the Red Cross doctors stationed in Erzincan, wrote the following on 3 March 1915: "No medical services can be properly provided due to the lack of all kinds of preventive medical measures. As a result of that, the casualties among the Ottoman soldiers are much higher than the Germans." The lack of medical services "is perishing the Ottoman soldiers in unbelievably great numbers." As a result, the Ottoman army had to struggle with the challenge of providing medical treatment to the withdrawing forces in addition to the military disasters it encountered.[10]

The report sent in March 1915 by the 3rd Army's Office of Medical Chief to the General Medical Inspectorate provides valuable information about the admissions to the hospitals attached to the 3rd Army for several diseases, as well as the deaths that occurred there. Those figures add credibility to the observations of the Red Cross doctors regarding the severity of the epidemic (see Table 4.2).

In 1915, just during March, 45 percent of the servicemen in the 3rd Army became ill with infectious diseases, and eventually the 3rd Army lost

Table 4.2. Red Cross hospital admissions records

Admissions to hospitals in one month	38,730 admissions	9,242 dead
Typhoid	1,243 admissions	654 dead
Spotted fever	2,109 admissions	1,116 dead
Recurrent fever	2,102 admissions	622 dead
Dysentery	2,250 admissions	846 dead
Influenza	677 admissions	50 dead

11 percent of its total strength due to diseases. Of those who caught diseases, 24 percent died.[11]

A study carried out at Istanbul University in 1999 calculated the incidence rate of the typhus epidemic that broke out in Erzurum in 1915, based on data provided by the monthly reports prepared by Dr. Tevfik Sağlam, the medical chief of the 3rd Army in the Great War. According to those calculations, in March of that year 2,478 soldiers of the 3rd Army became ill with typhus. In the aftermath of the severe epidemic, which broke out in late 1914 and became more severe in January and February of 1915, typhus remained a significant threat. Given that most soldiers took shelter in the villages following the defeat in Sarıkamış, and the infected soldiers could not be quarantined in their units, it would be reasonable to conclude that the actual incidence rate of typhus was greater than the calculated value. Toward the end of June, the incidence rate of typhus started to decline gradually, and in July the decline became steeper.[12]

According to the same study, the incidence rate of the recurrent fever affecting the 3rd Army units in 1915 was higher than that of typhus. The annual variations calculated for the two diseases, on the other hand, seem almost equal. As far as the epidemics of louse-borne diseases are concerned, more cases of recurrent fever were encountered than those of typhus. The epidemics of recurrent fever and typhus continued through 1916. Compared to the previous year, however, an evident decrease was observed in both diseases.

From the beginning of 1916 until mid-August of that year, the Ottoman Army was on the retreat, which, accompanied by fierce battles, caused the flow of great numbers of ill and wounded into hospitals. Nevertheless, despite large numbers of wounded flooding into hospitals and the great poverty that arose during the army's retreat, the incidence rate of both diseases did not increase noticeably in the first months of 1916. The increase observed in the spring was countered by a decrease during the summer. By the end of the year, however, a significant surge was observed in the incidence rates for both diseases. That surge from January 1916 on was interpreted as a second epidemic. Typhus was more frequently encountered when soldiers were in their barracks than in the months when military operations were being carried out. Because the barracks were overcrowded, lice more easily spread through the wards. As a matter of fact, no large-scale military operation was carried out in the 3rd Army's area of operation in 1917. Since the winter of 1916–1917 was very severe, however, a famine devastated the army. The incidence rates of typhus and recurrent fever, which had been increasing during the last months of 1916, started to decline and fell to a low 0.1 percent from January 1917 on.

The medical report for January 1917 narrates a wide-scale struggle against lice conducted throughout the month. The exercise grounds and the points of dispatch were completely cleaned of lice. The places where the patients had caught the disease were detected and disinfected. Clothing and belongings of 40,176 people on the frontlines and 62,478 people in the rear were cleaned during January, despite the shortage of fuel. The fight against lice continued through February and March. As of March, sixty-three mist boxes were available on the frontlines, and eighty-nine in the rear. During the same month, however, sudden deaths from malnutrition were encountered in the army. The army persistently continued to implement the measures against lice in July, and as a result, the soldiers deployed in the frontlines were almost completely free of lice. The figures on the disease rates in 1917, indeed, attest to the success of those efforts. Although the figures pertaining to the last months of 1916 were pointing toward an imminent epidemic, the incidence rates of diseases significantly decreased in the following months, a result of the determined efforts of the doctors and other medical staff working under the 3rd Army's Office of Medical Chief. In March 1918, the typhus epidemic resumed after the arrival of new reinforcements from Istanbul. Notwithstanding this development, overall, the incidence rates of typhus and recurrent fever were significantly reduced in 1917 and 1918.[13]

The high incidence rate of typhus in 1915 is confirmed by Table 4.3, which shows the number of deaths due to various causes among Ottoman medical officers working in the area.

Of the 300 medical officers who died between 1914 and 1918, 222 lost their lives due to typhus. That ratio of over two-thirds is unbelievably high. During the Great War, a large portion of Ottoman medical officers died

TABLE 4.3. Causes of death of Ottoman medical officers (1914–1918)

Typhus	222
Typhoid	17
Cholera	10
Malignant fever	7
Enteric fever	4
Freezing to death	4
Recurrent fever	3
Influenza	2
Dysentery	1
Paratyphoid	1
In hospital	2
On ship	1
Accident	1
In captivity as prisoner	1
Unknown	3
On the front	21
TOTAL	300

while they were struggling with infectious diseases. A direct and meaningful relationship was established between the incidence rates of the diseases and the distribution of deaths, which is obtained by tabulating the number of deaths into the years and months of their occurrence. The highest number of deaths was observed in 1915 (113 deaths). It was followed by 81 deaths in 1916; 57 deaths in 1917; and 21 deaths in 1918. Moreover, each year the number of deaths occurring in the first half of the year exceeded that of the second half: The number of deaths in the first half of the years in question were as follows: 101 deaths in 1915; 67 deaths in 1916; 45 deaths in 1917; and 16 deaths in 1918.

The number of medical officers who died during the first six months of 1915 accounts for one-third of the total number of medical officers who

TABLE 4.4. The months of deaths of the Ottoman medical officers

YEAR	JANUARY–JUNE	JULY–DECEMBER	TOTAL
1914	3	7	10
1915	101	12	113
1916	67	14	81
1917	45	12	57
1918	16	5	21
TOTAL	232	50	282

died during the entire war. This is indicative of the fact that in the beginning of 1915, the Ottoman medical officers were confronted with enormous epidemics which forced them to work in close contact with patients affected by the diseases for extended hours. The death toll the Ottoman Army suffered under these extraordinary conditions is very well documented by the statistical data regarding the deaths of medical officers.

When Dr. Tevfik Sağlam was assigned as the medical chief of the 3rd Army, Dr. Mayer, the deputy field medical inspector general, told him the following before he left Istanbul for Erzurum:

> The 3rd Army is in a grim situation. I don't know what the exact conditions in the region are, where and which hospitals exist, and how many patients need treatment. I could say for sure though that Erzurum is virtually in the middle of a fire. The responsibility incumbent upon you is to contain the disease where it is and prevent it from spreading further. Other than that, there is not much to be done in Erzurum.

Dr. Sağlam also narrates the following in his memoirs:

Past Niğde, we encountered isolated cases of spotted fever in many places. In most cases, however, the disease was diagnosed as influenza instead. Most of those cases thought to be influenza were in fact spotted fever. The spotted fever was very severe in Erzincan whereas the epidemic had not yet reached its peak level in Erzurum. Except for those who previously had spotted fever, almost all of the doctors were either ill, or were on convalescence leave.[14]

Aziz Samih, who was working at the 3rd Army Headquarters in Erzurum in January 1915, provides the following observations about the extent of the disaster encountered in the region:

> I was woken up at midnight by a phone call on 29 January. I went to pick up the phone. Avni Pasha, the Inspector of Army Stations, was calling. He told me that Hakkı Pasha had passed away at two thirty a.m. local time, and wanted me to ask Enver Pasha where to bury him. We went to Erzurum, and laid Hakkı Pasha to rest in Kars Kapısı. He had a diary with a black cover. At the headquarters, I used to see him writing something on it every day. They told me that in his will he had requested that his diary be taken by Captain Cemal, the Commander of the Headquarters, to his wife after his death.
>
> The diseases of typhus and recurrent fever, having spread to even the Army Commander, are causing too many deaths. Long and deep ditches have been dug in the north of Hasankale. The carriages constantly transport the dead bodies to the ditches every day. Staff Officer Şemseddin recently died of recurrent fever. Two doctors assigned to the Headquarters, Adil and Şükrü, also caught typhus. They were taken to the hospital.... That louse-born disease, which has no known method of treatment, follows its victims everywhere. No infectious disease specialist is available in Erzurum. Twenty doctors are ill.[15]

According to Dr. Sağlam, at the beginning of 1915 around twenty to thirty civilians per day were dying due to the disease in Erzurum. He provides the following observations regarding the conditions prevailing there:

> Erzurum was flooded by ill, wounded, and weak soldiers, as well as deserters. One could see many people suffering on the streets, in hotels, or in stables, waiting for their turns. Epidemics of typhus and recurrent fever have reached their utmost severity....
>
> Since all the ill and wounded could not be accommodated in Erzurum, the exhausted and ill soldiers were also placed in the villages of Ilıca, Kan, and İstavuk, located on the Erzurum Plain. Extreme poverty was prevailing in those places, and it was impossible to keep records of the deaths. The diseases diffused to the local people, causing around 20–30 civilian deaths a day in Erzurum. All the provincial officials volunteered in hospitals in the town and in the villages to help care for the patients. The number of deaths among them due to disease was not negligible.

At the time, the Ottoman authorities could not provide "exact figures" about the 3rd Army's epidemic-related losses in January 1915. According to the officials stationed in the area, it was not possible to keep track of the deaths. Most of the time, the IDs of the patients could not be registered, let alone diagnosing their illnesses.[16]

On 29 November 1914, some 139 officers and 5,646 recruits wounded in battle were transferred to Erzurum from the Caucasian front. As of that date, a total of 6,929 ill and wounded were receiving treatment in the hospitals in Erzurum and Hasankale, 4,985 of whom were in Erzurum. Dr. Nâzım Şakir, who was assigned to Erzurum then, narrates the following about the onset of the typhus epidemic:

One week after the commencement of the war, all of the 300 beds of the hospital were occupied by patients. The hospital offered extremely bad care and treatment services. Since no autoclave was available, all of us had lice on their bodies. The spotted fever, which already had existed in the town before the war, intensified and spread throughout the towns and villages and into the hospitals. One of the reasons behind the failure to prevent the spotted fever before the war, which was borne by the lice transmitted from the villages to the town, was the lack of preventive measures against the spread of lice. A second reason was the reluctance on the part of doctors to care for patients, since they believed that the disease was airborne.

The typhus epidemic turned into a real disaster with the arrival of the soldiers moving back and forth between the frontlines and the interior, as well as the ill and wounded being treated in the town. It was beyond our ability to care for all of the patients. In the meantime, young doctors who had graduated in 1914 were assigned to Erzurum. Since they were too young and inexperienced, they caught typhus before us. We could not provide them with the medical care they needed. The medical resources and personnel were inadequate. As typhus is one of those illnesses that become more hazardous the more they spread through body, [we knew that] any complication affecting especially the lungs and the heart would definitely end with death. Once that merciless disease entered the body, it was migrating to different organs freely, and settling in whatever organ it would choose, causing various clinical symptoms. The course of the disease was very severe, and 70% of the patients were dying. Only those who were receiving good care, who had a strong bodily constitution, or who were infected by viruses with lower levels of toxin could recover from the disease.[17]

Dr. Şakir, having caught typhus during the outbreak in Erzurum in the fall of 1914, had to undergo a long period of convalescence. After his recovery, he went back to the hospital only to burst into tears when he realized none of his friends were there: "After recovering, I went back to the hospital where I used to work. I could not see any of the people who I had known while working there. The doctors, nurses, and patients were replaced completely. I could not help crying."[18]

The typhus also took its toll among the inhabitants of Erzurum and Erzincan, in addition to the losses it caused in the army. Dr. Server Kâmil was appointed as the chief doctor of the Red Crescent Hospital in Erzincan, which was established through the contributions of the people of Konya. He commenced his duty on 26 March 1915. He later noted that eight of his colleagues, including Dr. Süfyan and Dr. Recai, died of typhus, and fifty to sixty deaths were observed daily among the soldiers.[19] The ill doctors lay with open bruises on their back which could not even be dressed.[20] Three doctors of the Hasankale hospital died one after another due to typhus. As the water pipes of the hospital bath were frozen, the patients could not be cleaned of lice. Burying the dead proved extremely difficult as it was almost impossible to dig the frozen soil.[21]

Dr. Sağlam, the former medical chief of the 3rd Army, made the following explanations regarding the disease-related deaths during the Great War, in a speech he delivered at the Gülhane Military Medical Academy on 8 January 1939:

> The number of admissions to hospitals during a period of 42.5 months between March 1915 and the end of 1918 was 564,498 in the 3rd Army. That makes an average of 13,250 admissions per month, and 435 admissions per day. Given that the average strength of the army was approximately 110,000 men, each month 12% of the servicemen were ill. On the other hand, a total of 44,234 wounded soldiers were admitted to hospitals, which implies a monthly average of 1,040 and daily average of 34. In other words, the number of the ill is 12 times greater than that of the wounded. As for the deaths, 107,761 soldiers fell victim to diseases. Whereas 3,801 servicemen died of wounds, 9,001 were killed in the course of fighting. Thus, the total number of deaths was 120,563.[22]

In the winter of 1914–1915, epidemics with high incidence rates broke out in and around Erzurum. The records of the 3rd Army's Office of Medical Chief regarding death rates in the military units deployed in the area reflect the following: A total of 9,485 individuals were admitted to hospitals, 5,842 due to illnesses and 3,643 due to wounds. Of those, 2,366 of the ill and 389 of the wounded died while in the hospital. The number of patients admitted due to spotted fever was 522, of whom 218 lost their lives. Of the 537 patients admitted for dysentery, 145 died. While 46 patients with erysipelas were hospitalized, 37 of them died. All 5 tetanus patients who were admitted to hospitals died. "Those numbers are definitely well below the actual figures." Even though the medical conditions had improved somewhat, and the effect of spotted fever had been alleviated by March 1915, still a total of 38,000 patients were admitted to hospitals during that month, 9,242 of whom died. Spotted fever alone accounted for 2,109 of the admissions and 1,116 of the deaths.[23]

As of 6 February 1915, the number of sick and wounded soldiers in various towns was as follows: 2,041 in Hasankale, 8,906 in and around Erzurum (Ilıca, Kan, Istavuk), 1,050 in Bayburt, 1,000 in Trabzon, 457 in Bulanık, 913 in Hınıs, 412 in Malazgirt, and 521 in Van. The total number of ill and wounded within the 3rd Army reached 20,000, including those admitted to hospitals in Erzincan, Elazığ, Muş, Bitlis, and Diyarbakır.[24]

After the 3rd Army lost half of its manpower in Sarıkamış in the winter of 1914–1915, the 37th Division and other detachments of the 13th Army Corps joined it in January 1915. However, since those detachments came from warmer provinces, they could not transfer all of their troops; the weakened and sick soldiers were left in various cities along the way: 539 in Malazgirt, 372 in Bulanık, and 381 in Hınıs; and 415 patients were sent back home from the hospital newly opened in Esmer. The vehicles carrying the mobile hospitals could not go beyond Diyarbakır, and most of the personnel from the medical company became ill. A hospital was set up in Mişki by the medical company, which was formed for a second time. Only one doctor was assigned to that hospital, and he had to care for 681 patients as of 16 February.[25]

According to the 3rd Army's statistics, the number of admissions to hospitals due to spotted fever (typhus) declined progressively from 1915 on, when a severe epidemic of typhus broke out: a 42 percent reduction in 1916; 75 percent in 1917; and 94 percent in 1918. During the period between March 1915 and September 1918, a total of 19,619 cases of spotted fever were recorded, 7,310 of whom died.[26] Another source provides the following data: a total of 93,000 typhus cases were encountered within the 3rd Army during the four years of war, 26,322 of which resulted in death. Those figures did not include the deserters or those who died away from their units, either on the roads or in various villages.[27]

Of the epidemic diseases occurring within the 3rd Army during the Great War, recurrent fever played a significant role from November 1914 on. As with spotted fever, recurrent fever caused the highest level of deaths in the winter of 1914–1915, according to hospital records from the 3rd Army's area of responsibility.[28] The statistics prepared in the early periods of the war show that enteric fever (typhoid) was also widespread. In July 1915, a small-scale "paratyphoid A" epidemic broke out in Erzurum.[29]

During the Great War, many cases of death from hypothermia occurred within the 3rd Army, due to the severe winter conditions prevailing in Eastern Anatolia. Most of those cases of hypothermia were encountered during the military operations carried out in winter.[30] In Sarıkamış, the casualties the Ottoman Army suffered under the command of Enver Pasha was caused more by cold and hunger than by the fighting. According to Guhr, the number of wounded was only around eighteen to twenty thousand. The rest of the troops were almost wiped out by typhus.[31] Liman von Sanders wrote the following on that incident: According to the official records, of the Army's total strength of ninety thousand men, only twelve thousand were able to withdraw. The remaining troops were either killed in combat, were taken as prisoners, died of hunger, or were frozen to death in military camps without any tents. "Then, an epidemic of spotted fever broke out, killing most of the remainder who had lost their bodily strength."[32]

Dr. Bentmann, a hygiene specialist, narrates the following assessment about the situation. "The typhus epidemic was like a strong desert fire burning down the entire country, which first surfaced among the ruins of the 3rd Army in the Caucasus in January 1915." From just the province of Sivas, 290,000 typhus cases were reported to the German authorities. That typhus epidemic later was accompanied by a cholera epidemic, which broke out in 1915. None of the later epidemics were as widespread as the one in the winter of 1915. In the aftermath of the battles taking place in 1916, a new typhus epidemic ravaged the area, similar to what had happened in 1915. In the course of that epidemic, which peaked in 1917, the ill soldiers died "like flies."[33]

A proposal sent from the Ottoman Ministry of Internal Affairs to the Ministry of War on 17 April 1914 stated that before taking necessary medical measures against cholera, which was seen widely in the military units, it would be more suitable to reach a joint decision of the military and civilian doctors under the authority of the Medical Directorate General, as was the case in the past. The same communiqué also stated that the doctors should be sent to the places with epidemics only after appropriate measures were decided upon according to the suggested procedure.[34] The cholera epidemic, which started in Lapseki in 1914–1915, also ravaged the provinces of Kale-i

Sultaniye and Hüdavendigar.[35] Right after the onset of the cholera epidemic in Erzurum-Hasankale at the beginning of 1915, all civil servants were reassigned to the hospitals to make up for the missing medical staff. They soon caught the disease, and all but a few lost their lives.[36] Another area plagued by cholera was the province of Aydın.[37] Since syphilis became widespread in Biga and its surrounding villages, as well as in the district of Çan in 1914, the government decided to implement a more intensive program to combat the disease in Kale-i Sultaniye.[38]

The greatest danger for the Ottoman Army and the people of Anatolia during the Great War was no doubt the typhus epidemic. Dr. Lütfi Aksu, who was sent to Van in the winter of 1911 in order to examine an epidemic that had started there, identified it as typhus.[39] During the first days of mobilization in 1914, the detrimental effects of typhus were already being felt at the Army's dispatch center in Konya and within the labor battalions in Sille.[40] During that epidemic in Konya, the Red Crescent Society distributed free medicine.[41] According to the American Missionary Board records, a very severe typhus epidemic started in Erzurum and Harput in the fall of 1914. The same epidemic also affected Mardin, Van, and Bitlis to varying degrees. In December, four hundred cases of military and civilian deaths per day were recorded in Erzurum. The medical personnel and medical facilities in the region were inadequate. The disease claimed the lives of seventy people per day in Harput. During the Armenian uprising in Van, five American missionaries caught typhus and one lost her life.[42] As several historical documents, reports, and the narrations of the missionaries indicate, as of 1915 the typhus epidemic started to spread all over Anatolia, and particularly in Konya.[43]

In late 1914, in response to the outbreak of a typhus epidemic in Balıkesir, the Medical Board of the Balıkesir Society of National Defence, the most influential nongovernmental organization in the area, issued two declarations on health conditions. The second of those declarations in particular was written in plain language which could be understood easily by the local people, and circulated in all villages by the gendarmerie.[44] The declaration of the Balıkesir Society of National Defence was as follows:

> Unfortunately, this disease has penetrated us. Due to our failure to take it serious, and implement necessary measures, it spread through our villages. Many people died, and many children were left orphans, and in destitution because of the disease. In some of the households nobody remained alive. The doors were closed. Many gallant young men, many old or young people perished due to the disease. In some villages only a few people died.

If we add up all those few people, however, we would reach a figure that can be expressed in hundreds. As a usual habit, we failed to pay attention to this problem. Nobody came to us and told that they were suffering from a disease in their village, neighborhood, or house. Although people travel from one village to another to seek advice when even one of their animals is ill, they have not done anything about this disease, affecting human beings. From now on, at least, please listen carefully to the advice given to you, and implement it. There is no excuse for rejecting any advice. On the contrary, if you implement them, you will be performing a good deed for the common good, and you will acquire merit in God's sight.[45]

The above declaration regarding the typhus epidemic in Balıkesir and its environs was dated 15 December 1914. It is a very important document indicating that the typhus epidemic was already affecting even a distant part of Anatolia during the first months of the war, which was far away from the battlefronts and not involved in the war. Despite this fact, some people attempted to explain the deaths from epidemics by referring to other causes, such as the negligent attitude of the local people toward diseases.[46]

The above-mentioned declaration is in no way the only document regarding the typhus epidemics seen in Anatolia. According to a military medical authority, the disease of typhus, which was then called "spotted fever," had existed sporadically for a long time in the eastern provinces. Only occasionally, especially in winter months, small- or large-scale epidemics of typhus had been observed. Before the beginning of the Great War, cases of spotted fever also had been recorded in various places in Anatolia. In April 1914, cases of spotted fever were observed in Sivas, Samsun, Merzifon, Amasya, and Bayburt; in June of the same year in Sivas and Tokat; in July in Sivas, Erzincan, Bayburt, and Trabzon; in September in Erzurum and Van; and in October in Hakkari, and Hasankale-Erzurum. To illustrate this point, we could look at a telegram dispatched on 14 August 1914 to the field medical inspectorate, by the then medical chief of the 3rd Army before Dr. Tevfik Sağlam took up that position. It stated that the "spotted fever, which had prevailed in Erzurum in the form of a widespread epidemic and had claimed the lives of many servicemen in the previous years, is now encountered here sporadically."[47]

Following the death of Hafız Hakkı Pasha from typhus on 30 January 1915, Mahmut Kamil Pasha was assigned as the 3rd Army commander. The new commander set off from Istanbul on 17 February, together with his headquarters personnel, and arrived in Ulukışla, the last railway station, two days later. The people traveling in this convoy came across cases of typhus on its way from Niğde to Erzurum. As of 27 February, the hospitals in Erzincan were full of patients affected by typhus. When the convoy members reached Erzurum on 9 March, they encountered similar scenes.[48]

Captain Hüsamettin Tugaç, who was captured by the Russians in Sarıkamış in the winter of 1914, later wrote that he had been taken to Samara (Kuybyshev) together with his friends and kept under quarantine there, due to the typhus epidemic existing in the town. The Ottoman war prisoners, after being kept in railroad wagons without water and food for several weeks, died of hunger, lack of water, and illnesses. Captain Tugaç, who had graduated from the war college with honors in 1910, also caught typhus in Samara. While lying ill in bed, he recalled some disasters that were caused by typhus epidemics and were buried in the depths of history:

> I remember that almost a hundred thousand soldiers and civilians died of typhus during and after the Balkan Wars. Hadn't we lost 40 doctors in Tekirdağ? Hadn't I heard that a total of 10,000 people, servicemen and civilians, fell victim to typhus in Van after the mobilization? Shortly before the outbreak of war, hadn't I observed how almost 80% of the troops of the company at the frontal area of Muş were in a miserable condition in their tents, unprotected from the burning heat of summer?[49]

Guze has the following observations about the winter of 1916–1917: "It was a very severe winter; it seemed as if a struggle was waged against hunger and cold."[50]

The typhus epidemics, which ravaged the battlefields after 1914, continued at various intervals until the conclusion of the war. The "second" typhus epidemic of 1916 is considered the continuation of the one in the winter of 1914–1915. The latter epidemic continued very severely through the winter of 1918–1919, notwithstanding short-term pauses.[51]

The typhus epidemics in Balıkesir and in the provinces of East Anatolia had started months before the Ottoman government made the decision in the spring of 1915 to resettle some of the Armenians in an area far from the battlefield controlled by Russia (the decision of deportation meant obligatory migration and resettlement of the Armenians). This decision was taken as a precautionary measure to protect the transportation and supply routes of the Ottoman Army and to ensure public order in the wake of the Armenian uprisings that occurred in Zeytun, Van, Muş, Sivas, and Şebinkarahisar.

Before the commencement of the Great War, typhus epidemics were observed in various places along a long line extending from the inner parts of Asia in the East, and from Samara to the Caucasus, to Anatolia, and to Serbia in the West. The conditions prevailing during the Great War triggered widespread typhus epidemics, as well as other local epidemics, causing mass movements of both troops and civilian people (in the form of migrations). Since those mass epidemics had extremely high incidence rates, they claimed the lives of millions of people from various nationalities and religions.

5

ORDEAL WITH DISEASES

> We are getting on for two months now since the August fighting—all that time we have been allowed to do nothing—literally, allowed to do nothing, seeing we have been given no shell. What a fiasco! The Dardanelles is not a sanatorium; Suvla is not South End. With the men we have lost from sickness in the past six weeks we could have beaten the Turks twice over.
>
> —General Ian Hamilton,
> *Gallipoli Diary*

Five short sentences an Ottoman officer serving in Gallipoli wrote in his diary are a succinct description of the conditions prevailing in the Ottoman Army during the four long years of the Great War. Not only at the Battles of Gallipoli, but on all fronts the army had to fight against epidemics of infectious diseases more than it did against the enemy:

> December 4, 1915…I was told that the Commander had arrived. I went to brief him. He told me that he had assigned 26 raw recruits to the company, and added that we were losing lots of soldiers. I answered by saying that most of them were lost due to diseases. He replied: "You are right, I am aware of that fact."[1]

Military Doctor Abdülkadir Noyan also had striking memories of the battlefield in the Gallipoli Peninsula:

> The first row of trenches had a very upsetting scene. Our martyrs and the dead bodies of enemy soldiers were lying so close to each other that they resembled people prostrating themselves during a Friday prayer in a mosque. This prostration was disorderly and one could see it in a multitude of people who had found eternal peace. The flies had laid their eggs on the noses and mouths of the dead, and the hatching worms, well nourished and

developed there, were marching towards the trenches with their white and fat bodies. The scene was unendurable. The dead bodies, having been there for days, were emitting an overpowering odor into the surroundings.[2]

Observing the same scene on the other side of the trenches, British Sergeant Johnston records in his diary:

As I made my way along the trench I passed many heaps of dead upon which the great ugly flies were feasting.
Wounded by the dozen were huddled in side trenches waiting for the time when it would be possible to get stretchers along to convey them to the base.[3]

As the battles in Gallipoli occurred mostly in the form of hand-to-hand bayonet fights between the combatants, the wounded mostly had to be left under the blazing sun in summer, exposed to the attacks of millions of flies. Following these attacks, they were abandoned to die without any treatment.[4] It also was observed that the viruses carried by those flies transformed into a mosquito-borne infectious disease called "dengue."[5]

Writing in 1956, forty years after the battles, Robert Rhodes James depicted the flies at the Gallipoli Front as follows:

By now the heat was almost unbearable. The trenches were like ovens; the grass had long since withered and vanished, and the hot wind stirred up the dust, which drifted across the Peninsula, covering everything, and horribly pungent with the stench of war and death. On the limpid sea the corpses of horses were churned up in the propellers; if they still refused to sink they were left to their own devices, and the hideously mangled carcasses often found their way back to the beaches.

Ashore, the bloated loathsome green flies—"corpse flies" the men called them—were becoming literally pestilential. Feasting on the corpses in No Man's Land, swarming hideously in the latrines, filling every trench and dug-out and covering the food, they were directly responsible for a virulent form of dysenteric diarrhea—generally known as "the Gallipoli Trots" or "the Gallipoli Gallop"—which spread rapidly through the army in July. It was particularly serious at Anzac, where the closely packed trenches and dugouts provided perfect conditions for the spread of disease. By the end of July Birdwood was losing as many men in a fortnight through sickness as would be expected in a major attack; in one week alone (July 21st–27th) 1,221 cases of acute dysentery were reported at Anzac, or nearly 5 per cent of the garrison, but these figures give no adequate indication of the [extent] of the epidemic....

In August, when it was at least conclusively proved by a team of Australian doctors that most of the men were suffering from dysentery and diarrhea, and some from a virulent form of paratyphoid, Birrell issued circulars on "The Prevention of Flies in Camps and Billets" and "The Prevention of Typhoid." As an embittered Australian doctor remarked, "you might as well have spat on a bushfire." By then, the Anzac force was melting away at the appalling rate of 10 per cent *per week*, and it was calculated that nearly 80 per cent of the Allied troops on the Peninsula were suffering to some extend from the disease.[6]

The British Official History of War, prepared by General C. F. Aspinall-Oglander in 1932, had the following assessment about the difficulties encountered in Gallipoli:

> A deterioration in the health of the troops, which, here as at Hellas, became more and more marked as the summer advanced, was aggravated by a constant shortage of water, a plague of loathsome flies, and a daily average temperature of 84 degrees in the shade.
>
> Though there was little fighting during June and July, and the normal daily number of casualties was small, the drain on the corps from sickness and the disease began to assume disturbing proportions as the summer heat increased. In July the number of men evacuated for sickness and wounds amounted to an average of 1,400 a week, of which approximately 75 per cent were sick.
>
> Even hard work and hourly risk of death could not relief the monotony of existence on those barren, sun-baked hillsides; and as week followed week with no change in the situation, and no sign of the promised advance from the south, it needed all the philosophy of which the troops were capable to keep their spirits from dropping. Cooped together in stifling trenches or shadeless gullies, tormented by flies, tortured by thirst, stricken by disease, and ignorant of the reasons which condemned them to activity, it was difficult to keep light-hearted as the early hopes of victory gave way to disillusionment.
>
> During the hot weather the troops were for the most part dressed in "shorts" and shirts, while workers on the beach would often be stripped to the waist. Many of the biggest men in the first contingent had already passed away.

On the 23rd August, his [General Ian Hamilton's] wastage from sickness was becoming abnormal, and his total losses, including sick, since the opening of the offensive amounted to over 40,000 men.[7]

In a note dated 3 July 1915, General Ian Hamilton, commander-in-chief of the Mediterranean Expeditionary Force, describes his personal condition as "very hot; very limp with the prevalent disease."[8]

Dysentery became widespread among the British troops by mid-July 1915. In a time span of fifteen days, the losses of the Anzac forces, under the command of General Birdwood, due to dysentery exceeded their combat-related losses. By that time, 80 percent of the troops already had been afflicted with infectious diseases.[9]

On 10 July 1915, the British commander-in-chief wrote the following in his diary:

We have refused the request made by His Excellency, Weber Pasha, who signs himself Commandant of the Ottoman Forces, to have a five hours' truce for burying their piles of dead. The British Officers who have been out to meet the Ottoman Parliamentarians say that the sight of the Turkish dead lying in thousands just over the crest line where Baikie's guns caught them on the 5th inst. is indeed an astonishing sight. Our Intelligence is clear that the reason the Turks make this request is that they cannot get their men to charge over the corpses of their comrades. Dead Turks are better than barbed wire and so, though on grounds of humanity as well as health I should like the poor chaps to be decently buried.[10]

Another British Commander, General Godley, noted in a letter to his wife on 5 September, "They are all quite worn out, and from my Division alone going sick at the rate of 100 a day."[11]

According to a memo sent by General Birdwood to General Hamilton, the losses caused from infectious disease were quite high during the last days of August 1915.[12] That month, 43,553 men were evacuated, of whom 12,968 were suffering from dysentery; the 1st Australian Division, which had landed 13,300 strong and received reinforcing drafts of 7,700 men, was now reduced to a total of 8,500; the evacuation rate for sick alone was 1.7 percent at Suvla, 5.1 percent at Hellas and 7.5 percent at Anzac.[13]

On 11 October 1915, General Hamilton informed General Robeck that their strength had already been reduced to half, and that a further 50 percent of that half-strength were ill.[14] According to a Turkish source, within

TABLE 5.1. Number of sick in a British brigade

DATE	NUMBER OF SICK
August 28	59
August 29	64
August 30	58
August 31	17
September 1	2
September 1*	6

*Note: In the original, September 1 appears twice, which is most likely a mistake.

the period of five months between July and the end of November 1915, the Ottoman Army suffered a total of 46,881 wounded, 31,420 of those in the Gallipoli front.[15] The British commander-in-chief wrote the following note on 14 October 1915: "Colder than ever. We are told that the winter will kill the flies and that with their death we shall all get hearty and well. Meanwhile, they have turned to winged limpets."[16]

Although General Hamilton was correct in his estimation about the reduction of cases of malaria, this time a new and totally different cause of death started to threaten the British Army:

> The nights of the 27th and 28th were nights of horror throughout the Suvla zone. In the front line many men had been drowned in the trenches. The severe cold following the floods proved an unbearable strain to men whose health had been undermined by the hardships of the summer campaign. Hundreds were dying from exposure and the 86th Brigade was practically out of action. All over the plain, streams of utterly exhausted men were struggling back to the beach, many collapsing on the roadside and freezing to death where they fell. The hospitals, ordnance tents, supply depots, and every place where any cover was available, were packed to overflowing; but more and more sick came pouring in, for which no shelter could be found. Night and day the doctors struggled devotedly to grapple with the situation. But the suddenness of the emergency had outstripped the means of dealing with it. It was impossible even to provide the men with warm food and drink, and while the storm lasted it was equally impossible to send them away from the peninsula or any help to arrive from outside. To make matters worse large quantities of winter clothing, which had only recently

arrived at Suvla and was now so sorely needed, by cruel error had just been re-embarked.

On the 30th November the wind abated, the frost disappeared, and for the next three weeks there was an almost unbroken spell of perfect autumn weather with the sun shining continuously, the sea a lake of turquoise, and the air like sparkling wine. But the blizzard had left its mark. At Suvla alone in the course of the three days' storm there had been more than 5,000 cases of frost-bite, and over 200 men had been drowned or frozen to death.[17]

According to Robert Rhodes James, cases of frostbite and exposure were encountered on several fronts: over 12,000 at Suvla, nearly 3,000 at Anzac, and about 1,000 at Hellas, where the conditions were relatively better. A total of 280 men died as a direct result of the storm and the blizzard.[18]

THE GALLIPOLI FRONT

In terms of the hygiene conditions on the Gallipoli front, the Ottoman side had the following facilities and constraints:

The health affairs were put under the responsibility of Directorate 5 (the Chief Doctor's Office) integrated within the organizational structure of the Fortified Position Command in Gallipoli. Before the war, the districts of Seddülbahir, Kumkale, Kilitbahir, Gallipoli, and Eceabat each had one infirmary of 25 to 100 beds. A 250-bed Mevkii (local) hospital also was in operation in Gallipoli. When the British forces appeared at the entrance of the Dardanelles Strait, the number of beds in the infirmaries was increased to around 150.

Certain factors adversely affecting human health in the area, however, could not be eliminated. Some of those factors include the following: The marshes in the region of Gallipoli, especially the ones located in the east of Kumkale and in the south which were formed by the Menderes stream, as well as the stagnant waters in other parts of the region were providing a very suitable environment for malaria, which had been frequently observed among the troops and the local people. Other diseases frequently encountered in the area were cholera, typhoid, and smallpox. Spotted fever (typhus), tuberculosis, pneumonia, and pleurisy were also common diseases in the region, whereas lice were very widely seen on the bodies of people. The living conditions of the soldiers were extremely poor. For one, the barracks were overcrowded. Because no bunk beds were available, soldiers had to sleep on the ground; nor did they have any bedspreads to cover their bodies. There was a shortage of water, and no water pumps were at the service of

Table 5.2. The numbers of ill and wounded treated in hospitals in Akbaş and Akdere

April 1915	25,065 wounded	207 ill
May 1915	16,298 wounded	1,192 ill
June 1915	15,031 wounded	953 ill
Total	56,394 wounded	2,352 ill

the soldiers. Severe difficulties were encountered in the provision of medical supplies. Shortly after the onset of the war, restrictions were placed on the use of tincture of iodine due to a shortage. Since the medical companies of the divisions had no transportation means at their disposal, the ill and wounded had to be carried to the medical units located behind the battlefront by the transportation convoys normally carrying ammunition.[19]

In May 1915, the capacity of the Ottoman Army hospitals in Gallipoli was increased to 5,050 beds. Additional hospitals to supplement the stationary hospitals run by the Inspectorate of the Army Stations were established. The wharf in Akbaş was modified into a transfer center for the wounded. All the ships arriving here from Istanbul were transporting the ill and wounded on their return. As a result, long queues were among the ordeals the ill and wounded waiting for transfer had to endure as their sheer numbers overwhelmed the capacity of the wharf in Akbaş.[20] Another source notes that the ill and wounded literally were crammed onto the ships going to Istanbul.[21]

From the start of the battles in Gallipoli on 25 April 1915 and continuing through 1 July, the numbers of ill and wounded treated in the hospitals in Akbaş and Akdere were recorded as shown in Table 5.2.[22]

Aptülahat Akşin, a foreign affairs officer by profession who then was serving as a reserve officer in the 1st Army, witnessed the cries of thousands of wounded who were "trying to clean their wounds of maggots by washing them with sea-water, or even by putting lime on those wounds" while waiting in crowded groups on the Akbaş wharf at Gallipoli, to be sent to Istanbul in the aftermath of the battle of Anafartalar.[23] Since Istanbul was the main medical center, the ill and wounded soldiers from various fronts were flooding into Istanbul, particularly in 1915. All official and private hospitals in Istanbul were packed, prompting the field medical inspectorate general to issue a declaration calling the army to halt the transfer of the ill and wounded to Istanbul.[24]

A document kept in the Turkish Military Archives provides the following information about the battles in Anafartalar:

> At the onset of the war, hospitals serving the various units deployed in the sector of the fortified position of Gallipoli had a 500-bed capacity. After the start of the mobilization, cases of typhoid, cholera, and meningitis started to be seen too. In response, the bed capacity of the existing hospitals was increased to 1,270. A total of 64 soldiers were killed and 9 were wounded when the enemy's navy conducted its first strike against the outer fortifications. Since the first aid center was located inside the fortifications, close to the ammunition dumps, they were frequently coming under fire. In addition, the means of transportation were inadequate to carry the wounded. Cases of cholera, dysentery and spotted fever were detected within the units. In the course of the enemy's naval attack against the Strait on 18 March 1915, 44 soldiers were killed and 70 were wounded. After the first landing of the enemy forces, large numbers of wounded soldiers began flooding to the medical companies. During the first hours of the battle, the number of the wounded arriving in the Mobile Hospital of the 9th Division alone exceeded 2,000, and that number later increased to 5,000. Since the hospital had only 300 beds available, additional hospitals were set up in 45 houses previously evacuated in Maydos. The beds and shields used in these hospitals were collected from the local people. During the enemy bombardment on 18 March 1915, however, these converted hospitals were also hit, and all of the equipment was destroyed. Several ships of the Şirket-i Hayriye (the company then running the city line ships in Istanbul), numbered 66, 67, and 70, as well as the ship *Gülnihal* were seconded to the Army to help with the transfer of the ill and wounded. They transferred the wounded to several hospitals set up on the coasts of Anatolia and Rumelia. Large casualties were suffered during the mutual offensives and counter-offensives carried out during the battles of Kerte, Zığındere, Kerevizdere, Kanlısırt, and Conkbayırı, as well as during the landing at Anafartalar. The corpses of thousands of soldiers were heaped in front of the trenches. Meanwhile, the dysentery epidemic continued to ravage the army, and cases of hypothermia began to occur after September.[25]

In August 1915, a report prepared by British military intelligence aroused new hopes in the British Command as it hinted that the Ottoman Army was as exhausted as the British Army. According to this report, the situation prevailing in the Ottoman Army was as follows:

Notwithstanding the satisfactory results achieved in August, General Liman von Sanders still regards the future with anxiety.... The wastage amongst the Ottoman troops was alarmingly high, and the danger was that they would gradually bleed to death.... Further formations were hardly likely to become available for Gallipoli. Drafts were coming in more slowly and their standard was growing worse. The increased size of the Army enhanced the difficulties of supply. Not only were the lines of communication barely able to meet the existing demands, but the resources of the capital appeared to be running short.[26]

Ekrem Şadi Kavur described the situation on the Gallipoli front as follows:

During the course of the battles in Gallipoli, one of the wounded I met in the hospital, a cadet, told me that it was like a hell in the Gallipoli Peninsula: it was entirely surrounded by a ring of fire encompassing the sea, air, land, and the underground sewers.

Despite the accumulation of a huge number of forces in a narrow area in Gallipoli Peninsula, no significant disease other than those such as malaria, dysentery, filariasis, recurrent fever, and scurvy were observed. As the battle was transformed into a trench war, more and more soldiers needed to be hospitalized.[27]

The troops of the 1st and 5th armies who, having survived the battles where hundreds of thousands were fighting, were sent to the Thrace for rest, had to fight the disease of typhus this time under conditions of extreme misery and poverty. The typhus epidemic, which proved to be a real disaster, could only be controlled after a month-and-a-half-long struggle. Some of those troops assigned to the 6th and 15th Army Corps were dispatched to the fronts at Romania, Austria, and Galicia. Though they were in a relatively better condition compared to those fighting on other fronts, they nonetheless were unable to escape the typhus, as it already existed among the Germans and Austrians there. On the other hand, the losses from diseases of the Russian armies fighting them were even greater.[28]

THE FRONTS OF DOBRUJA, GALICIA, AND ROMANIA

In the far north of Gallipoli, on the fronts of Dobruja and Romania in the Balkans, the hygienic conditions were relatively good:

The 7th Army Corps divisions had their own medical companies. They took no mobile hospitals there. During the first engagement with the enemy, 17 soldiers were killed and 49 were wounded. Soon, the number of wounded exceeded 1,200 who could not receive any treatment since no mobile hospital was yet allocated to the force. The Muslim residents in the area provided beds to help accommodate the patients. Later, the German Mobile Hospital 172 was assigned to the Ottoman Army, which contributed to the regularization of the transfer of the wounded. After some time, however, new difficulties were encountered in the transfer of large numbers of the wounded because the mobile hospital remained far behind as the Army Corps advanced further into the enemy lines. Although a Red Crescent Hospital was sent from Istanbul to the 7th Army Corps to alleviate these problems, the Bulgarian Government did not allow the Ottoman Army to set up a hospital in Dobruja. Despite sporadic cases of cholera and spotted fever seen among the troops, they did not transform themselves into epidemics. Since the Ottoman Army Corps suffered heavy casualties in the battles that took place in the North of Dobruja and Ortaköy, it was reinforced with the newly dispatched 26th Division. In the course of the battles, which turned into a trench war along the Seres River in the winter, severe cold caused an increase in the cases of hypothermia, 63 of which resulted in death. Three mobile hospitals and one Red Crescent Hospital sent from Istanbul became operational in Bucharest. In addition, the Muslim Community in Ruse set up another hospital. As of 1917, the cases of recurrent fever, spotted fever, and venereal disease increased significantly among the troops.[29]

The conditions on the Galician front could also be considered reasonable:

Before the 15th Army Corps was assigned to the Galician Front, dysentery, malaria, recurrent fever, and spotted fever existed among its troops. Although the divisions could transfer their medical companies to the frontlines, they could not take any mobile hospital. Upon their arrival in Zemlin via the route of Sofia and Belgrade, each division of the Army Corps was assigned one consultant doctor by the Austrian Government. The Austrian Government also provided the medical supplies. In response to the increase in the number of the wounded, two mobile hospitals were dispatched and put under the mandate of the Army Corps. Cases of dysentery, typhoid, and malaria were noted widely in the units.[30]

Overall, the medical services were maintained at reasonable levels on the Galician front from the beginning of the battles on. The evacuation of the dead and wounded from the battlefields, however, could be performed slowly and with difficulty as the large number of casualties overwhelmed the capability of the existing infrastructure. Meanwhile, typhus was recorded in one of the brigades.[31]

Because the Ottoman 6th Army Corps was ordered to leave behind its mobile hospitals in Turkey before setting off for the Romanian front, it faced great difficulties in evacuating casualties from the battlefield and providing treatment to the wounded in the course of the initial battles. The Ottoman medical doctors tried to treat their patients in the houses of the Turkish villages nearby. As the military units were constantly moving from one place to another, however, most of the time the patients in those houses had to be abandoned to their destiny.[32]

Already at the beginning of the operations, infectious diseases were detected among the Ottoman troops at the Macedonian front, the severity and depth of which caught the close attention of the German general headquarters. Shortage of beds and inadequate medical support in the hospitals were the main reasons behind the high rates of death. The 2,082 casualties the 20th Army Corps suffered are broken down as follows: 1,165 deserters and missing soldiers, 653 wounded, 173 combat deaths, and 91 deaths in hospital. The Ottoman detachment in Rumelia, on the other hand, suffered 1,655 casualties: 100 deserters and missing soldiers, 860 wounded, 410 combat deaths, and 285 deaths in hospital.[33]

Meanwhile, the situation in the fortified position on the Black Sea Strait was as follows:

> When the Black Sea Strait was bombarded by the Russian fleet for the first time in March 1915, no casualties occurred among the troops. The subsequent bombardments caused a few casualties in the army and among the residents. The most widespread diseases in the area were dysentery, malaria, recurrent fever, typhoid, and the venereal diseases.[34]

THE CAUCASIAN FRONT

In the previous chapter, "The Epidemic Disaster," the typhus epidemic and the cases of freezing in Eastern Anatolia are already discussed. Here, other diseases that emerged in the same region (cholera, dysentery, malaria, smallpox, tetanus, and erysipelas) are covered.

A communiqué issued by the field medical inspectorate general in mid-

August 1915 stated that a cholera epidemic had affected Tbilisi and Baku in the Caucasus first, and later spread to other parts of Russia as well as to the Tabriz, Hoy, and Urmia regions of Iran. This information prompted the medical authorities of the 3rd Army to take very strict measures against the danger approaching from the front. Considering the possibility that migrants, refugees, and prisoners of war could transmit cholera into the country, these groups of people were subjected to strict examination, disinfection, and isolation. A hygiene consultant and mobile laboratory were provided to each of the army corps. More importantly, a vaccination campaign against cholera was launched within the entire army. In order to meet the enormous demand for vaccine, the Erzurum institute of vaccine was reorganized to produce only cholera vaccines. By October 1915, vaccination of the entire army against cholera was completed.[35]

In November 1915, cholera epidemics broke out in three different centers within the 3rd Army's area of responsibility. The first of those epidemics broke out in Bayburt on 26 November. When an individual, who had not recently left Bayburt, died of a disease indicating the symptoms of cholera, his feces were immediately sent to Erzurum for analysis. In that material, which had the appearance of rice water, vibriones were found. Then, a recruit from the labor battalion in Bayburt became ill with diarrhea on 22 November and was sent to the hospital on suspicion of cholera. After the latter case, a bacteriologist and mobile laboratory were sent from Erzurum to Bayburt to investigate the extent of the disease there. The medical chief of the army also went there to review the situation and to ensure that all necessary measures were being implemented. In addition to these two cases, a recruit who came from Erzurum to Bayburt and a patient hospitalized since 17 November also showed symptoms of cholera. As a result, strict measures were put into place in Bayburt.[36]

The second province where cholera was recorded within the 3rd Army's sector was Trabzon. In Trabzon, the first case of cholera was seen in the 2nd Mobile Gendarmerie Battalion on 27 November 1915, the same day as the one in Bayburt. The fountain pool in front of the barracks was used by soldiers for drinking water or washing their hands and faces. Because a guest house was also located within the barracks, it was thought that a vibrione-bearing visitor might have contaminated the water. In 1,033 feces analyses conducted by 14 December 1915, a total of 337 vibrione bearers were detected.[37]

The third incidence of cholera started in Erzurum, where the first case was seen in the Morgof Hospital on 30 November. Soon after, the disease turned into an epidemic within the barracks, from where it spread into the

TABLE 5.3. Deaths from dysentery in the 3rd Army

YEARS	ADMISSIONS	DEATHS	PERCENT RATIO
1915 (9 months)	8,315	3,578	43
1916	3,002	1,615	54
1917	995	648	65
1918 (10 months)	330	101	30
Total	12,642	5,942	47

city.[38] After Erzurum was occupied by the Russians and the 3rd Army withdrew behind Erzincan, the cholera epidemic was carried into interior locations by the refugees. The first case of cholera in Erzincan as a result was seen on 27 February 1916.[39] Within a period of one month, 98 out of 151 cholera patients being treated in the Central Hospital of Erzincan lost their lives.[40]

Dysentery also ravaged the 3rd Army throughout the Great War, and is considered as one of the most damaging infectious diseases. Within a period of 42.5 months, a total of 12,642 patients were admitted to hospitals for dysentery, and the same disease accounted for 5,942 deaths in the 3rd Army. In other words, the admissions due to dysentery amounted to 2.3 percent of the total admissions, and the deaths caused by dysentery made up 5.4 percent of the total deaths from disease. The deaths from dysentery peaked in 1915. The largest numbers of admissions to hospitals for dysentery were recorded in March and April of 1915. Another increase was observed after August of that year. As is well documented, during the Great War dysentery mostly emerged in hospitals. According to the medical records of the 3rd Army, for instance, dysentery took a heavy death toll in 1915 in the Central Hospital of Erzurum. Within the same year, improved hygiene conditions in the hospital helped contain the disease.[41]

In October 1915, some 1,085 patients were admitted to the Central Hospital of Erzurum for diarrhea, 266 of whom died. In other words the death rate was 24 percent, which is high by any measure. In November of the same year, 784 admissions and 94 deaths (12 percent) were recorded. In December, there were 530 admissions and 19 deaths (only 3.4 percent), which indicates a progressive improvement in the conditions and treatment.[42]

In the 3rd Army's area of responsibility, the struggle against malaria could be initiated only in August 1917.[43] On the other hand, during the period between March 1915 and September 1918, smallpox accounted for

TABLE 5.4. Deaths from tetanus in the 3rd Army

YEARS	ADMISSIONS	DEATHS	PERCENT RATIO
1915 (9 months)	44	23	50
1916	69	45	65
1917	37	30	80
1918 (10 months)	32	20	62
TOTAL	182	118	65

TABLE 5.5. Deaths from erysipelas in the 3rd Army

YEARS	ADMISSIONS	DEATHS	PERCENT RATIO
1915 (9 months)	1,446	374	26
1916	1,246	287	20
1917	345	74	21
1918 (10 months)	62	1	1.6
TOTAL	3,099	736	24

346 of the admissions to the 3rd Army's hospitals, 40 of which (30 percent) resulted in death.[44] Tetanus was not common within the 3rd Army despite the fact that the army was involved in large-scale battles where many cases of local hypothermia occurred among troops. The low number of tetanus cases was due to dressing the wounds of the soldiers without delay and applying tetanus serum within the proper time frame on wounds that looked dirty and were suspected of tetanus infection. Another important observation reached after studying the records of the 3rd Army on tetanus is that tetanus-related admissions to hospitals were most common during the winter months, indicating that most of the cases of tetanus resulted from freezing rather than from the wounds that occurred in fighting. The annual figures about tetanus-related admissions and deaths, however, are significantly high.[45]

Erysipelas and the deaths it caused were also among the frequent problems the 3rd Army encountered during the Great War. Most cases could be found on faces, since the disease was caused by the chaps occurring on the skin due to cold and lack of care under those adverse conditions. Erysipelas patients were referred to hospitals mostly in winter and in the months when the battles proved to be more intensive. The admission-to-death ratio was quite high.[46]

THE HIJAZ FRONT

Other than malaria and sunstroke, no major epidemics threatened the troops deployed at the Hijaz front. However, the combat capabilities of the units were severely limited by several factors such as hot weather, lack of water, malnutrition, and lack of medical supplies and medicines. In one instance, the personnel of the 2nd Battalion of the 42nd Regiment deployed around Medina had to be taken to hospitals or infirmaries due to malaria.[47]

According to the records found in the Turkish Military Archives, the army came across scurvy frequently at the Hijaz front. For instance, in the 55th regiment subordinate to the 58th Division, twenty-five of the soldiers who visited the doctor on 21 February 1916 were found to have that disease. As malaria season approached, the recruits were obliged to take quinine twice a week. Epidemics of recurrent fever are known to have prevailed in the area from time to time. Some evidence demonstrating inadequacy of the medical services in the Yemen is uncovered as well. The Ottoman forces operating in the region faced these epidemics and their harmful effects both in the beginning and during the later stages of the war. In an environment where life-threatening heat, lack of water, malnutrition, and lack of care were prevalent, the tragic condition of the troops was described in a note sent on 30 January 1915 from the Regional Command of Operations in Taiz to the Army Corps Command:

> 1. The doctors I tasked to investigate the health conditions of the units in Mendep have returned. From the telegrams they had sent, it appeared that a total of 244 officers and recruits, as well as all but 15 recruits from the national battalion seemed to be exhausted, disabled, and absolutely unable to carry out their duties, who needed to be transferred to Moza for two months for medical reasons. Following my oral conversation with the returning doctors, I gave the necessary orders to the Mendep area commander for the transfer of the said personnel to Moza so that they can rest as quickly as possible. Given their ailing conditions, my own judgment was that keeping them in Mendep any longer would be to the detriment of the army rather than providing any benefits.

2. In addition to the above-mentioned points, it also was seen that the drinking water had a bad odor and contained salt, alum, and other organic materials. A general state of weakness, moreover, plagued the units, caused by the lack of vegetables, extreme fatigue, and the difficult weather conditions specific to Tehama.

3. The most common diseases are fever, enteritis, acute common cold, and scurvy. More than 400 ill and very weak soldiers were documented in Mendep.

4. In order to prevent the artillery batteries in Mendep from vanishing and becoming unable to fight, I found it necessary to include the artillery units in the rotation scheme initiated between the forces in Mendep and Moza. The necessary orders already have been given to the Command of Mendep Region to send a mountain battery to Dibap, so that the troops could drink fresh water, as much as they wish.

The Ottoman Commander also stated in his report that seventy infantry troops living under those conditions died in November and December of 1914, and added that a similar number of soldiers were about to die.[48]

THE SYRIAN FRONT

According to a document available in the Turkish Military Archives:

> Various hospitals were set up in the cities of Aleppo, Damascus, Jerusalem, and others in Syria, by appropriating the existing government and municipality hospitals, as well as the foreign hospitals. The total bed capacity of those hospitals was 4,400. During the Canal Operation, a medical depot was established in In, and convoys for the transportation of the wounded were formed, each composed of 8 camels. The army fighting on the Canal front had one medical section on both right and left wings, and two medical companies in the centre. At the rear were two mobile hospitals. Since those hospitals were close to the frontlines, they were targeted by the enemy's battleships, and as a result had to be relocated. The medical companies were both evacuating the wounded from the battlefield, and carrying water on the stretchers to the combatants. When the fighting ceased, the medical units were gathered in Keteb-ul Halil for the treatment of the wounded soldiers. During the Canal expedition, 196 soldiers were killed, and 565

were wounded. When the army was retreating, the wounded were evacuated in four convoys, together with the convoys charged with supplying water and provisions. During the retreat, cases of recurrent fever and scurvy were encountered. Since the infectious diseases could never be completely eradicated in the country, the cases of spotted fever, recurrent fever, smallpox, and dysentery seemed to have increased both among the civilians and within the army. In Jerusalem and Aleppo, epidemics of spotted fever broke out. In order to combat those epidemics, commissions of hygiene were established in the districts, and very strict measures were implemented; the vaccines produced in the Syrian hospitals were used during these efforts.[49]

The most widespread diseases seen on the Syrian front were typhoid, typhus, and cholera. Malaria and dysentery, on the other hand, stubbornly persisted in the region and could never be eliminated completely. Cholera and typhus mostly afflicted the local people. In an illustrative example, a Jewish village called Afule was completely evacuated and burned down under the orders of the military authorities, since it was a major breeding ground for typhus. The diseases mostly were erupting in the winter and during shortages of food supply. Deprivation, hunger, exhaustion, and lack of medical services caused mass losses during the long years of war. During those years, the number of doctors also was reduced drastically and the dentists, veterinarians, and pharmacists were assigned to their positions to meet the demand for medical doctors in the battalions or mobile hospitals. As the war continued, existing medical supplies either were used up or became unusable. The failure to resolve the clothing problem, combined with the shortage of food, aggravated the adverse conditions, providing a suitable ground for infections.[50]

The following sentences taken from the 26th Division's Journal of War reflect very well the dramatic conditions encountered by the military units from time to time throughout the war:

> Since the artillery units ran out of kerosene or candles, they were burning barks of trees to have some light to align their weapons.
>
> On the evening of 7 December 1917, sleet began to fall, accompanied by a severe cold. Most of the soldiers did not have any underwear, whereas others lacked raincoats and portable tents. Their feet were naked, and their clothes were ragged and worn out. The situation was communicated to the Army Corps, which ordered us to supply the required materials from the army station at the rear. An officer sent to the army station also was given a letter of pledge written by the Division Commander. We requested [the res-

idents] to give the bed sheets in hotels, and some of the carpets in mosques and churches to the soldiers who were defending them in rough terrain under great deprivation. Unfortunately those requests were of no avail.[51]

German Military Doctor Seuber recalls the following about his visit in 1917 to the 59th Division's tented camp area, located about 10 km south of Aleppo, which he visited in order to investigate an outbreak of cholera there:

> I went to the Division in question. Even though the infected battalions were quarantined, in fact the entire division was infected. Those who were slightly ill were lying on earth in front of the cone-shaped tents, unprotected against the sun, and without any cloth covering on them. The seriously ill were a little bit farther away; but they too were lying on the ground, writhing in pain.
>
> Even if one disregards the effects of cholera, the 59th Division was not in a condition to be used in any military mission. That Division seemed to me as a large group of delicate individuals, who were exhausted from hunger. The Deputy Commander was a German Lieutenant Colonel. He is sitting desperately in his tent located under a pomegranate tree; he seems to have surrendered to his fate, and detached himself from the whole world.[52]

The following scenes, depicting the plight of the 26th Division in its Journal of War, are indeed very tragic:

> Reduction of the bread ration to 0.400 grams affected the soldiers very badly. Approximately half of the personnel are in vain. The hospitals along the road and the army stations in the interior were overwhelmed by the ill soldiers. As was the case in other units, as soon as our Division wanted to take a rest, it fell victim to the epidemics of the diseases such as scurvy, anemia, and dysentery, caused by living under pathetic conditions for a long period of time (7–8 months). More than 20% of the total strength of the division was lost; many soldiers either died, or were sent on leave for medical reasons. Since the Division did not have its own mobile hospital and other means to treat the ill except for a medical company, it ran into serious difficulties.[53]

As of 17 November 1917, the last Ottoman and German troops had withdrawn from Jerusalem and headquarters were transferred to Nablus. As a result, the ill and wounded surged into the town, bringing with them the risk of cholera there. The first epidemic eventually surfaced among the Ottoman soldiers. The only method of disinfection that could be implemented against the epidemic was to spread chloride of lime around the tents of the patients diagnosed with cholera. The regiment infected with cholera could not be dispatched to a quarantine station. In fact, the local people rather than the soldiers were under the threat of that disease as they grew vulnerable over time. The health conditions of the local people had deteriorated enormously. Hunger was reigning in Palestine and in most parts of Syria.[54]

The struggle against malaria accounted for a large part of the army's activities on the Palestinian and Sinai fronts throughout 1915. In Jerusalem, the cisterns used for storing water became main sources of malaria as they were a suitable breeding ground for the mosquitoes of the anopheles type.[55] Another malaria epidemic was recorded in Der (Palestine) in 1917.[56]

Between the dissolution of the commanderships of the 4th Army and Sinai front on 28 September 1918, which were replaced by the Command of the Lightning Group of Armies, and the establishment of the Chief Inspectorate of the Lightning Army Stations, the medical services for humans and animals were carried out by both medical and veterinary units within the Office of the Deputy 4th Army Command.[57]

The official historical records published by the Turkish General Staff provide the following remark about the conditions on the Palestinian front during the period of 1917–1918: "[A]lthough a quite extensive medical infrastructure was in place, the treatment of the ill and wounded was far from satisfactory." Although a network of hospitals, infirmaries, and convalescent hospitals existed in cities such as Damascus, Beirut, Aleppo, Humus, Der, Zahle, Hama, and Baalbek, the medical services in those places had to be carried out with insufficient personnel. Moreover, the same records also emphasize that the cases of typhoid, typhus, cholera, malaria, and gangrene caused by wounds were so widespread that they overwhelmed the capacity of those medical institutions.[58]

THE IRAQI FRONT

The following medical measures were taken on the Iranian-Iraqi front, the battle area of the 6th Army forces:

> The precautions implemented were very primitive. The enormous need for tents, greatcoats, clothes, shoes, and the like could hardly be met. The insufficiency of food supplies further contributed to the bleak health conditions throughout the war. Even General Goltz lost his life due to an infectious

disease. Although each division was assigned a medical company and a mobile hospital, the shortage of specialist doctors, medical equipment and medicines resulted in great casualties.[59]

According to the Turkish Military Archives, during the four years of the war, 45,000 to 50,000 people were affected by infectious diseases, and more than 10,000 soldiers died on the Iraqi front. The number of soldiers who were killed in battle, on the other hand, was only 5,934.[60]

On the Çapakçur Front, the battle area for the 2nd Army, hunger, lack of proper clothing, and infection took a heavy toll, too:

> The 2nd Army units came from Pozantı on foot, and they did not receive sufficient food on the road. Cases of malaria, sunstroke, and cholera were widespread among those units. As a result of the atrocities committed by the Armenians, which took advantage of the Russian Army's offensive, large groups of refugees diffused through the interior areas, carrying with them infections of spotted fever and recurrent fever. The outbreak of a large-scale cholera epidemic was prevented among the military units, thanks to timely examinations to diagnose the carriers of disease, and routine vaccinations. On this front, though, insufficient nutrition, lack of proper clothing, and seasonal diseases caused large casualties.... The most common infectious diseases were cholera, spotted fever, smallpox, recurrent fever, and dysentery.[61]

The death toll within the 2nd Army tended to increase in the winter months. Again, insufficient nutrition and the lack of cleaning materials prepared a fertile ground for the outbreak of infectious diseases such as typhoid, typhus, and cholera. Moreover, many troops suffered from night blindness and lost their ability to move due to malnutrition. Most of the ill and wounded died while they were being transferred from the front lines to the rear bases on the backs of horses and mules or on oxcarts under miserable conditions. In 1916–1917, the 2nd Army lost 24 percent of its strength because of epidemic diseases.[62]

According to a document from the Turkish Military Archives:

> During the British offensive against Fav, 56 soldiers were killed but the number of wounded was unknown. Some of the units could not evacuate their wounded from the battlefield, as they had neither any doctors, nor any means to carry patients. Cases of dysentery, typhoid, spotted fever, smallpox and plague were encountered within the Army. The British Army, which surrendered after the siege of Kut al-Amarah, suffered 380 wounded

and more than 1,000 ill soldiers. Cases of dysentery and scurvy were widely seen among the British and Indian detachments. An Army Corps subordinate to the Ottoman Army moved to Iran and occupied Kirmanshah. Since initially no network of military stations was available behind the frontlines, 1,123 wounded had to be transferred to Hanikin. Later, a hospital was opened in Kirmanshah. Cases of spotted fever and recurrent fever arose within the units deployed in Iran. In the 6th Army, while trachoma and venereal diseases became widespread, cholera and dysentery also maintained their prevalence. Before the evacuation of Baghdad, about 8,000 ill soldiers were transferred to Samra first and then to Mosul, and the bed capacity of the hospitals in Mosul was increased to 5,000. Since the food rations given to soldiers were reduced drastically during the last years of the war, cases of scurvy surged and large number of losses occurred due to cholera and amoebic dysentery.[63]

On the Iraqi front, the epidemics of typhus, cholera, and amoebic dysentery posed great difficulties for the medical authorities of the Ottoman army. One study notes that the British forces, which used Basra as a logistics base after occupying it on 23 November 1914, also were impaired by infectious diseases, the most common of them being smallpox, cholera, dysentery, malaria, and typhoid.[64] When the British Army initiated its move northward in May 1915, the most adverse climate conditions were encountered, and 117 persons died in one day because of sunstroke alone. Some British officers were reported to have died in a few hours because they refused to cover their heads. After the fall of Amarah on 25 July 1915, the British also captured Nasıriyah. During that campaign, the British forces suffered fewer than 1,000 casualties including the dead and wounded, whereas those who died from diseases were several times greater.[65]

An order issued by the Ottoman Army Command on 16 February 1916 noted an ongoing typhus epidemic in Kut al-Amarah. Therefore it ordered that all refugees and prisoners from the region be taken to the headquarters directly, without being allowed to establish contact with anybody.[66] According to the list submitted by British forces surrendering to the Ottoman Army in Kut al-Amarah, the British prisoners included the following: 5 generals, a total of 481 officers consisting of 277 British and 204 Indian, a total of 13,309 recruits consisting of 2,592 British and 10,717 Indian, 43 artillery, 13,700 rifles, a large number of machine guns, 6 automobiles, and large amounts of equipment and supplies.[67] As of late April 1916, a total of 1,347 British and Indian soldiers were being treated in the hospitals of Kut al-Amarah, 400 of whom were wounded and the remainder ill; 308 of those patients were British, and 1,035 were Indian.[68] Their transfer to prisoner camps resulted in the notorious "death walk" of more than 500 miles, which started from Kut al-Amarah and later was subjected to British Parliamentary enquiry.[69]

A popular history magazine provides interesting information about that period. The Ottoman Army gained a victory in Kut al-Amarah, but it came at a great cost. As the battles were becoming fiercer, a new infection began to kill off the soldiers there. The air strikes of the British planes continued unabated throughout the summer, and under the effect of the extreme heat most of the soldiers were afflicted by trachoma. Nevertheless, the Ottoman Army continued to have everyone work to make the adobe bricks that were used in the construction of shelters for winter.[70]

In June 1917, in response to the incidents of cholera observed in Aleppo and Pozantı, the 6th Army Command circulated the following orders to its subordinate units:

1. The soldiers and units coming from Aleppo and Pozantı shall not be permitted to enter the town [Mosul] directly; they first shall be kept under observation in a military camp, to be set up on the left bank of the Tigris River, where the soldiers with diarrhea as well as the soldiers suspected of it shall be examined.

2. Contamination of the Tigris River, the only source of drinking and daily use water, shall be prevented by applying measures to be determined in collaboration with the civilian medical authorities and the Municipality of Mosul.

3. The recruits in the army units, as well as the inhabitants of those neighborhoods of Mosul where cholera was recorded, shall be vaccinated.

4. In the army units, and the residential houses where cholera was seen, examinations shall be made in order to detect carriers of the disease.[71]

In July 1917, based on 4,001 feces analyses performed in the laboratory of the army station hospital in Mosul, 293 individuals were found to be carrying cholera vibriones. Of those cases, 18 were troops from the 46th Division that came to Mosul via the route through Aleppo, while 27 of them belonged to the self-standing supply units, which also followed the same route. Eight cases were from the soldiers of the telegram company working on the way to Nusaybin, 9 were deserters, and 63 were among the troops from various detachments in Mosul. Though most of the latter belonged to

TABLE 5.6. Laboratories in the army stations in Mosul, Kirkuk, Shikrat, and Nusaybin (1917–1918)

PERIOD	SAMPLE FROM THE PATIENT	AMOEBIC CASE	PERCENT
September 1917	10,648	112	01.05
October 1917	8,635	256	02.96
November 1917	4,508	381	08.45
December 1917	1,433	450	31.40
January 1918	1,046	215	20.55
February 1918	910	197	21.64

the detachments in Mosul, in fact they constantly were shuffling between various army station posts.[72]

The biggest problem bedeviling the cities of Baghdad and Mosul in 1916–1917 was amoebic dysentery. Following the capture of Kut al-Amarah, some British patients with chronic diarrhea and some Indian soldiers with diarrhea, some of whom were in a state of cachexia, were found in the British Military Hospital. Those ailing British and Indian patients were returned to their countries with the permission of the Army Command, and 300 out of a total of 1,400 patients were transferred to Baghdad. In 1916, during a sporadic amoebic dysentery epidemic, 2,660 cases were recorded, and 35 to 40 percent of the patients died. In 1917, some 3,039 cases of amoebic dysentery were encountered. During the last months of 1917 and into early 1918, the dysentery epidemic continued on a large scale.[73]

In Kut al-Amarah, as early as March 1916, the medical companies, mobile hospitals, and Army Station Hospital in Kut admitted some patients for malaria. The cases of malaria were recorded under two categories, namely the common malaria and the malignant malaria; together, they exceeded the cases of other infectious diseases according to the hospital statistics. For instance, out of 250 patients whose blood analyses were completed in the Army Station Hospital in Kut in April 1916, 10 were found to have malaria parasites. During 1916, within the 6th Army as a whole, a total of 7,930 cases of malaria were recorded, 470 of which (5.9 percent) resulted in death. In 1918, the death ratio increased to 11.4 percent. According to Abdülkadir Noyan, the increase mainly was caused by the gradual deterioration of the food supply for the troops. He remarked: "[Though] the troops are working hard, and getting tired, they receive insufficient food." He added that "the troops should have been provided with sufficient food and clothing."[74]

The monthly statistical bulletins explain that venereal diseases and especially syphilis were widespread among the prostitutes in Baghdad and Mosul between 1916 and 1918, and that some of the soldiers and officers who had intercourse with them also caught those diseases.[75] During the war, bacillary dysentery affected all fronts, including several areas in Turkey.[76] Some cases of plague were seen at the ports of İzmir and Istanbul during the Great War.[77]

THE LIBYAN FRONT

In Libya, no health units could be formed within the organizational structure of the Sunusi forces, fighting against the British in the east, nor within the mujahedeen units resisting the Italians in western Tripoli (Homs, Tripoli, and Zouara fronts). During the Ottoman Army's military expedition in Libya, only four military doctors were available. In his memoirs, Lieutenant İhsan Aksoley, who was deployed in the headquarters of Prince Osman Fuat in 1918, states that the most vital needs of the Army in North Africa were medicines, doctors, and pharmacists. A doctor finally arrived much later, and a pharmacist arrived shortly before the Mondros Armistice. He also notes that no medicines, other than tincture of iodine and alcohol, were available. The activities in Tripoli had to be terminated before the doctor and pharmacist could start their duties.[78] On this front, in an environment where no medical services could be provided even to the humans, quite understandably, no veterinarians, veterinary equipment, and medicines were in place for the treatment of the animals.[79]

THE LAST EPIDEMIC

The greatest single epidemic in modern human history was the one of influenza that killed 21 million people at the end of the First World War.[80] At the end of the war, the world was shaken by this epidemic. It broke out during the last months of 1917 in the center of China, around the city of Chungking. It then passed across China and into Japan, then moved south and southeast until it reached India, Turkey, and the Near East. Another arm of the epidemic swept across Russia via Siberia, and then moved from the Baltic coasts to America on merchant ships. In the United States, the first cases of the disease were seen in the harbors of Boston and New York. In Europe, the epidemic spread from the Baltic coasts to Western Europe, France, and the coasts of the Atlantic Ocean. In that way, Western Europe was caught between two fires. The first cases of the disease in France were seen in April 1918. Later on, Great Britain, Germany, Spain, Portugal, and Italy were affected by the disease. The epidemic spread to Switzerland by June, to Denmark and Norway by July, to Holland and Sweden by August. Within a few weeks, it made its way into Greece and Turkey.[81]

Until the Great War, influenza had remained a "domesticated" pestilence with little clout and even less meaning. But starting in the spring of 1918, the flu abruptly turned on adults and buried more than 15 million people in eighteen months. The death rate stunned physicians. It took the battlefields of France fours years to kill 15 million men, but the flu did the same work in much less time. In the United States alone, more people died of the flu (550,000 adults) in 1918 than the U.S. Army's combat losses in both world wars, the Korean War, and the Vietnam War combined. In Alaska, whole Indian villages perished.[82]

All ten of the largest-scale influenza pandemics, which have broken out at different times since 1729, are found to have originated in Southeast Asia and then followed the route from Asia to Europe toAmerica. In response to the death of 20 million people in 1918, research into the causes of the epidemic was speeded up, and eventually the influenza virus, the main agent of the disease, was singled out in 1933.[83]

The ability of the flu virus to mutate and change shape every ten to fourteen years (the interval is not always this neat) also makes influenza highly invincible. Scientists have looked hard for the strain that caused the epidemic of 1918 but have never found it.[84] While France and Spain held each other responsible for the outbreak of that epidemic, the United States accused Eastern Europe, while Western Europe accused the United States for it. On the other hand, Allenby's armies claimed that the retreating Turks caused the epidemic.[85] The influenza pandemic of 1918 was called "Spanish influenza," as the disease first originated in Spain.[86]

In 1918, the influenza epidemics swept through wide areas of Europe as well as other continents, resulting in unprecedented levels of casualties. In some countries, the epidemics took a particularly high toll. In India alone, 8 million people died from influenza. The number of deaths from the same disease was 1.3 million in Africa, 1 million in North America, 1 million in South America, and 300,000 in Japan. It was not possible to obtain exact figures regarding the number of deaths in Siberia and Russia. According to several estimates, a total of 20 million people lost their lives during the influenza epidemic of 1918.[87]

Turkey, too, was afflicted by a severe influenza epidemic toward the end

TABLE 5.7. Deaths from influenza in some countries

COUNTRY	1918	1919	1920
Britain	112,329	44,811	10,665
Germany	187,884	42,254	17,855
France	91,465	35,326	10,382
Italy	274,041	31,781	24,428
Holland	17,396	1,550	2,454
Sweden	27,379	7,341	2,853
Spain	147,114	21,335	17,825

of the Great War.[88] One source, after stating that a total of 21,643,291 people died during the influenza epidemic of 1918, noted that "that epidemic caused a great loss in Turkey."[89]

The great influenza epidemic of 1918 broke out in the Ottoman Army for the first time on 6 August at the Army Station hospital in Nusaybin. An epidemic disease (called Spanish influenza) swept through patients, doctors, and other hospital personnel, who experienced a burning sensation in the nose and throat, followed by sneezing, coughing, and high fever. It is believed that railway workers brought the disease to the area, and it could not be contained since influenza is airborne and is transmitted easily by the sneezing and coughing patients. It further penetrated into the army automobile convoys and transportation units, as well as the people riding the *keleks* (a kind of raft mounted on animal skins filled with air). Well-protected places, such as the prison in Mosul, were affected from the disease last. The death ratio from the disease remained at a level of about 3.5 percent. The decline in humidity in August helped the disease lose its strength.[90]

As the Mondros Armistice was signed on 30 October 1918, the Directorate of Health in the Province of Aydın was waging a comprehensive struggle against influenza, which had spread widely within the province. The disease was so severe that the schools had to be closed for twenty days.[91] Meanwhile, some deaths due to influenza were recorded in the district of Seferihisar.[92]

The hardships the White Russian refugees were enduring further increased after the Commission of Refugees decided to transfer them. Many of the refugees waiting to be transferred at the ports of Istanbul and Samsun died of infectious diseases. At the port of Samsun alone, an average of one hundred refugees per day died of Spanish influenza.[93]

THE SITUATION IN ISTANBUL AND ANATOLIA

In 1918, as the first quarter of the twentieth century was coming to an end and the Turks were entering the last phase of a ten-year period of wars in their history, the situation in Anatolia was as follows. The inhabitants were deprived of any kind of infrastructure or any means to lead a decent life. The population largely was affected by various kinds of infectious diseases; many people became ill, died, or became disabled. More than half of the people living in Anatolia were afflicted with malaria, and at least one person in every few families had tuberculosis. Trachoma and syphilis were seen as disasters affecting certain regions. In addition to cholera, typhus, and typhoid, which spread throughout the country, other types of infectious diseases continued to affect the people sporadically.[94]

With the conclusion of the First World War, the city of Istanbul was confronted with a new humanitarian duty of struggling against epidemics. The epidemics were rampant especially in areas where the refugees coming from Russia were settled. Despite the outstanding efforts of the doctors, scarlet fever, typhus, plague, smallpox, cholera, and typhoid penetrated all around after November 1920. In December of the same year, a cruel epidemic of cholera breaking out in the Çilingir camps wiped out hundreds of people.[95]

In the novel, *Yüzbaşı Selahattin'in Romanı* (Captain Selahattin's novel), some cross-sections from the lives of the people were presented through the eyes of the novel's hero. It illustrates the everyday life of ordinary people during the process of decay and dissolution toward the end of the war in Istanbul. The large buildings in Anadoluhisarı were turned into hospitals. The soldiers receiving treatment in the outpatient clinics of those hospitals wandered around the streets every night, begging bread from the houses nearby because they were not given sufficient food. Furthermore, it was rumored that their senior officers—the sergeants, doctors, and officers—were stealing the already small amount of food supplies given to them. Many soldiers were dying from cold, hunger, and lack of care. What is more, all these incidents were occurring before the eyes of the entire public. Many officers, civil servants, soldiers, and tradesmen made a fortune in Istanbul by charging excessive prices for the goods they sold; on occasion they demanded five hundred kuruş for an object they had bought for five kuruş. Whereas a large part of the population was stricken by extreme poverty, a small group accumulated immense wealth, which amplified debauchery and all kinds of dishonorable conduct within the society.[96]

In 1918 a plague epidemic broke out in a prison in Trabzon, killing twenty-five people.[97] Dr. Feridun Frik notes that malaria, typhoid, and

TABLE 5.8. Deaths as found in the records of İzmir municipality

DISEASE	TURKS	JEWS	ARMENIANS	GREEKS	TOTAL
Enteric disease	203	42	10	305	560
Tuberculosis	165	16	12	222	415
Pneumonia	139	29	106	180	454
Malaria	73	7	2	80	162
Bronchopneumonia	37	9	3	111	160
Smallpox	38	16	2	97	153
Malnutrition	40	–	–	89	129
Spotted fever	17	7	–	22	46
Children's disease	21	8	–	10	39
Typhoid	10	3	–	25	38
Influenza	5	4	1	25	35
Plague	5	2	–	11	18
Acute Bronchitis	4	–	–	10	14
Infant deaths	5	–	–	8	13
Puerperal fever	5	–	–	3	8
Diphtheria	–	–	–	8	8
Erysipelas	–	2	–	3	5
Tetanus	–	1	–	2	3
Recurrent fever	1	–	–	1	2
TOTAL	768	146	136	1,212	2,262

tuberculosis were the diseases he encountered most frequently while he was a student at the Faculty of Medicine (1918–1923) and later while he was working in the army.[98] In the course of World War I, a disease known as the "hookworm infection" became prevalent in and around Hopa—a town on the Black Sea coast—during the Russian occupation, and then spread into other areas.[99]

Throughout the occupation of Istanbul in the aftermath of World War I, tuberculosis took the highest toll, although deaths among newborns and the deaths due to typhus, typhoid, diphtheria, and influenza reached strikingly high figures. In 1920 alone, a total of 2,640 inhabitants died of tuberculosis.[100] In 1922, one-sixth of the 16,256 deaths in Istanbul were also caused by tuberculosis.[101] On the other hand, between 1917 and 1920 a total of 1,522 individuals were infected with recurrent fever in Istanbul, 15 of whom died.[102] During the same period (1917–1920), a total of 313 patients were diagnosed with smallpox in Istanbul, 183 of whom died.[103] Ahmet Emin recalls how he became ill with typhoid in 1922, on his return to Istanbul from Malta.[104]

TUBERCULOSIS

During World War I, economic difficulties, poverty, and disastrous incidents of the war caused a sharp increase in the number of deaths from tuberculosis.[105] In 1918 an organization called the Ottoman Society of Combat against Tuberculosis, under the chairmanship of Dr. Besim Ömer Pasha, was established with the aim of reducing the deaths from tuberculosis. After the occupation of Istanbul in 1920, however, the organization had to suspend its activities.[106]

According to the statistical data given in a pamphlet entitled *Verem Tehlikesi, Veremle Mücadele* (Danger of Tuberculosis, Struggling with Tuberculosis), published in 1919, tuberculosis-related deaths constituted 10.8 percent of the total deaths in 1918 in Istanbul, which had a population of 940,000, which is a very high percentage by any measure.[107]

The statistics pertaining to the period of 1901–1923 further show that an average of 2,800 individuals were losing their lives due to tuberculosis annually in Istanbul, which accounts for 15.8 percent of the total number of deaths in the city. Between 1892 and 1914, a total of 14,700 individuals died from tuberculosis in İzmir, which had a population of about 200,000. In other words, the percentage of deaths from tuberculosis in İzmir was equal to that in Istanbul, which was 15.8 percent. In 1919, the number of tuberculosis-related deaths in Istanbul was three times greater than the number of deaths from other diseases, which had to be reported to the relevant authorities.[108]

TYPHUS

Dr. Feridun Frik notes that typhus was prevalent both within the army and among the civilian population during the Great War.[109] Cases of typhus already had been encountered in Istanbul in the wake of the Balkan

TABLE 5.9. Data relevant to various diseases encountered in Aydin Province (March 1919)

DISEASE	RECOVERY	DEATH	TOTAL
Spotted fever (Typhus)	32	12	44
Tuberculosis	0	43	43
Puerperal fever	0	1	1
Meningitis	0	8	8
Smallpox	0	2	2
Recurrent fever	2	1	3
Typhoid	1	5	6
Measles	0	1	1
Plague	2	1	3
Erysipelas	0	1	1
Scarlet fever	0	1	1
Ordinary diseases	0	213	213
Contagious diseases	0	6	6
TOTAL	37	295	332

Wars. After World War I, it resurged again in Istanbul and spread all over the country. In 1915 a typhus epidemic broke out in the School of Reserve Officers in Yakacık, Istanbul, caused by the widely spreading lice.[110] During the period of 1915–1916, typhus was also widely prevalent in Urfa, which was located on the route of the convoys coming from the north.[111] Finally, in the third year of the war (1917), large-scale typhus epidemics were encountered on the Syrian and Iraqi fronts.[112] Between 1917 and 1922, a total of 10,806 people became ill with typhus in Istanbul, 1,181 of whom lost their lives. In 1919 a public bath (*hamam*) was rented in Kasımpaşa, and two mobile and one stationary public baths were set up in Tophane, so that people could bathe.[113] When the typhus epidemic broke out in Istanbul in 1917, the Mediterranean Fleet was not affected greatly, thanks to the doctors' diligent endeavors to make necessary arrangements with the hospitals nearby. For instance, the common practice of giving uniforms of dead soldiers to others was abandoned in the case of typhus-related deaths.[114] Typhus persisted throughout the War of Liberation; during the stressful days of the Battle of Sakarya, particularly the hospitals in Polatlı and Ankara were flooded with thousands of typhus patients.[115]

Between 1919 and 1922, a total of 3,425 cases of typhus were encountered in the armies of the Turkish Grand National Assembly, 552 of which resulted in death.[116] According to the statistical data published in *Sıhhiye Mecmuası* (Medical Journal), only 333 cases of typhus were seen in Turkey in 1925. In subsequent years, the number of typhus cases gradually decreased: 184 cases in 1926; 179 cases in 1927; 106 cases in 1928; 117 cases in 1929; 254 cases in 1930; 181 cases in 1931; and 97 cases in 1932. A marked increase, however, was observed in 1934, due to the outbreak of another epidemic of typhus in which 3,943 cases were recorded.[117]

TRACHOMA

Trachoma had existed endemically only in the southern and eastern provinces of Turkey until the beginning of the Great War. The migrations caused by the war, however, facilitated the spread of trachoma up into the Central Anatolia. According to some records, around seven hundred children staying in the orphanages in Istanbul were diagnosed with trachoma in 1919.[118] Throughout the war, epidemics of trachoma further spread all over Anatolia, causing many people to become blind.[119] Other countries also encountered similar problems and took various measures against trachoma. In that context, for instance, the United States declined to issue residence permits to those wartime emigrants who were found or suspected to have the disease upon medical examination. In the British and American armies, soldiers diagnosed with the disease were sent to treatment centers.[120]

SYPHILIS

As the war was coming to an end, a new wave of infectious diseases, including syphilis, ravaged Istanbul and other ruined towns and villages of Anatolia. Although the venereal diseases of gonorrhea, syphilis, cancroids, and scabies were infrequent in Istanbul before 1914, they soared after the war began. Even Anatolia came under the threat of those diseases. The regulations issued in 1915 with the aim of controlling venereal diseases found the existing norms "extremely liberal." According to drafters of the new regulations, ethical norms were insufficient. The primary purpose of those regulations was to track the carriers of the VD and treat them before they transmitted their illnesses to others.[121]

During discussions on the health budget for the year 1918 in the Ottoman Cabinet, Şemsettin Bey, deputy from Ertuğrul, brought up the issue of syphilis, underlining that "the country was being destroyed from inside by a real enemy, and that the very existence of the nation was constantly being threatened."[122] Fevzi Bey, the deputy from Diyarbakır, also pointed out that syphilis was spreading not only in Istanbul, but also in other parts of the country, including his own province, at an enormous speed.[123]

Just after World War I, Red Crescent health teams were dispatched to several parts of Anatolia. The personnel who went to Trabzon kept very detailed notes on their journey as well as observations about the situation there in their reports. The team, after stopping in İnebolu on 29 June 1919, arrived in Giresun on 1 July. The first scene they witnessed was the coastal buildings that were reduced to rubble by the bombardments. Hunger and poverty prevailed in every corner of the city. Though the cases of recurrent fever were infrequent in and around Giresun, a syphilis epidemic, gonorrhea, and scabies were widespread. The Giresun municipality doctor told the team members that about 20 percent of the people in Giresun were ill with syphilis. The situation in Trabzon was no different. At the country hospital, which was located in the center of the city and administered by the municipality, one entire ward was allocated to patients of syphilis. The non-Muslims had better conditions. The Greek Red Cross regularly examined and gave free medicines to the non-Muslim patients. During their first days in Trabzon, the Red Crescent team offered to work together with the Americans; but the Americans responded by saying that although they did not discriminate on the basis of race or religion, they would prefer to continue helping only the Armenians and Greeks, since they needed help more than others. According to the reports of the Red Crescent team during their first days on duty, a total of 270 malaria cases, 9 cases of syphilis, and many cases of scabies were encountered in the polyclinic they opened in Trabzon. In Bayburt and its environs, the districts and villages attacked by the Armenian militia needed help desperately. When the Armenian militia had heard that the Ottoman Army was approaching, they put thousands of Muslims seeking refuge in Bayburt into large buildings and burned them alive.[124]

The Red Crescent team dispatched to Erzincan in 1919 had more or less the same impressions as those of the team sent to Trabzon. A total of 15,000 patients were examined and treated at the outpatient clinics opened by the Red Crescent team. According to statistics prepared by the team, the diseases of malaria, scabies, recurrent fever, syphilis, and other skin diseases were frequent in the area. The Red Crescent team in Erzincan did not discriminate between the local people, and provided underclothes and provisions also to 78 Armenian and 40 Greek families living in the area. In Harput, too, the Armenian and Turkish orphanages were provided with 500 sets of underclothes each.¹²⁵

MALARIA

In her book *Türk'ün Ateşle İmtihanı* (Turk's Ordeal with Fire), Halide Edip describes the epidemic of malaria, which spread all over Anatolia in the 1920s and also afflicted her, as follows:

> We were all glad since none of us had caught a malign kind of malaria which had diffused through Ankara. Later, I caught the most dangerous type of that disease in Ankara, although I had survived through the severest malaria epidemics in Syria.¹²⁶

During the Balkan Wars and World War I, three quarters of the Ottoman population suffered from malaria. Other than distributing quinine to patients, no measure could be implemented. During the war years, moreover, due to the difficulties encountered in importing quinine from European countries and the increase in prices, the amount of quinine distributed to patients had to be further reduced.¹²⁷ Whereas malaria existed as an endemic disease in the Ottoman Empire prior to World War I, it turned into epidemics in various places after the war.¹²⁸

According to the results of a study carried out during the war by Dr. Tevfik Sağlam, the medical inspector of the 3rd Army, malaria affected parts of the Black Sea coastal area extending from Tirebolu to the west of Canik Sanjak (a subdivision of the province in the Ottoman Empire), to certain parts of Tokat and Amasya Sanjaks of Sivas province, to the Kuruçay district of Erzurum, and to the provincial center and İncesu district of Kayseri.¹²⁹ The observations by the medical units of the Turkish Army indicate that malaria was widely prevalent on the battlefields. During the course of the War of Liberation, the rate of occurrence of malaria was 40 percent in the Ottoman Army.¹³⁰ A report prepared by Dr. Ekrem Hayri in 1921, the general director of hygiene, stated that a total of 172,000 cases of malaria were recorded in and around Antalya; at the time, the population of Antalya was estimated to be 200,000. During the same period, the rate of malaria reached 70 percent in some parts of Anatolia.¹³¹ In 1924, a daily published in Antalya wrote that the number of deaths, which had previously been twice the number of births, showed a further increase in 1921 and became two and a half times the number of births, causing a large decrease in population. The same daily also reported that in the villages of the Finike district of Antalya, the rate of malaria among the population was 70.3 percent, while in some of the villages of Elmalı, another district of Antalya, the rate was 62.3 percent.[132]

Throughout the War of Liberation, the number of deaths from diseases exceeded the number of soldiers who died on the battlefields. According to a study on the casualties suffered during the two-year-long war, whereas 8,505 soldiers died in combat, 22,543 people died in hospitals.[133]

In December 1921, for instance, despite all measures taken before the launch of the Grand Offensive, a total of 16,953 soldiers had to be admitted to the hospital. That figure further increased to 29,193 in March 1922.[134] As of April 1922, the total number of ill soldiers was 27,834.[135]

In 1920, at the time of the establishment of the Ministry of Health, only one bed per 4,100 persons was available in Anatolia.[136] When the new Turkish Assembly, established on 23 April 1920 in Ankara, was in the process of laying out the fundamentals of its health policy, it passed the 1921 Law on Syphilis as part of its attempts to combat epidemic diseases.[137]

As pointed out by Dr. Ömer Besim Pasha, who authored various studies on Turkey's population policy, malaria continued to exist in Anatolia in its severest form during the years immediately following World War I. It not only reduced childbirths, but also greatly increased the number of deaths.[138] The research carried out by the medical units of the army during World War I had revealed the prevalence of malaria epidemics all over Anatolia. After the conclusion of the war, soldiers returning to their homes from battlefronts in Hijaz, Iraq, and other places with hot climates brought with them malaria, particularly malaria tropic, and spread it throughout the country.

In places where malaria reaches endemic proportions, the rate at which it spreads is measured by the spleen size of people. If the ratio of individuals having enlarged spleens is less than 10 percent in a certain area, malaria is considered to be partially endemic there. Ratios of 10–25 percent indicate that malaria is endemic at a medium level, while ratios of 25–50 percent indicate highly endemic malaria. Ratios above 50 percent are accepted as an indication of hyperendemic malaria. According to reports prepared by the medical units for the period between 1917 and 1925, changes of about 80–90 percent had been recorded in the spleen indexes in Ankara, Balıkesir, Denizli, Istanbul, Mardin, and Seyhan. During the period 1917–1926, the spleen indexes measured in some of the cities were as follows: 90 percent in Denizli, 80 percent in the Çekmece region of Istanbul, 40–90 percent in Ankara, 20 percent in Bursa, and 70 percent in Eskişehir.[139]

During the War of Liberation, malaria was widespread among the

Turkish soldiers (40 percent). That ratio was even higher among the civilians (50 percent). In some regions, the ratio of malarial patients even exceeded the average: 70 percent around Samsun, 44 percent in Söke, and 50 percent among the laborers working on tunnel construction in the Taurus Mountains. Those figures were obtained based on tests made on the blood samples of the people. In other places, the number of deaths due to malaria epidemics was twice the total number of births.[140] Malaria was so widespread in Anatolia that even Mustafa Kemal Pasha had occasional fevers, which meant his military doctor, Refik Saydam, had to accompany him at all times.[141] Indeed, the war increased the cases of malaria in Ankara. When construction work started on the Yahşihan railway line, the laborers arriving from other places and suffering from malaria transmitted the infection even further in the region. In the years 1923 and 1924, almost everybody in Ankara was affected with malaria.[142]

INFANT DEATHS

During the First National Medical Congress, held at the Grand National Assembly between 1 and 3 September 1925 in Ankara, the subjects that received the most attention were the population policy, prevention of child deaths, and the public health.[143] A paper entitled "Infant Deaths," presented by Prof. Dr. Asaf Derviş Pasha and Dr. Hamit Osman, provided numbers of deaths and births among the Muslims, Jews, and Armenians living in Istanbul, based on the official records. The authors noted that acute infectious diseases of diphtheria, whooping cough, scarlet fever, and measles were the prime causes of infant deaths. Syphilis also killed infants in their first three months. In cities such as Adana and Mersin, malaria, too, was causing many infant deaths. The paper also included information regarding the ratios of births and infant deaths for various cities. It noted that compared to other cities, the infant deaths were particularly high in Erzurum, which had a cold climate, as well as in Mersin, which had a hot climate. It was also noted that 95 percent of the infants were breast-fed. The death ratio was five times greater among infants fed with artificial formulas than among those fed with breast milk.[144]

The Ottoman armies fought five different wars between September 1911 and September 1922, where young people from Anatolia shed their blood in Europe, Africa, and Asia. The poverty and deprivation caused by those wars put its mark on the lives of people from all sectors of society throughout Anatolia. The most destructive of those wars, however, were the ones waged in Anatolia. In eastern Anatolia, the Great War had two dimensions: the

TABLE 5.10. The epidemics and deaths in Turkey (number of cases / number of deaths)

DISEASE	1925	1926	1927	1928	1929
Scarlet fever	971 / 245	1,102 / 155	1,567 / 273	1,791 / 882	2,693 / 527
Smallpox	483 / 69	492 / 117	99 / 6	47 / 8	1,146 / 870
Measles	2,878 / 168	3,900 / 314	2,572 / 340	3,242 / 234	3,008 / 197
Puerperal fever	48 / 11	39 / 12	52 / 26	59 / 37	38 / 11
Diphtheria	336 / 56	567 / 74	790 / 113	1,120 / 189	889 / 135
Typhoid	607 / 59	751 / 63	974 / 154	982 / 738	1,058 / 106
Spotted fever	333 / 26	184 / 23	179 / 17	106 / 15	117 / 14
Recurrent fever	33 / –	185 / 3	53 / –	23 / 2	3 / –
Yellow malaria	34 / 11	34 / 12	29 / 12	38 / 12	163 / 68
Amoebic dysentery	56 / 2	711 / 22	126 / 15	398 / 43	494 / 33
Whooping cough	239 / 25	781 / 15	188 / 16	666 / 34	322 / 13

Russian occupation and the civil war. The defeat the Ottoman forces suffered on the Ottoman-Russian border between November and December 1914 was followed by the uprisings of the Armenians and the Nestorians in Van in April 1915. During the same period, the Kurdish tribes, capitalizing on the domestic chaos, conducted raids and attacked particularly the Christian communities. During the three years of war between the Turks and the Russians, control over agricultural lands was not sustained long enough to get the crops harvested. Every time the villagers had to move again, they became vulnerable to hunger, enemy armies, and the incessant raids of the Kurds; as a result, many villagers lost their lives.[145]

The Russian Army started to withdraw in November 1917, and an armistice was signed with the new Russian regime on 16 December 1917 in Erzincan. Armenian militia forces started a campaign to massacre the Muslim people in the areas evacuated by the Russian Army in the Eastern front. The Ottoman forces started a new offensive on 12 February 1918 to halt those massacres. In the course of that expedition, some Turkish soldiers froze to death. By the time the Turkish forces entered Erzurum on 12 March 1918, the Armenian militia had massacred half of the civilian population.[146]

Ahmet Refik, after visiting the region in May 1918, reported his observations about Erzincan in his book entitled *İki Komite İki Kıtal* (Two Committees, Two Massacres):

> Hunger and death were everywhere. Between the frightening rocks on the banks of the mournfully purling Euphrates River, one could see a hungry dog tearing the flesh of a Turk, killed and thrown onto the roadside by the Armenians, or skulls of children with grinning teeth in the villages.
>
> The entire Erzincan looks like a graveyard for the Turks. The neighborhoods of the city were in ruins. The destruction in the walls of the houses indicated that the fiercest clashes between the Armenians and the Turks had taken place there. The houses of both the Turks and the Armenians were razed. The cemeteries of both the Turks and the Armenians also were in a terrible condition. The fresh bodies lying in streets and inside wells, which were still warm, and whose wounds were still bleeding, belonged to the poor Turks shot dead by the Armenians. The courtyards of the Armenian houses known for their nice gardens with blossoming trees, and well-decorated paved courts were full of bloodstains. A very heavy smell was coming out of the narrow wells in the gardens, making one dizzy. One could see the poor Turks' hair and pieces of their clothes which stuck on the inner walls of those wells.
>
> The ruined buildings, the burned down houses, and grounds near the walls were full of dead Turkish bodies; pieces of arms, skulls, greasy leg bones, and the corpses not yet decayed spread all around. The residents were in great sorrow, exhaustion, and misery. The ones wandering around in the marketplace were poor and hungry creatures, who no longer looked like human beings. They had no shoes on, their faces were darkened under the sun, and they were all in ragged clothes. Most of the shops were closed down; and the remaining ones were selling only herbs as foodstuff for the people. Except for the Army Command, bread was not available anywhere. If the commander had not provided food, even the mutasarrıf (governor of a sanjak) would surely die of hunger.[147]

By 1918, even those who were committing raids and plunders must have fallen hungry, because practically no livestock was left by then to be seized. The people grew entirely helpless and hunger-stricken, and the diseases of cholera, typhus, influenza, and dysentery took the lives of many. Despite the misery on both sides, one more fight was fought between Turkey and the Republic of Armenia in 1919.[148]

The battles in the west were ignited by the Greek Army's invasion of İzmir in May 1919. The war extended to the areas beyond the battlefronts where the Turkish and Greek armies engaged each other. As had been the case in eastern Anatolia, the Turco-Greek war soon turned into a civil war between the two nations of the Ottoman Empire. This time, combatants were the Muslims and the Greeks. Most of the deaths and destruction that occurred in the course of the war resulted from the attacks conducted by different Ottoman subjects, who aimed at taking revenge for the evil actions performed or believed to be performed against them, either recently or centuries before. They failed to observe the laws of war in this conflict.[149]

6

UNBURIED CORPSES

> Now snowflakes thickly falling in the winter breeze
> Have cloaked alike the hard, unbending ilex
> And the grey, drooping branches of the olive trees,
> Transmuting into silver all their lead;
> And, in between the winding lines, in No Man's Land,
> Have softly covered with a glittering shroud,
> The unburied dead.
>
> —Malcolm Ross,
> "The Unburied"

MUCH HAS BEEN WRITTEN about various episodes in history, characterized by the extreme ruthlessness, unrestricted behavior, and oppressive aims of fighters. Humanity has faced mass exterminations, conducted during times of war, which continued through generations. Attila the Hun used to raze the places he passed through in order to mark his victories. The concept of "all-out war" was part of daily life for the people living in the medieval towns surrounded by high walls, and a defeat always meant migration, destruction, and death.[1]

The Great War, which lasted for four long years from 1914 to 1918, demonstrated similar characteristics to previous wars. It was in many ways the continuation of a recurrent pattern in history. Although it shared many commonalities with other major wars in history, it still had unique features as far as the territories occupied during the course of war, the technological intensity of battles, and its comprehensiveness. This war is rightfully known as the first "global war" in military history, and as a result the losses it caused were incomparably higher than previous wars.

According to Eric Hobsbawm, the First World War Involved *all* major powers, and all European states except for Spain, the Netherlands, the three Scandinavian countries, and Switzerland. What is more, troops from

TABLE 6.1. French, German, Belgian, and American death ratios

NATIONALITY	DEATHS IN COMBAT (%)	DEATHS DUE TO DISEASES (%)
French	13.5	2.0
German	13.7	1.0
Belgian	8.5	3.0
American	4.5	1.7

overseas were sent to fight and work outside their own regions, a phenomenon not generally seen in previous wars. The Canadians fought in France; a distant peninsula in the Aegean—"Gallipoli"—became part of the national myth of the Australians and New Zealanders; and more significantly, the United States acted against George Washington's warning to avoid "European entanglements" and sent its soldiers to fight there, which determined the course of twentieth-century history. Indians were deployed to Europe and the Middle East, Chinese labor battalions were brought to the West, and Africans served in the French army. Although military operations outside Europe were insignificant, except for the battles in the Middle East, the naval war was once again global: the first naval battle was fought in 1914 off the Falkland Islands, and several naval campaigns were decisive of the war's outcome, such as the fighting between German submarines and Allied convoys on and under the seas of the North and mid-Atlantic.[2]

THE CASUALTIES OF THE GREAT WAR

According to a study carried out in 1920, the total number of deaths during the war is estimated at 35 million. In addition to the battlefield deaths, epidemic diseases such as typhus and influenza took a heavy toll among both troops and civilians. The influenza epidemics alone accounted for the lives of millions of men and women. According to the same source, combat-related casualties were 13 million.[3]

The statistics in Table 6.1, published in Paris in 1925, provide valuable information on the ratio of deaths that various armies suffered from battles and diseases. These statistics, however, do not include the Ottoman army.[4]

One British source in 1934 claimed that the exact figures on human losses during the Great War would never be established. Various factors complicated obtaining correct figures. For instance, in some countries, such as Russia and Turkey, statistical information gathered was unreliable. France,

TABLE 6.2. Total war casualties according to Cruttwell

COUNTRY	DEAD	WOUNDED	PRISONER	TOTAL
England	747,023	2,493,906	19,652	3,260,581
France	1,385,300	447,000	446,300	2,278,600
Italy	460,000	947,000	530,000	1,937,000
Russia	1,700,000	4,950,000	2,500,000	9,150,000
USA	115,660	205,690	4,526	325,876
Germany	1,808,545	4,247,143	617,922	6,673,610
Austria-Hungary	1,200,000	3,620,000	2,200,000	7,020,000
Turkey	325,000	400,000	1,565,000	2,290,000

on the other hand, did not publish a total number of wounded. Germany did not include the slightly wounded in its casualty lists. Many countries involved in the First World War could not ascertain the number of casualties and prisoners. The borders of many countries, moreover, were changed after the war. The number of recorded deaths was calculated at 10,004,771, while the estimate of additional, unrecorded deaths was 2,991,800, which together add up to 12,996,571. Deaths from diseases are included in this figure.[5]

As shown in Table 6.2, prepared based on information provided in 1934 by the abovementioned British source, Germany leads in terms of the number of dead (1,808,545). It ranks second in terms of the numbers of wounded (4,247,143) and prisoners (2,200,000), and third in total casualties (6,673,610). Russia ranks second in terms of the number of dead (1,700,000), but it sits at the top of the list in terms of the numbers of wounded (4,950,000) and prisoners (2,500,000), as well as in total casualties (9,150,000). In terms of the number of dead, Germany and Russia are followed by France (1,385,300), Austria-Hungary (1,200,000), England (747,023), Italy (460,000), and Turkey (325,000).[6]

The same source admits that the figures pertaining to Turkish losses are incomplete. In another study published nine years later, Colonel A. G. Butler of the Australian Army established that Turkey's losses during the war were greater than previously estimated. According to this 1943 study, Turkey's battle-related human losses were 948,447, whereas the losses occurring outside battles were 3,967,000. Turkey's losses from epidemic diseases were not included in A. G. Butler's tables, either. As in the British study, the number of deaths was given as 325,000.[7]

These studies bring to mind several questions. In estimating the human losses of war, should we take into account only those killed in combat? As the case of World War I demonstrates, epidemics took the lives of not only troops but also of a great many people living within the boundaries of the Ottoman Empire during the war years. It is obvious that those deaths occurring due to epidemics need to be included in an estimation of the total losses of that country. Indeed it would be useful to give figures on deaths from epidemics separately, to better differentiate between deaths in combat, either by wounds or by epidemic diseases.

According to William H. McNeill, "In the course of World War I, huge waves of typhus, striking from time to time, were destroying armies, deserting prisons, and badly hitting houses of the poor. About 2–3 million people lost their lives due to epidemics."[8] And Hanson Baldwin stated, "An enormous scale of destruction was brought to light by typhus, chickenpox, and the plague. Hunger became more prevalent than ever. The views of babies with swollen bellies made those who saw them lose their sleep."[9]

During the Great War, the number of disease-related casualties among troops of all the nations involved was about 1.5 million. The French journal *Drapeau* estimates the number of casualties due to diseases at 3,115,000, which is generally considered to be a highly inflated figure. In fact, epidemic diseases did not cause such a big damage in Europe. The effects of epidemics were felt most severely within the Ottoman Army.[10] Within the European continent, the other exception in that regard was the Serbian Army. In the very early stages of the war, a typhus epidemic killed a large number of soldiers serving in the Serbian Army.

New advances in medicine, developments in the eradication of lice, and improvised mobile hygiene measures in military units were the main factors that helped reduce the number of deaths from epidemics in the West.

> In the decade before World War I another important medical discovery that altered the epidemiology of European armies profoundly was between 1909 and 1912, when the role of the louse in spreading typhus fever was understood. This, together with a systematic immunization against other common infections, was what made the unexampled concentration of millions of men in the trenches of northern France, in 1914–1918, medically possible. Passing men and clothing through delousing stations became part of the ritual of going to and returning from the front; and this prevented

typhus from playing the lethal role on the Western Front that it did, sporadically but dramatically, in the East. Even when typhus did break out on the Eastern Front in 1915, disease losses in the ranks remained well below the losses from enemy action, as long as organization and discipline remained intact.[11]

In his study on the Ottoman Army's experience with deaths and desertions in 1914–1918, Eric Jan Zürcher emphasized that the ratio of deaths among patients was about 50 percent in the Ottoman Army, whereas that ratio was only 10 percent in the German Army.[12]

Another study, published by Tevfik Sağlam, the medical chief of the Ottoman 3rd Army during the Great War, lends support to the assessment that epidemic diseases caused extreme damage to the Ottoman Army compared to other armies. According to his study, during the four years of World War I, the German Army suffered 1,651,072 deaths, 87 percent of which were caused by wounds or other external factors, whereas epidemic diseases accounted for 11 percent of total deaths, corresponding to 177,162 individuals. The total strength of the German forces in the war was 6,400,000 men. That means, an average of 2,953 deaths per month occurred due to diseases. When that figure is compared with that of the Ottoman 3rd Army, it appears that the ratio of deaths from disease in the Ottoman Army was nearly fifty times higher.[13]

According to information provided by the Military Health Administration of the Ottoman Armies, during the four years of the war, 47 percent of the servicemen were hospitalized, 17 percent of whom died in the hospital.[14] Colonel Butler's study, entitled "Australian Army Medical Services in the War of 1914–1918," published in 1943, included detailed statistical data regarding the casualties of the belligerents in the Great War. Colonel Butler took the figures on the casualties from the military publications of the respective countries.[15]

Austro-Hungarian Casualties

When the numbers of dead, wounded, and prisoners of the participants in the Great War are compared to their total populations, Austria-Hungary appears to have suffered the highest casualties. According to the official explanation made in late May 1918, the total casualties of the Austro-Hungarian Army amounted to 4 million, consisting of 800,000 dead and 3.2 million wounded. When 1.8 million prisoners are added to that figure, the total casualties reach 5.8 million.[16]

A total of 300,000 soldiers from the Austro-Hungarian Army died due

TABLE 6.3. Total war casualties according to Colonel Butler

ALLIED COUNTRIES	NUMBER OF TROOPS	DEAD	WOUNDED	PRISONER AND MISSING	TOTAL CASUALTY	RATIOS
England	8,485,926	897,780	2,085,377	266,700	3,249,857	38.30
France	8,194,150	1,457,000	2,300,000	478,000	4,235,000	51.68
Russia	15,123,000	664,890	3,813,827	3,950,000	8,428,717	55.73
Italy	5,615,000	650,000	947,000	600,000	2,197,000	39.13
USA	2,040,000	51,606	234,300	4,500	290,406	14.24
Japan	800,000	300	907	3	1,210	0.15
Belgium	267,000	13,716	44,686	34,659	93,061	34.85
Serbia	707,343	45,000	133,148	152,958	331,106	46.81
Montenegro	50,000	3,000	10,000	7,000	20,000	40.00
Romania	750,000	335,706	120,000	80,000	535,706	71.43
Greece	261,890	5,000	21,000	1,000	27,000	10.31
Portugal	191,362	7,222	13,751	12,318	33,291	17.40
TOTAL	42,485,671	4,131,220	9,723,996	5,587,138	19,442,354	45.76
AXIS COUNTRIES						
Germany	13,387,000	1,061,740	5,397,884	771,659	7,231,283	54.02
Austria	7,800,000	1,200,000	3,620,000	2,200,000	7,020,000	90.00
Turkey	2,850,000	325,000	400,000	250,000	975,000	34.21
Bulgaria	1,200,000	87,500	152,390	27,029	266,919	22.24
TOTAL	25,237,000	2,674,240	9,570,274	3,248,688	15,493,202	61.39

to freezing and disease. The deaths from various epidemic diseases are broken down as follows: tuberculosis (43,000), enteric fever (24,000), cholera (16,000), dysentery (11,000), and malaria (3,000).[17] A Turkish source writes that 171,601 individuals became ill with typhoid in the Austro-Hungarian Army, 17,399 of whom (10.14 percent) died.[18] Just as the Serbs in 1915–1916 and the Russians in 1917–1918, Austro-Hungarians suffered from epidemic-related deaths both in the military and among the civilians.[19] In the Austro-Hungarian Army, despite prolonged exposure to the epidemic of typhus

TABLE 6.4. Austro-Hungarian casualties (1914–1918)

Dead	800,000
Wounded and ill	3,200,000
Prisoner	1,800,000
TOTAL	5,800,000

TABLE 6.5. French casualties (1914–1918)*

Soldiers on the front	8,410,000
Combat deaths	674,700
Deaths from wounds	250,000
Wounded	2,300,000
Missing / dead	225,300
Prisoner	252,700
Total casualties in battle	3,702,700
Deaths due to diseases	175,000
Recovered from diseases	800,000
TOTAL CASUALTIES	4,677,700

*From Butler, *Australian Army Medical Services*, 870, taken from Table 6.

raging in Serbia, disease-induced losses never exceeded 50 percent of the losses from enemy action.[20]

French Casualties

The total French losses during the war are estimated at approximately 5 million, approximately 1,400,000 of whom were dead or missing. Of those casualties, 175,000 soldiers died of disease. In the French Navy, there were 4,000 who died from Spanish influenza, which together add up to 179,000.[21] Of the 124,991 soldiers who were infected with typhoid, 15,211 (12.17 percent) died.[22]

By 1917, the French Army had suffered 1 million dead, and after another disastrous offensive in Champagne in April, half of its servicemen under arms refused to obey further orders to attack. The episode, loosely described as mutiny, was in a sense a large-scale military strike against an operation which had no chance of success. By the conclusion of the war, four out of nine Frenchmen under arms either died or were wounded.[23] By November 1918, France had lost 1.7 million out of a population of 40 million.[24]

Russian Casualties

In the Russian Army, a total of 395,000 soldiers died from either freezing or disease. Russian sources give the numbers of dead and wounded at about 1.7 million and 5 million respectively. Other sources estimate the actual number of dead at closer to 3 million.[25] Typhus continued to plague Russia after the war, as well; during the period 1918–1922, about 20 to 30 million cases of typhus were recorded in that country.[26] According to W. E. D. Allen and Paul Muratoff, the operations against the Ottoman 2nd and 3rd armies during 1916 resulted in heavy costs for Russia's Caucasian Army. Losses for the period between June and September 1916 amounted to some 50,000 (mostly in General Baratov's forces), due mainly to sickness.[27]

Russian troops on the western sector of the front could rest in the comparatively clement valleys of the Kelkit and Karasu, but those on the Dersim and Bingöl Mountain could only shelter in the wild alpine valleys of the Endres (at 1500–1700 m elevation) and the Ognot (at 1800–1900 m) In these valleys the frost was as severe as on the upper ridges and the snow, piled in great drifts by driving gales, lay even deeper. Despite their winter equipment, troops of the 2nd and 4th Plastun Brigades and 4th and 6th Rifle Divisions suffered terribly; many patrols were frozen to death, and casualties from frostbite were heavy. All these units had fought hard and suffered severe losses in the fighting of late summer, and by January 1917 their ranks were gravely thinned. There were periods when the men of the 4th Caucasian Rifle Division were receiving only half a pound of bread daily and horses only one and a half pounds of barley. There was no meat and no conserves, and men were boiling soup from the flesh of donkeys, cats, and dogs. Only in February did headquarters find it possible to relieve this excellent unit and bring it into reserve at Erzurum. Slightly better were the conditions of the 66th Infantry Division on the southern slopes of the Şerafettin Mountains. But here, in March, typhus broke out, imported perhaps from the neighboring town of Muş.[28] As noted in General Maslovsky's study, *The Caucasus Front*, the Russian Army lost 100,000 of its soldiers in the winter of 1917 due to hunger, illness, and severe cold. Even though the Russians' depots were full of foodstuffs, the Russian troops had to eat the meat of donkeys and dogs, due to the fact that none of the wheeled vehicles could be used. Fahri Belen also notes that in the winter of 1917, the two armies lost a total of 20,000 men because of cold, illness, and malnutrition.[29]

Toward the middle of the war, the Russian army, whose exact casualties never were established, began to "vote for peace with its feet," as Lenin metaphorically put it. Without the military catastrophes that the Tsarist army experienced in East Prussia, Poland, and the Ukraine, Lenin and his comrades hardly would have achieved the political victory in the October revolution in Petrograd in 1917.[30]

British Casualties

The Entente Powers deployed around 500,000 troops in Gallipoli in 1915, some 410,000 of which were British and 79,000 were French. Of this total, 43,000 British officers and recruits either were killed, taken prisoner, posted as missing, or died of wounds or disease. The total British casualties, including those evacuated sick, amounted to 205,000; French casualties were 47,000.[31] According to another source, the total casualties of the British Army in Gallipoli were 213,980. Of those, 145,154 died from diseases. Dysentery caused the highest number of deaths; it alone accounted for 29,728 deaths. It was followed by diarrhea with 10,373 fatalities. The number of those who died from enteric fever was 9,423, whereas 15,000 men froze to death during the extreme cold in November 1915. Some British soldiers, on the other hand, died in accidents. According to the same source, the official figures for the Ottoman casualties are cited as 251,000. The Ottoman records, however, are not reliable, and according to other sources, the total Ottoman casualties were about 350,000.[32]

According to German General Hans Kannengiesser, in Gallipoli the Entente deployed 539,000 expeditionary forces, whereas the Turkish defense lines involved 310,000 men. Where total British casualties, including dead, wounded, missing, and prisoners, equaled 180,282 men (33 percent of the forces), the Turks lost 165,371 men (53 percent). The sick, moreover, numbered as high as 85,938 men on the Ottoman side, where similar figures for the British forces were not available.[33]

During the Great War, the medical standards of the British Army were clearly superior to its rivals. Some experts even defined the war as "the war of engineers and doctors."[34] For instance, on the Gallipoli front, the equipment left behind by the retreating British forces clearly showed the superiority of the British Army. Liman von Sanders noted that the British forces abandoned five small ships and more than sixty transportation boats on the coast of the area extending from the Suvla Bay to Arıburnu. In addition, many narrow-gauge railway cars, telephones, materials used in installing woven wire, all kinds of tools, depots of medicines, various sorts of medical equipment, water filters, ammunition used by infantry and artillery units, limbers, equipment used in parking vehicles, various kinds of weapons, boxes full of hand grenades and machine-gun barrels, canned food, sacks of flour and barley, and high piles of wood were left behind by the British. The corpses of many horses killed by the British because they could not be taken back on the ships were also strewn around.[35] Although the British troops were relatively well supplied, they suffered from other problems. The main problems the British forces had to overcome were the heavy psychological stress and very bad hygienic conditions caused by being tightly packed together in a narrow area.

Sir William Robertson, the British chief of staff, makes an important confession, in his study entitled *Soldiers and Statesmen, 1914–1918*, with regard to the melting away of his soldiers due to diseases: In August 1915, even before the intensification of the clashes, they already had lost 24 percent of their strength due to diseases. According to the information communicated by the medical officer, during the medical checks made of seven Anzac battalions in September (one month later), 50 percent of the troops had been observed to have heart disorders, while 78 percent had been suffering from diarrhea and 64 percent from dermal sores. From time to time, it was necessary to transfer a total of one thousand patients in one day. Though patient care improved in October, by then the troops had been so physically and psychologically worn out that they were not able to endure a battle lasting more than twenty-four hours. In Sir Robertson's words, "The British Army, in its entire history, had never suffered from so many and bitter casualties from infectious diseases."[36]

In the above-mentioned historical study, the spreading of fatal diseases all over Anatolia and the mass annihilations caused by them in the winter of 1914–1915 and all through 1916 were explained in detail and proven by documents.

Throughout the Great War, the British Empire suffered 3,260,581 casualties, of which 947,023 were dead or missing. When those figures were disclosed to the British citizenry after the war, public opinion came to view the war as a great disaster. An intense feeling of panic spread throughout the country. Granted, Great Britain was able to overcome the trauma generated by the war casualties more swiftly compared to its allies.[37] Of the 1 million soldiers lost by the British Empire during the war, 700,000 were recruited from the British Isles, which had a total population of 50 million.[38]

The British chief of general staff notes that the ratio of the sick for the British soldiers serving on the Mesopotamian front was very high: "When the expenditures made for the ill in different camps in the East are added, the numbers obtained become very high." The figures on health expenditures

TABLE 6.6. British Army hospital admissions in November 1916

French Front	433
Egyptian Front	656
Salonika Front	1,036
Mesopotamian Front	2,135

TABLE 6.7. Casualties suffered up to October 1917*

Deaths in combat and from wounds	1,138,768
Deaths from disease	85,088
Prisoners	387,979
Missing	263,043
Heavily wounded	652,021
Wounded	328,431
Slightly wounded	1,829,820
Other wounded	315,263
TOTAL	5,000,413

* From *Statistics of the Military Effort of the British Empire*, 354.

also indicate that compared to the other fronts, the British army fighting on the Eastern front had a higher number of casualties due to diseases. The same report also adds that "the number of deaths caused by disease on the French Front was slightly more than the number of ill in Great Britain in peacetime."[39]

Syphilis was a major disease the British military medical personnel had to cope with during the Great War. As a syphilis epidemic spread through the British soldiers, the doctors initially failed to respond effectively, with moral weakness, rather than medical reasons, causing the delay in intervening in the epidemic.[40]

German Casualties

Germany's persistence to the very end, despite the loss of more than 2 million people from a prewar population of 70 million, is all the more remarkable.[41] The German Army lost 188,000 of its soldiers due to noncombat-related

TABLE 6.8. German casualties according to Colonel Butler (1914–1918)

Number of soldiers on the front	13,387,000
Combat deaths	772,687
Deaths among wounded	289,053
Deaths from gas	80,000
Wounded	5,397,884
Missing/prisoner	771,659
Total casualties in battle	7,311,283
Deaths due to diseases	150,000
Recovered from diseases	21,498,303
TOTAL CASUALTIES	28,959,586

deaths. Excluding the deaths caused by accidents, suicides, or murders, the number of soldiers dying from diseases was 150,000. As far as fatalities are concerned, pneumonia ranked first among the various diseases (27,000 deaths). It was followed by tuberculosis (20,000), influenza (14,000), and typhus (11,000).[42] According to a Turkish source, 112,364 soldiers became ill with typhus in the German Army, 11,405 of whom (10.15 percent) died.[43]

According to the German press, German war casualties (as of 1 November 1918) consisted of 1,600,000 dead, 203,000 missing, 618,000 prisoners, and 4,064,000 wounded, adding up to 6,485,000.[44] These figures show a similarity with the figures given by another source (Wolf Bureau) about the casualties suffered through 30 April 1919.[45] The figures published in a journal, *Majority Socialist*, on 6 January 1920 also are in compliance with the above-mentioned figures. That journal further adds that the number of casualties among German officers was 210,812.[46]

Casualties Of Other Countries In The Great War

According to an official statement made on 1 April 1920, the fatalities in the U.S. Army were as shown in Table 6.9.[47] The 325,876 casualties the U.S. Army suffered are broken down as follows: 115,660 dead (including deaths from diseases), 205,690 wounded, and 4,526 captive or missing. One of the documents published by the medical section of the U.S. Army further notes that a total of 60,000 deaths occurred due to diseases within the U.S. Army and Navy during World War I.[48]

Table 6.9. U.S. Army fatalities

Combat deaths	35,560
Deaths among wounded	14,720
Deaths due to diseases	57,460
Deaths from miscellaneous reasons	7,920
TOTAL NUMBER OF DEATHS	115,660

Table 6.10. Bulgarian casualties (1914–1918)

Number of soldiers on the front	768,000
Combat deaths	48,917
Death among wounded	13,198
Deaths caused by accidents	888 (?)
Deaths due to diseases	24,497
Missing	13,799
Wounded	152,390
Prisoner	10,623

In the Bulgarian Army, too, diseases took a heavy toll, with 24,000 deaths from various diseases. According to a document prepared by the Bulgarian War Cabinet, an even greater number of soldiers had to be called off from combat zones because of illness.[49]

Italy joined the war nine months after Britain. Except for their involvement in operations in Salonika and later in France, their major military operations were confined within the borders of Italy. Despite this fact, however, the number of casualties reached a figure as high as 460,000. This figure equals half of the total casualties suffered by the British Empire in the entire land and sea battles the British military fought.[50] It was even speculated that the Italian Army's casualty figures during its eleven abortive offensives over the Alps against the Austrian Army in May 1915 reached suicidal proportions: as many as one million. There came a point where the soldiers began refusing to obey the orders given by their commanders. In the end, the Italian Army was demolished by a joint attack of the Germans and Austrians;

TABLE 6.11. Casualties of Ottoman Empire according to a British source

Combat deaths	50,000
Deaths among wounded	35,000
Deaths due to diseases	240,000
Wounded	400,000
Total	725,000
Prisoners, deserters, missing	1,565,000
GENERAL TOTAL	2,290,000

Italy was then practically out of the war until the armistice. It lost 600,000 of its people out of a total population of 36 million.[51]

According to a British source, 53,000 individuals died of diseases in Italian hospitals. Another 32,000 died from diseases while waiting to be drafted into the army. The total Italian casualties due to diseases were 85,000. On the other hand, in the Romanian Army, 30,000 soldiers died from disease. In the Belgian, Greek, and Portuguese armies, the numbers of deaths due to diseases were 2,300, 16,994, and 1,002 respectively.[52]

TURKISH CASUALTIES

At the international level, the first statistics regarding Ottoman casualties in the Great War was published in 1922 by British military authorities. According to those statistics, a total of 85,000 Ottoman soldiers died in combat and from wounds. Diseases took a further 240,000 lives, for a total altogether of 325,000 dead. When 400,000 wounded are added to that figure, the total number of casualties reaches 725,000. The same study estimates the number of prisoners, deserters, and missing at 1.5 million. Based on those figures, the British military authorities claimed that the Ottoman Army suffered 2,300,000 casualties.[53]

A second foreign study on Ottoman Army losses in the Great War was published by a French officer, Commandant Larcher, in 1926, whose estimates approximate those of the British statistics published in 1922. When the Ottoman Army's total losses of 2,300,000 are subtracted from the number of soldiers recruited throughout the war, it appears that at the time of the signing of the Mondros Armistice in 1918, Turkey still had 560,000 soldiers at its disposal. Larcher notes that those official figures are based on a decree issued by the Ottoman government on 30 January 1919, and they could only give a rough estimate of the losses. According to Larcher, given that in Gallipoli alone 55,000 soldiers died, the Ottoman total fatality figure of 325,000 may actually have been closer to 500,000 to 600,000. Larcher also remarks that in Anatolia, 500,000 Muslim migrants coming from the East, 800,000 Armenians, and 325,000 Greeks lost their lives due to massacres, deportation, and the adverse living conditions in the labor battalions.[54]

Professor Hikmet Bayur discusses the statistical data made available by Larcher. Bayur observes that since Lieutenant Colonel Nihat, who translated Larcher's study into Turkish, corrected some of the factual mistakes concerning Turkey, those figures might be assumed to be reliable (up to the year 1928).[55] It is not unusual that in the 1930s several translators of the foreign studies on military history or the memoirs of foreign individuals made some corrections or additions. As far as Larcher's study goes, another thing that catches one's attention is that whereas the numbers of Armenian and Greek losses are exaggerated unreasonably, the Turkish losses were remarkably lower compared to the actual figures. This makes us think that as of 30 January 1919, the entire statistics regarding the four-year-long war had not been gathered in the Turkish Military Archives yet (see Table 6.12). The differences in figures provided by foreign and national studies could be explained by the fact that in the early 1930s, the statistical data regarding the deaths that occurred in the Great War could not be uncovered fully since the documents being kept in separate folders in the Turkish Military Archives had not yet been classified. That confusion in the data also continued in the following decades.

In a speech he delivered at a conference held in 1950 at the Turkish War Academy, Tevfik Bıyıklıoğlu stated that the Ottoman Army deployed around 700,000 men in Gallipoli; of those, 190,000 were either killed or wounded and another 70,000 became sick.[56] Based on his research on the documents available in the Turkish Military Archives, Fahri Belen argues that the total Ottoman losses in Gallipoli amounted to 190,000, consisting of 55,000 dead, 100,000 wounded, 10,000 missing, and 25,000 sick.[57] Belen also writes that the British losses in Gallipoli consisted of 43,000 dead and 72,000 wounded. When the French losses, which totaled 30,000, are added to that, the overall losses of the Entente Powers are found to be 145,000.[58]

Apart from those studies, some figures also could be obtained from various individuals' memoirs or personal reflections on the wartime conditions. For instance, Münim Mustafa notes that a total of 21,498 Turkish soldiers died due to illnesses at Gallipoli.[59] However, the British author Alan

TABLE 6.12. Total casualties of the Ottoman armies (1914–1918)

Under treatment	2,167,941
Disabled	891,364
Dead	501,091
TOTAL	3,560,396

TABLE 6.13. Deaths in the nine Ottoman armies

YEARS	DEATHS FROM DISEASES	DEATHS FROM WOUNDS	TOTAL DEATHS
First year of war	57,462	21,988	79,450
Second year of war	126,216	21,986	148,202
Third year of war	133,469	8,081	141,550
Fourth year of war	84,712	7,407	92,119
TOTAL OF FOUR YEARS	401,859	59,462	461,321

Moorehead states that at Gallipoli, the Ottoman side buried 76,000 of its soldiers, 55,000 killed in battle and 21,000 died from disease. According to Moorehead, apart from those who died, the Ottoman side had 100,000 wounded, and had to send 64,000 soldiers to the rear areas because of illness. When another 10,000 missing also are added, the Ottoman Army's cumulative casualties reach 250,000.[60]

A study published by the Turkish General Staff in 1935 argues that the total number of deaths in the Ottoman Army was 650,000, of which 240,000 were caused by various diseases.[61] That figure confirms the estimations made by Larcher in 1926 about the number of deaths.[62] As stated, the first official statistical data regarding the Ottoman Army's casualties in the war was provided by a decree issued by the Ottoman government on 30 January 1919 (see Table 6.12). This decree stated that a total of 2,850,000 soldiers were drafted into the army during the war. By November 1918, military force available to the Empire had fallen to only 60,000 men. A total of 800,000 individuals, moreover, were disabled in the war. Most of the disabled were unable to earn a living, and their number is high compared to the numbers of disabled in other countries involved in the war.[63] An article prepared by the medical department of the Turkish General Staff and published by

Dr. Osman Şevki in the daily *Tasvir-i Efkar* on 15 December 1921 also included similar statistics.[64] According to that article, the Ottoman fatalities amounted to 500,000. A total of 891,336 soldiers and officers, moreover, were discharged from the army due to various reasons, such as recreation, weakness, or retirement.[65]

Ahmet Emin published a book in 1930 based on the data he obtained from the Department of Health of the Ministry of National Defense, which included very detailed statistical information.[66] This study provides fatality figures on nine different Ottoman armies that fought on different fronts. When the figures about self-standing units and other fronts are also added (64,100 deaths from diseases and 8,916 deaths from wounds), we obtain a total of 466,759 deaths due to diseases and 68,378 deaths due to wounds. Accordingly, the grand total of fatalities according to the military health department is around 535,137. In evaluating these figures, one must bear in mind that the author himself underlines that the losses in Gallipoli were not included in these statistics. Based on the figures given by Ahmet Emin, we see that in the Great War the Ottoman Army suffered 60,000 combat deaths, whereas another 400,000 died of diseases. The total fatalities of the Ottoman Army, excluding those in Gallipoli, were as much as 460,000 men.[67]

The same source also gives valuable information as to the distribution of the deaths caused by various diseases. As can be seen from Table 6.14, the ratio of deaths caused by typhus and dysentery (especially typhus) was considerably high (as much as one-third).

In addition to the records of the regular armies, various military formations and enlistment stations that served during the Great War reported the following cases of sickness and death: Among the causes of sickness, malaria came first, with 461,799 cases and 23,351 deaths. Next was dysentery with about 147,000 cases and 40,000 deaths. The figures for intermittent fever were approximately 103,000 cases and 4,000 deaths; for typhus, 93,000 cases and 26,000 deaths; for syphilis, about 27,000 cases and 150 deaths.

According to Ahmet Emin, the total loss of life due directly to the Great War is variously estimated at between 1.5 and 2.5 million. As narrated by Ahmet Emin, Rıza Nur, on the other hand, suggests a figure closer to 3 million. Despite the disagreements on the exact figures, however, it is agreed that of all the able-bodied men who were under arms during the war, only 10 to 20 percent returned to their villages. Yalman even contends that without the mass desertions that took place during the last part of the war, the survival of the Turkish nation might have become problematical.[68]

TABLE 6.14. Distribution of deaths by various diseases

DISEASE	NUMBER OF DEATHS	NUMBER OF CASES
Malaria	23,351	461,799
Dysentery	40,000	147,000
Recurrent fever	4,000	103,000
Typhus	26,000	93,000
Syphilis	150	27,000

Niall Ferguson in 1999 and Edward J. Erickson in 2001 published their own estimates on the Ottoman military casualties. In *The Pity of War,* Niall Ferguson calculates that Ottoman losses were around 804,000 dead, 400,000 wounded, and 250,000 prisoners. He also notes that this total of 1,454,000 is the most recent estimate; the actual number of Ottoman casualties may range between a minimum of 970,000 and a maximum of 2,290,000.[69] According to Edward J. Erickson's own estimates, the Ottoman military casualties were 771,844 dead or missing (comprised of 243,598 deaths in combat, 61,487 missing in action, and 466,759 deaths from diseases), and a total of 763,753 wounded, including 303,150 seriously wounded.[70] Like other scholars, Erickson adds a note of caution that the exact costs of defeat in the First World War for Turkey remains hard to calculate. In spite of meticulous records kept by the wartime Turkish staff, none of Turkey's official histories contain consolidated casualty statistics for the entire war.[71]

As part of a research project, the records available in the Turkish Military Archives in Ankara were carefully analyzed in 2004. In particular, the statistical data regarding the losses of the Ottoman Army due to diseases were examined. It appeared that a special commission formed by the Army Health Department at the end of the war prepared those statistics after careful consideration. It also appears that Ahmet Emin's above-mentioned study partially draws on those documents, but until the publication of the current study, the information contained in those documents were not analyzed systematically. Granted, those statistics still have some shortcomings: they were prepared based on the records found in the military hospitals operated by the Army Health Unit and contained information about the admissions and discharges of patients only to those hospitals. They therefore do not reflect the entire deaths caused by diseases because several undocumented

TABLE 6.15. Ottoman military casualties according to hospital records (1914–1918)

FRONTS	HOSPITALIZED ILL	HOSPITALIZED WOUNDED	DEATHS FROM DISEASES	DEATHS FROM WOUNDS	COMBAT DEATHS
Caucasus front	628,953	60,983	116,290	2,968	–
Çapakçur front	377,316	41,754	67,414	–	–
Iraqi front	217,609	41,133	33,247	5,939	–
Syrian front	788,135	44,449	65,205	1,823	–
Gallipoli front	354,634	343,648	44,407	7,756	56,127
Galician front	7,115	10,326	124	522	3,859
Romanian front	17,511	13,106	809	681	2,132
Bosporus Strait's opening to Black Sea	18,525	29	615	3	1
Macedonian front	4,804	376	671	82	105
Casualties in Hijaz	8,571	36	1,166	9	–
Casualties in Asir	4,176	–	218	–	–
Casualties in Yemen	4,162	392	630	58	16
TOTAL	2,431,511	556,232	330,796	19,841	62,240

deaths or illnesses due to epidemics did not make it to this list. Notwithstanding, the statistics prepared by the army medical experts are no doubt the most detailed and most reliable official records about the losses of the Ottoman Army due to epidemics in the Great War.

According to those records, a total of 2,500,000 soldiers were admitted to hospitals on all fronts during the Great War. Whereas the numbers on admissions might not be accurate because multiple records for a single ill soldier are likely, the exact numbers on deaths could be estimated from the hospital records. When the combat deaths (330,000) and deaths from wounds (20,000) are added up, total deaths in hospitals comes to 350,000.

The statistical data documenting the deaths of Ottoman recruits due to disease during the Great War also provide useful information on the regions mostly affected by epidemic diseases and the extent and severity of those diseases in the afflicted regions. The provinces in eastern and southeastern Anatolia, as well as Syria and Iraq in the Middle East (outside the borders of today's Turkey) were beset by epidemics most severely. Beyond question, the epidemics also created numerous victims among civilians living in those regions, as well as among the convoys of Muslim and Christian refugees, who were uprooted by the war and had to take long and dramatic journeys to reach their new areas of settlement.

In 1915, during the first year of war, the number of Ottoman Armenians subjected to deportation due to security reasons was 500,000, whereas the Russian Armenians who took advantage of the Russian invasion of East Anatolia forced 1 million Muslims to flee from the Caucasus and East Anatolia to safer areas in central Anatolia. Those numbers indicate that during the entire course of the war, about 1.5 million Muslim and Christian civilians were constantly on the move in the combat zones, such as the Caucasus, Çapakçur (Bingöl), Iraq, and Syria, as well as in the central and southern regions of Anatolia. When the 2 million recruits of the Ottoman Army and the soldiers from the enemy forces are added to that figure, the number of people in flux in these geographical areas exceeded 4 million. In such a setting, deserters wandering around, new recruits and army units being dispatched to the frontlines, and civilians constantly displaced no doubt created a very suitable breeding ground for the spread of epidemics.

Hospital records also include detailed statistical data on the 1st, 2nd, 3rd, 4th, 5th, 6th, and 7th armies. Deaths from epidemic diseases are ranked as follows: The 3rd Army deployed in East Anatolia (116,000 dead); the 5th Army deployed in Gallipoli (68,000 dead); the 2nd Army deployed in Bingöl (67,000); the 4th army deployed in Syria (65,000 dead); the 6th Army deployed in Iraq (42,000 dead); and the 1st Army deployed in the Balkans (26,000 dead). Variations across years were encountered: the units of the 3rd and 5th armies had the highest death rates in 1915 while mainly the 2nd and 3rd army units accounted for the greatest number of deaths in 1916 and 1917, and the 6th Army in 1918.

When the figures about deaths from diseases based on hospital records on different fronts (330,000) are compared to aggregate figures based on different armies (387,000), the latter exceeds the former by 57,000. That difference might have arisen due to the difficulties of estimating the number of deaths from disease on different fronts. An army headquarters might be in a better position to maintain the records of losses occurring within its units. When units from two different armies are assigned to the same front, however, it might naturally be more difficult to estimate the losses according to the armies.

According to hospital records, the Ottoman Army suffered 387,000 losses due to infectious diseases, excluding deaths among the army deserters.

TABLE 6.16. Deaths in hospitals among the 1st Army units (1914–1918)

YEARS	ADMISSIONS DUE TO DISEASES	ADMISSIONS DUE TO WOUNDS	DEATHS DUE TO DISEASES	DEATHS DUE TO WOUNDS
1914	77,491	3	813	1
1915	127,771	190,372	8,239	3,033
1916	27,605	4	945	1
1917	84,204	812	4,789	33
1918	88,147	524	11,313	20
TOTAL	405,218	191,715	26,099	3,088

TABLE 6.17. Deaths in hospitals among the 2nd Army units (1914–1918)

YEARS	ADMISSIONS DUE TO DISEASES	ADMISSIONS DUE TO WOUNDS	DEATHS DUE TO DISEASES	DEATHS DUE TO WOUNDS
1914	35,159	–	517	–
1915	68,378	24,208	5,033	171
1916	111,939	15,916	26,298	2,539
1917	153,690	1,072	34,226	210
1918	8,250	554	1,340	2
TOTAL	377,416	41,750	67,414	2,922

TABLE 6.18. Deaths in hospitals among the 3rd Army units (1914–1918)*

YEARS	ADMISSIONS DUE TO DISEASES	ADMISSIONS DUE TO WOUNDS	DEATHS DUE TO DISEASES	DEATHS DUE TO WOUNDS
1914	29,201	17,929	6,121	901
1915	327,329	23,016	54,463	530
1916	103,018	18,484	23,720	1,814
1917	139,110	1,614	21,864	342
1918	81,703	2,421	10,014	147
TOTAL	680,361	63,464	116,182	3,734

* From *Statistics of the Military Effort of the British Empire*, F. 3-3.

Table 6.19. Deaths in hospitals among the 4th Army units (1914–1918)

YEARS	ADMISSIONS DUE TO DISEASES	ADMISSIONS DUE TO WOUNDS	DEATHS DUE TO DISEASES	DEATHS DUE TO WOUNDS
1914	40,986	592	441	105
1915	134,828	81	13,744	–
1916	278,835	10,362	20,605	341
1917	247,064	17,636	18,403	821
1918	120,101	14,795	12,014	556
TOTAL	821,814	43,466	65,207	1,823

Table 6.20. Deaths in hospitals among the 5th Army units (1914–1918)

YEARS	ADMISSIONS DUE TO DISEASES	ADMISSIONS DUE TO WOUNDS	DEATHS DUE TO DISEASES	DEATHS DUE TO WOUNDS
1914	–	–	–	–
1915	136,548	144,802	28,009	4,151
1916	178,052	–	19,924	–
1917	167,696	3	13,673	–
1918	95,818	–	6,424	–
Total	578,114	144,805	68,030	4,151

Table 6.21. Deaths in hospitals among the 6th Army units (1914–1918)

YEARS	ADMISSIONS DUE TO DISEASES	ADMISSIONS DUE TO WOUNDS	DEATHS DUE TO DISEASES	DEATHS DUE TO WOUNDS
1914	21,049	–	886	–
1915	21,736	12,433	5,080	413
1916	59,408	11,967	7,938	1,280
1917	64,366	16,605	9,564	1,147
1918	52,267	892	11,851	86
Total	218,826	41,897	35,319	2,926

TABLE 6.22. Deaths in hospitals among the 7th Army units (1914–1918)

YEARS	ADMISSIONS DUE TO DISEASES	ADMISSIONS DUE TO WOUNDS	DEATHS DUE TO DISEASES	DEATHS DUE TO WOUNDS
1914	–	–	–	–
1915	–	–	–	–
1916	–	–	–	–
1917	4,350	5,206	158	398
1918	7,907	2,597	498	138
Total	12,257	7,803	656	536

No figures are available on the deserters who might have fallen ill from infectious diseases, and eventually died. It is not unusual during wars that army deserters, deprived of all medical services, including vaccinations, are completely helpless against epidemics and act as agents of transmitting disease germs.

Even more than the deserters, migrants played a major role in transmitting diseases in the battlefields of Anatolia, the Caucasus, Syria-Lebanon, and Mesopotamia. The ratios on military fatalities from diseases can be used to make a rough estimate about the losses among Muslim and Christian migrant groups who were constantly moving within the same geographical area.

When the deaths from diseases in the Ottoman Army during the Great War are broken down, typhus appears to be the most fatal one, followed by dysentery and malaria. The death ratio among patients with typhus was just over one-fourth (28 percent). For dysentery, the same ratio was about the same (27 percent). Obviously, these ratios are quite high.

The military units literally melted away in the face of infectious diseases. Striking examples of such cases during the Great War are well documented. One is narrated by General Hans Kannengiesser, one of the German commanders of the Ottoman Army who served in Gallipoli:

> A characteristic picture in this connection is given by a report of losses of the 16th Army Corps, at the same time an indication of what the Ottoman War Office was continuously called upon to send reinforcements to the Gallipoli front. Between the 14th October and 9th December, 1915, the losses of the 16th Army Corps were 509 killed, 2,158 wounded, 3,386 sick

TABLE 6.23. Deaths in hospitals (1914–1918)

	ADMISSIONS DUE TO DISEASES	ADMISSIONS DUE TO WOUNDS	DEATHS DUE TO DISEASES	DEATHS DUE TO WOUNDS
1st Army	405,218	191,735	26,099	3,088
2nd Army	377,416	41,750	67,414	2,922
3rd Army	680,361	63,464	116,182	3,734
4th Army	821,814	43,466	65,207	1,823
5th Army	578,114	144,805	67,848	4,151
6th Army	218,826	41,897	35,319	2,926
7th Army	12,257	7,803	656	536
8th Army	18,065	5,589	978	182
9th Army	27,227	1,483	1,892	88
Thunderbolt Group of Armies	15,840	28 (?)	6,344	1,071
TOTAL	3,155,138	542,020	387,939	20,521

and 2,159 having a change of climate…making a total loss of 8,212 men during a period of two months, from an army Corps of three Divisions approximately 12,000 strong. In considering these figures it must be taken into account that the bodily resistance of the Turks is generally much less than that of the Europeans. The reasons for this, apart from climatic reasons, are insufficient nourishment and care of the body, the lack of any kind of hygienic arrangements and the terrible amount of vermin.[72]

Tevfik Salim Sağlam, medical chief of the 3rd Army, discusses the reasons behind the tragic fate of the Ottoman soldiers on the Eastern front. He, too, notes that such a huge amount of casualties was caused by four factors: adverse climate conditions, the insufficiency of roads and lack of transportation vehicles, inability to provide good clothing for the troops, and the malnutrition of the troops.[73]

Adverse climate conditions

The 3rd Army's sector was mostly a mountainous region with high altitudes, having long and severely cold winters. In winter, the temperature was almost always below 0°C. In comparison, the plains and some of the valleys also located in the 3rd Army sector were very hot in summer. In the early summer of 1915, it was said that on the very same day, a soldier became ill due to the excessive heat in the valley, while another soldier froze to death in the mountains.

Insufficiency of roads and lack of transportation vehicles

Other than a few paved roads, the 3rd Army had no roads available in its sector. The closest railway station to the front was in Ulukışla, which was about 900 kilometers away from Erzurum. The troops were transferred on foot. As the Black Sea was not controlled by the Turks, even in the coastal areas major seaborne transportation was impossible. Goods and supplies between proximate coastal areas could only be transferred by small motorboats or sailboats at great risk. The 3rd Army had almost no motor vehicles. Only on the paved road extending from Ulukışla to Erzurum could some trucks be operated. Even the automobiles allocated to high-level officers could rarely be used due to the insufficiency of roads, or the lack of gasoline and other supplies. Therefore, oxcarts, packhorses, camels, and donkeys were the only available means to transport provisions and ammunition. At times, as discussed before, even those primitive means were unavailable, and the food and ammunition had to be carried long distances on the backs of the soldiers and civilians.[74] Similarly, a few cars, sent to the 3rd Army sector from Istanbul for the transportation of the ill and wounded, could never be used due to lack of roads, gasoline, and other needed supplies for automobiles. The ill and wounded had to be carried mostly in carts and on packhorses, but most of the time on foot.[75]

Poor clothing for the troops

The troops of the 3rd Army never could be dressed suitably for the severe climate conditions of the region. When the Ottoman Empire entered the war in November 1914, some of the soldiers stationed in the plains of Erzurum were still in their local clothes and had no military greatcoats. Even then, no vehicle could be found to bring the greatcoats from the military depot in Gümüşhane to Erzurum. The acting commander-in-chief ordered that three out of six depot battalions in Erzincan should be sent to Gümüşhane so they could wear the uniforms to be sent from Trabzon by the inspectorate of the army station. Each soldier, moreover, would wear five military greatcoats in order to transport them to Erzurum. Difficulties in the supply of clothes could not be overcome during the entire period of the war, which no doubt played a major role in the frequent occurrence of "the problems and diseases connected with cold, such as local freezing, death from freezing, pneumonia, and the like."[76]

Malnutrition of troops

The problems encountered in the food supply for the 3rd Army could never be eliminated. As the war progressed, the diminishing food stocks and unavailability of transportation vehicles turned the food supply for the army into an ever-growing problem.

> The factors related to food supply in the area set the limits to military concentration on that front. Even when large numbers of troops were brought to the area, the difficulties encountered in supplying foods, as well as the adverse climate conditions, forced the authorities to decrease the strength of the army to affordable levels. Even the well-dressed and strong-looking recruits of the 5th Army Corps, who were assigned to the 3rd Army Front on their return from Gallipoli, soon became undistinguishable from the 3rd Army's own recruits.[77]… The huge number of illnesses encountered among the 3rd Army troops, therefore, was the result of the miserable conditions endured by the troops, who were dressed unsuitably and fed insufficiently in the middle of a long and bloody war, carried out in a harsh climate, and in an area where the roads and means of transportation could rarely be found. It should always be kept in mind that as long as those conditions remained the same, any military concentration in that area would have the same fate with the 3rd Army.[78]

The same historical records also indicate that the 3rd Army suffered the greatest number of losses due to epidemic diseases. Apart from the tragic incident where many soldiers were frozen to death at the very beginning of the war, the same army was afflicted with further losses in subsequent years under the continuous "attacks" of infectious diseases. Table 6.24, prepared by Tevfik Sağlam, summarizes the effects of the epidemics succinctly. The table clearly shows that during the course of bloody battles on the 3rd Army front, the diseases also ravaged the forces, and the sick soldiers were consuming the efforts of the Army's medical unit much more than the wounded.[79]

Between the years 1915 and 1918, within a period of 42.5 months, 9,001 soldiers of the 3rd Army were killed in the battles while a total of 109,562 soldiers died due to diseases or wounds in hospitals. In other words, the number of deaths due to diseases was 27.8 times greater than those due to wounds and 12 times greater than those that occurred in the course of fighting. Given the total strength of the 3rd Army, it appears that approximately

TABLE 6.24. The ill and wounded in the 3rd Army (1915–1918)

YEAR	SICK	WOUNDED	TOTAL
1915 (10 months)	206,793	8,939	215,902
1916	136,722	31,200	167,942
1917	139,110	1,654	140,764
1918 (9 months)	81,703	2,421	84,124
TOTAL (42.5 MONTHS)	564,328	44,214	608,732

TABLE 6.25. Admissions to hospitals from the 3rd Army

YEAR	ADMISSIONS DUE TO DISEASES	MONTHLY AVERAGE	DAILY AVERAGE
1915 (10 months)	209,793	20,979	688
1916	136,722	11,394	375
1917	139,110	11,593	381
1918 (9 months)	81,703	9,078	297
TOTAL (42.5 MONTHS)	567,328	13,349	433

2.5 percent of that strength was lost due to diseases and 0.08 percent (eight in ten thousand) due to wounds. The ratio of those killed in combat was .19 percent (19 per ten thousand). Those figures unequivocally show that the losses caused by diseases rather than the casualties suffered in combat wore down the 3rd Army. In the German Army, on the other hand, 78.8 percent of deaths occurred in fighting or due to wounds while 12.2 percent of them were caused by diseases. The monthly ratio of deaths due to diseases in the Ottoman Army, 2.5 percent, is 54 times greater than in the German Army.[80]

During the same period, the number of admissions to hospitals in the 3rd Army was 567,328, which makes an average 13,349 patients per month, and 433 per day. In other words, each month 12 percent of the total strength of the army was hospitalized.[81] The largest number of casualties due to infectious diseases occurred in 1915, when the number of wounded admitted to hospitals was 8,939—an average of 894 wounded per month and 29 per day.[82]

The figures from Turkish and foreign sources discussed so far all point the same direction: during World War I, Turkey was the only country in which deaths from disease well exceeded combat fatalities. In the course of that war, one-third of the recruits fell victim to disease. Furthermore, only about 10 to 20 percent of the young people drafted into the army were able to return to their homes after the war.

7

UNEXPECTED RESULTS

Sad scenes of exodus all along the road.... Those poor women and children, having loaded a few dirty quilts on an oxcart, and driving one or two scrawny cows and calves in front of them, are going barefoot toward unknown horizons. Similar scenes were repeated after every retreat of the Army.

[JANUARY 1915] The large convoy of refugees is going toward Erzurum. There are men old, disabled, or carrying their mothers on their backs. Women have their children wrapped in quilts on their shoulders, and babies in their arms. Small children are trying to walk behind the oxcarts. If you asked them, they would not know where they are going. They are trying to protect their lives and honor from the Russian troops and from the attacks of the Armenians. Only God knows how many of those poor people are dying under the ruined roofs in the empty villages.

The Governor of Erzurum estimates the number of deaths up until now at 15,000.

—Azız Samıh,
Büyük Harpte Kafkas Cephesi Hatıraları

EMPHASIZING THE UNIMAGINABLY STRONG LINK between epidemics and mass destruction in both classical and modern history, one expert defines a great disaster as "a common denominator in the process of bringing a dramatic character to the calamities badly affecting the Ottoman subjects." He further states that "there is one and only one single factor which could turn a drama into a tragedy, and a high mortality ratio into a mass destruction, and it is the disease of the plague." The disaster he was referring to took place in the Ottoman city of Akka in the late eighteenth century, where "all the conditions which could enable mass annihilation of a people came together," such as "extreme poverty, hunger, drought, a high concentration of refugees and troops, and the like."[1]

The disaster at Akka, described by Daniel Panzac, which occurred on a small scale there, indeed turned into a real tragedy of huge dimensions for millions of people, both servicemen and civilians, during the Balkan Wars and the Great War. The Balkan Wars adversely affected the Ottoman Empire in every respect. The epidemics that broke out in Anatolia in the aftermath of the Balkan Wars continued to prevail during the Great War not only in Anatolia, but also in Palestine and Syria.[2] The huge number of casualties caused by epidemics that spread from Edirne to Istanbul, and then to the whole of Anatolia, is especially noteworthy. The Muslim subjects of the Empire, still remembering the sufferings caused by the Balkan Wars, became distressed when the Caliph (Sultan) declared a jihad at the beginning of the Great War. Instead of a general feeling of excitement, usually seen in such events, there was a frightening silence in the air, caused by the contemplation of the imminent hardships.

In his book *Death and Exile*, Justin McCarthy describes the story of a bloody tragedy as well as a historical truth. He states the following:

> The deaths of Muslims, like the deaths of Armenians in the same period, occurred primarily while they were refugees. There are few descriptions of the well being of the eastern Anatolian and Caucasian refugees, whether Muslim or Armenian, but one can assume their condition to have been worse than that of refugees in Europe and western Anatolia in the same period. During World War I, there were no established refugee camps for Muslim refugees from the east. The government Refugee Commission did what it could to offer succor to the refugees, but how much could a government that could not even clothe its own soldiers do for a million refugees. Moreover, the refugees from the east moved through the worst terrain in Anatolia. The region contained neither adequate roads nor railroads. Many areas that received refugees could only be reached by horseback and pack animals. Even had food been available, transportation conditions would have insured that little of it reached the refugees.
>
> By looking at a map of Anatolia and considering the economic state of its regions, one can see that refugees from Van, Erzurum, or Bitlis would have been forced to make long journeys before they found adequate transportation facilities, large population centers, or fertile fields. For most, such journeys were impossible.
>
> On the eastern Anatolia front in World War I and then later during the Turco-Armenian War there was such a mass of peoples on the move that contemporary accounts give the impression that the peoples of eastern Anatolia and the southern Caucasus were all refugees.... The majority

of eastern Anatolians, both Muslims and Christians, either died or were forced from their homes.³

The common characteristic of those migrations caused by the war was an "impulse to get protected from massacres." On that issue, Justin McCarthy quotes a British document, what he calls "one of the rare honest European accounts of the refugees, a British Military report from Baku (1 July 1919)." The report stated that "during the war Armenians fled from Muslim areas and Muslims from Armenian areas. Both groups 'fled to avoid massacres and from massacres.'"⁴

W. E. Allen and Paul Muratoff also illustrate this feeling well in their study:

> Natural difficulties were made worse by the fact that the Young Turk policy of deporting the Armenian population of the surrounding areas had been carrying out only too effectively. At the beginning of the war Ottoman supplies had been drawn from the fertile and well-cultivated upland basins of Eleşkirt, Erzurum, Muş and Mamahatun. All these had fallen into the hands of the Russians, while the Armenian cultivators had been driven off from the valley of the Murat-Çay and the great plain round Harput. At the same time the Turkish peasants had, at the approach of the Russians, trekked into the interior of Anatolia. The eastern vilayets had been depopulated to the extent of about seventy-five per cent of their inhabitants (and they have never since recovered their former degree of prosperity).⁵

ARMENIAN CONVOYS AND THE EPIDEMICS

Besides the "spontaneous" migrations stemming from wars, "planned" and forced population displacements due to security reasons were also common throughout history. The most disputed example of the latter is no doubt the one imposed on the Armenians. In the spring of 1915, the Ottoman government used its constitutional powers and decided on the relocation of some of its Armenian subjects to Syria.⁶

The weekly military intelligence report for the week of 14–21 September 1915, prepared by the British Army Command in Egypt, compares the events of 1894–1896 during the reign of Sultan Abdülhamid to the events that took place in 1915. The report identifies an important distinction between the two periods in its following assessment: unlike the events of 1894–1896, the "deaths" occurring in 1915 started after the "victims" were sent into exile, many of whom lost their lives from starvation and disease.⁷

Another nuance that needs to be taken into account is the fact that a considerable portion of the Armenians subjected to deportation by the Ottoman government during the Great War consisted of individuals who had joined foreign armies as "volunteers," in particular the Russian Army. In addition, a large number of Ottoman Armenians are found to have migrated to other countries and become citizens of those countries.[8]

The biggest problem faced by the Armenian convoys was fatal epidemics, which had always accompanied wars and intensive migrations throughout history. One disease, for instance, which emerged among the Ottoman Armenians who migrated via the Mediterranean route, was called "Maladie Armenienne" (the Armenian Disease) first by the French doctors who diagnosed it widely among the Armenians in Marseille. When the same disease was also seen among the Jews and other peoples living around the Mediterranean basin later, the name was changed to the "Periodic Disease."[9]

Deaths among the Armenians due to epidemics were not limited to the Armenians living in the Ottoman provinces. According to the information communicated to the UK Foreign Office from American sources, each month one-seventh of the Armenian refugees in the Caucasus were losing their lives due to various reasons (hunger, typhus, and cholera).[10] According to a ciphered telegram, 30 percent of the population living in Yerevan became severely ill with Spanish influenza, and as a result, a total of 1,870 individuals lost their lives in the streets, in their homes, and in the civilian hospitals between 24 December 1919 and 4 January 1920. A significant number of deaths also occurred in the provincial areas of Armenia, causing the death of 20 percent of the entire population.[11] Based on those numbers regarding the death rates in and around Yerevan, it would be reasonable to expect that great numbers of people living in the cities and rural areas of Anatolia and other parts of Caucasus also lost their lives.

The Armenian convoys deported from eastern Anatolia in fact encountered infectious diseases long before reaching their new places of settlement, while they were still in Anatolia. For instance, in a note sent to the Governorate of Konya on 2 November 1915, it was stated that out of 200 Armenians, 50 were severely ill and 150 were slightly ill, mainly from dysentery and malaria. The governorate was requested to put the Armenians into empty houses in the town immediately.[12]

Kress von Kressenstein, one of the important witnesses of the war, observed the infectious diseases borne by the Armenian deportees moving along the River Euphrates in Aleppo in 1915. Around the same time, troops coming from the north were also traveling through Aleppo en route to Palestine, and infectious diseases were posing a great danger to these military units. According to hygiene specialists, recurrent fever and typhus epidemics were threatening the Syrian front in 1915. Though Cemal Pasha attempted to improve the conditions of the Armenian deportees somewhat, it was of no avail: his efforts to send food to the Armenian convoys bore no significant results since even the Turkish troops had a grave shortage of food supplies at the time.[13]

German Commander General Goltz recounts the following about the Armenian convoys sent on 22 November 1915 to the places where they would be resettled under the government's relocation plan. He tells how those convoys passed through the Taurus Mountains, and what happened to them afterward:

> The longest tunnel was passed through the next morning. After that, the convoy started to descend toward the Syrian Plain.
>
> At this point, the sad view of the Armenian deportees strikes the eye. The plan is to settle them at the southern foot of the Taurus Mountains. However, since it was impossible to provide sufficient humanitarian care to such a large number of people, they are living in an endless misery.
>
> We are witnessing an enormous disaster involving an ethnic group. Many people are dying on the way, and are abandoned there for a long time, unburied. Though one is saddened when he sees the entire scene, there is nothing to be done for them. The disasters caused by this ominous war are innumerable; and it is impossible to foresee what disasters those people will be enduring in the coming days.[14]

A dysentery epidemic broke out among the Armenian deportees upon their arrival in Syria, which was aggravated by the food and water shortages. That epidemic posed a significant problem not only for the Armenian deportees themselves, but also for the 4th Army forces stationed there. With the vaccines supplied by the efforts of Neşet Ömer, director of hygiene in Jerusalem, urgent measures could be undertaken against the epidemic. In 1915, out of the total strength of 142,802 of the 4th Army, 6,430 were admitted to hospitals, 159 of whom died.[15]

Spotted fever afflicted Syria and Palestine mainly in winter months. Even though the spotted fever did not affect the German units because of the preventive methods implemented, combined with the impact of ever-continuing problems of hunger and exhaustion, it took a heavy toll among the Ottoman units.[16]

As the war progressed further, the epidemics also escalated in Aleppo. The typhus epidemic spread by the Armenian convoys being transferred from East Anatolia caused growing distress within the army and among the local people. In order to alleviate the problems, the half-built French hospital in the neighborhood of Cemile was completed in 1915 within a period of one week by a labor battalion of five hundred men, who in fact had been tasked to construct the military barracks in Aleppo. Upon completion, the hospital was put into service with a bed capacity of 850.[17]

On the Syrian front, the typhus epidemic also caused many losses among the troops and within the labor battalions. In Aleppo, the disease spread largely among the Armenian convoys deported to the region, as well as among the troops. In order to struggle against the epidemic, strict measures were adopted; a medical crisis center headed by Cemal Pasha was formed, which enforced compulsory isolation and treatment.[18]

A ciphered telegram, dispatched from the Ministry of the Interior on 17 October 1915 to the director of immigrants in Aleppo, talked about the cases of spotted fever and dysentery among about 20,000 migrants in Hama, which killed about 70 to 80 people each day. The same communiqué ordered local officials to dispatch the migrants promptly to their final places of settlement.[19]

As the statistics prepared after the British Army established its control over Mesopotamia show, large numbers of deaths due to epidemics continued to occur in the Armenian and Syrian refugee camps. The most widely seen illnesses among the refugees were dysentery, diarrhea, pneumonia, and bronchitis.[20]

As of 1 October 1919, a total of 39,191 refugees were held in the Ba'quba refugee camp; 5,089 of these refugees lost their lives, 2,161 left the camp, and 369 were taken to the Farm of Jasmiyah to work there, while another 2,117 individuals were taken into the newly formed Assyrian Battalions.[21] Of the refugees in the Ba'quba refugee camp, 14,612 were Armenians—519 were from Istanbul, 675 from Cilicia, 10,341 from Van and the Caucasus, 547 from Bitlis, and 2,530 from Azerbaijan, according to their own statements.[22]

On 1 July 1920, a British vice-consul in Hamadan had communicated the statistical data provided to him by an Armenian doctor serving in the American hospital there. The data were related to the patients referred to the hospital because of diseases like malaria, influenza, bronchitis, and dysentery.[23]

CONDITIONS ON THE MESOPOTAMIAN FRONT

Bacillary dysentery, which is known to be widespread in Syria, was also encountered during the Balkan Wars and the Great War due to the movement of troops and people.[24] Before the Great War, dysentery had rarely been encountered in cities such as Istanbul, İzmir, Ankara, and Bursa; but after the

TABLE 7.1. Deaths that occurred in the Ba'Quba Refugee Camp (September 1918–October 1919)*

MONTHS	ARMENIANS	SYRIANS	MEN	WOMEN	CHILDREN	TOTAL
September	193	75	69	69	130	268
October	768	675	318	521	604	1,443
November	515	462	231	363	383	977
December	379	451	225	351	254	830
January	196	265	134	172	154	460
February	115	130	69	100	76	245
March	73	102	50	57	68	175
April	53	54	31	38	38	107
May	49	50	30	23	46	99
June	53	50	36	30	38	104
July	52	74	54	34	38	126
August	76	65	44	42	55	141
September	56	58	35	32	41	114
TOTAL	2,578	2,511	1,326	1,832	1,931	5,089

*From UK ARCHIVES, T 161/50, Table 2, dated 1 October 1919, 34.

commencement of the war, it became more prevalent in those cities and in the whole of Anatolia.[25]

In the years of 1916 and 1917, typhus was widespread in the city of Birseba within the army units and among the local people.[26] The headquarters of "Operation Lightning" was transferred from Nablus to Nasıriyah on 17 December 1917. At that time, a typhus epidemic emerged in Nasıriyah due mainly to the lack of measures against lice at the frontlines and the insufficiency of hospital infrastructure. The spread of typhus from Damascus to other places could not be prevented, which significantly decreased the strength of the military units.[27]

Although the city of Aleppo had great strategic importance especially for the battles taking place in Iraq, Palestine, and Sinai, the health conditions there posed a great threat to the troops. The hospitals in the area were in a much worse situation than in Palestine. The attempt to put all typhoid patients into one hospital could not be achieved because the Muslims did not want to leave their women in hospitals. Nor could medical checks in houses be conducted because the people viewed this as interference with their privacy. As a result, Cemal Pasha's efforts in this regard yielded limited results. Kress von Kressenstein provided interesting details regarding the conditions prevailing in hospitals: "One hospital had no doors and windows which would protect patients against cold; in another one, 30 patients were using the same glass to drink water. Another hospital accommodating 500 patients had only three body thermometers."[28]

Infectious diseases also found breeding ground in the labor battalions in Syria, which had around twenty thousand men. Since the members of these battalions were deprived of any care and had weak bodily constitutions, epidemics of typhoid, typhus, and cholera spread very easily among them; on an average day, a minimum of five hundred soldiers were hospitalized.[29]

In January 1915, a health commission consisting of three German Navy doctors reached the conclusion that the most widely seen epidemics within the army were recurrent fever and typhus. As a result of this discovery, urgent measures were taken, baths and autoclaves were put into service, water channels were repaired, and a vaccination campaign was initiated against typhoid and cholera. The reports published in Germany about these studies were full of praises for 4th Army Commander Cemal Pasha, who had achieved great success in his efforts to struggle against infectious diseases.[30] For one, Kress von Kressenstein, who closely observed Pasha's extraordinary efforts in this area, praised "Cemal Pasha's awareness and energy with regards to the improvement of medical services" and emphasized that that awareness manifested itself most visibly in the case of measures he took to protect the individuals deported from eastern Anatolia against diseases. After the assassination of Cemal Pasha in 1922 by Armenian militants in Tbilisi, von Kressenstein noted, "All of the Germans who had worked together with Cemal Pasha would speak highly of his organizational talents."[31]

In order to supplement the Central Military Hospital in Damascus, which was located in the 4th Army sector, the Mezze neighborhood was entirely evacuated and turned into an infectious diseases hospital with one thousand beds. In Aleppo, too, a very large building was turned into a hospital, and a church and a mosque were temporarily used as hospitals in order to meet the growing demand for hospitals.[32]

The 4th Army also set up a hospital for the Armenian convoys arriving in Aleppo. Dr. Altunian from Aleppo was assigned as the chief doctor of that hospital. The 4th Army also founded two orphanages and put them under the direction of Dr. Altunian's daughter and a German nurse.

Another orphanage for one thousand Armenian children was opened in the Aya Tura Abbey in Lebanon. Dr. Captain Lütfi, who was an eye specialist, was assigned as the director of that orphanage. Since the 4th Army directly assumed the responsibility for taking care of orphans, it opened a fourth orphanage in Damascus.[33]

MUSLIM CONVOYS AND THE EPIDEMICS

The Muslim people of the areas occupied by the Russians following the retreat of the 3rd Army migrated to the inner parts of Anatolia. In 1916 and 1917, especially after the fall of Bayburt, Trabzon, and Erzincan, the army had to deal with a huge wave of refugees. Since no civilian organization existed to take care of the health problems of such a large number of people, the army also had to assume that responsibility beginning in mid-July 1916. Out of 5,424 refugees who became ill and were taken to refugee hospitals, 2,300 recovered and 1,529 died. According to Tevfik Sağlam, "Since civilian authorities could not take proper measures for the transfer and settlement of the refugees, much of the suffering, which could in fact have been prevented to a certain degree, could not be avoided."[34]

Turkish writer Halide Edip describes some scenes of the great misery she witnessed in Konya in 1916, while she was traveling to the Syrian front together with Hamdullah Suphi, upon the invitation of Cemal Pasha:

> The train station in Konya was full of scenes of suffering. Refugees from Eastern Anatolia with their families and their bundles engulfed the station. They were standing together closely under the station lamps, in ragged but brightly colored clothes. They were waiting for the train with their eyes looking empty and meaningless; the eyes of those who were uprooted, and had to migrate. A strange smell of misery and helplessness coming from them. No, that smell isn't coming only from the physical dirt; crowds in a spiritual misery have a smell of their own.[35]

Justin McCarthy identifies two waves of Muslim migrations during the Great War, which took place at different times in the eastern provinces of the Ottoman Empire. The first period of Muslim migration was sparked by the Armenian uprising in Van, and ended with the retreat of the Russians in the summer of 1915. The second wave started with the Russian offensive in 1916, which was more successful than the previous one, and resulted in the Russian occupation of the entire province of Erzurum, as well as large parts of the provinces of Van, Diyarbakır, Ma'muret'ül Aziz, and Trabzon. As a result of the Russian occupation as well as the clashes between the Muslims and Armenians, many of the peaceful Muslim and Christian inhabitants in the rural areas started to migrate in search of security. Because of those migrations, the cities held more firmly by the Ottoman Army in the south and in the west were flooded by these refugees. The luckiest among those refugees were the ones who could reach the Trabzon province on the north and Erzurum province on the northeast, since they later could move farther into the central and western Black Sea regions, where control of the central government was more firmly established and security conditions were better. Some of those refugees were sent to central Anatolia, similar to the procedure applied to those coming from the southern part of Trabzon province and from the Erzurum province. Those coming from the provinces farther east were less lucky since they had to flee southward to the provinces of Elazığ, Diyarbakır, and Van, where they could receive little help. Most of those refugees migrated in various stages. After leaving their homes, they moved to safer areas, only to stay there until the next forward movement of the Russians and Armenians, and then they had to flee again. Most of the refugees from around Erzurum had to go to places such as Maraş or Adana, which meant a journey of more than 600 km on foot.[36]

The Turkish military medical records relevant to the period between 15 August 1916 and 18 December 1917 reveal that cholera epidemics broke out among the Muslim refugees, posing a great threat to the army: "In the wake of the retreat of the Army, an enormous wave of migration started, which surpassed the capacity of the civilian authorities. The Army, therefore, had to assume the responsibility for the refugees.... The duty of struggling with epidemic diseases encountered among the civilians living in the Army sector was given to the Army's Chief Medical Officer."[37]

The problems encountered in the resettlement of the Muslim people migrating toward the inner parts of the country, and the conducts and behavior of the civilian authorities that exaggerated those problems somewhat, were well documented in the reports prepared by the military medical units. General Fevzi Çakmak, acting commander of the army, who was on an inspection tour in the Black Sea region, stated the following in a telegram he dispatched to the Ministry of the Interior on 5 May 1917:

> During my inspections around Samsun, I saw the refugees in impoverished conditions. Based on a medical inspection I had instructed to be carried out, we found out that the people living in the districts and villages were a

breeding ground for infectious diseases and therefore creating a great risk for the military personnel who were sent to Ordu. They are not provided with any food or shelter. Even the children and women are on the run under miserable conditions. Naturally, no sanitary measures could be put into practice; and they are spreading infections to various towns and villages as they randomly wander around.[38]

In his report from October 1917, the army medical chief states the following:

Many people from the District of Alucra are departing for coastal areas together with their families, hoping to find something to eat there. The Governorates of Karahisar Sanjak and Sivas Province could not care for these people.... The conditions of the refugees arriving in the coastal areas are heartbreaking too. Though it is not possible to give an exact figure, obviously the losses of our country, in terms of human lives and material, are enormous.[39]

When the defterdar (the official who heads a provincial treasury) of Trabzon delayed aid to the refugees on the pretext that he had not yet received the money sent for that purpose on 19 December 1917, Vehib Pasha, the 3rd Army commander, sent the following telegram to the defterdar, to be communicated to Cavit, the minister of finance:

Please communicate my order to your Minister Cavit. If he were also in Trabzon, he would do nothing but follow my order. Those migrants and refugees who are dying from hunger are not the sons of Israel; they are all Muslims. I am strictly determined to resort to any measures, when necessary the use of force, in order to allow those people to live. The orders of your Minister cannot contravene my orders. That should be understood very well.[40]

The chief doctor of the Recovery House in Çorum stated in his report dated 22 December 1917 that the refugees, especially the women and children, were living in great misery. Four women had frozen to death during the last four days and both the governorate and the municipality had been completely indifferent to the suffering of those people.[41]

In a telegram he sent to the 3rd Army's chief medical officer, the governor of Çorum referred to the extraordinarily severe winter conditions as an excuse for the failure to help the refugees; but he also confessed another bitter fact.

A winter as severe as this year's has not been encountered for many years, the effects of which are beyond imagination. On the roads to Merzifon, Çorum, Yozgat, and Ankara, one could see many animal corpses, as well as dead human bodies, all frozen to death. Some exhausted soldiers are also seen among those dead. Since it is absolutely impossible to bring firewood from the mountains, some of the local people and most of the government workers and refugees were left without any wood. The government offices have no wood either. On the other hand, the refugees continue to come to Çorum via Amasya and Merzifon. Yesterday, another convoy of refugees arrived from Niksar. They are naturally in great poverty. In fact, even the basic need for food and clothing of the refugees living in destitution in town can not be met sufficiently.[42]

DEPORTATION OF THE GREEKS AND THE EPIDEMICS

In January 1917, the Supreme Command Headquarters of the Ottoman Armies deemed it necessary to relocate the Greeks living in the coastal areas of Trabzon Province behind a line extending 50 km south of the coastal areas. Due to severe winter conditions and the lack of transportation means available to those refugees, that decision also led to the outbreak of a great misery. When the military authorities learned that about 1,500 people had gathered in a village called Pürk, located on the plain of Suşehri, some of whom were ill, they immediately sent doctors to the village; about 200 sick, 150 of whom had fever, were separated and placed under treatment. The army could only provide limited support for those people in the form of treating and feeding the sick among them.[43]

When the Greeks revolted in December 1917 and burned down Bafra, the Army Command ordered that the Greeks living in Bafra and Samsun be sent to the interior toward Ankara. Upon that order, health stations for the refugees were immediately set up in Kavak, Havza, and Merzifon, where the migrating people had to undergo medical examination. Here, those with infectious diseases as well as lice on their bodies were cleaned, and their clothes were disinfected. Moreover, all of the refugees were vaccinated against smallpox, cholera, and typhoid. Refugees' feces were examined in Merzifon and Çorum to verify any vibrione-bearing individuals among them.[44]

EPIDEMICS IN SYRIA, MESOPOTAMIA, AND ANATOLIA

According to Donald Matthew's findings, the spread of diseases is least likely in those places where most of the population lives in rural areas and small towns, with little communication between them.[45] Although that observation might be true under normal conditions, several extraordinary factors play a role in the spread of diseases in times of war. The migrations caused by fighting take the lead among these conditions. Moreover, the diffusion of epidemics is also affected by other factors such as geographical location and climate conditions. For instance, the conditions in swamps and rivers are accepted as the major source of malaria. As early as the first century B.C., Varro emphasized the dangers posed by swamps.[46]

The strip of land lying between the Euphrates and Tigris rivers, which varies between 1 and 7 km in width, remains underwater only during flood seasons. However, the land between Korna and Basra, as well as the delta portion, consists entirely of marshes. The Garaf Canal (Shattul Hay), serving as a spillway draining the excess water of the Tigris River to the Euphrates and connecting the two rivers to each other, separates from the Tigris River near Kut al-Amarah. It cuts the plains of Lower Mesopotamia lying between the two rivers in a north-south direction. Then it splits into many branches before flowing into the marshes in the Nasıriyah region. In summer, a large part of its bed becomes dry. In the Lower Mesopotamia, many canals and swamps, similar to the Euphrates River, surround the Tigris River. In the lands of Lower Mesopotamia, innumerable small lakes and swamps can be seen along the rivers Tigris and Euphrates. As the level of the water rises during the flooding season, it is impossible to determine the boundaries of those swamps, whereas in July and August and on into autumn, those swamps become smaller and shallower as a result of intense evaporation. Some of them even dry up completely. Generally, the swamps are covered with rushes. Plenty of canals connect the swamps to each other and to the rivers. This large marshy area is called the Sinpha Swamp, extending from south of the Euphrates River to east of Nasıriyah to Basra. The area starting from south of Hille and extending along the right bank of the Euphrates River to Qurnah is also covered with swamps of various sizes. There are also other swamps located on either bank of the Euphrates River after passing Al-el-Gharbi, the largest among them being the Ebu Kelam Swamp. Southeast of Kut al-Amarah are the swamps of Samargha and the Large Huwaiza, also called el-Azim, into which the Karha River flows. North of Kut al-Amarah there is the Suwaija Swamp. The largest marshlands of Iraq are located south of Kut al-Amarah, in the area extending from the Qadir Tomb to Basra and covering the lower beds of the Euphrates and Tigris rivers. This large area is almost entirely covered with marshlands, with the exception of the few small strips of dry land, which could be found along the banks of the Euphrates and Tigris rivers. In general, those marshlands remain wet during six months of the year (between November and June), becoming dry in

August and expanding again after November. In such areas, the escalation of malaria is quite natural and unavoidable; so are large casualties suffered by the military units.[47]

Dr. Abdülkadir Noyan, the medical chief of the 6th Army, provided the following information regarding the hygiene conditions in Mosul:

> Anyone who observes the environmental conditions and the inhabitants of Mosul will easily appreciate that in a city where nobody knows the meaning of hygiene, even the military would remain helpless in establishing order and control, let alone the civilian authorities. The only source of drinking and utility water for both the local people and the soldiers is the Tigris River. In almost every neighborhood of the city by the river, while the dirtiest clothes and objects are being washed on the riverbank, drinking water is also supplied from the river. Many houses have no toilet. The inhabitants, therefore, are using the streets and roofs as toilets. One could smell human faeces in the dusts of the city, which form clouds in the blowing wind. One could see toilets or toilet pits only in the houses of the people with higher educational level. The foodstuff being sold in market places are covered with flies in almost every season of the year.[48]

Malaria is a commonly encountered infection in Syria and Mesopotamia, particularly in the areas lying between 45 degrees north and 40 degrees south latitudes. This tropical disease has a closed transmission cycle. For the human-to-human transmission of malaria, the involvement of mosquitoes is necessary. Therefore, malaria can easily turn into an epidemic in marshlands, which have suitable temperature conditions for the breeding of the anopheles type of mosquito.[49] During the war years, malaria epidemics escalated in Syria following the arrival of the convoys, which came in automobiles via the route of the Taurus Mountains and the plains of Adana.[50]

Recognizing that malaria was a disease threatening the very existence of the local people during the Great War, a German bacteriology laboratory was transferred to the Taurus Mountains region in July 1917. That place was chosen because Pozantı was located at the crossroads of the routes leading to Palestine and Mesopotamia. By locating the lab in that area, the military units going south could be subjected to a last medical check. It also would be helpful in the fight against malaria, which was prevalent in that region, too, by applying medical checks on the troops returning to Anatolia. In some of the villages in Anatolia in those days, 75 to 90 percent of the children between the ages of one and five were reported to have died from malaria. The vast marshlands in the Taurus Mountains region particularly

TABLE 7.2. Infectious diseases and deaths recorded in the hospitals of Pozantı (August 1917–July 1918)

Malaria	2,798	188 deaths
Recurrent fever	244	19 deaths
Dysentery	202	82 deaths
Typhus	156	18 deaths
Typhoid	10	5 deaths
Cholera	7	5 deaths
Smallpox	3	1 deaths

facilitated the spread of malaria even further. Moreover, it was observed that the malaria was causing greater damage in the mountainous regions than in the plains. In the summer of 1916, a severe epidemic of malaria broke out in Çamlıhan and Belemedik in the Taurus Mountains region. At the time of the epidemic, thousands of soldiers and railway workers were in the area. In Çamlıhan, 53.3 percent of the soldiers in one German military unit of 689 men caught malaria. When the German mobile bacteriology laboratory arrived in Pozantı in August 1917, the malaria epidemic was at its height.[51]

Table 7.2 shows the distribution of the deaths from various infectious diseases, which occurred in the seven military hospitals in the Taurus Mountains region between August 1917 and July 1918.[52]

Typhus and cholera were other epidemic diseases that affected the convoys struggling to exist under the hard conditions of migration and deportation. The Ottoman government, as a result, had to appropriate new resources to facilitate the struggle against the epidemics. For instance, the bill the government submitted to the Assembly of Deputies on 16 October 1915 regarding funds to be allocated for the fight against the cholera epidemics seen in Istanbul as well as in certain other provinces[53] was passed by the Senate. According to that bill, a further sum of 3 million kuruş was allocated for that struggle, in addition to the 8 million kuruş which formerly was approved to be spent in three different installments.[54]

In 1915 a cholera epidemic broke out in Anatolia. In 1916 a total of 31,465 soldiers were checked for cholera in a mobile laboratory set up by the Germans in Ankara[55] on 23 November 1916 in response to the outbreak of cholera in that city, where large numbers of military personnel were stationed.[56]

Dr. Abdülkadir Noyan, the medical chief of the 6th Army, also could not escape from the typhus epidemic:

> When I arrived in Baghdad on 12 November 1915 and started to inspect the hospitals as well as the military units in the city centre, I saw many patients with dysentery and malaria. However, I became ill before examining the type of the dysentery encountered here. No cases of spotted fever were observed in Baghdad during the summer and the first months of the autumn. That disease was diagnosed here first in the two patients sent to the Central Military Hospital in Baghdad on 16 December, by the 15th Division, which was dispatched from Erzurum. Around the same time, a soldier from Hijin Cavalry Regiment, which came from Aleppo, was also found to have spotted fever. It therefore appears that the typhus was brought to the 6th Army by the troops from Erzurum and Aleppo.[57]

Dr. Abdülkadir Noyan goes on recall the following from his memoirs:

> The Jewish School, close to the Central Military Hospital in Baghdad, was allocated for typhus patients. A total of 12 cases of spotted fever were reported in the hospital statistics from November 1915. By December, the number of patients increased to 128; and in February [1916] a total of 744 cases were reported, which indicated an alarming escalation in the occurrence of the disease. Cases of typhus also were seen among the doctors. It was necessary to initiate an urgent program for struggling against lice.... It was the rainy and the coldest season of Iraq. A large epidemic of spotted fever was likely.[58]

Moreover, among the Russian prisoners of war transferred to Baghdad, spotted fever was recorded in 1916.[59] In April 1917, cases of typhus were observed in Tikrit.[60]

Külz notes that the "Genius Epidemicus" was relatively mild in Mesopotamia. Indeed, the typhus epidemics seen in Mesopotamia generally were not as severe as epidemics elsewhere.[61] For cholera, however, the situation was completely different. The first case of cholera encountered in the Mosul area was an army deserter who was captured on the second day of July 1916.[62] Because the mobile bacteriology laboratory set up in July 1917 by the Germans in Pozantı was sent back to Istanbul after the war ended, the troops returning home from the south brought cholera to Anatolia.[63] The answer to the question of how the cholera reached Mosul in July 1917 is important, for it also would reveal the main source of cholera on the eastern front.

Dr. Noyan gives an important clue regarding the origin of the cholera epidemic (Pozantı-Tarsus) which broke out in Mosul in 1917:

> The investigations made within the 46th Division showed that all its troops were in good health condition when the division left Istanbul. When they reached Tarsus via the land route, some cases of diarrhea started to be seen among the troops. The patients were left at the hospitals of the army stations along the way. Since no cases of cholera were diagnosed among the troops in any of those hospitals, the units continued their journey over land until they reached Derbisiye. They left many patients with diarrhea at the hospitals on their way. From almost each battalion, 60–70 patients of diarrhea were left behind.
>
> Since the military doctors in the units did not receive reports of any diagnosed cases of cholera from the hospitals, the cases of cholera remained unnoticed. As the ill soldiers were left behind at the hospitals, luckily, the disease did not escalate into an epidemic among the troops. As soon as the 145th Regiment of the above mentioned Division arrived in Mosul, bearers of cholera vibrione were detected among the soldiers having diarrhea. As a precaution, all of the soldiers were checked to diagnose carriers of cholera among them. A great disaster, thus, was prevented by separating the vibrione-bearers from the others.[64]

One of the reasons leading to the sudden outbreak of cholera epidemics is water contamination.[65] The epidemics of cholera are mostly seen in and around places close to flowing water sources such as rivers, streams, brooks, or canals. The severity of an epidemic depends on the population density in the area, as well as the nutrition and physiological conditions of the people.[66] In Baghdad, as well as in many other settlement centers in Iraq, the Tigris River is the main source of water for drinking and for daily utilization. At the places where the Tigris River passes through, there are certain points used constantly by the local people for obtaining water and for cleaning purposes. The water usage habits in the region are reflected in the saying: "flowing water does not get dirty." However, the Tigris River, which naturally was contaminated while passing through large settlement centers, caused great epidemics during the war by spreading the infections of cholera and dysentery, as well as the amoeba and bacilli dysentery. Microorganisms borne by the troops caused the cases of cholera observed in Baghdad. The troops went there from Syria through the Jerabulus-Euphrates route, which was the most direct between Syria and Baghdad.[67]

In eastern Anatolia, the cholera which initially came from Russia emerged in Erzurum in 1915 and spread through contacts, whereas in Trabzon it became widespread due to contaminated waters. That epidemic spread later to the coastal areas and to the Sivas province as a result of migrations. Throughout 1916, cholera persisted mostly in the form of isolated cases or small-scale epidemics. In 1917 it was seen in Sivas, Trabzon, Canik, Kayseri, and Ankara. The total number of admissions to hospitals in the above-mentioned places due to cholera was 192 in Sivas, 110 in Trabzon, 56 in Canik, 5 in Kayseri, and 21 in Ankara.[68]

The cholera epidemic was brought to Sivas on 7 March 1916 by the migrants, and from there it spread to Kayseri. Again from Sivas, it was transmitted to Tokat and Amasya; it also spread along the Black Sea coast as a result of the movements of the immigrants. Cases of cholera were observed in Giresun, Ordu, Fatsa, Ünye, and Samsun, all located on the Black Sea coast.[69] In October 1916, a small-scale cholera epidemic broke out in the Recovery House in Merzifon. During that epidemic, twenty-seven admissions and eleven deaths due to cholera were recorded within a period of twelve days.[70]

Another outbreak of cholera occurred in İzmir in the summer of 1916. That disease, which had been diagnosed sporadically at various army stations for months, turned into an epidemic in İzmir and took a heavy toll among people from all segments of society in a very short time. Rahmi Bey, the governor of İzmir, recognized the imminent danger in time, however, and granted full authority to German Major Dr. Rodenwalt to fight against the cholera outbreak. In addition to their service in İzmir, the German doctors also were sent to the province of Aydın where they participated in the efforts to contain the cholera, spotted fever, and malaria epidemics.[71]

A ciphered telegram sent by the Governorate of Trabzon to the Ministry of the Interior on 14 July 1916 stated that the cholera was spread by refugees arriving from Giresun.[72] In mid-June 1917, when the 9th Division approached Bayburt, a cholera epidemic broke out among its troops. Sending those troops into the battlefield could have risked spreading the epidemic within the whole army. The division was sent to the combat zone after intensive efforts by bacteriologist Hulusi, who separated about five hundred carriers from the rest of the troops through medical examinations. Although the danger of a new cholera epidemic arose on the return of the division from the battle due to fatigue and other difficulties caused by the war, the efforts expended by Dr. Tevfik Sağlam prevented the diffusion of the epidemic and the likely damage it could have caused.[73]

From March 1917 on, cholera cases were on the rise again, mainly due to the deportation of Greeks from the coastal areas to the interior, who carried the disease as they went.[74] Another factor contributing to the spread of that cholera epidemic was the decision to forbid the refugees from returning.

> Because the refugees returning back to their homes were falling into deep misery, and many of them were dying on the roads even before reaching their homes, and the areas allocated for the resettlement of refugees were entirely full, the civil authorities issued an order forbidding further migrations and ordering the refugees to remain at their current locations. However, since the opportunities for making a living were very limited in İspiye, Giresun, Ordu, Fatsa, and Ünye, the people moved in large convoys to Terme, Çarşamba, and Samsun, despite the orders. Because migration was forbidden officially, the Government did not take necessary measures to facilitate those migrations. As a result, immigrants entirely got out of control, and people became dispersed in various villages in an uncontrolled manner. Only after the Deputy Army Commander and the Army Medical Chief took serious action regarding this matter that the migrants could be returned to their destinations in regular convoys, and receive some medical services. Because of the initial uncontrolled movements of the refugees, the epidemic existed until October 1917, mostly along the coastal areas.[75]

The 3rd Army sector remained safe from cholera for about nine months. But in July 1918, the disease broke out again in Batum, which was brought from Tbilisi, and spread among the people creating another epidemic. In August, cases of cholera began to be encountered in Samsun, having been brought there by the Greeks who moved from Sohumkale to Çarşamba. Throughout September, the cholera epidemics continued in both cities.[76]

Epidemics of bubonic plague broke out in Baghdad during the spring of 1915, and also in Beirut in October of the same year.[77] Another 22 cases of recurrent fever were encountered in Baghdad between 15 December 1915 and 7 January 1916. By March of 1916, the number of recurrent fever cases increased to 629. As a precaution, obtaining blood samples from each soldier having a high fever and sending those samples to laboratories was rendered compulsory in military units and hospitals. Since a sufficient number of microscope slides was not available in the medical depot, window glasses were cut in the form of slides and were distributed to hospitals and military units.

In 1916, insufficient nutrition and drinking of uncontrolled waters caused an escalation in recurrent fever at the Iraqi front. According to the 6th Army's hospital records, within a period of four months between November 1915 and March 1916, 107 of 264 typhoid patients died. In 1916,

Table 7.3. Deaths in the 6th Army attributed to recurrent fever*

Ratio of deaths due to recurrent fever	17%
December 1915–November 1916	1,644 persons
November 1916–November 1917	2,141 persons

*From Noyan, *Son Harplerde Salgın Hastalıklarla*, 63.

Table 7.4. Deaths in Baghdad and Mosul attributed to typhoid*

PERIOD	NUMBER OF PATIENTS WITH TYPHOID	NUMBER OF DEATHS	PERCENT
November 1915	7	–	–
December 1915	15	10	66.7
January 1916	74	35	47.3
February 1916	138	62	44.9
March 1916	12	4	33.3

*From *Türk Silahlı Kuvvetleri Tarihi*, 9: 400.

in ten months until the end of December, 11 out of 33 typhoid patients died. In 1917, a total of 8 out of 15 patients with typhoid died within twelve months. In 1918, the total number of patients with typhoid dropped to only two. Though the hospitals recorded the above-mentioned statistical data for cases of typhoid, Dr. Noyan was of the view that those were in fact cases of typhus. According to him, epidemics of typhoid were rare because of the successful vaccination campaign against typhoid.[78]

In the 3rd Army sector, venereal diseases showed an enormous escalation in the years of 1916 and 1917, "which was particularly common in coastal areas and among refugees. The fight against venereal diseases proved to be unsatisfactory."[79] An increase was also observed in smallpox epidemics between July 1916 and June 1917. Those cases were caused largely by the enormous number of admissions to hospitals among the refugees, who then transmitted the disease to the army personnel.[80]

From 1917 on, the duty to protect the civilians from infectious diseases was given to the army units. According to the records of the 3rd Army, a total of 1,417,014 civilians were vaccinated against smallpox, which corresponds to 44.8 percent of the total population then living in that area.[81]

Meaningful results were obtained from analyses of the amoebic dysentery in the Mesopotamia region, within the 6th Army sector. In January 1918, tests in the Mosul hospitals on eighty-five dysentery patients having amoeba in their feces revealed that thirty of those patients had dysentery as the primary sickness, twenty of whom were troops from the heavy machine gun units who recently had joined the army sector. It was also established that those soldiers caught the disease "during their travel which lasted for 7–8 days on the desert road between Nusaybin and Mosul." The other ten patients were soldiers already deployed in Mosul. As for the remaining fifty-five patients, their illnesses were connected to the amoebic dysentery that they previously experienced. It was understood that eighteen of them had caught the same disease once, twenty-three of them twice, fifteen of them three times, one of them four times, and three of them five times before.[82]

Another important finding obtained from the medical records pertaining to the sector of the 6th Army concerns the distribution of dysentery cases and the death ratios of patients in different regions. The hospitals kept track of the ratios of the soldiers coming from Anatolia, Syria, and Iraq who caught amoebic dysentery. The results show that the disease was most common among the soldiers coming from Anatolia and Rumelia, and that the death ratio among them was also higher. The soldiers coming from Iraq were mostly appointed to the station commands to carry out some routine work, and some of them had meals in their homes. Since they also were used to the climate and local traditions, they rarely became ill.[83] Thus, these results also indicate that people coming to the region from other places, such as the Armenian deportees from eastern Anatolia, were at greater risk of catching infectious diseases and dying.

BRITISH BLOCKADE AND THE DEATHS FROM HUNGER

Of the many disastrous events encountered in the Ottoman territories during World War I, both on and off the battlefield, two were particularly important in terms of the high human cost: locust infestations, and famines. Although the locust infestations were not directly related to the war, they had serious effects on both the army and civilians by causing famine and hunger.

Before World War I, the Ottoman territories had twice been infested with locusts, in 1850 and 1880.[84] Daniel Panzac writes that the mystery surrounding those locust infestations was partially solved in 1920–1925. According to the information included in Panzac's study, the locust species of *Schitorceca gregaria* belongs to the Acrididas family, in the Oaliferes class of the orthoptera order of insects. The locusts of this species live alone and change their locations at night by moving short distances. In certain ecological conditions, such as abundant rainfall, high temperature, soft alluvial soil, special kinds of plant communities, and desert areas, they reproduce in unbelievably large numbers. When a large number of them come together and reach a certain population density (the details of that process are not yet sufficiently known), they begin to live in swarms, which are carried long distances by hot winds that allow migration from one place to another. They move during the day, and descend to ground in the evening. The locusts are about 7–8 cm long and can reach a population density of 200 insects per square meter. That indicates a density of 200 million locusts per square kilometer. Considering that sometimes locust swamps are seen to spread across an area of dozens of square kilometers, it could be said that the density of locust populations in these limited swampy areas creates a real catastrophe.[85] In the course of the eighteenth century, a total of seven periods of drought occurred in Syria as a result of locust infestations. Various parts of Syria were affected more than others, but deprivation caused by those infestations was high.[86]

During the First World War, enormous groups of locusts caused great tragedies in the Ottoman territories. For instance, the infestation of Moroccan locusts in 1914 greatly damaged the crops. The next year, another type of locust known as the Sudanese locust infested the cultivated lands. A commission was established to exterminate the insects. In order to implement the decisions of the new commission, an organization for combating locusts was set up jointly with the Ministry of War. Thirteen of the labor battalions were assigned to carry out the work.[87]

The Ottoman Assembly of Deputies, following long debates during its sessions held on 11 June, 13 June, and 20 June 1914, passed the bill on the locust extermination.[88] Another bill was passed on 19 February 1916, which introduced awards of 250–1,000 kuruş to anyone who would provide timely information about locust infestations to the authorities.[89] In 1918, the issue of the extermination of locusts and combating them was brought before the Assembly of Deputies once again. In 1917, intensive locust infestations had been recorded within the boundaries of the Çeşme District and Manisa Sanjak (a *sanjak* is a subdivision of a province), as well as in Alaşehir; it reached such a high level that Saruhan Deputy Mustafa İbrahim Bey once said, "my province is famous for its locusts."[90] Despite all the measures taken at the beginning of the war, the crops for the year 1915 were badly damaged by locusts.[91] In 1914 and in subsequent years, many places in the country were afflicted with losses caused by locusts, including Karesi, Kütahya, Karahisar-ı

Salip, Istanbul, Burdur, Denizli, Aydın, İzmir, Menteşe, Antalya, Karaman, Halep, Urfa, and Zor.[92] Furthermore, just as the war was beginning, Syria was very badly hit by an unbelievably intense locust infestation.[93]

Cemal Pasha, the general governor of Syria and the commander of the 4th Army, wrote the following:

> In mid-April we encountered an unexpected disaster. Syria was wholly covered with locusts. The infestation was so intense that by the end of May and June, it was impossible to see even a single tree, the leaves of which had not been eaten up by locusts, in Syria. The greedy locusts consumed the grains, which had not yet eared. Being badly upset by this natural disaster, we were pessimistically thinking how we would spend this year.[94]

Next year, the problem was further deepened by a new disaster. In June 1916, a hot wind blowing constantly from the east for one week badly affected the grains grown in Havran, Humus, and Aleppo, reducing the yield of wheat that year.[95]

Famines can be caused by a number of things, mostly involving natural disasters such as floods, fires, droughts, earthquakes, epidemics, and excessively hot or cold weather conditions. Famines also are closely related to political and social events. For instance, famines can occur in a certain region that remains within an area of fighting between great powers, or in areas located on the routes of moving armies, or at times while a battle is taking place. During periods of widespread banditry, revolts, or internal disorders caused by a variety of reasons in the country, the inhabitants might have to suspend agricultural activities and leave the area, or their crops might be destroyed. Such incidents are in most cases followed by a famine. On the other hand, after long-lasting famines, it generally takes a long time for the people to resume their normal lives.[96]

In the reports sent by the French consul in Aleppo (dated 1 September 1757, 3 March 1758, and 6 September 1758), it was stated that most of the residents of Mosul, Diyarbakır, and Urfa had migrated to other places due to a famine, and they had to sell all of their children, particularly their girls, in Aleppo for prices less than two kuruş, or half a kuruş. No comparable poverty had been observed elsewhere before. Since the living conditions deteriorated even further in Aleppo in the winter, every day about fifteen to twenty poor people were dying on the streets from hunger and cold. The population decreased dramatically under the effect of the "malign fever, causing the body to decay." Typhus, dysentery, and infections related to malnutrition found a very suitable breeding ground.[97]

During World War I, the supply of foodstuff was severely limited in the Ottoman Empire as a result of several factors such as the closure of trade routes, the insufficiency of the transportation system within the country, the reduction of agricultural production, the lack of an organization for coordinating food supply, and the rapid consumption of the stocked supplies. The crisis was felt only in the big cities in the beginning, but later escalated further and badly affected the rural areas.[98] As in every other corner of the Ottoman Empire, in the region controlled by the 4th Army, too, the prices of various goods exceeded the values of banknotes or gold. That situation was the result of partly the rules of economics, and partly the groups that emerged under war conditions to take advantage of others' suffering.[99]

An officer who had been assigned to a duty within the 6th Army during the war wrote later, in 1942, the following about the dimensions of the food supply crisis:

> From November on, one of the biggest hurdles was the food supply.... A while ago, the 13th Army Corps already had reduced the amount of barley given to the animals to half. Later, even supplying that amount became very difficult. As the animals, especially the horses used in pulling the gun carriages, became very tired and unable to do the same work any more, two guns were withdrawn from each battery at the front lines. Furthermore, the cavalry brigade within that army corps had to be sent to Mosul on November 2 due to severe shortage of food supply. Also, by getting the approval of the Army, some new arrangements were made in the deployment of those Army corps. On the Tigris Front, the food supply crisis caused the withdrawal of 5,812 men and 1,819 animals from the supply forces, and 139 officers, 3,217 rifles, 45 machine guns, and 16 field artilleries from the combatant force.[100]
>
> In late 1917, and at the beginning of the following year, the food supply crisis continued very severely. As time passed, that crisis caused even bigger and more distressing problems, which forced the armies and army corps to ignore all kinds of military rules. They were obliged to reduce to minimum levels the strength of even the units fighting at the frontlines, and to dispatch their reserves to very remote areas behind the front. Even those measures were not effective in saving the troops from hunger....
>
> Increased rates of diseases, deaths, and desertions among troops were the natural consequences of that crisis. Besides, many soldiers eating grass due to hunger were poisoned. The soldiers were so tired and exhausted that it was impossible to use them even for digging graves for those who died of hunger, let alone making them carry out their routine duties. The dead were

just thrown into holes, which were covered with stones and bushes. Here, I can't help telling my memories about the ill and exhausted soldiers who were taken to hospitals. They were complaining to the high-ranking officials inspecting the hospital and to the doctors by saying: "We stayed alive, though we were wounded many times in the Caucasus and Iraqi fronts, and now, are you going to kill us with hunger?" The words of the soldiers made the inspectors and others listening to them shed tears of sadness. It was possible to see soldiers killing their friends just for a piece of bread. Again, there were many soldiers, who deserted from the army in order to find something to eat, by forming convoys and going into areas well behind the front, most of the time taking their arms and equipment with them....

As the civilians living in areas controlled by the Army were faced with the same trouble of hunger, the death ratio among them was high too. Due to hunger, uprisings and robberies became common in various places.

In the face of that terrible crisis, the Army resorted to several measures such as reducing the number of troops and animals. At the same time, it applied to the Lightning Group of Armies and to the Supreme Command Headquarters requesting them to provide the 2nd Army with five million kilograms of food supply. In response, the Supreme Command Headquarters advised purchase of provisions from the inner parts of Iran in cash. The Lightning Group of Armies, however, even did not take that request into consideration.[101]

The following lines from the "situation report" prepared by Kara Kemal, Istanbul representative of the Union and Progress Party, offers a great insight into the dimensions of the crisis, which suddenly broke out at the beginning of the war and challenged Istanbul significantly:

While the declaration of the war caused stagnation in our foreign trade, the mobilization launched in the country prioritized the needs of the army, which was considered to be a sacred institution, over the daily needs of the people. Most of the transportation vehicles, and all of the foodstuff and commodities waiting in the port were confiscated by the military authorities as part of the efforts to meet the needs of the mobilized army. Unfortunately, since we used to import most of our basic needs, even the most trivial ones, from Europe and to supply even wheat, our basic element of food, partially from Anatolia, but mostly from Romania, Russia, and even from Marseilles, after the declaration of mobilization, flour became the most badly needed commodity in the country. A flour shortage started to be felt in Istanbul, especially after the Dardanelles was closed to traffic, and Russia entered the war. Other factors also exacerbated the problem and as a result the shortages became severer: most parts of the railways in Anatolia were allocated to military transportation purposes, the flour prices increased in Romania, and the army continued to confiscate goods for itself.[102]

Besides the war, other disasters such as famines, hail, floods, infestations of locusts, and epidemics adversely affected yields, and contributed to food shortages throughout the war.[103]

Turkish Commander Ali Fuad, who was working under Cemal Pasha in the 4th Army, tells the following about the people dying of hunger in Beirut, then an Ottoman province:

> At nights, the peace and silence in Beirut could be disturbed only by the whimpers of those dying of hunger. In fact those voices would not last long, as the poor people would die soon. Before dawn, while the city was still asleep, the dead from the night were collected and heaped on carts by employees of the municipality, and then were carried to a ditch opened to bury all of them together. The streets were cleaned of corpses long before the sun began rising gloriously over Lebanon's mountains, which are almost always covered with snow.
>
> Some nights, the whimpers on the street were suppressed by the music coming out of the luxurious houses brilliantly shining in electric light. Quite possibly, in those large houses the rich merchants were happily showing off their wealth, or the expensive nightgowns and diamonds of their wives. Indeed, they were making their wealth by selling the wheat set apart from the provisions of the armies fighting at the Sinai Front or Medina; or they were running the railway cars being used in the shipment of that wheat to Lebanon and Beirut, though those railway cars were needed for transportation at the Sinai or Hijaz Fronts.
>
> When the Acting Commander-in-Chief came, a banquet was given in his honor in the garden of the Municipality, which lasted about an hour. While the guests were eating and drinking, none of them heard the voices of hungry people shouting "juan," "juan" (we are hungry, we are hungry). Nor did the guests see those poor people's hands, trembling and puckered from hunger, extended over the iron fences around the garden, begging for a small piece of bread.[104]

In her memoirs, Halide Edip also emphasizes that hunger was the biggest problem causing difficulties for Cemal Pasha during his tenure as the general governor in Syria and the 4th Army Commander.[105] General Ali

Fuad, who was one of the closest witnesses of the period, draws attention to a different aspect of the problem:

> Britain's position was of particular importance. It is an interesting fact that whereas the coasts of Hijaz, encouraged by Britain to revolt against the Ottoman Empire, was excluded from the British blockade, and the Muslim cities in that area could find all kinds of food sent by Britain at cheap prices, the Christian people of Lebanon were not even allowed to receive a shipload of wheat sent by the King of Spain. The British sank the barges and the sailboats bringing provisions for the Lebanese people from other ports of Syria.[106]

In his memoirs, Cemal Pasha, Commander of the 4th Army, writes that the food supply crisis that broke out in May and June 1916 escalated rapidly to reach terrible dimensions in the months of August and September, and "due to malnutrition many inhabitants looked like skeletons":

> Though I previously had written that I would not use the army's food stocks for relieving hunger among the local people, in view of the miserable conditions they are in, I could not help providing assistance to them within our limits. I provided one year's food supplies to all state schools, American School in Beirut, the families that are citizens of the states we are fighting, the spiritual leaders of Maronites and other sects, state officials, as well as the public and private hospitals, either free, or at a reasonable price. Especially for the Maronite Patriarch, and for the orphanages and religious organizations under his patronage, I provided three hundred thousand kilograms of grain free of charge in 1916. In 1917 too, I provided grains and monetary assistance to them.
>
> This aid, however, was of little help for the huge population of Beirut and Jabal Lubnan (Mount Lebanon). I intended to secure private relief to be extended from outside, for example from Spain or the USA. To that end, I had Maronite Patriarch write a letter to his Holiness the Pope, and had our Ambassador to Switzerland presented it to the Pope. I also communicated our requests for relief to Mr. Wilson, the US President, through Dr. Blis, the President of the American University. I repeatedly wrote to Istanbul, and noted that five to ten thousand tons of grains and medical supplies should immediately be sent to Beirut from any source whatsoever, and through anyone, be that the King of Spain, the American President, or the Pope. I told that otherwise, the innocent people in Beirut would fall into a deep misery, and that it would be impossible to prevent terrible mass deaths due to hunger or epidemics. Once, a very small amount of aid was

sent to Jaffa by the American Zionists in order to be distributed among the poor living in Jerusalem; compared to the huge need that amount was a joke. Besides, those who brought that comical amount of aid also had many printed materials with them for Zionist propaganda. That was of course a very inappropriate behavior.

One day, again, we were informed that two thousand tons of grains were about to be sent to Beirut through the initiatives of the King of Spain and the American President. We even were told that the ships carrying the food already had reached Alexandria. At that point, however, the Entente Powers intervened, claiming that we would seize the grain as soon as they reach Beirut, and would use them towards the needs of the Army. The Entente Powers refused to release the ships before securing a guarantee that all the grains would be distributed to the civilians. After intense correspondence, eventually…they asked me if I would give permission to the presence of the Pope's Representative to Beirut, as well as one or two Americans in a commission to be established for the distribution of the grains, when they reached Beirut.

I immediately replied by saying: "Once those grains reach here, I can form a delegation consisting only of American, British, and Italian members for their distribution. I even can accept one or two individuals to be assigned by the Entente Powers to inspect the distribution. My only wish is to get the grains here as soon as possible so that the people could be saved from hunger. Because I have become very tired of seeing everyday those innocent people dying on the streets."

My answer also was communicated by Enver Pasha to Mr. Elkuse, the US Ambassador, which also proved ineffective. On the contrary, the blockade imposed by the navies of the Entente Powers was further intensified. Then, I made an attempt to use sailing ships for carrying foodstuff to Lebanon and Beirut from the coasts of Syria. However, I had not taken into account the activities of the enemy's spies. The navy ships of the enemy were taking pleasure in hunting those sailing ships and sinking them.

In those days, I opened an orphanage in Aya Tura Abbey, in Jabal Lubnan (Mount Lebanon), to provide shelter to a thousand Armenian children. Also, I was supplying foodstuff from the army's stocks to many Armenian orphans and widows in Damascus.[107]

As a general rule, epidemics and famines mutually trigger each other. The epidemics can also emerge in the aftermath of natural disasters like floods and earthquakes.[108] As discussed so far, hunger caused by the war conditions was quite widespread within the boundaries of the Ottoman Empire. To give yet another example, in the "Political and Economical Intelligence Brief" dated 15 September 1918, prepared for the British War

Cabinet, it was noted that in the winter and spring of 1917, hundreds of Armenians died of hunger in Damascus.[109]

The situation in Mesopotamia during the winter of 1917–1918 was depicted very clearly by a German source:

> A general state of utmost deprivation could be seen all over Mesopotamia. During the winter months of 1917–1918, masses of people lost their lives from hunger. Even cannibalism was observed. An Arab couple was found out to be selling the meat of the children they were stealing and killing. Between the dates of 1 September 1917 and 13 April 1918, a total of 12,735 Turkish officers and soldiers died due to malnutrition.[110]

Another German source states that from January 1918 on, thirty to sixty individuals were dying every day of hunger in Mosul.[111] Memoirs of a Turkish officer also include similar observations:

> Hunger was prevailing everywhere. We were collecting foodstuff from the civilians either for free, or by paying their costs to prevent hunger among soldiers; this however further contributed the shortages among the local people. In Mosul, the price of bread first increased to one silver mecidiye (one lira), and later to three liras. The people could not afford to buy bread. Incidents of death from hunger started to be encountered. Nothing could be done for those women, men, children, and elderly people dying on the streets, moaning bitterly. About 10–12 people were executed for selling the flesh of dead children in butcher's shops as sheep or lamb meat, or serving those meats in the restaurants.[112]

According to a document from the British Archives, the year of 1914–1915 was recorded as a period of rapid escalation of infectious diseases in eastern Anatolia as well as in the Caucasus and Iran. Unfortunately, as it also was seen in the case of Urumia, the deaths occurring from epidemics in the area were presented as a massacre of the Christians by the Muslims as part of the war propaganda efforts. The British admitted that fact later.[113]

Another document from the British Archives notes that Gordon Paddock, the American consul in Tabriz, denied the reports that a massacre took place around Urumia; he instead clarified that a typhoid epidemic in the region caused the death of many local people and American missionaries, as well as many Armenians living in the villages nearby.[114]

Justin McCarthy reaches the following conclusion: "Judged on the basis of the general wartime mortality of the Ottoman eastern provinces, more than one-half of the internal refugees in eastern Anatolia must be dead." He also adds the following:

> The precise numbers of Muslim dead are not in themselves important; their importance lies in their depiction of the enormity of the Muslim loss in the east. In the provinces in which the war was primarily fought, Van, Bitlis, and Erzurum, at least 40 percent of the Muslims were dead at the war's end. The depth and breadth of the suffering that such figures imply is beyond comprehension. The death rate is well beyond that of most of the great disasters in world history, such as the Thirty Years' War and the Black Death. Of course, Muslims were not the only ones to die. The Armenian death rate was at least as great, and Armenian losses cannot be ignored. But the world has long known of the suffering of the Armenians. It is time for the world to also consider the suffering of the Muslims of the east and the horror that it was. Like the Armenians, Muslims were massacred or died from starvation and disease in stupefying numbers. Like the Armenians, their deaths deserve remembrance.[115]

Joseph Pomiankowsky, the Austrian-Hungarian Empire's military attaché to Istanbul, also is of the opinion that a minimum of one million Muslims, including many military personnel, died during the Great War as a result of the infectious diseases transmitted by the internally displaced Armenians:

> The deportation of the Armenians in Anatolia by the Government of the Young Turks suddenly left the country deprived of its tradesmen, craftsmen, merchants, and agriculturists. As a shortage of grains, animals, and all kinds of provisions arose within the country soon, it became very difficult to find food supplies for the Turkish military units constantly moving within Anatolia. In Armenia [i.e., Turkey's eastern provinces claimed by the Armenians], about a hundred thousand Turkish troops were badly afflicted by hunger. On the other hand, the convoys of the Armenians, being deprived of any basic facilities, such as hygiene and medical services, spread the infectious diseases wherever they went. The infection of spotted fever, also brought by those convoys, caused the death of around one million Muslims.[116]

One German source describes the Ottoman soldiers suffering from insufficient nutrition as the "weak bodies and sunken cheeks" and "hungry ghosts."[117]

A German doctor named Liebert wrote the following from Elazığ: "It can be easily seen how fragile those weakened and feeble individuals are. Taking or not taking them to surgery doesn't change anything. They are dying anyway."[118]

Eric Jan Zürcher also writes that among both the Armenian and the Muslim refugees, many fell victim to infection, especially typhus: "Particularly in winters, eggs of the lice were easily transmitted onto the clothes and other personal belongings, and caused typhus. That disease was killing the deported Armenians, Muslim migrants and others."[119]

According to Zürcher, excluding the losses that occurred on the battlefields, one-seventh of the total strength of the army at mobilization capacity died due to various diseases such as malaria, dysentery, and typhus.[120]

8

UNARMED WARRIORS

PROFESSOR H. BRAUN, A GERMAN DOCTOR, delivered a lecture at Istanbul University on 18 November 1933, entitled "Microbiology, Parazitoloji, and Epidemics." After defining some basic concepts, he gave his audience a *tour d'horizon* by providing information on a vast range of subjects, from the causes of epidemic diseases, to the importance of hygiene in daily life, to the unbelievable impact of diseases on the course of history. Toward the end of that "historical lecture," the voice of the German professor was echoing in the lecture-hall:

> At a time when hygiene was not yet established as a science, the famous French Philosopher J. J. Rousseau said the following: "Hygiene should be treated as a virtue, rather than a scientific discipline." Though somewhat exaggerated, those words entail an element of truth in them.
>
> The two basic components of hygiene, namely scientific and ethical, should be observed both in education, and in practical life. A doctor should possess immense knowledge, and should always be ready to make sacrifices without expecting any benefit in return. The famous Viennese internist Dr. Nothnagel once finished his first lecture with the following sentence: "Only a good person can be a good doctor." This is especially true for the doctors involved in the struggle against infectious diseases. The main desire of true doctors is to help patients and serve the public good.[1]

The performance of the Turkish doctors in their struggle against infectious diseases during the wars of the Ottoman Empire in the nineteenth century, and during the Balkan Wars and the First World War, present some very bright, as well as very bitter, examples of the history of Turkish medicine.

In his book called *Başımıza Gelenler* (What Happened to Us), Mehmet Arif, the former first secretary of the Ottoman Extraordinary Commissariat in Egypt, provides the following assessment about the typhus epidemic that broke out during the Ottoman-Russian War of 1877–1878:

> The condition of our troops in Erzurum worsened due to typhus. In addition to the patients already being treated in our hospital, the doctors examined every day about three to four hundred patients coming from the fortifications on the frontlines. An average of 100–150 of those patients was being hospitalized. The number of deaths increased so much that religious personnel in the hospital, though working non-stop from the morning till the evening, became unable to wash and shroud all of the dead [according to Islamic tradition]. As a result, the corpses of the dead soldiers had to be piled one over the other like a heap of wood. At one point, even it became impossible to find shrouds for the dead, and some of the corpses had to be buried in their underclothes. Then, some of the tradesmen helped us by providing, on credit, sufficient amount of cloths to be used as shrouds. What was even worse was that many of doctors, who already were insufficient to meet the demand, also caught the disease. Many of our doctors, of every rank, from the chief doctor to the young ones at the rank of captain, lost their lives. About twenty to twenty-five doctors were taking care of eight to ten thousand patients.[2]

During the Ottoman-Greek War of 1897, which followed the Ottoman-Russian War of 1877–1878, "The military encampments turned into graveyards due to infectious diseases." In the war of 1897, the Ottoman Army lost some 30,000 men as well as many doctors. Among the doctors who died during that war was Dr. Major Hasan Zühtü Nazif, who had attended courses on microbiology at the Pasteur Institute in Paris in 1892.[3]

The struggle against infectious diseases during the Balkan War was discussed in Chapter 2 in this study.[4] An interesting detail regarding the War of Tripoli should be mentioned here. The Red Crescent Organization's 1913 yearbook reports a typhoid epidemic that broke out in 1911, during the War of Tripoli. While the Ottoman, German, and British medical organizations were jointly struggling against that epidemic in the region of Garian, two doctors from the German Red Cross, as well as two nurse's aides from the Red Crescent, lost their lives. None of the Red Crescent doctors from the Ottoman minorities went to Tripoli to serve there during the war.[5]

At the start of the Ottoman-Russian battles on the eastern front on 29 October 1914, the medical conditions in the 3rd Army were as follows:

The establishment of the army stations at the rear could not be completed yet. The hospitals in those army stations were lacking sufficient number of beds and medical equipment. The army, deprived of the means of disinfection, was vulnerable to epidemics at any moment. Indeed, the first signs of an epidemic already had been observed.

After the beginning of the war, two battles took place in Köprüköy within three weeks, which were very bloody. By 26 November, a total of 139 wounded officers and 5,646 soldiers were brought to the hospitals in Hasankale and Erzurum. Then, a period of one month until the battle of Sarıkamış passed in relative calm. In general, during the intensive military movements made in the course of war, diseases and epidemics are encountered rarely. This situation is in fact temporary and might be misleading. The severest diseases and epidemics occur during the calm periods that follow a tiring and intensive war involving a lot of movement. That was the case encountered here too. A terrible misery was prevailing everywhere. Spotted fever [typhus] became widespread. The doctors also were falling sick due to illness one after another.[6]

The medical organization on the Caucasian front consisted of one medical company in each division, and three mobile hospitals in each of the army corps. The cavalry divisions had no medical companies or mobile hospitals. The battalions on the front, as well as the gendarmerie battalions, had no medical units, either, other than the medical infrastructure established in the field. In Erzurum, a 900-bed hospital was subordinated to the fortified post command, and a total of 1,950 beds were available in the hospitals located within the entire sector of the army stations at the rear (250 beds in Trabzon, 300 in Bayburt, 500 in Erzincan, 200 in Elazığ, 200 in Diyarbakır, 200 in Van, 200 in Muş, and 100 in Bitlis). For an army with the strength of 189,000 men, a total of 4,650 beds were prepared, 1,800 on the frontlines and the mobile hospitals, and 2,850 at the rear. The most crucial hospitals at the rear, given their proximity to the front, were those in Erzurum, Bayburt, and Trabzon. The total bed capacity of those hospitals was 1,650.[7]

By March 1915, all of the mobile hospitals had become entirely full, and no free beds were available for wounded soldiers in case of war.[8] The 3rd Army's core strength was concentrated in the north, around Erzurum. It was expected that Erzurum would have to shoulder the biggest burden, which indeed turned out to be the case during the war. Considering the centrality of Erzurum to the Ottoman war plans, previously a total of ten to twenty thousand beds were calculated to be necessary there. Despite those prewar diagnoses, only nine hundred beds could be made available in Erzurum, whereas the hospital in Erzincan had only five hundred beds. Bitlis Hospital, on the other hand, was a station hospital of secondary importance. As for the hospitals in Muş, Elazığ, and Diyarbakır, they would be able to meet only the local needs and admit only the soldiers being transferred to other places. Of the fourteen newly established station posts, only the ones in Erzincan, Kelkit, and Bayburt were appointed doctors. None of those posts had any medical establishment. No medical unit could be set up on the roads to be used in the transfer of ill and weak soldiers. The detachment, which was ordered to be formed in Bayburt to carry out the mission of transferring the ill, could not be formed. Meanwhile, the medical detachment having the same transfer assignment in Erzurum could receive only eight carriages after 5 November, all of which were in need of repair. There were three medical depots in Erzurum. The medical depot of the station was not yet operating. As of 6 November, the medical detachment of the 17th Division had twenty-nine horses, twenty-two mules, and ten animals used for riding, while the 1st mobile hospital of the 9th Army Corps had twenty-four two-wheel carriages, and forty-eight oxcarts.[9]

On the Caucasian front, a particularly important problem was the shortage of war packages. The war packages sent from Istanbul (36,700 for the infantry, 1,794 for the artillery units) were not only inadequate, but also most of them did not even reach the area.[10]

RESEARCH FOR THE DIAGNOSIS AND TREATMENT OF DISEASES

Although recurrent fever had been known since the ancient times, it was differentiated from typhus in 1843, and its spirochetes were identified in patients' blood samples in 1868.[11] In Turkey, Dr. Süleyman Numan was the first to classify recurrent fever in 1905.[12] As with typhus, lice play an important role in the human-to-human transmission of recurrent fever. In the case of armies, it was found out in 1909 that lice were responsible for the transmission of typhus. Outbreaks of recurrent fever and trench fever, in 1910 and 1917, respectively, were also understood to be transmitted by lice.[13] Recurrent fever was widespread throughout the world, and during World War I it was encountered in Eastern Europe, particularly in Poland, the Balkans, and Russia, as well as in the Far East, in India and China, and in North Africa and Central America.[14] In untreated cases, the death ratio from that disease could be as high as 50 percent.[15]

Ekrem Kadri notes that in the national and international medical literature, "louse typhus" (typhus exanhematicus), "epidemic typhus," and "spotted fever" are used interchangeably.[16] It is also known that during the Great War typhus was called "spotted typhoid" or "army fever." In the past, typhus used to be confused mostly with typhoid. Some of the diseases referred to as typhoid were likely to be typhus.[17] During the Balkan Wars, the first case of spotted fever (typhus) in Istanbul was diagnosed in the Gülhane military hospital.[18] Dr. Major General Abdülkadir Noyan explains how a typhus epidemic that broke out in 1904 was diagnosed to be typhoid:

> An epidemic of a feverous disease broke out in Karaköse. A medical delegation headed by Dr. First Lieutenant Haydar was sent from Istanbul to diagnose the disease. Although the delegation members reached the decision that the disease was typhoid, it was rather unusual. An outbreak of typhoid was impossible at that time of year—under severe winter conditions. Indeed, the disease in question was showing all typical symptoms of "typhus exanhematicus," a louse-borne disease. Unfortunately, at that time typhus was not yet known or understood.[19]

In order to conclude the debate among the Ottoman doctors about the distinction between typhoid and typhus, the Ministry of War set up a medical commission in March 1913. That commission, composed of Dr. Ferik Hacı Emin Pasha, the field medical inspector, as well as Dr. Fevzi Pasha, Dr. Neşet Ömer, Dr. Selim Ali, Dr. Server Kamil, and Dr. Abdülkadir Noyan, reached the decision that the epidemic disease seen in the army was typhus and rejected the diagnoses of typhoid made by other doctors.[20]

A cholera epidemic also spreading to the Bulgarian Army hastened the signing of a ceasefire between the Ottomans and the Bulgarians on 3 December 1912. Around the same time, cases of typhus were seen in the trenches of the Ottoman Army along the Çatalca line. The military doctor Tevfik Sağlam, who worked at the Yassıviran Hospital, later described the situation in the hospital as follows: "The patients lay side by side on mattresses placed on the floor very close to each other. They have their own clothes on them. Their bodies are covered with lice."[21]

Although he had diagnosed the disease as measles on his first encounter, Dr. Sağlam later thought—when his friend Dr. Şekip Habip also became ill showing the same symptoms—that it could in fact be typhus. After a short while, he caught the disease, too.[22] In his book *Büyük Harpte 3: Ordu'da Sıhhi Hizmet* (Medical Services in the 3rd Army during the Great War), Dr. Sağlam writes the following about the dispute regarding the diagnosis of infectious diseases:

> It was not easy to have everyone agree that the cases of illness were spotted fever (typhus). Some of the doctors, including several well-known medical experts, were claiming insistently that the disease was typhoid. In order to have them recognize the real nature of the disease, I had to carry out an intensive study, based on clinical findings, blood analysis results, and autopsy findings. My opponents had to accept my thesis, after a conference held at the Faculty of Medicine on 1 May 1913. The text of my speech in the conference was published in 1913 in pamphlet form.[23]

The discussions between the Ottoman doctors about the diagnosis of typhus were quite normal at that time.

Dr. Noyan took part in the struggle to control spotted fever encountered among the labor battalions in Kandıra in March 1915. He successfully got the typhus epidemic under control within only ten days through the "bakery method" he developed there, and described his method in a report he sent to the field medical inspectorate. He also offered the method of operation to the army.[24] The bakery method was then rapidly put into the form of a simple project, and a pamphlet was published about it entitled "Oven of Disinfection through the Flow of Hot Air."[25]

He later published the following observations about how he came to develop this new method:

> I was assigned to Kandıra on 3 March 1915 in order to combat an epidemic of spotted fever which had broken out among the labor battalions there. When I arrived in Kandıra, I found more than 3,000 members of the labor battalion busy chopping wood, who were in civilian clothing, and who seemed to be in a miserable condition. Almost all of them were dirty and were infested with lice. Every day, I was encountering 10–15 new cases of spotted fever I had no means to combat against. The patients were being treated in a hospital, which seemed rather like an infirmary. Some of them were also transferred to the Military Hospital in İzmit. The death ratio was very high among the patients. Under those conditions, I seriously wondered what to do.
>
> When I was wandering around in the market place of Kandıra, I saw plenty of bakeries. They reminded me of my first place of appointment—Serviburnu—after becoming a doctor. I remembered how I had had hard-baked breads, as well as their sacks, cleaned in the military ovens to fight against cholera in the Quarantine Establishment in Serviburnu.
>
> I became very relieved when it occurred to me that I could use the bakeries in Kandıra as hot air stoves for disinfection, and could have the

soldiers cleaned in the baths to be set up in tents. I immediately talked to the Kaymakam (district governor) of Kandıra, and the Commander of the labor battalion. Leaving sufficient number of bakeries to meet the needs of the people, I had three bakeries located side by side to each other emptied. The market place was located on a straight, long, and wide street. I had three baths set up in tents just across the bakeries. There was plenty of wood. Water was going to be boiled in large cauldrons to be placed beside the tents of bath.

Since it was my idea to clean the clothes and other belongings of the soldiers by using that method, and I was the first one to implement, I worked together with the bakers in heating the ovens and adjusting the temperature. I personally measured the temperature by throwing a white paper into the oven and then closing its door. When the temperature was high, the paper would become black. In that case, it would be necessary to open the door of the oven for a while in order to lower the temperature. If on the other hand, the paper was found to have a yellowish color, then wet sackcloth was spread at the floor of the oven and the objects to be sterilized were put on those cloths by using the bakers' peels. In the beginning, I implemented all these steps personally, with the help of the bakers and some soldiers. Later, when I served in Çanakkale and Iraqi fronts, I saw in many places military units building field ovens and combating lice by the method of dry-heating.[26]

A very intensive campaign was launched against epidemics of spotted fever and recurrent fever from the very moment they were encountered. Initially, disinfection was carried out in field ovens (Noyan's method) and in tandirs (ovens consisting of a clay-lined pit or an earthen jar buried in the ground). In 1916, Ahmet Fikri invented the method of vapor chest, which formed the very basis of the fight against lice. Cleaning houses were set up at various places, and eventually the army was successful in getting rid of lice. As a result, spotted fever and recurrent fever no longer turned into new epidemics. Very severe epidemics of cholera, however, broke out several times both within the army, and among the civilian population, which mostly broke out as a result of contacts between individuals. In two cases, through, they were transmitted through water. Through an intensive struggle based on diagnosing the carriers and waging extensive vaccination campaigns, the army was saved from a great disaster. As a result of the measures implemented, cholera ceased to be a threat to hinder the movement of the army in some places. An effective struggle also was carried out against the diseases of typhoid and dysentery.[27]

Dr. Hüseyin, the chief doctor of Tokat Hospital, also invented a mobile barrel of vapor in 1916. The barrel, manufactured in Tokat, was mounted on two wheels, to be pulled by a horse or an ox.[28]

The following was written by Guze about the availability of disinfection means in other military units: "It was impossible to dispatch the mobile hot-air stoves to many of the units, as they could never be taken through the snow-covered passages. The units stationed in the Aras Valley and around Erzurum at least had the chance of making use of the hot water springs in Hasankale and Erzurum."[29]

In 1917, still another simple device was invented by Dr. Ahmet Lütfi, the consultant of hygiene for the 4th Army Corps, subordinated to the 2nd Army. That device, which was called a "vapor boiler" by its inventor, could be used in places where no hot air stoves or vapor chests were available for disinfection.[30]

Ottoman doctors' successful work in the field of military medicine and in combating infectious diseases during the long years of war should also be underlined here.[31]

REŞAT RIZA

Three doctors, who separately instigated typhus vaccination within the Ottoman Army during the Great War—namely, Dr. Tevfik Sağlam, Dr. Server Kamil, and Dr. Abdülkadir Noyan—stated that they borrowed the idea of vaccination from Dr. Reşat Rıza. The first typhoid vaccination in Turkey was applied in Gülhane Military Hospital by Dr. Rıza and Dr. Mustafa. Dr. Rıza was also a key figure in the search for a typhus vaccination in Turkey. One year before the publication of an international study on typhus in 1916, he had drawn the shape of the rickettsia that caused typhus in his notebook, but had not published it. Dr. Rıza first developed the idea of preparing a prophylactic vaccine against typhus by using the blood of patients who had the disease. He proved the harmlessness of the vaccine by experimenting it on himself and Dr. Musa Kazım. On 25 April 1915, Dr. Rıza and Dr. Mustafa Hilmi submitted a report pertaining to the results of their joint study to the field medical inspectorate, entitled "An Experiment of Vaccination against Spotted Fever." That report was presented before the Supreme Medical Assembly in July, which approved it for publication in the *Sıhhiye Mecmuası* (Medical Journal). Dr. Rıza's and Dr. Mustafa's studies were both published the same year.[32]

The vaccines produced from the blood of patients following Dr. Rıza's research were tested in the 3rd and 6th armies. Although the efforts of vaccination performed by using those vaccines produced positive results, they remained of limited value. The three doctors executing the tests, Hayri, Recai, and Süfyan, died in quick succession in March 1915, with an interval of one week between their deaths.[33]

The first vaccine against typhus containing Rickettsia prowazekii was used in the Ottoman Army. The method for preparing that vaccine was designed by Dr. Rıza. Considering the fact that the typhus agent exists in the blood when the patient has a fever, and that it dies at the temperature of 60°C when heated for one hour, this distinguished microbiologist proposed to inject 5 cc of blood taken from typhus patients during the feverish stage of the disease and heated at 50 to 60°C for one hour after defibrination. The same method was also implemented by Dr. Sağlam in early 1915 and by Dr. Noyan in 1916, yielding positive results in both cases.[34] The Germans first studied and tested Dr. Rıza's method of vaccine preparation at the Romanian front.[35] In subsequent studies carried out in Germany, the vaccine was modified and it was syringed three times. No definite findings, however, could be obtained regarding the immunity provided by the vaccine. It was thought to be due to the fact that the blood used in the preparation of the vaccine was taken from patients after they had recovered from the disease.[36] The method of vaccination used previously by the Ottoman doctors was based on injecting the blood of individuals who had recovered, or still were recovering, from the disease, either to patients or for prophylactic purposes to healthy individuals, because no medicines were available against typhus then.[37]

The Ottoman Army had no institution of vaccination in 1914.[38] Dr. Captain Hamit Osman, the bacteriologist of the army station hospitals in Erzincan, Dr. Hamdi Suat, who was assigned by the General Directorate of Health as the inspector of communicable diseases, and the Red Crescent delegation used the method of vaccine preparation developed by the Ottoman doctors against typhus after some modifications. Dr. Osman vaccinated 20 soldiers on 9 March with the blood he had taken from patients newly recovered from spotted fever and still convalescing. He used that blood without inactivating it. None of the soldiers vaccinated by him caught typhus, whereas 4 of the 8 soldiers who lived under the same conditions with the others but were not vaccinated, caught the disease. After evaluating these results, Dr. Osman decided to obtain the blood to be used for vaccination from patients at the beginning stage of the disease—within the first ten days. He vaccinated 112 persons with that blood, again without inactivating it. The results were again positive. Then, Dr. Osman vaccinated 304 individuals with the unheated blood taken from typhus patients during the most acute stage of the disease. Out of those 304 individuals, 114 remained healthy, while 190 of them caught typhus. Based on his own vaccination efforts, Dr. Suat gave the same figures as 310 and 136, respectively, and stated that 49 individuals died due to typhus. On 9 May 1915, Dr. Osman went on leave from Erzincan to Istanbul due to severe family problems, and there remained in a hospital for one and a half years due to a mental disorder. He, therefore, could not personally follow the health conditions of some of the individuals he had vaccinated. The fate of these individuals was followed instead by Dr. Captain Ahmet Hamdi who was sent to Erzincan. In 1919, because of the special conditions following the armistice, the vaccination studies were highly questioned, and the directorate of health made a decision to investigate the matter as well as the methods of applying the vaccinations. The results of that investigation were published in a report.[39]

Turkish military doctor and typhus specialist Abdülkadir Noyan vaccinated all of the officers and doctors in Baghdad with the vaccine he had developed. However, Dr. Noyan's vaccination caused much dispute among the German doctors and hygiene specialists. While some of them accepted the benefits of the vaccine, others questioned its effectiveness. Marshal Goltz's doctor refused to vaccinate the German marshal, and a few weeks later both the marshal and the doctor lost their lives. On the other hand, all of the vaccinated soldiers and officers remained healthy.[40]

HAMDİ SUAT

Before the war, Dr. Hamdi Suat, one of the first interns at the Gülhane Military Hospital, was sent to Germany where he successfully defended a thesis on "bubonic plague." On his return to the Gülhane Military Hospital, he set up and directed a laboratory for pathologic anatomy. This distinguished medical figure, described by Tevfik Sağlam as a "great patriot," joined the Red Crescent's medical delegation voluntarily when World War I broke out, and he went to Erzurum. He continued his studies on typhus there, during the fiercest stages of the war.[41]

Besides serving as a military doctor, Suat also carried out significant research on typhus throughout the war. Although he was dismissed from the university during the University Reform in 1932, he did not display his disappointment openly, and accepted Dr. Refik Saydam's offer to work at the Gureba Hospital, where he was able to continue his studies.[42]

During the Great War, Dr. Suat performed some tests in Erzurum by using vaccines prepared with serums, which were kept on ice for 24 hours after being taken from typhus patients when they reached the acute phase of the disease. The results of the research he carried out in Erzurum were published in 1916 in *Zeitschrift für Hygiene und Infektionkrankheiten*.[43]

Ekrem Şadi wrote the following about Dr. Suat:

> Students of the Military School of Medicine were assigned to various duties; first and second year students at the rank of medical corporal, and students of higher grades at the ranks of medical sergeant. I was also assigned as medical corporal first at Beykoz, Serviburnu, and later at the Hospital in sheds at Yeşilköy. I was given appointed to the shed allocated for typhus patients. The Chief Doctor of the hospital was Dr. Major Hulusi. When I was there, I heard once that Dr. Major Tevfik Sağlam and Dr. Major Hamdi Suat had come to the hospital, and by using scissors, cut out typhus exanthemas from the backs of the typhus patients, to analyze them. Then I was assigned to the Beylerbeyi hospital where the seriously wounded soldiers were treated. The doctors working in that hospital were retired military doctors of the ranks of lieutenant colonel or colonel."[44]

Dr. Sağlam, who was a colleague of Dr. Suat, explains the following about the results obtained from the tests completed in 1915 on a vaccine, which was developed by the Ottoman doctors in order to combat an epidemic of spotted fever that broke out in the 3rd Army sector during the Great War: "I was talking to Dr. Reşat Rıza about the measures to be taken against the severe epidemic of spotted fever that existed in the 3rd Army sector before my departure to join the 3rd Army in February 1915. He offered me to use a vaccine—to be prepared according to the method he was planning—on the 3rd Army." Under the existing conditions, however, the vaccine could not be applied widely. It had to be prepared by using blood taken from patients infected with spotted fever. Therefore, in order to apply the vaccine, a patient with spotted fever was needed. The blood taken from one patient was only sufficient to create vaccine for a maximum of two to four individuals. Consequently, the vaccine was applied only on the individuals at greatest risk during epidemics, such as doctors or nurse's aides.

> I personally prepared the first vaccine for spotted fever on 28 March 1915 in Hasankale, and applied it to 9 officers, 5 of whom were doctors, who volunteered for it. Later on, my associates vaccinated 510 individuals in Erzurum, 130 in Bayburt, and 156 in Sivas. Together with the ones I had vaccinated earlier, a total of 805 individuals were vaccinated. None of those individuals showed any symptoms to indicate a transmission of the disease caused by

the vaccine. Later on, the harmlessness of the vaccine was further proven when used in the 3rd Army, and [later] during the War of Liberation. The vaccine was causing minimal reaction in the soldiers vaccinated.

As for the immunity provided by the vaccine, results of comparative studies have proven that the vaccine developed immunity against the disease. However, since those results are based on observations that covered a period of no longer than about 3–4 months, it has not been possible to acquire an accurate idea about the duration of that immunity. In my personal opinion, that vaccine is perfectly effective for the time being [as of 1941], and therefore it should be applied to the individuals at the greatest risk of catching the disease by the time a superior treatment is developed.

Dr. Tevfik Sağlam went on to note that:

As I write these lines [1941], many foci of spotted fever continue to exist in our country. Unless those foci are completely eliminated, and the people are completely cleaned of lice, spotted fever will continue to threaten us in any future mobilization and war, causing terrible disasters. In order to get rid of the spotted fever, we should eradicate the lice in our country.[45]

The above-mentioned studies were published and took their places within the scientific literature.[46]

İBRAHIM TALI AND TEVFİK SAĞLAM

Dr. İbrahim Tali and Dr. Tevfik Sağlam had very bright professional careers as medical administrators within the army during the war, and are recognized as two important figures in Turkish medical history.

Dr. Tali was appointed as the deputy chief of the Army Department of Health during the general mobilization declared in 1914, and served in that position for five months until his promotion to the rank of colonel in June 1915. He served first in Çanakkale and Seddülbahir, and later on the front in Diyarbakır. When the army headquarters he was serving in was renamed the Inspectorate of the Caucasus Group of Armies, he became its medical inspector. After the abolition of this headquarters, he returned to Istanbul and was assigned to the duty of inspecting the health conditions of the ill and wounded officers and soldiers being treated in Germany. During his stay in Germany, he attended two medical congresses on infectious diseases and surgery, and represented the Turkish Military Medical Organization together with other Ottoman doctors. Later, he was assigned as the medical chief of the Eastern front which was established in June 1920 to coordinate the military expedition against Armenia.[47]

Dr. Sağlam also earned an honorable place in Turkish medical history, particularly for his intensive efforts in the 3rd Army sector during the war. He designed several research projects and was involved actively in their implementation. Guze, who was the 3rd Army's chief of staff, wrote that the Army's medical chief was a "very capable person." According to German Major Guze, Dr. Sağlam "had done everything which could be done under the conditions of those days."[48]

TURKISH MEDICAL PUBLICATIONS IN WAR TIME

Dr. Akil Muhtar and Dr. Besim Ömer, who were the chief of board of the Civilian School of Medicine and the chief of the General Health Council, respectively, published a 233-page study on the cholera epidemics that occurred within the boundaries of the Ottoman Empire in 1912, entitled "A Guide for the Measures to Be Taken against the Disease of Cholera."[49] Ziya Nuri translated into Turkish Henrique da Rocha Lima's 1915 study on typhus in 1916.[50] A considerable increase was observed in the number of scientific articles on infectious diseases published in the *Journal of Darülfünun Faculty of Medicine* (Istanbul) in 1916. This trend continued during the years of 1917 and 1918.[51]

Dr. Server Kamil published the results of the studies he carried out by using the "Weil Felix" method in Sivas in 1916. In an attempt to develop a serum for the treatment of one particular disease, he conducted experiments on goats and calves.[52]

The results of research carried out by German hygiene specialists in the Ottoman Empire during the Great War were published in various German medical journals in the Weimar Republic, and after 1933. To give a specific example, one could mention Prof. Hans Ziemann's book, also written on the subject of tropical diseases. In that book, called *Malaria and Black-water Fever*, Prof. Ziemann details his experiences in southern Anatolia, Syria, and Palestine during his assignment there as the medical advisor to the Ottoman armies in Palestine.[53]

According to the records pertaining to 1909, a total of 600 doctors, 130 pharmacists, 170 midwives, and 200 vaccination officers were serving in the Ottoman Empire, about half of whom were non-Muslims.[54] When the mobilization was declared in 1914, the military doctors were distributed throughout the army, according to the importance of the various army corps.[55]

TABLE 8.1. Ottoman medical officers shown according to their ranks*

RANK	1914	1915	1916	1917	1919	DEATH	RESIGNATION
Brigadier general	1	1	2	2	4	–	–
Colonel	11	12	12	13	11	1	4
Lieutenant colonel	26	53	80	58	102	7	17
Major	267	317	428	449	436	45	39
Captain	1,198	1,030	811	800	808	278	77
First lieutenant	143	129	141	72	102	3	14
Lieutenant	–	–	–	–	101	–	7

*From ATASE Archives, from no. 1/63, box 1327, file 11, fih. 1–116, 1–117, in *Türk Silahlı Kuvvetleri Tarihi*, 9:613.

According to Ahmet Emin, the number of physicians serving in the entire health service amounted to 2,555. According to the official figures, 2,998,321 men were enrolled in the army during the four years of war. Although the total soldiers under arms never exceeded 1,200,000 at any one time, the medical staff were still extremely insufficient compared to those numbers. The 1,202 active army surgeons were broken down as follows: 1,173 Turks, 9 Greeks, 17 Armenians, and 3 Jews; whereas the 1,353 reserve surgeons were composed of 528 Turks, 331 Greeks, 229 Armenians, 116 Jews, and 79 Catholic Maronites. The army medical corps suffered heavy losses during the Great War: 163 active surgeons and 186 reserve officers lost their lives either during the fighting or due to sickness, amounting to a 13.66 percent casualty rate.[56]

Dr. Tevfik Sağlam set off from Istanbul for Erzurum on 17 February 1915, together with Mahmut Kamil Pasha, who was assigned as the commander of the 3rd Army, and started his duty as the medical chief of the army on 14 March. On his way to Erzurum, he observed the medical situation and organization along the main line of the army stations, extending from Ulukışla to Erzurum. Upon his arrival at Erzurum, he received the following information from his predecessor, Dr. İbrahim Tali, on the medical situation in general: "Various diseases, particularly spotted fever and recurrent fever have caused the death of many doctors and pharmacists, and most of those who have recovered from those diseases are either at the stage of convalescence, or they are still in a very weak condition." As of mid-March 1915, the 3rd Army had a total of 255 doctors, 194 of whom were healthy, whereas 42 were sick and under treatment in the hospital, 12 were convalescing, and 7 were on sick leave and were sent to other places for a temporary change of environment. Furthermore, a total of 21 doctors from the army corps either had been taken as prisoners by the enemy or were missing. Most of the 44 new doctors, who were sent from Istanbul and started their duties in Erzurum after their journey between February 20 and March 5, soon became ill with spotted fever.[57]

The Ottoman Army put into place an interesting practice. Süleyman Numan, the field medical inspector general, understanding the difficulties borne by the doctors in Erzurum and appreciating the intensive efforts they spent despite all the difficulties and the diseases afflicting most of them, had promised to implement an exchange program between the doctors in Erzurum and in Istanbul. It was indeed disturbing to see those self-sacrificing individuals fulfilling their duties in a devoted manner although they just had recovered from illness and hardly had the power to stand. Besides the doctors, many officers had only recently recovered from spotted fever and were in need of sick leave and a temporary change of environment. Because the epidemic was still raging, however, replacing the doctors and officers who had recovered from spotted fever with new ones from Istanbul meant that almost all of those new personnel would catch the disease after a short while, that about one-third of them would lose their lives, and that the rest would not be able to work for a long time. These considerations forced the army authorities to make a tough decision: the army eventually agreed to keep the officers, and particularly the medical officers, who had recovered from spotted fever and had therefore gained a permanent immunity against that disease in their present posts, and not to call them back to Istanbul. Regardless of their suffering and desire to go back, they were kept and spent their convalescence period where they were stationed, resuming their duties after recovering. Although that particular military decision put a heavy burden on the shoulders of those personnel who had the disease, it also saved many new people from becoming ill and losing their lives.[58]

Under war conditions, some people could demonstrate unusual behavior. When the acting commander-in-chief Enver Pasha was visiting a hospital after the disastrous defeat of the Ottoman Army in Sarıkamış, he observed the tragic conditions of the patients, many of whom were lying together on the ground. These scenes made him angry and led him to accuse the doctors, thinking that they were responsible for that tragedy. He ordered tearing of the epaulets of Major İbrahim, who was the chief doctor at the hospital. The doctor, who was sent back to his unit as a private and on foot, died from sorrow on his way.[59]

Just as other Ottoman officers were fighting against the enemy, the

TABLE 8.2. Medical officers who died from disease*

YEAR / MONTHS	DEATHS
1914 months 1–6	3
1914 months 7–12	7
1915 months 1–6	101
1915 months 7–12	12
1916 months 1–6	67
1916 months 7–12	24
1917 months 1–6	45
1917 months 7–12	12
1918 months 1–6	16
1918 months 7–12	5

* Quoted from Kızılay Archives in Çapa, *Kızılay Hilal-I Ahmer Cemiyeti,* 120–121.

Ottoman medical officers were also involved in an intensive war; theirs was against a different kind of enemy, diseases. During that war, they never hesitated to sacrifice their own lives. From the Red Crescent delegation sent in 1915 to Erzurum, Dr. Mustafa Şakir, Dr. Mehmet Emin, research assistants Dr. Tacettin and Dr. Hasan Selahaddin, nurse's aides Fehim and Cevdet, and privates at the medical service named Mehmet (son of Mustafa) and Halil (son of Tahir), all lost their lives from disease.[60]

Many of the German medical personnel serving within the 2nd Army also became ill and would never see their homeland again. During the typhus epidemic in February 1916, a total of 42 Ottoman doctors lost their lives due to that disease alone.[61] Of the 163 medical officers who died on the Eastern front, there were 125 doctors, 24 pharmacists, 1 dentist, 6 surgeons, and 7 final-year students from the Faculty of Medicine. There were 124 Muslims, 19 Greeks, 17 Armenians, and 3 Jews.[62]

On the marble monument erected in 1946 by Dr. General Nahit Tunaşar, then medical chief of the 3rd Army, at the entrance of the Marshal Fevzi Çakmak Military Hospital in Erzurum, are the names of a total of 164 conscripted medical officers who died during World War I.

Different figures exist regarding the number of Ottoman medical officers who died while fighting against infectious diseases, particularly typhus, during the period of 1914–1917. According to one source, the number was 215.[63] Another list published in 1997 gives the same number as 301.[64] Because the names of some of the Ottoman medical officers listed in the first source mentioned, published by Mazhar Osman, were not included in the second source, we could reach the conclusion that the number of martyrs among medical officers was more than 301.[65]

EFFORTS TO SUPPLY HUMANITARIAN AID IN WORLD WAR I

On 4 February 1918, the acting commander-in-chief sent a telegram to the 3rd Army Command saying that, "in view of the massacres conducted by the Armenians and the Georgians, the 3rd Army is afforded the freedom to carry out offensive operations to protect our people living in the area, on the condition that such moves should not violate the truce made with the Russians." Upon receiving this message, the army moved forward on 12 February in the direction of Erzincan-Bayburt. During the course of that movement, the army recaptured several towns: Erzincan on 13 February, Bayburt on 19 February, Mamahatun on 22 February, Trabzon on 24 February, Erzurum on 12 March, Ardahan on 3 April, Van on 8 April, Batum on 14 April, Kars on 25 April, Gümrü on 15 May, and finally Karakilise on 26 May. At the end of May, an agreement was signed in Batum with the Azeris, Georgians, and Armenians. At that time, the numbers and conditions of the Russian and Georgian army personnel in Batum were as follows: 12 officers, 158 wounded soldiers, 11 wounded officers, and 180 ill soldiers. Also available were 46 doctors, 11 pharmacists, 24 medical noncommissioned officers, and 274 nurses and privates in the medical service. All of those personnel were released. Only the doctors among them, who previously had served as field medical officers, were assigned to the medical services of the other prisoners of war. They were also used in the fulfillment of various other medical duties. Other medical personnel were given the freedom to choose either to stay in Batum or to return to the Caucasus or elsewhere at the first opportunity.[66]

The Red Cross delegation in Batum was not formed as a hospital delegation; it rather consisted of smaller delegations accountable to the Russian Red Cross, and had carried out activities on the front and at the rear before the arrival of the Ottoman forces. As the members of the delegation were eager to continue their activities after the control of the city passed to the Ottoman army, they were offered the opportunity to organize themselves under the auspices of a hospital. In addition, as they were not paid by their headquarters, the Ottoman government decided to pay their salaries as long as they continued to work in the service of the Ottoman Army. Of the doctors taken into the service of the Ottoman army, or who continued to work for the Red Cross, the chief doctors were paid a salary equivalent to the salary of a major in the Ottoman Army, while other doctors were paid a salary equivalent to that of a captain (including any extra payments and increases in salaries).[67]

After the disaster caused by the epidemics in 1915, the Chief Doctor's Office of the Army also was given the responsibility to combat the infectious diseases affecting civilians living in the 3rd Army sector. As of 1917, the army was directly involved in the health conditions of the people living in the area, including refugees. The children, who were orphaned as a result of the migrations, were taken under the protection of the army, which saved the lives of many of them.[68] Within a period of ten months, the 3rd Army's health organization assumed the care of 17,116 children.[69]

As a result of the huge wave of migration in the wake of the fall of Erzincan, many children were abandoned along the roadsides, parentless and in miserable conditions. Under the orders of the Army Command, those children were taken into the custody of the army health authorities, and were provided with food and shelter starting from Suşehri on 28 July 1916. Of the first group of children taken under care, the ill were treated by the military whereas the healthier ones were sent to Sivas. By the end of July 1917, more than 700 children were gathered in Sivas under this program. The ongoing demand made expansion of the organizational structure for these activities necessary. On 28 August 1917, the following order was sent from the 3rd Army High Command to the Army Corps Commands: "The little homeless children wandering around in hunger and misery, or sleeping at inappropriate places within the army corps sector, shall be taken to hospitals and treated in order to save their lives. Following their recovery, those who have parents shall be returned to their parents, and the rest shall be sent to the station hospitals in the interior." In October 1917, on the orders of the Army, Talas and Zencidere hospitals admitted 200 and 100 children respectively, and later on, other hospitals also admitted more children. Within a period of nine months, the 3rd Army cared for a total of 16,416 children, providing them with clothes, food, and medical services; 1,527 of these, unfortunately, died. As of April 1918, some 5,403 children were still under the care of the army's health organizations.[70]

The 3rd Army, upon the request of the Chief Doctor's Office, presented a new proposal to the Supreme Command Headquarters on 9 June 1918 regarding the future of the orphaned children:

Currently 5,000 orphans are being cared for by the 3rd Army's health organization, half boys and half girls. Those who are old enough to attend junior reserve officer schools already do so. The rest have been sent to the recovery houses in Merzifon, Talas, and Zencidere. Allocation of these houses to these children would mean that their lives will be saved from absolute poverty. This practice will also benefit the Army; the boys could be raised to become future military officers, and the girls to become the nurses for the military hospitals. Should this proposal be found acceptable, we consider that it would be necessary to appoint a high-ranking officer as director to each of these institutions. In addition, sufficient number of teachers, governesses, and medical personnel to ensure the health of the children, as well as maids to do the housework and personnel to care for the infants will be required. It also is considered appropriate to put the administration of those houses under the authority of the Ministry of War. This arrangement would be the best option to respond to the difficulties to be encountered by those houses during the gradual withdrawal of the 3rd Army's back-up forces stationed at the rear. We firmly believe that if this proposal is approved, our country will have 5,000 well-educated young men and women in 10–15 years' time. Our intention is that our country will benefit enormously from these young people. I therefore kindly request you to order necessary measures for the realization of this important and beneficial project.[71]

Unfortunately, following the signing of the Mondros Armistice, this valuable humanitarian project could not be realized.

During the war years, several other humanitarian projects were carried out in the 4th Army sector, too, under the efforts and guidance of Cemal Pasha. Those activities focused mainly on children. Novelist Halide Edip, who personally participated in the efforts to find orphan children and bring them under the protection of the 4th Army sector, explains the following:

I have rarely felt the same spiritual self-satisfaction as I did during my efforts for the Aya Tura Orphanage. It was because those in great suffering were all children. All of them were in an unbelievable state of helplessness and misery, and they had done nothing to deserve being in that condition. When the group coming from Istanbul started to work here, in the first week of January, the orphanage was unbelievably dirty and deprived of resources. Nothing was in order. The administration of the orphanage was entrusted entirely to two good-hearted but incapable women, a few men, and a dozen soldiers. More than five hundred of the eight hundred children were ill. Every child, the beds (some of them were being used by three children), and everything was infested with lice. Even when you were walking along the stone corridor, you would step on the lice flowing along the corridor.... The children, small, older, ill, or healthy, could no longer be defined as young human beings. Just like animals, they were relieving themselves anywhere, publicly, in their beds, in other places. It was impossible to tell the boys from the girls by looking at their faces or clothes....

Seeing these conditions had made the people from Istanbul astonished, even scared. However, they still attempted to do something about the almost unendurable situation. First of all, the Director requested a hot air drying stove, and started to use it for disinfection. He spent every effort to boil everything, which could be boiled. In those days, our best chance was to have someone like Doctor Lütfü with us. He was sent from the front to help us. Through his efforts, all the lice were eradicated, and the filthiness, which had become virtually an epidemic of different diseases, was cured as much as possible, though the children remained in their previous strange condition.... I had stated that if the parents of the children in the orphanage came and proved their identities, I would give them their children.... Many Armenian women came and claimed their children. However, since very few Kurds or Turks were living in Beirut and Lebanon in general, no one came from among them.[72]

Edip recounts a very touching scene of a meeting, which reminds us of the fact that the war was full of very dramatic stories and suffering of people and families of every nationality and religion living in a wide area:

On my last visit to Aya Tura, as I was walking out the door, a man with a woman near to him came close to me. Looking at their clothes and faces, they did not seem to be from an Arab region. They asked me at which orphanage the Kurdish children were being kept. They took a neatly folded paper out of their pocket and showed it to me. They had come from Erzurum. They had moved from there when the Russian army led by General Antranik occupied the city. During their fleeing, they had lost their son, Hasan. After losing their son, they had walked from Anatolia to the Arab region, and had asked for their son at every orphanage along the way. On the paper in their hand, various orphanages wrote the following sentence: "Hasan was not brought here." Ours was the last orphanage that they could ask for their child. When Dr. Lütfü went into the orphanage with that piece of paper in his hand, my heart was also pounding as fast as that couple's. After half an hour, Dr. Lütfü came back. He was holding the hand of a little boy, who seemed quite clean, having nice clothes on, and carrying a bundle in his hand. I still remember clearly. It was evening time. Beneath the sky's scarlet colors of the sunset, the father and mother knelt down and raised their arms. The child came running, and threw himself into the arms of his parents. There, a father called Ramazan, son of Abdullah, met his lost son again.

Edip goes on to tell the following:

As I was returning back to Istanbul in March, together with a group of teachers after the schools were closed for vacation, Dr. Lütfü Bey and many teachers remained in Aya Tura. I requested Dr. Bliss and his son-in-law Mr. Dodge to put Aya Tura under the protection of the Red Cross as soon as the military operation starts in the area. Thanks to the Kaymakam (district governor) Kemal's efforts, enough food supply for the next four months was available. I also requested them to put the Armenian children in Aya Tura under the protection of the Red Crescent. They promised to do so, and kept their promise.[73]

9

EPILOGUE

An ounce of prevention is worth a pound of cure.

—Ben Franklin

The Turkish military doctor Osman Şevki made the following assessment of the Ottoman Muslim community:

> The cities were dirty, and the people were unaware of observing hygienic measures. As they had no knowledge about diseases, they did nothing to avoid them. The people believed that both health and illness were dependent on God's will, and trying to be protected from disease would be tantamount to defying God's authority. The entire country had become a nest of infectious diseases, particularly the plague.[1]

Kiesling, who also had in-depth knowledge of the Middle East, explains that the typhus epidemics which occurred during the Great War had a lot to do with the Muslims' tendency to refrain from killing insects. He goes on to add that the dirtiness also contributed to the rapid spread of the disease to wide areas.[2]

Writing In 1837, Moltke made interesting observations on the Balkan people's ways of approaching disease:

> The Turks believed that saying the name of a disease loud would invite that disease and infect them. The disease of plague was called "scamp." They thought that if they avoided saying the actual name, plague, they would be protected from that disease. Whereas, the Greeks believed that Panaiya would have mercy on them and not send any illness. Bulgarians viewed the disease as a witch. For example, a Bulgarian woman could be heard saying "the witch of the night has taken my man and children, leaving me alone."[3]

Another well-known Turkish medical authority, Professor A. Süheyl Ünver, also wrote that the Turks' fatalism caused them not to take any measures even in the face of the most lethal epidemics:

> The fatalism of the Turks makes them believe that human beings can never change their fate which is determined unalterably by God. So they see the measures taken by the Europeans not only as useless, but also as an immense sin. None of them, however, appear to feel disgusted while caring for their beloved ones who became ill, and they never abandoned the sick to their fate.[4]

In the early twentieth century, some strange practices prevalent in Ottoman society regarding diseases were even reflected in the minutes of parliamentary debates. Speaker Ahmet Rıza's address during discussions on the health budget for the year 1918 in the Meclis-i Ayan (Ottoman Senate House) was revealing:

> Mr. Director claims that during this year typhus has slowed down in our country compared to the previous year, and he tries to prove his claims by presenting numerous graphics and statistics. Indeed, the disease appears to have decreased among the civilians compared to the previous year, but it has increased within the Army. The increase was almost twofold. Although that gentleman is the Director General of Health, he doesn't seem to be taking into account the situation in the Army. We should remember that the army members are also our citizens, and we should be concerned about their health.

Speaker of the Senate Rıza continued his speech by explaining the reasons behind the decrease in typhus cases in the cities under Ottoman rule:

> The decline in the typhus in our country is related to two factors. I would request Mr. Director to correct me if I am wrong. One of those reasons is, as Mr. Director also admitted, the doctors' tendency to hide the cases of typhus. Mr. Director says that when typhus is encountered in a house, our own doctors do not record it as typhus. That means we don't know the exact number of patients with typhus. Furthermore, as stated by Mr. Director again, the patients' families also prefer to call doctors who they think will hide the disease. What could be their reason for doing this? It could only be because they think that if the doctor informs the official authorities

about the disease, the patient would immediately be taken to a hospital. And, considering the current situation of our hospitals, who wants to go to a hospital? It would be equal to accepting to die! Of course, both the patient and the patient's families prefer to hide the cases of typhus because they reason that: "let's hide the disease from the government authorities and the Directorate of Health. If they hear about the disease they will immediately take the patient to an unspeakable place by taking them on a very bad stretcher, and they will kill the patient there." So, the information given about the low number of cases of typhus must be based on the two reasons I've just told you.[5]

Rıza also said the following about the inadequacy of the statistical data presented by Dr. Adnan Adıvar, the general director of health, and about the deaths occurring within the army due to typhoid:

I'm not claiming that these are all lies. The point I am making is that those authorities don't have sufficient means to record information. In fact, they admit it too. Therefore, I could say that the information they have presented to us is not wrong, but rather inadequate.

The actual number of patients might be ten times more than what we are told. Furthermore, they only have talked about civilian hospitals, and please forgive me for using that term, civilian patients. Nothing has been said about the military patients. In fact, the largest number of illnesses and deaths from infections are seen among the members of the army. This year, the illnesses of the civilians appear to have been more benign than those affecting the military personnel. Every day many deaths are occurring in the army due to diseases. Mr. Director said that only 6 cases of disease were encountered in Heybeliada. This is not true. The disease exists on Heybeliada, and on the other islands.[6]

ACHIEVEMENTS AND FAILURES

Staff Lieutenant Colonel Köprülülü Şerif, who took part in the Battle of Sarıkamış, had a significant assessment regarding the sources of failures: "Unless the civilian administration is run through a modern and scientific approach, the military organization cannot be maintained properly in case of a mobilization. Therefore, every preparation should be made in peacetime."[7]

The Ottoman Empire could not put into practice this principle when the general mobilization was declared on 20 July 1914. It would, however, be unfair to say that the state authorities did not take any measures. As a matter of fact, just before the beginning of the Great War, various kinds of infectious diseases had become widespread over most of Istanbul. Typhoid, cholera, and smallpox were prevalent in the neighborhoods of Kartal, Tuzla, Yakacık, Soğanlık, Maltepe, Ayastefanos, and Makriköy in that city. In order to prevent the spreading of those diseases to the army units, as a precautionary measure, the troops were stationed in tents, which were set up in areas quite far away from towns and cities.[8] Moreover, the cruises between Yalova and Istanbul were cancelled temporarily,[9] and the Quarantine Establishment in Sinop was prepared to be ready for the ships sailing to the Black Sea.[10] Following the declaration of mobilization, the Office of the Army Medical Chief, in cooperation with the 2nd Army, started to combat the infectious diseases encountered in the northern Anatolia region.[11]

At the beginning of 1915, the major activities of the Ottoman Army's medical units involved not only the treatment of the ill and wounded, but also the fight against infectious diseases, which were spreading through the rear areas of the 3rd Army sector and Istanbul and its environs.[12] It needs to be noted that these measures could be taken and implemented only in and around Istanbul. No significant and effective measure could be taken in other Anatolian cities, along the transportation routes, and particularly on the battlefields.

In the wake of the Ottoman Army's retreat in eastern Anatolia in 1916, the people living in the areas evacuated by the army poured into the roads, creating extremely miserable scenes. Since there was no civilian organization in place to deal with the health needs of the hundreds of thousands of refugees, the military doctors had to assume the duty of providing for the medical examinations and treatment of those people. After the Russian occupation of Erzincan, the first station for examining and quarantining the refugees fleeing from Karahisar and Erzincan was set up on 27 July 1916. At various stations established for the same purpose, a total of 65,778 individuals were examined, 22,499 of whom were given the first cholera vaccine, 9,607 were given the second dose of cholera vaccine, and 11,999 were vaccinated against smallpox.[13] During the same year, when infectious diseases such as plague, tuberculosis, typhus, cholera, recurrent fever, dysentery, typhoid, paratyphus, and syphilis began to spread all over the country, the Ottoman government allocated an additional amount of 3 million kuruş to the special budget for contagious and infectious diseases.[14]

On 7 January 1917, the General Directorate of Health assigned the primary responsibility for fighting against infectious diseases in the provinces of Ankara, Sivas, Erzurum, and Trabzon, as well as in the sanjaks of Niğde,

Kayseri, and Canik to the 3rd Army's Office of Medical Chief. At a time when almost all of Anatolia was suffering from epidemics, an extremely insufficient struggle was being carried out against them. The General Directorate of Health had no capabilities to conduct an effective struggle against those epidemics. The army, as a result, had to get involved actively in securing the health conditions in the military sector. However, "no matter how much the army cleans itself from the infections, unless the villages and the people living in the same area are cleaned too, the soldiers in contact with those people would eventually catch diseases, or the soldiers from the supply units passing through those villages would render the army vulnerable to those diseases."[15] The migrations, on the other hand, served as a catalyst for spreading diseases such as cholera, spotted fever, and even smallpox. Tasking the army with the responsibility to combat against epidemics affecting the civilian population was indeed an appropriate decision. Those parts of Trabzon and Erzurum provinces which were not occupied by the Russian forces, as well as the provinces of Ankara and Sivas, and the sanjaks of Niğde, Kayseri, and Canik fell within the 3rd Army sector. These were the main areas where the army units carried out intensive struggle against infectious diseases of many kinds: the louse-borne diseases such as spotted fever and recurrent fever, the diseases that are transmitted by agents found in the intestines, such as typhoid, paratyphoid, cholera, and dysentery, and other infectious diseases such as smallpox, diphtheria, measles, and scarlet fever. Malaria and syphilis, too, were endemic in the area.[16]

Despite the extensive efforts spent during World War I, the medical services on the frontlines remained far from responding effectively to the needs because of the difficulties caused by the war, as well as many other challenges. The large distances between the fronts also amplified problems due to logistical issues. Great difficulties were encountered in transferring patients, medical personnel, medicines, and the necessary medical equipment needed for treatment. Poor roads and primitive means of transportation also complicated the transfers. Not only munitions, but also medical supplies were used up. The tents used as shelters by soldiers were worn out. What is more, as those tents were badly ventilated and dark inside, they were having a bad effect on the health of the soldiers.[17]

Another adversity of the Great War that affected the medical conditions in the Ottoman Empire was the suspension of imports of medicines and medical equipment. This crucial historical fact was underlined by the German pharmacist Helmut Becker, who studied the situation in the Ottoman Empire in terms of the services provided by the hospitals, and the hygiene conditions as of 1914.[18]

MILITARY HOSPITALS

Liman von Sanders observes the following about the situation in the Ottoman military hospitals prior to the war:

> Most of the Turkish military hospitals were in terrible conditions. An extreme dirtiness and all kinds of bad odors made the overcrowded hospital wards virtually unendurable to stay in. Clinic patients of internal and external diseases were being placed in the same wards, and even were sometimes lying in the same beds. Since the number of beds was insufficient, most of the patients were lying on cushions, or on army blankets placed on the floor in closely spaced rows in the corridors.
>
> Most of those soldiers, already in a weakened condition, were dying even before receiving any treatment. Because I openly expressed my displeasure of the situation during my visits to such hospitals, and even reported the doctors who caused the problems to the Ministry of War, I made a fame for my fussiness.[19]

Dr. Abdülkadir Noyan, too, provides valuable insight into the conditions of the military hospitals in Mosul and Baghdad, which were located in the 6th Army's sector. Writing in December 1915, he also recorded striking examples that reveal the inadequacies of those hospitals:

> The situation of the hospitals in Mosul was terrible. The patients were lying on mattresses placed on the floor side by side. Nor were they sorted according to their diseases. The patients as well as the hospital beds were infested with lice. I had to sit on those beds to examine the patients one by one. Most of the patients were showing symptoms of spotted fever. I prepared a long report in order to inform the Field Medical Inspectorate of the situation.
>
> Since the Military Central Hospital and the Red Crescent Hospital in Baghdad were unsatisfactory for treating the ill and wounded, after the Selmanpak Battle, new hospitals were established in large summer palaces, called "Kasır," on the banks of the Tigris River. Five hospitals, having a total bed capacity of 1,300, were opened in those Kasırs. I visited all of those hospitals. The most damaging infectious disease I encountered among the patients in every hospital was spotted fever and dysentery. The patients carrying those diseases were put into the Jewish School.[20]

A note the military hospital in Mosul sent to the 6th Army Command in February 1916 stated that the reason why the army suffered a large number of deaths was not due to the fact that the patients were not treated in the hospital. Rather, the real cause of the deaths was the fact that the troops arriving from Istanbul, or from other places far away from Iraq, had to walk for months in the rain. The reserve soldiers, who were not used to walking such long distances, were particularly affected. Those long walks in the rain naturally invited many diseases. For example, battalions of the 6th Regiment had a total of twelve hundred men when setting off from Istanbul. By the time they reached Mosul, however, they had had to leave half of their men at various locations along the road. Another reason for the high number of deaths occurring in the military hospital was, according to the same report, the lack of medical personnel. The hospital doctors were also ill. A doctor serving in Baghdad died because of an illness around that time. A doctor and a pharmacist in Nusaybin became ill with typhoid. One of the civilian doctors in Mosul was being treated for spotted fever. The number of patients per doctor was about two hundred.[21]

During the retreat of the Ottoman Army in eastern Anatolia in the face of the Russian offensive, mentioned earlier, the insufficiency of transportation made the suffering of the patients in hospitals particularly acute. A total of 18,080 patients needed to be transferred from Erzurum to Erzincan during the coldest days of February before the occupation of Erzurum by the Russians. Dr. Nazım Şakir, who was tasked to oversee necessary preparations for that transfer, reports the following:

> Since ill and wounded from the front were flowing constantly, we could not sleep for three days. Especially I will never forget the difficulties we met during our ceaseless efforts to load patients wrapped in quilts onto carts to send them to Erzurum in a severe snowstorm in our last night in Erzurum.
>
> When we left Erzurum to go to Erzincan via the route of Ilıca, Yeniköy, and Tercan the next day, I did not see any of those carts on the road. I was saddened thinking that they must have died in temperatures below minus twenty degrees. In addition, the sorrow I felt at leaving our country to the enemy was making my heart bleed.[22]

Commenting on the same incidents, Dr. Tevfik Sağlam wrote the following in his report from March 1916:

> Although we were obliged not to leave many patients back in Erzincan, our means for the transfer of patients were insufficient. Under those conditions, we had to send most of the patients from Erzincan to Sivas on foot. Despite

the establishment of medical centers at close distances to each other along the road, those distances could still take a minimum of 15–20 days given the walking speeds of the patients. These patients could be given nothing more than bread and hot soup at those centers. Those limited means put them into an unavoidable misery on the roads. The ill and wounded sent to Sivas under those conditions were usually very exhausted when they arrived there. Even in Sivas, despite all the efforts of the chief doctor, the miseries of the patients did not cease because of the lack of care and assistance that should have been provided by the governorate. As a result, large numbers of patients remained in great deprivation, and their health conditions deteriorated further.[23]

GERMAN DOCTORS IN OTTOMAN ARMIES

During the Great War, several German military doctors and health specialists were serving in the Ottoman armies. The German medical team sent to Trabzon under very adverse conditions in January 1915 consisted of five doctors and six nurse's aides. After working for five months in Trabzon, the team went to Istanbul and carried out its duties there until the signing of the Truce.[24] During 1915 and 1916, three German doctors served in Erzincan, one of whom died from typhus. The other two continued to work until they became very ill and were unable to work any longer. Two nurse's aides served in Erzurum at a time when the typhus epidemic was very severe.[25] During the period of 1914–1918, the main priority of several Red Cross teams serving on the battlefields was to fight against typhus, and a number of them died as a result of the adverse conditions they were working in.[26]

The German doctors provided a great contribution especially in the field of bacteriology. A German Mobile Bacteriology Laboratory, which arrived in Ankara in the fall of 1916, was located in a place equidistant to each of the six hospitals in the city. The mobile laboratory remained in Ankara for eight months, and during that time a total of 10,190 individuals underwent medical examination there. Ninety percent of the patients examined in that laboratory consisted of army members who were either ill or checked voluntarily in the laboratory, while 10 percent consisted of civilians. In addition, those examinations provided information about the situation in the hospitals. The disease causing the greatest number of deaths within the army was typhus. Though a specific study was not performed regarding the civilians, many of them were also losing their lives from typhus. During the first six months of 1917, about 51 percent of the cases of typhus in hospitals resulted in death. Recurrent fever was the next most fatal disease in Ankara. About the same time, the bacteriologists were expecting an outbreak of malaria around Ankara.[27]

It appears that German doctors also had political and military duties during the Great War. A typical example of the political duties carried out by the German doctors between the years of 1915 and 1918 is illustrated in a note written regarding the appointment of a German doctor to the medical office of the railways administration in Konya. That note, sent on 25 July 1915 to the German Navy Headquarters, emphasized the following: "Appointment of the German doctors to such positions will make it possible to influence large numbers of people." Therefore, the German authorities deemed it appropriate to appoint a naval doctor, Dr. Börnstein, who was a gynecologist and surgeon, to that position in the railways administration. Although Dr. Börnstein's main duty was to fight against typhus, he was also caring for the general health of the civilian population.[28]

"ONE MILLION PATIENTS OF TYPHUS"

Andre Raymond observed the spread of infectious diseases in Cairo in the years 1718, 1759, 1785, and 1789. Al-Budayri also observed the same phenomenon in Damascus in 1743 and in Aleppo in 1787. Hunger was a very key factor in accelerating the spread of dysentery and typhus.[29] A similar effect of hunger was also observed in the Ottoman Empire during the Great War. A significant correlation exists between typhus and extreme poverty. Typhus epidemics have broken out mostly during periods when people not only had little to eat, but also had very limited opportunities to clean themselves up and were living in adverse conditions.

An authoritative source refers to the large number of Ottoman casualties suffered on the Caucasian front due to diseases and hunger as follows:

> Despite the very serious losses at Dardanelles, the effective strength of the Ottoman army reached its maximum in November 1915: 800,000. By 1 March 1917 it had fallen to 400,000 and it never again exceeded this total (200,000 in March 1918). In the summer of 1916, out of a total of fifty-two Ottoman divisions, twenty-six were fighting the Russians. Out of the 400,000 lost by the Turks during the period November 1915 to March 1917, not less than 300,000 must be accounted to the campaigns against the Russians (including prisoners and casualties from epidemics and desertion). If the losses at Gallipoli seriously shook the military power of the Ottoman empire and prevented, at a crucial moment, the mounting of any effective

offensive against the Transcaucasia frontier, the subsequent losses against the Russians in 1916 were decisive in destroying the remaining strength of the Ottoman army and prepared the way for the British victories in Iraq in 1917–18 and in Palestine in 1918.[30]

With the beginning of the war in 1914, the entire Ottoman territories became susceptible to the outbreak of epidemics. During the four-year-long war, louse-borne diseases—typhus being the most significant one—were encountered most frequently in the country and accounted for the greatest number of losses. Being caused by a certain type of rickettsia, it starts with a headache and high fever and causes exanthema on the skin. It lasts for about two weeks and can often be fatal especially for the elderly people. For centuries, typhus has caused the death of large numbers of people. In medical literature, various names have been used for typhus: spotted fever, classical typhus, and European typhus. In the Ottoman Empire, typhus was mostly confused with typhoid and was frequently referred to as typhoid fever.[31]

Rickettsiae, the agents of typhus, have been the insidious enemies of humanity throughout history, always hiding themselves during healthy and strong periods in the history of various societies, then reappearing during their weakened times. Therefore, typhus epidemics have broken out during wars, migrations, and other conditions that cause people to be thrown into deep poverty. As a result, typhus came to be considered an infectious disease, widespread throughout the world, turning into epidemics during times of war, extreme poverty, and hunger. Those are times when human societies mostly are uncared for, become susceptible to diseases, and are unable to implement the basic rules of hygiene. The underdeveloped countries, in that sense, can never completely get rid of typhus. In the epidemiology of typhus, the louse, which is one of the human parasites, appears as the most important means of transmission. A connection between typhus and the weather also has been widely recognized in the literature. In the cold months of autumn, the number of patients starts to increase. The epidemics spread even further toward the end of winter, reaching their maximum level in the months of February and March. After that, a gradual decrease is noted in the number of patients. Lice, the main agent spreading the disease, do not like light, hot environments, and open air. Due to the fact that during the cold seasons people are in greater contact with each other, and many of them live together in the villages, in houses, or in barracks, the rickettsia-bearing lice can easily cause epidemics and pandemics. During the Great War, a minimum of one million people caught typhus.[32]

Typhoid is another important infectious disease raging widely during wartime, and it is closely related to the hygienic conditions of water and food supplies. It, too, is common within the armies. Throughout history, typhoid epidemics of various scales of severity have been observed in the course of almost every war. Typhoid epidemics are also connected to seasonal conditions. The infection appears in early July and rapidly spreads through August. After reaching its peak level in October, it starts to decrease.[33]

Recurrent fever, one of the diseases most frequently encountered during the Great War, has been in existence since very early times. It has been confused mostly with typhus and thought to be a mild type of typhus. One thing that adds to that confusion is the fact that the epidemics of recurrent fever generally start at almost the same time as typhus epidemics. This is mainly because the conditions preparing the ground for outbreaks of recurrent fever are the same as the ones seen in the cases of rickettsia infections. Lice and ticks also transmit recurrent fever.[34]

CARRIERS OF DEATH

Another way through which diseases spread during the years of the Great War was by the movement of prisoners of war, deserters, and refugees. The Ottoman soldiers, transferred to India or Siberia after being taken prisoner by the British in Iraq and by the Russians in the Caucasus respectively, were severely hit by typhus. Especially many among those who were carried on trains to Siberia died during the long voyage due to lack of any medical care and medicine. Their dead bodies quickly hardened because of the extremely cold weather after being thrown out on the rails like logs, and were devoured by the wolves and dogs.[35]

The deserters from the Ottoman Army also played a crucial role in spreading infectious diseases. Since the number of deserters reached very high figures, they posed severe and permanent dangers. In 1938, General Ali Fuat Cebesoy explained the reasons leading to the increase in desertions (from 30 to 50 percent) in 1916–1917 as follows:

1. After two years passed since the beginning of the war, nobody was given home leave.

2. Although the battles incessantly continued in unendurably hot or cold weather conditions, none of the essential needs of the soldiers could be met, in even a simple and primitive way. Moreover, food was scarce and of low quality. Most of the time, even, no food could be served. To put it briefly, unimaginable misery and deprivation were prevalent.

3. Excluding the battles of Çanakkale, none of the Ottoman units fighting on the front was exchanged with other units from time to time; on the contrary, those units were kept permanently at the trenches with the intention of holding the fronts with a smaller force.

4. Though the armies were constantly losing in strength because of illnesses and desertions, further officers and soldiers were being drawn from them in order to set up new organizational structures.[36]

The soldiers sent from their units to other places for medical reasons and the deserters were carrying the disease to the interior. Diseases spread along the main line on which the military stations were located, and also on the roads between Erzurum-Kiği-Palu-Maden-Diyarbakır and Erzurum-Erzincan-Harput-Diyarbakır, as well as in the surrounding villages.

The winter of 1916–1917 arrived early and was bitterly cold. To the Ottoman 2nd and 3rd armies, this particularly severe winter proved disastrous and accelerated their disintegration, which had begun as a result of their failures in the field. Deserters became a social problem of the first order. Those who could not get work in the villages—and they found a less friendly welcome as the hard highland winter came down on the pauperized peasantry—took to the hills where they formed armed bands whose only livelihood lay in brigandine. In October at least fifty thousand deserters were wandering in the rear of the Third Army. Actual number of troops had fallen to less than thirty thousand despite the fact that the contingents of the 53rd Division issued new drafts to fill in gaps in the different corps. Heavy snowfall at last checked desertions and many men returned to take advantage of the meager rations they could find in their units. The number of soldiers under Vehib Pasha's command again began to grow, but typhus and cold offset these again.[37]

Refugees were the most dramatic victims of the war. They could also be seen as the unluckiest sector of society, considering the very heavy losses they suffered and the role they played in the transmission of infectious diseases. As discussed in Chapter 7, Joseph Pomiankowsky, the then Austrian military attaché in Istanbul, made interesting remarks on the role of the Armenian convoys deported to Syria in spreading infectious diseases.[38] Similar to the diffusion of typhus to the 4th Army sector by the Armenians, who were settled in Syria, Muslim refugees escaping from the Russian forces in 1916 also brought the same diseases to the places they took shelter in. The spread of typhus rapidly accelerated after the Russians occupied Erzurum on 16 February 1916, Bitlis on 3 March, Muş immediately after that, Trabzon on 18 April, Bayburt on 15 July, Gümüşhane on 20 July, and Erzincan on 24 July.[39]

With the arrival of the Armenian deportees in Syria in September 1915, the typhus epidemic, which previously had been confined to Gazze and Aliye, spread all over the 4th Army sector. At that time, Dr. Mühlens, the medical consultant of the 4th Army, was in Germany, and Dr. Galip, the medical chief of the 4th Army, was undergoing medical treatment in Istanbul. Therefore, Dr. Neşet Ömer, the chief of the Red Crescent team in Suez, was appointed as the acting medical consultant of the 4th Army at the rank of major. After he took office, Dr. Ömer convened all the doctors and briefed them about typhus. He also ordered the publication of booklets in Turkish and Arabic on the measures to be taken. Aleppo was divided into eighteen medical zones, and two doctors were appointed to each of them. Nine military detachments having the duty of cleaning individuals were appointed to a cleaning station. There, each day around three thousand individuals were cleaned and those infected with typhus were separated and sent to the hospital for epidemic diseases. Those measures bore some fruits, and the incidence rate for typhus, which previously had been 250 cases per day, was decreased to a level of 10 cases per month.[40]

CRITICAL QUESTIONS

Justin McCarthy believes that the ratio of Turkish widows, according to the 1927 census in Turkey, offers a good indicator of the military and civilian casualties suffered by the Turks during the Great War (1914–1918) and the War of Liberation (1919–1922). According to McCarthy's calculations, the provinces where the ratio of widows was higher than 30 percent among the entire adult female population were located in the areas on the route followed by the advancing Greek army, in western and central Anatolia where the battles had taken place. None of the other countries involved in the Great War suffered as much as Anatolia. Britain, France, and Germany did indeed experience a real and drastic "lost generation." Nonetheless, a population increase was recorded in the case of both the United Kingdom and Germany between the years of 1911 and 1922, whereas a decrease of only 1 percent occurred in France. On the other hand, Anatolia lost 30 percent of its population: 10 percent through emigration to other countries and 20 percent due to death.[41]

These figures naturally raise the following question: What led the Ottoman military and civilian elites to join World War I? A study published by the Turkish General Staff in 1970 offers significant insights to this question. Based on a detailed analysis of each component of overall fighting power, the study argues that as of 1914, given its combat power the Ottoman Army was not in a situation to initiate a war, nor to sustain a war on its own should it find itself in a war. Its geopolitical and strategic position, however, made it impossible for the Ottoman Empire to remain neutral in a world war. Given the inevitability of being drawn into war, the Ottoman policymakers reasoned that the most prudent course of action in the case of a world war would be to ally with a strong European country that would willingly provide sufficient support and equip the Ottoman Army. "To that end, after negotiations with each of the blocs, eventually an alliance was formed with Germany."[42]

This account of the Ottoman Empire's decision to join the war on the side of Germany in 1914 is succinct and reasonable. Nonetheless, the debate on the outcomes of that war, and the complete dissolution of a very large empire, has been going on for many years. An unequivocal explanation of *why* the Ottoman Empire took that course of action, which would satisfy everyone, is unlikely to be offered, as various individuals and organizations have their own views on the subject. No doubt, disagreements also may arise regarding the total numbers of military and civilian casualties suffered due to various incidents that occurred during the war. Such disagreements are likely to be settled over time through new and more elaborate scientific studies. It is also hoped that through a fresh evaluation of history in light of the new findings obtained, we would also develop a better insight into the causes of those casualties.

Based on my research, in this study I have shown that an extremely high number of deaths occurred in Anatolia, Syria, the Thrace, and Iraq, particularly due to diseases. The study has also illustrated the connection between various epidemics that accompanied different wars. For instance, the typhus epidemic of 1915 that spread all over the region was a result of dispatching large number of troops at the end of the Balkan Wars. Despite a decline in the number of cases of typhus, after the general mobilization was declared at the beginning of World War I, severe typhus epidemics quickly resumed.[43] The movement of refugees, deportees, and deserters was the main factor behind the spread of the disease during the Great War. In particular, the discharged soldiers coming from Erzurum and its vicinity, where that disease was endemic, played the major role. In fact, every individual living in Anatolia in 1915 was at great risk, since typhus and cholera existed everywhere and were spread both by the deportees and by the Ottoman troops.

Moreover, throughout the book I have endeavored to show that not only the dead, but also those who survived had to endure hardships and miseries of war and epidemics. For one example, Mrs. Christie, the director of the Tarsus American School, recounts her experiences with contagious disease epidemics in her notes from 13 November and 28 November 1915.[44] Mrs. Christie and William L. Nute could not escape the epidemics that spread all over Tarsus. As they did not trust the doctors in Tarsus, they went to the Missionary Hospital in Adana for treatment.[45] Most of the people of any nation and religion living in the Ottoman territories under the war conditions, however, were not as lucky as the teaching staff of the Tarsus American School. Lieutenant Ragıp Bey, the son of the chief clerk from Kayseri, witnessed the following scene in Suşehri on 30 March 1915:

> In a ruined garden located in a high place at the entrance to the city, we saw the bodies of many Turks, who lost their lives due to illness and poverty. They were lying on snow, either naked, or in very old clothes. Since no organization to deal with their burial was available, they were still lying on the ground, arousing feelings of distress in those who see them. Because of that frightful scene, we started to lose our courage.[46]

EPIDEMIC CASUALTIES

According to Dr. Major General Ekrem Şadi, those who died from illness during the Great War constituted 18.3 percent of all the dead.[47] During the war, a total of 25 million individuals became ill with typhus, 6 million of whom lost their lives.[48] The severest epidemics of typhus were encountered on the Ottoman eastern front.[49] Within the 3rd Army fighting on the eastern front, out of a total 12,642 individuals who became ill during 1915–1918 with dysentery, 5,942 lost their lives.[50] Malaria was another disease causing many deaths. While three quarters of the Ottoman population was already suffering from malaria, the outbreak of the war further increased the seriousness of the problem posed by that disease. Within a period of four years, a total of 412,000 soldiers became ill with malaria, 20,000 of whom died.[51]

As was discussed in Chapter 4, a study has showed unequivocally that the Sarıkamış Battle was one of the main factors in triggering the spread of infectious diseases at the beginning of the Great War. The disaster of Sarıkamış lasted for eighteen days, between 22 December 1914 and 9 January 1915. The army virtually melted away due to complete exhaustion and severe cold as it was fighting against the enemy under great difficulties. When the 9th and 10th army corps finally made it to Sarıkamış, they consisted of a handful of exhausted soldiers. When the intelligence arrived on 29 December indicating that the Russians were in retreat, the Ottoman Army could not find the power to start an offensive. It was so cold that even the feet of the army's chief of staff, the medical chief, and the first aide-de-camp were frozen. "The winter and the deprivation, which perished several divisions, certainly did the same to the medical companies and the mobile medical units."[52] During the severe epidemics that spread in the aftermath of the Sarıkamış Battle, 53 percent of the typhus patients, 52 percent of the typhoid patients, 37.6 percent of the dysentery patients, and 29 percent of the recurrent fever patients lost their lives.[53]

Dr. Tevfik Sağlam, the medical chief of the 3rd Army, offers the following assessment in regard to the medical services and organization:

> [Based on our experience at the Battle of Sarıkamış], the most important point which should be underlined is that medical precautions had been ignored entirely before launching such an important military operation, which was carried out during the coldest days of winter and under the most adverse conditions. The orders given for carrying out the military preparations and for starting the offensive in Sarıkamış contained no reference to the medical pre-arrangements. During the military operation, the medical services on the front became completely out of control. The operation was destined to end in a disaster, and that disaster indeed happened. The failure to appreciate the value of establishing a hospital system, which would operate in good order both on the frontline and at the rear areas, and arranging roads to be used for transportation during the planning stages of military campaigns has always been punished by such a disaster.[54]

For Dr. Sağlam another lesson of the Sarıkamış Battle was the following: in such a military operation, many wounded and many ill would certainly be inevitable, especially during severe winter conditions. Indeed, the army was besieged entirely by infectious diseases:

> The medical organization at the rear, however, was far from responding to the needs. No arrangement was made to set up roads to be used in the transfer of the ill and wounded. To sum up, before launching such a large-scale military operation, the medical issues were never given sufficient attention.[55]

İsmet İnönü also offers valuable observations on how a typhus epidemic spread throughout the army immediately after the Battle of Sarıkamış:

> We suffered heavy casualties at the Battle of Sarıkamış, and had to retreat and go back to our positions on the border. Immediately after the battle,

our army fell entirely into the clutches of typhus. In those days, typhus was accepted as a great disaster which could happen at times of war.[56]

Even after the tragic experience of the disaster of Sarıkamış, while a military buildup in Erzurum was being planned, the orders given contained no reference to medical measures or medical organization. The only order was the following: "after the disasters suffered previously, gather the troops and provide military training for them." However, no thought seems to be spent "on the disasters which could occur as a result of a military campaign carried out under such adverse conditions, and on how many of the troops gathered in this way the army could use effectively."[57]

In December 2004, in commemoration of the ninetieth year of the Sarıkamış disaster, General Hilmi Özkök, the chief of general staff, issued a message. The message included an important lesson derived from the Sarıkamış experience: "When evaluated in terms of the management science, the Sarıkamış incident constitutes a very good example that illustrates well the distinctions between fantasy and truth, and between unmanageable and manageable risks."[58] The risk management referred to by the chief of staff certainly pertains to the infectious diseases that broke out in the aftermath of the Sarıkamış Battle. The Supreme Command Headquarters of the Ottoman Armies failed to take into account that important factor during the planning phase of the campaign.

As this study demonstrated, other armies that fought in the Great War also suffered significant casualties. In the case of the Ottoman Empire, however, the numbers, as well as the level of the suffering due to the epidemics, were beyond comparison. To reiterate yet another example, we could look at a joint American-Armenian report prepared in 1918 regarding the deaths that occurred during the typhus epidemic in 1915, which reflects the bitter truth very clearly:

> In 1915 Typhus fever caused the death of around 200,000–300,000 people. Several hundred of the physicians sent by the Turkish government to cope with it became infected and died. In Erzurum region, where around 60,000 to 100,000 people died, soap, water, and fuel could hardly be obtained anywhere during the epidemic.[59]

A report Senator Henry Cabot Lodge submitted to the American Senate, dated 13 April 1920, emphasized that the male population between 20 and 35 years of age was strikingly low in Anatolia, due to the fact that only about 20 percent of the Turkish villagers recruited into the army were able to return back to their homes, and that the number of Ottoman soldiers who died from typhus alone was as high as 600,000.[60]

My research has helped lift a "blackout of war" that has been imposed for ninety years on the academic literature concerning the military and civilian losses caused by infectious diseases in Anatolia, Syria, Mesopotamia, and the Caucasus. It also provides new insight into the medical conditions at the Ottoman battlefronts in the Great War, as well as the medical status of the civilian populations under war conditions. The findings put forth in this study are thought provoking, and are full of bitter lessons for anyone longing for the establishment of a sound cooperation between nations and governments around the world. As the study has shown, the egregious disasters did not afflict narrowly defined "national" communities. Rather, the devastation of World War I, including the diseases and epidemics that sprang from it, affected every nation that was involved in the conflict. Instead of casting blame on one nation or another, let every nation and every government heed the lessons to be learned from the bitter and tragic consequences of the Great War.

APPENDIX 1

A TESTIMONY OF THE TURKISH RESERVE OFFICER ON TYPHUS EPIDEMIC AT OTTOMAN ARMY, IN 1915**

"Our Armies Were Defeated by the Winter Cold and Typhus"

INTERVIEWER: Mr. Cindoruk, you are a man who fought on those fronts, under the most merciless conditions of war. I know that your life could be the subject of an entire book, but now, in a short conversation between us, I would like to discuss, at least a small part of your past experiences. Particularly I should like to listen to your memories about what happened to our armies fighting on the East Anatolian Mountains, and about your experiences there. When did you join the army?

MR. CINDORUK: My dear son, I was called to the military service in 1915, when I was 20 years old. I was a student then at the high school of Cartography within the Darülfünun (university). First, I was taken to the drill ground in Yakacık. There, I started to receive military training.

INTERVIEWER: The drill ground in Yakacık, was it something like today's reserve officer schools? How were the conditions then?

---

* Vasfi Cindoruk, who had fought in the Great War, was born in Istanbul in 1895. He was drafted into the Army in 1915, when he was a student of cartography at the School of Engineering. He lost one eye because of typhus. After the war, he could not continue his university education since his school had been closed. However, he became a topographical engineer by taking the external examinations. Following the foundation of the Republic, he worked as a topographical engineer, and prepared the development plans of various cities. He also worked together with the well-known German Architect Jansen, who had prepared the development plans for Ankara. In 1960, he retired from his duty as the director of the Cartography Department of Vilayets Bank. This historical interview was done with his nephew Emin Çölaşan, and was first published in the Turkish daily newspaper, *Hürriyet*. Vasfi Cindoruk, who was the father of Hüsamettin Cindoruk, the ex-speaker of the Turkish Grand National Assembly, died on 1 April 1990. / HÖ.

Mr. Cindoruk: As you also know, we were then allies with the Germans. We had Turkish and German commanders there, but in general we disliked the German officers. One day, a German Lieutenant Colonel named Herr Rabe gathered all of us together and, apparently he was angry about something, he shouted at us, "You ass," In response, all of us standing there on the drill ground, as if it had been planned beforehand, shouted back at him saying, "You're the ass." Eventually, some of our friends were arrested for "provoking others to revolt." I mean we were not very fond of the German officer.

Interviewer: What did you eat and drink at the drill ground? What sort of food were you given by an Empire fighting on so many different fronts?

Mr. Cindoruk: Our foods! Suffice to say that may God protect not only us, but also our enemies from experiencing those things again. In the mornings, tea with a thin layer of oil on it was served to us in a cauldron. Each of us could drink only one glass of tea. Since the cauldrons were never washed up, and the tea put in them had a layer of oil on it as I just told you. We used to drink that tea with a few slices of bread. We had called the tea given us as the "chestnut juice."

Interviewer: Were you eating nothing else for breakfast?

Mr. Cindoruk: Nothing at all. Of course the ones who had some money were buying something like bread and cheese. We were given cabbage stew or fava bean soup at lunch and dinner. Though they sometimes added some meat to the fava bean dish, it had plenty of water, and we used to see the fava bean bugs and worms floating on its surface. That's why we used to call that meal as the "fava bean soup." Once a week, we were given haricot beans with meat. That was a lavish meal for us. Sometimes we were given olives and bread at lunch.

Interviewer: Was that all, sir? You're saying that the soldiers who would soon be sent to the battlefront to fight were being fed like that?

Mr. Cindoruk: What would you expect under those conditions, during those days, my child? The enemies were attacking us on many fronts at the same time. How could a country such as ours, being in great destitution, give more than that?

INTERVIEWER: In the Great War, all of the males were drafted. Was your family affected much when you were taken into the military service?

MR. CINDORUK: My elder brother Ali Selim Bey, sixteen years older than me, was a military doctor. He served first on the Yemeni Front. On his return from Yemen in 1914, he was appointed to the 2nd Army Corps headquarters, in Edirne. When that Army Corps was transferred to the Gallipoli Peninsula in order to fight in the war, my brother also went there. Ahmet Şadi Bey, my other brother, was 7 years older than me. He was a last year student in Darülfünun's (university) Faculty of Law. When the war broke out, he was immediately taken to the drill ground. As a candidate officer (reserve officer candidate), he was appointed to a regiment located at the Selimiye Barracks. He was given a half-day leave on Fridays. When he came home on one of his leaves, it was one of the last days of April, he told us that his unit was going to be sent to one of the battlefronts on a ship, and he would be leaving on 1 May. He said he didn't know where they would be sent.

That morning, our father gave me and my younger brother Hasan Kemal some money and told us to give it to our brother who was going to the front. We went to Üsküdar, where we saw the ship docked and being loaded. While the troops were boarding the ship, we tried to give our brother the money sent by our father. He took only two *mecidiye* (Ottoman silver coins) of that money upon our insistence. He said to us: "Take the rest to our father; our family needs that money." I still hear very clearly speaking with my brother that day. I feel deep inside me the tragic destiny and all the sufferings of my elder brother Ahmet Şadi Bey. We later learnt that his regiment had been transferred to Gallipoli, and from there, without giving a rest, sent to Anafartalar. On 6 May, when his identification tag was brought to us, we understood that he had become a martyr. Imagine the situation of our family then. One of the sons is a military doctor in Gallipoli. The other martyred in Anafartalar, and then, I was also sent to the front. I am telling you all this as an answer to your question. That war had affected our family like that. We also lost our father a short while before I left for the front.

INTERVIEWER: Were you sent to the Eastern Front directly from Istanbul?

MR. CINDORUK: No. Before leaving, we trained the raw recruits at a place near to Istanbul. Then we went to Bandırma by ship, and continued by train to İzmir. One day, we were told that our division would go to the Caucasian Front. We went to Manisa and took the train there, and then we headed for the Eastern Front.

INTERVIEWER: How many days did it take to reach the Caucasian Front?

MR. CINDORUK: I'll tell you. It took precisely 57 days. We went as far as Ulukışla by train. There, the railway ended. The train that took us there was running on wood, since it was impossible to find coal in those days. Therefore, we had to gather sticks and twigs all the way along to use them as fuel in our train. Or, we were taking to the train board fences, hedges, and everything that could be burned, almost everywhere we passed through. Indeed it was not easy to find such fuel for our train, since a great many military convoys that had passed through the same places before us had already used them up. We were actually walking faster than the train; therefore, it took about 15–20 days to reach Ulukışla. From there on, we started walking.

INTERVIEWER: Were you carrying the necessary equipment yourselves?

MR. CINDORUK: The transportation columns in the carriages were carrying light things. The heavy equipment was loaded on trucks in Ulukışla. Our other ally, the Austrian Government, had sent those trucks. I saw trucks there for the first time in my life. After we passed through the Gülek Pass by walking and went down the mountain, we got on a train once more and reached a station called Mamure. At that place, there was a mountain called Gavur Mountain. We restarted walking there. We set up a camp with tents at the top, near the village of Hasanbeyli. The next day, we walked down the mountain, to İslahiye. Then, we continued walking until we reached Diyarbakır. Meanwhile, two soldiers who had deserted from their units were captured. The regiment commander ordered the whole regiment into formation for fighting, made a speech, and then had those two deserters tied to the telegraph poles and executed by shooting. The court martial was convened after the execution of those deserters and signed the decision of execution. Anyway… then we set off again from Diyarbakır, and after a four-day walk towards the north, we arrived in Palu. After walking further for a few days, we eventually reached our front. Our whole journey had lasted 57 days.

INTERVIEWER: Where was the exact location of your front?

MR. CINDORUK: It was located at a place called "Karir" then. Today, it is called the top of the Şerafettin Mountains. We took up position at a place with an altitude of 2,500–3,000 metres. Though we took up a position against the Russians, there were also Armenians against us. They were stabbing our army in the back.

INTERVIEWER: They were acting in cooperation with the Russians, weren't they?

MR. CINDORUK: Of course they were, and the Armenians were even more dangerous than the Russians, since they were stabbing us in the back.

INTERVIEWER: What was the season when you took up your positions?

MR. CINDORUK: As soon as we arrived at the front, winter set in. First, it was snowing in the form of dust. Later, the thickness of the snow reached the height of a man. There was a terrible cold. In fact, very few clashes occurred with the Russians when I was there. Only once we attacked them.

INTERVIEWER: Why weren't you fighting?

MR. CINDORUK: The Russians had also taken up positions on the mountains opposite us, but my son, it was impossible to fight under those weather conditions. Nevertheless, the Russians were in much better conditions compared to us, and the difficulties they had to endure were probably one thousandth of ours. We were learning how from the Russians who were taken prisoner by our forces. In those severe winter conditions, our troops only had *çarıks* (a type of sandal made of rawhide) on their feet. Many of our soldiers were frozen to death, and the feet of so many of our soldiers were amputated.

INTERVIEWER: Why were their feet amputated?

MR. CINDORUK: Their feet were becoming gangrenous. The frozen feet were becoming gangrenous. Let me give you an example. Our positions were at the top of the mountain. On the ridge of mountain just opposite us, the positions of the Russians were located. There was a river passing between us. That river was just between the positions of ours and the Russians. Therefore, both of the parties were sending their reconnaissance patrols to the river. Our soldiers were always begging us to be sent on that mission, which was the most dangerous of all, with the hope of killing an enemy soldier, should a clash occur. That was because they could take the boots, the greatcoats, and the furs of the enemy soldiers who would be killed. Or they could take the sugars, chocolates, and other foods from the pockets of the enemy. There was nothing else our soldiers could do then. Under those conditions, I served as the aide-de-camp of the battalion commander.

INTERVIEWER: Were the conditions very bad, sir?

MR. CINDORUK: My child, just imagine a mountaintop in Eastern Anatolia in the midst of winter. Then, add to that scene an army, lacking even proper boots and weapons to give its troops. Of course we did not have then anything like a thermometer with us. However, it was so cold that when we spit, we used to see our saliva immediately freezing. Tears that came to our eyes because of cold were freezing as soon as they came out of the inner corner of our eyes and were sticking on the surface as they were falling. The inner parts of our noses used to freeze down to our lungs. Naturally under those conditions the military duties could not be fulfilled properly. All the officers, including myself, were trying to do our best at least to protect the soldiers from becoming frozen. But what could be done for those soldiers who lacked proper clothing?

INTERVIEWER: What were their clothes like?

MR. CINDORUK: They were just terrible. If we were defeated on that front, we were defeated not by the enemy, but by the snow, the winter, and the typhus. Most of the soldiers had çarıks on their feet. As to their uniforms, they were provided by Germany to be worn in summer. There was nothing on their feet, like shoes or boots. We were wearing only greatcoats and because of the lice, we were wearing them with difficulty.

INTERVIEWER: What were the officers' shoes?

MR. CINDORUK: Our shoes were good, but I was feeling great pity for the soldiers. Imagine my child, how difficult it was to have those simple shoes on one's feet in snow. It was terrible and I think of the merciless people who caused all this. I still feel a very deep sorrow whenever I remember our soldiers there. Therefore, I blame Enver Pasha a lot. Under such conditions, our soldiers were running away, only to be killed in the ambushes set up by the Armenians and Kurds just for taking our soldiers' weapons. Those mountaintops had witnessed many bitter events in those days, especially after the severe winter set in.

INTERVIEWER: Was the Ottoman Administration in Istanbul unaware of the adverse conditions you were in?

MR. CINDORUK: While we were at the front, Enver Pasha came for an inspection. At the time he came, the thickness of snow exceeded the height of a man. Our commander İzzet Pasha, the commander of the 2nd Army, said to Enver Pasha, "Sir, the Russians have withdrawn to the Pasinler Plain to remain there until the end of winter. They left only some small detachments against us. Under your orders, we could also withdraw our army to the Murat Valley, and remain there during the winter. It is impossible to fight here under the existing weather conditions. At least we could save our soldiers from getting totally annihilated." Hearing that proposal, Enver Pasha said: "You cannot know, Pasha. Russians could come here hiding under the sheepskin, and occupy all these territories. Then, we'll lose all the country." That was the response of Enver Pasha; İzzet Pasha could say no more. Then, as you know, our armies were completely annihilated.

INTERVIEWER: How were the sentries' duties being arranged in such cold weather?

MR. CINDORUK: We had shortened the durations of watches to 15 minutes. We were sending two soldiers together on duty. However, many of our soldiers still froze to death in the cold of probably minus 40 degrees centigrade.

INTERVIEWER: I wonder where you sheltered during those severe winter days, and at the top of a mountain. Where and how were you sleeping?

MR. CINDORUK: Each squad was digging an underground shelter of its own. It was like a cave; we were digging the ground and entering into the cave, which we made. In that long and narrow hole under the ground, 10–15 persons could take shelter.

INTERVIEWER: Were those shelters completely covered?

MR. CINDORUK: Only the doors were open. If we could find a canvas tent, we hung it on the door. The canvas tent did not let in the snow, though it did not protect us from the cold.

INTERVIEWER: Was there anything like beds in those shelters?

MR. CINDORUK: Oh, my son. How could we have beds there? During all those months we spent there, we could see beds only in our dreams. Everybody was spreading their greatcoats on the earth and lying on them. That was the only thing you could do. The bodies of the people lying there warmed each other. Or, we were trying to get warmed with our breath.

INTERVIEWER: I suppose you didn't have anything like a stove?

MR. CINDORUK: We didn't have any. We were sometimes burning sticks and twigs, if we could find them. Of course, they produced too much smoke, but we were willing to have the smoke, instead of being frozen.

INTERVIEWER: How were you washing or cleaning yourselves under such conditions?

MR. CINDORUK: We had great difficulty in doing that. We were bringing snow from outside and putting it into a cauldron. If we could find some sticks and twigs we were burning them in order to heat the cauldron a little bit and melt the snow. We were using that water only to wash our hands and faces. We were not able to clean ourselves any further. We did not have any hot water for months.

INTERVIEWER: Did you spend all day in those underground shelters at the top of the mountain?

MR. CINDORUK: Unless we were on duty, we spent all day in those shelters, many of us together in such a small place. None of us could go outside in that very severe cold. Under those conditions, naturally the lice spread and increased in number. The dirtiness and all those adverse conditions invited the lice. Besides the cold weather, a second factor which destroyed our armies there was typhus. As you know, typhus is a fatal disease transmitted by lice.

INTERVIEWER: How did the people become infested with lice?

MR. CINDORUK: The soldiers brought the lice there. I don't know where they were brought the lice. In fact, the lice were already widespread in our country then. In the underground shelters, everyone easily became infested with lice. It was impossible to protect yourself. You could never clean yourself completely from the lice on your body. Even in that cold weather, I had to take off my jacket. They were plenty. You cannot imagine at all. When you stroked one side of your shirt or jacket, you could see hundreds of lice falling to the ground. Then we were crushing them with our feet, but they were too many to be eradicated by crushing. You cannot imagine how badly they could bother you and make you itch. One could go insane.

INTERVIEWER: What were you eating and drinking under those conditions?

MR. CINDORUK: That was another tragedy. A total of 27,000 animals were sent to the front from the rear, and were frozen to death before reaching the front. Therefore, the army had to seize all the flour which could be found in the area. Everyone was given a hundred grams of flour each day, and that was all. When we lit a fire in the underground shelter, we were placing a thin piece of sheet iron on the fire in order to bake a kind of bread with the flour wetted with snow.

INTERVIEWER: Were the officers eating the same thing?

MR. CINDORUK: There was no difference in that regard between the officers and the soldiers. We were eating the same things as the soldiers.

INTERVIEWER: Were the officers given meat from time to time?

MR. CINDORUK: We were never given any meat, but if the 27,000 animals I have mentioned had reached the front without being frozen, their meat would have been fried and preserved. If it had been done, we wouldn't have a shortage of food for quite a long time.

INTERVIEWER: To tell the truth, Sir, what you're telling me makes my hair stand on end. Once more, I see very clearly the enormous costs paid to bring this country to the present.

MR. CINDORUK: May God never show again the miseries of those days to our country, or to anybody.

INTERVIEWER: How was the transportation to the front carried out?

MR. CINDORUK: Camels were being used for transportation. In fact, we know camels as animals living in warm climates, don't we? But in those days, the camels had proven to be more resistant to the severe cold than the horses and the mules.

INTERVIEWER: Then, you had also caught typhus, didn't you?

MR. CINDORUK: That's right. As I told you before, typhus is a contagious and fatal disease transmitted by lice. It is also called as spotted fever. In those days, typhus could not be cured. It was starting with a severe nausea. Then the body temperature increased. I showed the same symptoms when I caught the disease. In the beginning, my body temperature was not very high, it was around 38°C. There was no doctor on the mountain, in our post, but there was a pharmacist. When he informed the commander of my situation, I was sent down the mountain accompanied by a soldier sent to accompany me. We walked down. The horses belonging to our division were waiting at the foot of the mountain. In order to keep them in a warmer place, a cave to be used as a stable had been dug out on that side of the mountain. The animals had been given more food than us. Imagine that under those conditions, an animal could be more valuable for the army than a soldier at the front. Anyway, together with the soldier, I set off for Lice on the back of a horse.

INTERVIEWER: What was there in Lice?

MR. CINDORUK: There was a stone-built school building in Lice. The building had been turned into a military hospital. There was a very terrible winter. First, we went down the mountain and arrived in Çapakcur. It took two days to reach Çapakcur on horseback. Then, we continued our way and crossed the Murat River. In that severe cold, there was only my uniform on me while passing the Murat River through a ford, which was not very deep. We spent two more days on the road, and finally reached the military hospital in Lice. I later learnt that two military doctors with typhus had arrived there before me. One of them was Captain Nail Bey; and the other was a Jew, the name of whom I had forgotten. I learnt that both of them had died. When I first arrived in that hospital, there were a few young officers also ill with typhus like me. I witnessed the deaths of all of them. I heard that after my departure, the chief doctor of the hospital had also died of typhus.

INTERVIEWER: Sir, you have just mentioned a military doctor who was a Jew. Were the members of minority groups taken to the military service then?

MR. CINDORUK: Members of certain professions needed by the army were taken. For instance, there were not many Turkish doctors then. Therefore, doctors belonging to the minority groups were taken to the Army. The Chief Doctor of the hospital in Lice was a Jew named Jak Efendi, and the Doctor Major who treated me in the hospital was an Armenian. I don't remember his name now. I learnt from others that I had been treated in that hospital for two months.

INTERVIEWER: Don't you remember the days that you received treatment in the hospital?

MR. CINDORUK: I remember only our arrival in that hospital, and my last days there. They told me later that I had lost my consciousness immediately after our arrival. The soldier who accompanied me to the hospital continued to stay there with me. He told me later that one night I had unconsciously stepped down the stairs of the hospital and lain on the snow outside. My body temperature had been 40–41 degrees centigrade then. After I had lain on the snow for a few hours, I had been found and taken inside by the soldier accompanying me. Lying on the snow had decreased my body temperature somewhat and saved me from dying. When they told me all this later, I didn't believe at first, but when I saw that all the typhus patients were dying in the hospital, I believed that unconsciously going and lying in the snow had saved my life. Of course that had happened because of God's will.

INTERVIEWER: Was typhus the most widespread of the infectious diseases?

MR. CINDORUK: Typhus was the disease which caused the largest number of deaths within our Army. Besides that, plenty of deaths occurred because of the cold, and there were also many who froze to death. During a period of 2–3 years, the Ottoman armies were defeated by irresponsibility, cold, and typhus. About a hundred thousand young citizens of this country had been lost on our front only. History books also write the same thing.

So, my son. Our division was 17,000 strong when it first arrived at the Eastern Front. On our way back, we were only 2,000. Particularly the cold and the typhus had caused the death of totally 15,000 officers and soldiers from our division alone. All those people had died for nothing. Even now, whenever I remember those days, I feel a deep sorrow. I cannot understand the reason for what happened there. Therefore I blame the late Enver Pasha a lot. May God's mercy be upon the souls of all who died.

Appendix 2

Reconstruction in Turkey

A Series of Reports Compiled for the American Committee of Armenian and Syrian Relief

RECONSTRUCTION IN TURKEY

A SERIES OF REPORTS

COMPILED FOR

THE AMERICAN COMMITTEE OF ARMENIAN AND SYRIAN RELIEF

1 Madison Avenue, New York City

WILLIAM H. HALL
Editor

For Private Distribution Only

1918

HEALTH AND SANITARY CONDITIONS IN TURKEY.

The material presented in this summary was taken from reports prepared by the following persons:

Harpoot district: Rev. H. H. Riggs, Professor of Science, Euphrates College, Harpoot, Turkey.

Adana district: Rev. Thomas A. Christie, President St. Paul's Institute, Tarsus, Turkey.

Syria district: Professor William H. Hall, Syrian Protestant College, Beirut, Syria.

Mesopotamia district: Rev. A. N. Andrus, Missionary, American Board of Foreign Missions, Mardin, Turkey.

Konia district: Dr. Wilfred Post, American physician attending hospital at Konia, Turkey.

Smyrna district: Professor John K. Birge, International College, Smyrna, Turkey.

Jerusalem: Dr. E. W. G. Masterman, F. R. C. S., D. P. H., Medical Superintendent of Camberwell Infirmary and (before the war) Medical Superintendent of the English Mission Hospital, Jerusalem. (Report published in the Lancet, London, February 23, 1918.)

No effort was made to elaborate on the facts presented in these reports. The information was merely systematized. So far as possible the original expressions used in the separate reports were incorporated in the account which follows.

Sewage Disposal.

Syria. Sanitary conditions in Syria are said not to differ materially from those of other parts of the empire. Sewers are open. The streets are used as public water closets. There are swarms of flies. In cities of the type of Beirut a certain amount of street cleaning takes place. Elsewhere practically nothing is done. Screening of doors and windows, or even the covering of food in the shops to protect it from flies, is unknown. There have been sporadic attempts on the part of the government to have meat kept behind wire screens. Houses in both cities and villages have their own privies. Generally these have a vault, some deep, some shallow; but often they are without any vault, the contents being thrown into the garden, or allowed to drain into the public way. The intense sunshine of Syria is her greatest purifier. Along the sea coast the very heavy downfall of rain on the steep slopes washes a great many impurities into the sea before they have a chance to become lodged in the soil.

Mesopotamia. The method of sewage disposal is described as too meagre to meet the requirements of decent sanitation. In villages there is an utter absence of sewage systems, while the cities and large towns are also conspicuous for their imperfect systems or the want of any system. In many places cesspools constitute the only method of sewage disposal. Taken as a whole the sewage produced in Mesopotamia is found on the surface. The sun is the only disinfectant. Much of the disease of this large part of the country is directly traceable to these conditions.

Harpoot district. In some cities a local and inefficient sewage system exists. Such sewers as are found merely carry the sewage outside of the city, and discharge it in the open air. The point of discharge of the sewer frequently is the center for the most prosperous market gardening, the sewage furnishing abundant fertilizer. In the matter of plumbing traps are almost unknown, so that the sewers generally have a draft upward towards the city and fill the houses and streets with a stench from the sewers and cesspools. In most villages there is no attempt whatever at sewage disposal. Each house at best has a shallow cesspool opening on the street where from time to time men shovel up the sewage and carry it to the fields. No attempt is made at covering or screening. The air of the streets is apt to reek with stench, and to be filled with flies which swarm about open cesspools. Most frequently it is reported there is not even an attempt to provide cesspools or any other kind of disposal. The streets and the hillsides serve as public water closets. It is said to be difficult to conceive of any conditions less favorable for health so far as sewage disposal and water supply are concerned than those found in the Harpoot district.

Konia district. Sewage is usually disposed of by the dry closet method and carried away in carts and thrown upon the open fields as fertilizer.

HEALTH AND SANITARY CONDITIONS. 69

Smyrna district. In most of the quarters of Smyrna itself underground sewers are found. In the Turkish quarter, however, the dirty water from sinks and washing places runs through the middle of the street. In the smaller cities around Smyrna the streets are commonly built with a gutter in the middle through which sewage is running most or much of the time.

Garbage Disposal.

Syria. Garbage is emptied in the streets. Wagons go about and daily collect the waste which property owners have dumped into the highways. It is sold to gardeners who pile the refuse into corners of their gardens where it remains for months to rot. Later it is spread on the ground where green vegetables are raised for the city markets. These piles of fertilizers, which contain dirty rags and other sorts of filth, are breeding places for flies and other insects. Street dogs have long been the city scavengers and they have aided materially in the disposal of garbage. Lately the government has been disposing of these dogs without providing any adequate substitute for the service they have rendered.

Harpoot. Household garbage is here as elsewhere thrown into the streets where dogs and birds are the only scavengers. Cattle are slaughtered in the streets, the blood being permitted to drain away across the roadbed.

Water Supply.

Syria. The water supply in all parts of Syria is on the whole good. Usually it is a village fountain enclosed in masonry, and fairly well protected from drainage. Beirut and Damascus now have water in iron pipes from the mountains. Damascus, however, still has the open rivers from which the people continue to draw water to some extent. Aleppo has a small supply of piped water. Aleppo is, however, reputed to be chiefly supplied from deep wells. Jerusalem is dependent on cisterns of rain water. Often a village is supplied by water brought in a channel from a distant spring. This channel is generally closed with slabs of rough stone with the object of keeping the soil of the hillside from being washed into it, rather than as a hygienic precaution. These stone coverings are never tight enough to prevent the infiltration of surface drainage.

Mesopotamia. With the exception of Diarbekir not a single city or town in all Mesopotamia has a water system under government control. In many of the communities the water supply is too meagre to meet the requirements of decent sanitation.

Harpoot. The water supply of various locations varies greatly as to purity and abundance. In mountainous places, such as Harpoot, Arabkir, and Egin, etc. the water comes from springs, and is pure and good. In other places, such as Malatia, Palu, Diarbekir, and many of the Harpoot villages, the water supply coming from distant places in underground water sources not well protected is liable to serious contamination. In Malatia the water supply is abundant, but in almost every other place in this district the supply of water is limited, expensive, or inaccessible, so that the people do not ordinarily have water in sufficient quantity for sanitation. In the city of Harpoot the local supply is so limited that even for common laundry work the people are obliged to go outside the city sometimes a distance of a mile or more. The use of water for adequately flushing closets and drains is impossible.

Konia. The main line of improvement of unsanitary conditions is stated to lie in the supervision of the water supply. In the city of Konia typhoid fever is comparatively rare owing to the piping of the water from the mountains and its distribution from a covered reservoir throughout the city, but wherever the people drink from their own wells typhoid fever and dysentery are the natural consequences. In the city of Karaman, which lies on the railroad and should boast of a certain degree of intelligence, the people still drink irrigation water which runs from the fields through the streets. These fields it should be remembered are extensively fertilized by means of sewage collected by the dry closet method. The vicious circle of contamination is thus said to be daily completed. At Eregli the same is true, and in both places malaria and typhoid abound. A special sanitary commission to control the water supply of the province, and to eliminate the mosquito would do more for the health and comfort of the million or more inhabitants than dozens of hospitals.

Housing.

Mesopotamia. In most of the cities and towns there has been much overcrowding in the houses of the poor and middle classes.

HEALTH AND SANITARY CONDITIONS.   71

This has been aggravated by the tendency on the part of the poor and oppressed villagers to drift into the towns and cities so that they may find work or beg for a precarious living.

Harpoot. In the larger cities houses are built with some regard to the possibilities of light and sanitation, but in the country villages, and in a large degree in cities also, the houses are low, damp, dark, and ill-ventilated. In the villages the houses are built in continuous rows, and even in solid blocks without any windows whatever, the chimney being the only means of ventilation. The walls and floor are usually of mud, and the ceiling of rough logs with brush over them and mud plastered over the brush to make the roof. With such construction it is hardly to be wondered at that vermin abound in all houses. When lack of care and cleanliness is superadded it is to be expected that diseases carried by vermin should be extremely devastating. The habit of the people even where windows exist is to plaster or otherwise seal them up during the winter, resulting in total absence of ventilation. Add to this the fact that the people are very much overcrowded in their houses, and usually live a sedentary life during the winter, and it will be understood why, in spite of their good habit of living out of doors in summer, tuberculosis in its various forms is very common.

The Prevalence of Disease.

Typhus fever. In 1915 this disease caused the death of from 200,000 to 300,000 people. Several hundred of the physicians sent by the Turkish government to cope with it became infected and died. In the Erzroom region where from 60,000 to 100,000 died, soap, water, and fuel could hardly be obtained anywhere during the epidemic.

Typhoid fever. Typhoid is prevalent through the country. It assumes epidemic proportions in the summer and fall months. Great carelessness prevails in caring for patients, who have been seen dying of typhoid in rooms directly overlooking a courtyard where tons of dried beef were prepared for shipment to Constantinople.

Asiatic cholera. This disease runs its course in terrible fashion in a given region, and then seems to leave it for several years. It seems to be as much dreaded as any disease. The people look upon it as a sort of hopeless terror. As a rule little effort is made to quarantine cases. Quarantine where resorted to, generally consists of painting a streak of yellow paint on the door post of the afflicted homes. Kindly disposed neighbors of the sick, however, are said to absolutely disregard the sign. Orders to eat only cooked fruits and vegetables are not obeyed. The ignorance of the population with respect to the disease and the manner of its conveyance is indicated by the fact that when accused of indifference in disobeying orders concerning the cooking of fruits the reply is made that the fruits do not seem to be any different in the present year (of the epidemic) than in former years. The eye cannot detect disease, hence the ignorant public reasons there can be no disease. Fear of personal injury from offended persons often prevents city physicians from insisting on the observance of rules for protection against cholera.

Smallpox. This disease is especially prevalent in village communities. More than half of the population is said to show pock marks. The mortality from the disease does not seem to be high. It is, however, the cause of innumerable cases of blindness among children. In this respect it ranks second only to gonorrhoeal infection. Vaccination is practiced in larger towns and cities and in the army. Only in the army is it systematically carried out.

Malaria. Malaria is prevalent in all the low lands of the country. It is the cause indirectly of thousands of deaths annually. When infected the custom is to take a few doses of quinine, and so to partially control the disease which may run on for years, make its victim physically unfit, and so a prey to other diseases. It is so common that quinine sulphate is a household remedy known to everyone by the name of "sulphato." It is used more than any other drug in the country. The native physician gives the remedy by mouth or intermuscularly. The result is, however, rarely controlled by miscroscopic examination of the blood. Netting over beds is used by some people solely as a matter of convenience to obtain sleep. No efforts were discovered to destroy mosquito larvae, or to screen houses.

Tuberculosis. The disease is present everywhere. It is found in every city, town, and village of the country. The houses themselves have become infected, so that family after family occupying them acquire the disease. In spite of a great natural dread of the disease the people take almost no precautions against its spread.

HEALTH AND SANITARY CONDITIONS.   73

The tubercular patient is found in the same room with other members of the family. His bed on the floor will be shared in common with others in the family. He will perhaps take the precaution to keep an open tin cup beside the bed into which he expectorates. Even in well advanced cases the patient will be found eating with the family from the common dish. A diagnosis of tuberculosis by a physician in the minds of the family sounds the death sentence of a patient. Owing to the limited knowledge of the people concerning germ infection the advice of physicians as to means for protection against the disease is apt to lead them to miss the most important point. The forms of tuberculosis which are not common in the United States are said to be exceedingly common in Turkey. This is true of tuberculosis of the bones and joints, of the spine, kidneys, bladder, and of tubercular glands and tubercular peritonitis. There are no sanatoria for tuberculosis in the interior of the country.

Syphilis. In some of the villages this disease is found among 80 to 90 per cent. of the population. Medical men have accounted for its wide prevalence largely by the manner of living of the village people. They are huddled together using common eating and drinking utensils. The disease is thus carried from one to another in the same manner as any infectious disease, and is referred to as the so-called " innocent " syphilis. In these districts the disease is not associated in the minds of the people with immorality. Syphilitic ulceration of the skin, the so-called chronic syphilide, is a commonly seen form. In the large cities, and especially in the coast cities the social evil is reported to be flagrant. Because of the relatively costly treatment for the disease it is generally allowed to run its course. Mercury fumigation is a form of native treatment considerably used. Unfortunately, however, it often results in mercurial poisoning, so that it is not at all rare to see cases of extensive necrosis of the jaw bone as a sequel. Hospitals in the interior are as a rule not equipped to do the Wasserman test. No scientific study of the situation seems thus far to have been made.

Gonorrhoea. This disease is found more in the large centers than in the interior. It is probably the cause of more unhappy homes than any other disease in Turkey. It is considered one of the greatest misfortunes in Turkey to have a wife that cannot bear a child. It is even held to be a legitimate ground for divorce.

Gonorrhœal pelvic infection, as is well known, is frequently the cause of the childless home. As a cause of blindness in infants the disease holds first place. Because of the ignorance and uncleanly methods of the midwives of the country little is done to protect against this source of blindness.

Infant mortality. Medical men conversant with the situation have found it hard to estimate, but it is thought to be over rather than under 50 per cent. Almost inconceivable conditions surround the birth and care of the infant. Very little preparation is made in the ordinary home for the new born child. Frequently it is regarded as merely an additional burden. Maternity cases rarely reach the hospital. The midwife usually attends. The practice of native midwives is described as absolutely brutal and oftentimes criminal. Medical men report cases of contracted pelvis in which the strength of several midwives served to break the pelvis with fatal result to both mother and child. The induction of criminal abortion is common, and results in untold misery from the consequent infection.

The present care of the child follows the lines laid down by earlier generations. The new born child is wrapped in swaddling clothes with a sort of finely pulverized earth in place of the napkin. It is nursed whenever it cries, and is given a " comforter " made of a piece of Turkish sweet wrapped in a rag. By the time the infant is one year of age it is given bread, and a little of almost anything to eat. Sometimes it may nurse until it is two years or older.

The infectious diseases of childhood, such as measles, scarlet fever, etc., cause the death of large numbers of children. As soon as the rash is faded the child is allowed to go out and play in the streets with the result that it frequently dies from complications, such as pneumonia, nephritis, etc.

Surgery. The needs of Turkey in the way of surgery are great. Cases are most frequently seen in their aggravated form. Patients come great distances to the American hospitals. So great is the demand, and so limited the capacity and staff of these hospitals that their work has become largely surgical in nature.

Eye, ear, nose, and throat troubles. The situation as to these is pitiful. Trachoma is widely prevalent. An incalculable amount of defective vision with resulting inefficiency is found. Among the most frequent operations which surgeons of the American hospitals

HEALTH AND SANITARY CONDITIONS. 75

have been called upon to perform are those for entropion and trichiasis, — the end results of trachoma. The prevention of blindness by the control of trachoma, gonorrhœa, ophthalmia, and smallpox is looked upon as one of the greatest blessings which may be given to Turkey. The blind are objects of great pity. They are apt to be turned out as unproductive members of society. People consider themselves poor enough without taking care of the blind, the deaf, the crippled, the aged, and the insane. Cataract is common. The native eye surgeons still practice dislocation of the lens with needles with the ultimate loss of the eye as a consequence.

Deafness and mutism, the result of neglected ear diseases are frequent. Mastoid disease and diseases of the antrum, the accessory sinuses are common. Dental trouble is likewise almost universal. It is said to be a rare exception to find a well kept mouth among the middle class in Turkey. Pyorrhœa is the rule. Native dentists are very mediocre, while the village people allow their teeth to rot uncared for until because of pain they have them pulled.

Flies, filth and vermin. These seem to be found throughout the interior of Turkey. The roadside inns are notorious in this respect. Foreigners find it necessary to provide travelling beds in order to keep away from the vermin. It is a common sight to see the village traveler sitting by the roadside picking the lice from his underclothing. Fleas are taken for granted as a necessary evil. They are everywhere in evidence. Bed-bugs infest practically every home in the interior, and in such numbers as to make calling in the homes most disagreeable.

The general statement concerning disease in Turkey contained on the preceding pages may be supplemented by brief additions referring to definite localities.

Jerusalem. The diseases of Jerusalem are many, — variola, varicella, measles, enteric, typhus, scarlet fever, influenza, pertussis, and cerebro-spinal fever all occur in epidemic form and claim large numbers of victims. Until recent years it is said scarlet fever was distinctly uncommon. Such diseases as acute rheumatism, pneumonia, broncho-pneumonia, chronic rheumatic arthritis are all common. Tuberculosis both pulmonary, and in the glands, joints, and bones is at present (1918) very common all over Palestine. There seems to be some reason to believe that it was rare here formerly.

76   RECONSTRUCTION IN TURKEY.

Appendicitis and gastric ulcer are uncommon. Carcinoma is thought to be much less common among the Syrians than among Europeans.

The greatest scourge of Jerusalem is malaria, which in the autumn months is almost universal. On examination of some 4,626 children actually attending school in Jerusalem 27.3 per cent. had malarial parasites in the blood, and of 7,771 persons of all classes and conditions 26.7 per cent. had the parasites. Among poor Jews the percentage was 40.5 per cent. Among Mohammedans 31.1 per cent. Among native Christians 16.4 per cent., and among Europeans 7.2 per cent. Medical men state that there is no reason whatever to doubt that with proper organization this pest could be reduced to very small dimensions.

Blackwater fever is not uncommon in other parts of Palestine. Several fatal cases have been known to originate in Jerusalem itself. Dengue fever occurs in rather frequent epidemics. Recurrent fever due to spirochaetae is found occasionally. There are many sufferers from tropical boil in Jerusalem. Most of them are said to come from Aleppo, and its neighborhood, and from Bagdad. A local variety of this disease is known as Jericho boil. It occurs in the Jordan valley.

Jerusalem is one of the four centers in the holy land where lepers congregate. The majority fortunately are segregated in the Moravian leper hospital. A considerable number, however, still live in a row of miserable cottages in the lowest part of Kedron valley. During the travelling season they come in from other parts of the land. Several cases of bilharzia have been found. It was not believed, however, that the infections had been received in Palestine. Hookworm disease, if present must be very rare, as frequent examination of stools has not revealed a single case. This fact is considered remarkable because of the wide prevalence of the disease in Egypt. In Palestine not 10 per cent. of the population have absolutely sound eyes.

Taking Syria as a whole, certain of the most serious diseases endemic in this part of Turkey are typhoid, smallpox, malaria, dengue fever, and tuberculosis. There are frequent epidemics of cholera and typhus. Bubonic plague is almost always to be found in some more or less restricted area.

Adana. Malaria is prevalent owing to the large extent of

HEALTH AND SANITARY CONDITIONS. 77

uncultivated land on the plain and many marshes near the coast. There have been three epidemics of cholera within thirty years. In every instance the disease was brought by pilgrims returning from Mecca. The neglect of the most ordinary sanitary precautions in the towns and villages always aggravate the scourge.

Smyrna. Asiatic cholera is the principal disease troubling the inhabitants of this district. There is an outbreak almost every year on so extensive a scale as to necessitate a quarantine of the city. Since the war began typhus and typhoid have also been common. In some interior cities malaria is very common.

The Control of Disease.

The reports already referred to contain incidental statements and suggestions with regard to the control of disease. These have been brought together on the following pages.

Efforts seem to have been made for a good many years to arrest the introduction of disease into the country by pilgrims as well as the spread of disease by pilgrims on their return. As early as 1881 a German physician was engaged at the quarantine station of Khanekin on the Turko-Persian frontier with a view particularly to preventing the introduction of disease. Owing to the fact that all devout Mohammedans seek to bring their sick to be cured, or take them for burial in holy ground, a constant procession of pathological types of all kinds passes along the routes of pilgrimages. The Mohammedans are said to be very skillful in evading the law. Often entire caravans manage to cross the frontier at some unprotected place. Fragments of human skeletons are concealed about their personal baggage in a highly ingenious manner.

Since the construction of the Hedjaz railway Syria has had a new avenue to disease opened. There were always a good many pilgrims to and from Mecca by the old caravan route. The railway has, however, multiplied the number many times, and so greatly increased the well known dangers of infection coming from Mecca. Palestine is also a menace to Europe for thousands of pilgrims from Christian lands visit the various sacred places every year and live in the great public hospices. These two pilgrimage centers are a constant source of danger, and especially so because no adequate system of quarantine or disinfection has ever been organized.

78   RECONSTRUCTION IN TURKEY.

Various writers have described the exaggerated and fanatical regulations which on various occasions have been enforced in Turkish quarantine ports. At some places it was the custom to incarcerate all travelers for a week, — sometimes even to subject them to fumigation in a closed chamber. Quite a number of writers claim that the evil aspects of Turkey, both with regard to sanitary conditions, and with respect to the characteristics of the people have been persistently exaggerated in occidental countries. Some writers go so far as to claim that great injustice has been done Turkey largely from political motives. It seems to be generally admitted, however, that on account of native indolence and general ignorance sanitary conditions within the Empire are in a very backward state.

Syria. Practically nothing has been done to combat the various infectious diseases which prevail in this district. There is needed a widespread and systematic campaign of popular education on the value of cleanliness and the simple methods through which disease may be prevented. This work should be backed up by proper laws relating to public hygiene and their systematic enforcement.

Mesopotamia. To relieve the great overcrowding in the cities and towns of this region the suggestion has been made that the villagers can only be gotten back to the soil if they are assured of security of life and of property, and of immunity from oppression.

Harpoot. Popular ignorance with regard to the most elementary principles of hygiene make the health conditions of this region worse even than external circumstances would seem to suggest. Superstition takes the place of medical science, and the absolute indifference in regard to the frightfully high mortality, especially among children, paralyzes any effort to improve conditions. It is not at all uncommon, for example, to see a young baby of a few months sucking or chewing a raw cucumber. The average rugged health of the people is interpreted by one writer as the result of a most pitiless application of the principle of the survival of the fittest through which all who are not naturally rugged die in infancy.

Adana. The missionary hospital at Adana is said to have done immense good in improving the health of the people. The same is said to be true of the work of the medical missionary in Mersine. The infant mortality among the Mohammedan population in par-

HEALTH AND SANITARY CONDITIONS.

ticular is enormous. The summer heat on the great plains is extreme. Those who can afford it go to the mountains or to the vineyards near the towns.

Konia. It is reported that as a result of German thoroughness smallpox, typhoid fever, and cholera have been largely eliminated from the army. This reform it is suggested should be made compulsory for the civilian population. It is believed that reasonable methods and instruction, oral rather than written, is necessary to the introduction of compulsory vaccination, especially in view of what is described as "the present intellectual condition of the country." The main line of improvement in this region is said to lie in the supervision of the water supply. Attention to stagnant water it is believed would "accomplish wonders." It is useless to appoint commissions and publish literature if the people are unable to read or understand the instructions given them. The establishment of medical schools, clinics, and hospitals is also looked upon as an important step.

Smyrna. During the time of cholera plague lime is sprinkled on the streets, and since the war began a systematic attempt has been made to have the people vaccinated against cholera.

Notes

Chapter 1. Introduction

1. Jared Diamond, *Guns, Germs and Steel: The Fates of Human Societies* (New York: W. W. Norton, 1999), 197.
2. William H. McNeill, *A World History* (New York: Oxford University Press, 1967), 172.
3. Ralph Jackson, *Roma İmparatorluğu'nda Doktorlar ve Hastalıklar*, trans. Şenol Mumcu (Istanbul: Homer B., 1999), 126, 131. For original edition, see Ralph Jackson, *Doctors and Diseases in the Roman Empire*, 4th ed. (London: British Museum Press, 1995).
4. M. F. Flinn, "Avrupa ve Akdeniz Ülkelerinde Veba," trans. Necmiye Alpay, *Tarih ve Toplum* 39 (March 1987): 25–26.
5. Arif Müfid Mansel, *Ege ve Yunan Tarihi*, 6th ed. (Ankara: TTK Pub., 1995), 321.
6. Feda Şâmil Arık, "Selçuklular Zamanında Anadolu'da Veba Salgınları," *AÜDTCF Tarih Dergisi* 15, no. 26 (1990–1991): 57.
7. H. Braun, *Mikrobiyoloji, Parazitoloji ve Salgınlar Bilgisi*, trans. Vefik Vassaf (Istanbul: Yaltırık Pub., 1936), 277–278.
8. Andrew Nikiforuk, *The Fourth Horseman: A Short History of Epidemics, Plagues and Other Scourges* (London: Fourth Estate, 1991), 10.
9. J. McPherson, *Battle Cry of Freedom*, in John Keegan, *A History of Warfare* (New York: Alfred A. Knopf, 1993), 360–361.
10. Tostantin Mutusis, "Mikrop Harbi," *Istanbul Tıp Fakültesi Mecmuası*, no. 3 (1952): 1158–1159.
11. Nikiforuk, *The Fourth Horseman*, 11.
12. Jean-Noël Biraben, *Les hommes et la peste en France et dans les pays europeens et Méditerranéens*, in Daniel Panzac, *La Peste dans l'Empire Ottoman 1700–1850* (Leuven: Editions Peeters, 1985), 187.
13. Ibid., 187.
14. Helmut Becker, *I. Dünya Savaşı'nda Osmanlı Cephesinde Askerî Tababet ve Eczacılık* (Istanbul, 1983), 6.
15. Salim Koca, "Türklerin Göçleri ve Yayılmaları," *Türkler* (Ankara: Yeni Türkiye Pub., 2002), 1:654.
16. UK FO 424/67 – Confidential (3598), 267–269, from no. 612/1: Bilâl N. Şimşir, *Rumeli'den Türk Göçleri, Belgeler* (Ankara: TTK Pub., 1989), vol. 1, doc. no. 185, 322–325.
17. Ekrem Kadri Unat, "Kış ve Bulaşıcı Hastalıklar," *Dirim* 55 (7–8) (July–August 1980): 249.

18. Inci Hot, Sıhhiye Mecmuası'na Göre Ülkemizde Bulaşıcı Hastalıklarla Mücadele, 1913–1996 (Istanbul University, Unpublished Thesis, 2001), 188.
19. Keegan, *A History of Warfare*, 361.
20. E. K. Unat et al., *Unat'ın Tıp Parazitoloji*, 5th ed. (Istanbul: Cerrahpaşa Tıp Fakültesi Vakfı Pub., 1995), 258.
21. A. Weiss, "Le typhus exanthematique pendant la Deuxieme Guerre Mondiale en particulier dans la camps de concentration," in Ekrem Kadri Unat, "Birinci Dünya Harbinde Türk Ordusu'nda Tifüs Savaşı," *Cerrahpaşa Tıp Fakültesi Dergisi* 20, no. 2 (April 1989): 256.
22. Yurkens, "Lekeli Tifo Epidemiyolojisi," in Mustafa Karatepe, *I. Dünya Savaşı'nda Kafkas Cephesi'nde Tifüsle Mücadele* (Istanbul University, Unpublished Thesis, 1999), p. 46–47.
23. Ahmet Özdemir, "Milli Mücadele'de Üserâ Taburları," *Atatürk Yolu* 5 (May 1990): 141.
24. Ekrem Şadi Kavur, "Askeri Hekimliğin Sıhhiye Hizmetlerinde Bir Etüd," *Dirim* 49, no. 8 (August 1973): 194–195, 378.
25. Tolga Ersoy, *Tıp, Tarih, Metafor*, 2nd ed. (Ankara: Öteki Pub., 1996), 142–143.
26. M. S. Anderson, *The Eastern Question, 1774–1923* (London: St. Martin's Press, 1966), p. 314. For the Treaty of Alliance, see M. S. Anderson, ed., *The Great Power and the Near East, 1774–1923: Documents of Modern History* (London: Edward Arnold, 1970), 157.
27. Sarkis Karayan, "An Inquiry into the Number and Causes of Turkish Human Losses during the First World War," *The Armenian Review* 35, no. 3–139 (August 1982): 284.
28. Ibid., 286.
29. Erik J. Zürcher, "Between Death and Desertion: The Experience of the Ottoman Soldier in World War I," *Turcica*, no. 28 (1996): 235–258. See also Zürcher, ed., "The Ottoman Conscription System in Theory and Practice," in *Arming the State: Military Conscription in the Middle East and Central Asia, 1775–1925* (London: I. B. Taurus, 1999), 89–94.
30. Stanford J. Shaw, *Idea to Realization: My Study of Ottoman History* (Ankara: Türkiye Bilimler Akademisi Pub., 2003), 72.

Chapter 2. Between Two Fires

1. Mehmet Yavuz Erler, "XIX: Yüzyıldaki Bazı Doğal Âfetler ve Osmanlı Yönetimi," *Türkler*, vol. 13 (Ankara: Yeni Türkiye Pub., 2002), 764.
2. Panzac, *La Peste dans l'Empire Ottoman*, 11.
3. Ibid., 13, 38–39.
4. Quoted from William Witmann, *Travels in Turkey, Asia Minor, Syria and Across the Desert into Egypt During the Years 1799, 1800 and 1801 in Company with the Turkish Army, and the British Military Mission* (London, 1803), in Şefik Görgey, İngiliz Cerrah William Witmann'ın 19. Yüzyıl Başında Istanbul, Yafa ve Mısır'daki Gözlemleri, Uygulamaları ve Raporları (Istanbul University, SBE, Unpublished Thesis, 1989), 28, 30, 35, 39.
5. Kemal Özbay, *Türk Asker Hekimliği Tarihi ve Asker Hastahaneleri* (Istanbul, Yörük Pub., 1976), 1:29.

6. Osman Şevki, *Osmanlı Tababeti, Türk Tarihinin Ana Hatları Eserinin Müsveddeleri,* vol. 2, no. 16 (Istanbul: Akşam Pub., n.d.), 55.
7. Osman Şevki, "Kırım Muharebesi," *Askerî Tıbbiye Mecmuası* 1, no. 4 (March 1919), 115–117, in Oya Dağlar, "Kırım Savaşı'nda Orduların Sağlık Durumu ve Bir Belge," *Tıp Tarihi Araştırmaları* 12 (2004): 50.
8. Kemal Özbay, "Tarihte Lekeli Humma-Tifüs ve Ordularımızda Tahribatı," *Dirim* 54, no. 3–4 (March–April 1979): 114; and Özbay, *Türk Asker Hekimliği,* 1:41.
9. Unat, "Birinci Dünya Harbinde Türk Ordusu'nda Tifüs Savaşı," *Cerrahpaşa Tıp Fakültesi Dergisi* 20, no. 2 (April 1989): 255.
10. Özbay, "Tarihte Lekeli Humma," 114.
11. Joseph O. Baylen & Alan Conway, *Soldier-Surgeon: The Crimean War Letters of Dr. Douglas A. Reid, 1855–1856,* in Dağlar, "Kırım Savaşı'nda Orduların," 42n3.
12. M. Zühdi Berke, *Tıbbî Viroloji* (Ankara, 1974), 2:1285.
13. Osman Şevki, *Osmanlı Tababeti 3, Türk Tarihinin Ana Hatları Eserinin Müsveddeleri,* 81–82.
14. Ekrem Şadi Kavur, "Askerî Hekimliğin Sıhhiye Hizmetlerinde Bir Etüd," *Dirim* 48, no. 2 (February 1973): 96.
15. Arslan Terzioğlu, "Kırım Harbi Esnasında Osmanlı Hastahaneleri ve Dünya Hastahaneciliğine Etkileri," *Toplumsal Tarih* 85 (January 1991): 42.
16. Özbay, *Türk Asker Hekimliği,* 1:39.
17. Aziz Kalyan, ed. *Kırım Savaşı* (Istanbul: Milliyet Pub., 1975), 78.
18. S. Payzın et al., *Sağlık Hizmetinde Mikrobiyoloji II, Özel Mikrobiyoloji* (Ankara: Tıp Fakültesi Pub., 1968), 660.
19. Özbay, "Tarihte Lekeli Humma," 114.
20. Şevki, *Osmanlı Tababeti 3,* 86.
21. Nedim İpek, *Rumeli'den Anadolu'ya Türk Göçleri* (Ankara: TTK Pub., 1999), 89–90.
22. Bilâl N. Şimşir, *Rumeli'den Türk Göçleri, Belgeler* (Ankara: TTK Pub., 1989), 427, 406–408.
23. İpek, *Rumeli'den Anadolu'ya,* 91.
24. Justin McCarthy, *Death and Exile: The Ethnic Cleansing of Ottoman Muslims, 1821–1922* (Princeton, N.J.: Darwin Press, 1996), 80.
25. İpek, *Rumeli'den Anadolu'ya,* 92.
26. Ekrem Şadi Kavur, "Askerî Hekimliğin Sıhhiye Hizmetlerinde Bir Etüd," *Dirim* 48, no. 3 (March 1973): 148.
27. Şevki, *Osmanlı Tababeti 3,* 87, 90.
28. Özbay, "Tarihte Lekeli Humma," 115.
29. [Major G. v. Hochwaechter], *Türklerle Cephede,* trans. Fahri Çeliker (Ankara: Askerî Tarih Bülteni Eki, August 1979), no. 8: 47, 50, 51–52, 55, 57–58, 61–62.
30. Ekrem Kadri Unat, "Osmanlı İmparatorluğu'nda 1910–1913 Yıllarındaki Kolera Salgınları ve Bunlarla İlgili Olaylar," *Yeni Tıp Tarihi Araştırmaları* 1 (1995): 58.
31. Şevket Süreyya Aydemir, *Makendonya'dan Ortaasya'ya Enver Paşa* (Istanbul: Remzi B., 1971), 2:363.
32. *Alemdar,* 90–155, from 11 November 1912, in Ahmet Halaçoğlu, *Balkan Harbi Sırasında Rumeli'den Türk Göçleri, 1912–1913,* (Ankara: TTK Pub., 1995), 97.
33. Kızılay Arşivi, File no. 211 (4 December 1912), in Halaçoğlu, *Balkan Harbi Sırasında,* 96.

34. Dersaadet'in 1913 Senesine Mahsus Sıhhî İstatistiki, *Şehremaneti Dergisi* (Istanbul, 1913), in Halaçoğlu, *Balkan Harbi Sırasında*, 99.
35. Ekrem Şadi Kavur, "Askerî Hekimliğin Sıhhiye Hizmetlerinde Bir Etüd," *Dirim* 48, no. 4 (April 1973): 193.
36. Seyhülislam Cemaleddin Efendi, *Siyasî Hatıralarım*, trans. Ziyaeddin Engin (Istanbul: Tercüman 1001 Temel Eser, 1978), 110.
37. A. Nazilmof, *Bulgar Süvari Tümeninin Harekâtı* (Ankara: Genelkurmay Pub., 1935), 155–156.
38. Abdülkadir Noyan, *Son Harplerde Salgın Hastalıklarla Savaşlarım* (Ankara: Tıp Fakültesi Y., 1956), 3–5.
39. Abdülkadir Noyan, "İntani ve Salgın Hastalıklara Karşı Tıbbın Eski ve Yeni Durumu," *Istanbul Tıp Fakültesi Mecmuası*, no. 4 (1947): 13–14.
40. Behiç Onul, *İnfeksiyon Hastalıkları*, 5th ed. (Ankara: Tıp Fakültesi Pub., 1974), 688.
41. Ekrem Şadi Kavur, "Askerî Hekimliğin Sıhhiye Hizmetlerinde Bir Etüd," *Dirim* 48, no. 4 (April 1973): 193–194.
42. Cemil Topuzlu, *İstibdat-Meşrutiyet-Cumhuriyet Devirlerinde 80 Yıllık Hatıralarım*, 2nd ed., ed. Hüsrev Hatemi-Aykut Kazancıgil (Istanbul: Cerrahpaşa Tıp Fakültesi Pub., 1982), 118, 125.
43. *Osmanlı Hilâl-i Ahmer Mecmuası*, in Seçil Karal Akgün and Murat Uluğtekin, *Hilâl-i Ahmer'den Kızılay'a* (Ankara, 2000), 1:121.
44. Ahmet Zeki İzgöer, "Osmanlı'nın Yıkılışı Öncesinde Hind Hilâl-i Ahmer Yardımları ve Dr. Ensari'nin Faaliyetleriyle İlgili Bazı Notlar," *Yeni Tıp Tarihi Araştırmaları* 8 (2002): 18.
45. Zekeriya Türkmen, "Balkan Savaşlarında Hilâl-i Ahmer Cemiyetinin Osmanlı Ordusuna Yönelik Sağlık Hizmetleri," *Belleten* 68, no. 252 (August 2004): 483–518.
46. Nazilmof, *Bulgar Süvari Tümeninin Harekâtı*, 155–156.
47. Noyan, *Son Harplerde Salgın Hastalıklarla*, 9.
48. Unat, "Osmanlı İmparatorluğu'nda, 1910–1913," 62.
49. Leon Trotsky, *Balkan Savaşları*, trans. Tansel Güney (Istanbul: Arba Pub., 1995), 257.
50. Ibid., 320.
51. Noyan, *Son Harplerde Salgın Hastalıklarla*, 13–14.
52. Ibid., 15–17.
53. Ibid., 17–18.
54. Ibid., 18–20.
55. Ibid., 22.
56. Aydemir, *Makedonya'dan Ortaasya'ya*, 2:364–365.
57. Noyan, *Son Harplerde Salgın Hastalıklarla*, 10.
58. Unat, "Osmanlı İmparatorluğu'nda 1910-1913," 64.
59. Rıfat N. Bali, "Edirne Muhasarası Sırasında Tutulmuş Bir Günlük-I," *Tarih ve Toplum*, no. 190 (October 1999): 43; no. 191 (November 1999): 16; no. 193 (January 2000): 34.
60. Noyan, *Son Harplerde Salgın Hastalıklarla*, 29–30.
61. Ibid., 23–24.
62. Ibid., 38–39.

63. Operatör Cemil Paşa, *Canlı Tarihler* (Istanbul: Türkiye Pub., 1945), 8:81 ff.
64. Ekrem Şadi Kavur, "Askerî Hekimliğin," *Dirim* 48, no. 4 (April 1973): 194.
65. Özbay, *Türk Asker Hekimliği*, 1:123.
66. Ekrem Kadri Unat, "Türkiye Cumhuriyeti'nde Bulaşıcı Hastalıklarla Savaş," *Cerrahpaşa Tıp Fakültesi Dergisi* 12 (Sp. Issue, 1981): 384.
67. Nuran Yıldırım, "Tanzimat'tan Cumhuriyet'e Koruyucu Sağlık Uygulamaları," *Tanzimat'tan Cumhuriyet'e Türkiye Ansiklopedisi* 5:1332.
68. "Emraz-ı Sariye Mücadelesi," in Hot, *Sıhhiye Mecmuası'na Göre*, 4.
69. BOA DH UMVM File 11/43, no. 3, in Mehmet Temel, "Birinci Dünya Savaşı ve Mütareke Yıllarında Türkiye'deki Bulaşıcı ve Zührevî Hastalıklara Karşı Alınan Önlemler," *Çağdaş Türkiye Tarihi Araştırmaları Dergisi* 3, no. 8 (1998): 332–336.

Chapter 3. Under the Crescent

1. Jorge Blanco Villalta, *Atatürk*, Translated from Spanish by William Campbell (Ankara: TTK Pub., 1991), 104.
2. Yusuf Halaçoğlu, *Osmanlılarda Ulaşım ve Haberleşme (Menziller)* (Ankara: PTT Pub., 2002), 7.
3. Ahmet Emin, *Turkey: In the World War* (New Haven, Conn.: Yale University Press, 1930), 86.
4. Turkish Military History Council, *Birinci Dünya Harbi'nde Türk Harbi, İran-Irak Cephesi* (Ankara: Genelkurmay Pub., 1979), vol. 3, part 1, 800.
5. Necmi Seren, "Yılların Ötesinden," *Harp Tarihi Mecmuası*, no. 210 (June 1982): 77.
6. Jonathan S. McMurray, *Distant Ties: Germany, the Ottoman Empire, and the Construction of the Baghdad Railway*, (Westport, Conn.: Praeger, 2001), 118.
7. İ. Hakkı Sunata, *Gelibolu'dan Kafkaslar'a* (Istanbul: T. İş Bankası Pub., 2003), 243.
8. ATASE, no. 6/4517, box 5240, H-3, in *Birinci Dünya Harbi'nde Türk Harbi*, 1:577–578.
9. Münim Mustafa, *Cepheden Cepheye*, 2nd ed. (Istanbul: Arma Pub., 1998), 15–17, 146.
10. Noyan, *Son Harplerde Salgın Hastalıklarla*, 50.
11. Cavid, *Harb-i Umumi Vesaikinden Irak Seferi, İttihad Hükümeti'nin Hayâlât ve Cehâlet-i Siyâsiyessi*, in Orhan Avcı, *Irak'ta Türk Ordusu, 1914–1918* (Ankara: Vadi Pub., 2004), 268–269.
12. Necdet Sakaoğlu, "Bir Osmanlı Neferinin I. Dünya Savaşı Anıları," *Tarih ve Toplum* 11 (November 1984): 49–50.
13. Ibid.
14. Ibid.
15. Tevfik Sağlam, *Cihan Harbinde 3: Orduda Sıhhî Hizmete Ait Küçük Bir Hulâsa* (Istanbul: Askerî Tıbbiye Pub., 1940), 3.
16. Noyan, *Son Harplerde Salgın Hastalıklarla*, 50.
17. Seuber, *Yıldırım*, trans. Kaymakam Nihat (Istanbul: Askerî Pub., 1932), 16.
18. Hamdullah Suphi [Tanrıöver], "Boğa Dağları," *Türk Yurdu*, vol. 7(14), no. 156 (1918) (Ankara: Tutibay Pub., 2000), 139, 140.
19. Seuber, *Yıldırım*, 32.

20. Sunata, *Gelibolu'dan Kafkaslar'a*, 251.
21. Kress von Kressenstein and Friedrich Freiherr, *Mit den Türken zum Suezkanal* (Berlin: Borhut-Verlag, 1938), 255, 265.
22. Noyan, *Son Harplerde Salgın Hastalıklarla*, 57–59.
23. von Kressenstein and Freiherr, *Mit den Türken*, 122.
24. Liman von Sanders, *Türkiye'de Beş Yıl*, trans. M. Şevki Yazman (Istanbul: Burçak Pub., 1969), 303.
25. The original old Turkish words used in the title were "iaşe and ibate," which meant "providing food and shelter."
26. *Türk Silahlı Kuvvetleri Tarihi, Birinci Dünya Harbi, İdarî Faaliyetler ve Lojistik* (Ankara, Genelkurmay Pub., 1985), 9:577.
27. Ekrem Şadi Kavur, "Askerî Hekimliğin Sıhhiye Hizmetlerinde Bir Etüd," *Dirim* 48, no. 6 (June 1973): 288.
28. Aziz Samih, *Büyük Harpte Kafkas Cephesi Hatıraları* (Ankara: Büyük Erkânıharbiye Y., 1934), 3–4.
29. ATASE Archives, no. 5/3771, box 4156, H. 7 from F. 1-129: *Birinci Dünya Harbi'nde Türk Harbi*, 1: Annex-1.
30. Noyan, *Son Harplerde Salgın Hastalıklarla*, 77–78.
31. Akşin Somel, "Türk Ordusu ile Filistin'de," *Toplumsal Tarih*, no. 66 (June 1989): 58.
32. ATASE Archives, K. 3612, D. 41/30, in Avcı, *Irak'ta Türk Ordusu*, 270.
33. Özbay, "Tarihte Lekeli Humma," 118.
34. Onul, *İnfeksiyon Hastalıkları*, 329.
35. *Birinci Dünya Harbi'nde Türk Harbi*, 1:575.
36. ATASE Archives, A. 1-217, D. 517, F. 2-2.
37. *Birinci Dünya Harbi'nde Türk Harbi*, 1:34.
38. Sağlam, *Büyük Harpte 3. Ordu'da*, 14.
39. von Sanders, *Türkiye'de Beş Yıl*, 68.
40. Ibid., 69.
41. Fahri Belen, *20: Yüzyılda Osmanlı Devleti* (Istanbul: Remzi Pub., 1973), 279.
42. ATASE Archives, no. 4/3671, box 2950, in *Birinci Dünya Harbi'nde Türk Harbi*, 1:54.
43. Samih, *Büyük Harpte Kafkas*, 43.
44. Arif Baytın, *İlk Dünya Harbinde Kafkas Cephesi* (Istanbul: Vakit Pub., 1946), 127.
45. von Sanders, *Türkiye'de Beş Yıl*, 303.
46. Sağlam, *Büyük Harpte 3. Ordu'da*, 16.
47. von Kressenstein and Freiherr, *Mit den Türken*, 205.
48. Samih, *Büyük Harpte Kafkas*, 11.
49. Carl Mühlmann, *Das Deutche-Türkische Waffenbündis İm Weltkriege* (Leipzig, 1940), from p. 256: Veli Yılmaz, *1 nci Dünya Harbi'nde Türk-Alman İttifakı ve Askerî Yardımlar*, (Istanbul: Cem Pub., 1993), 220.
50. *Birinci Dünya Harbi'nde Türk Harbi*, 1:192.
51. Ibid., 2:653–654.
52. Guze, *Büyük Harpte Kafkas Cephesindeki Muharebeler*, trans. Hakkı, *Askerî Mecmua*, no. 20 (January 1931): 60–61.
53. *Birinci Dünya Harbi'nde Türk Harbi*, 1:60.
54. Sağlam, *Cihan Harbinde 3. Ordu'da*, 6.
55. Sağlam, *Büyük Harpte 3. Ordu'da*, 18.

56. Ibid., 26–27.
57. Ibid., 28.
58. von Sanders, *Türkiye'de Beş Yıl*, 158–159.
59. Ibid., 159.
60. Ibid.
61. Ibid., 160.
62. Becker, *I. Dünya Savaşı'nda Osmanlı*, 26.
63. Sağlam, *Büyük Harpte 3. Ordu'da*, 14.
64. Ibid., 49–50.
65. *Türk Silahlı Kuvvetleri Tarihi*, 9:577.
66. Hafız Hakkı Paşa, *Bozgun* (Istanbul: Tercüman 1001 Temel Eser, n.d.), 58.
67. Salih Mayakuşu, *Golç Paşa'nın Hatıratı*, in Faruk Yılmaz, ed., *İmparatorluk Döneminde Türk-Alman İlişkileri* (Ankara: Berikan Pub., 2004), 62.
68. *Goltz Paşa'nın Hatırası ve Hâl Tercümesi*, trans. E. General Pertev Demirhan (Istanbul: Askerî Pub., 1953), 35. For German edition, see General Pertev Demirhan, *Generalfeldmarschall Freiherr von der Goltz* (Göttingen: Göttinger Verlagsanstalt, 1960).
69. Kolonel Lamouche, *Türkiye Tarihi*, trans. Galip Söylemezoğlu (Istanbul: Kanaat K., 1943), 2:468n3.
70. From Mayakuşu, *Golç Paşa'nın Hatıratı*, 163–164.
71. Noyan, *Son Harplerde Salgın Hastalıklarla*, 53–54.
72. Belen, *Birinci Cihan Harbinde Türk Harbi*, 4:83.

Chapter 4. Epidemic Disaster

1. İlhan Selçuk, *Yüzbaşı Selâhattin'in Romanı* (Istanbul: Remzi Pub., 1975), 1:118.
2. *Birinci Dünya Harbi'nde Türk Harbi*, 1:536.
3. Ibid., 535–536.
4. Fevzi Çakmak, *Büyük Harpte Şark Cephesi Hareketleri* (Ankara: Genelkurmay Pub., 1936), 80.
5. Sağlam, *Cihan Harbinde 3. Ordu'da*, 6.
6. von Sanders, *Türkiye'de Beş Yıl*, 6.
7. Sağlam, *Büyük Harpte 3. Ordu'da*, 78.
8. Ibid., 79.
9. Guze, *Büyük Harpte Kafkas Cephesindeki Muharebeler*, trans. Hakkı (Istanbul: Askerî Pub., 1931), 60–61.
10. von Sanders, *Türkiye'de Beş Yıl*, 68.
11. Sağlam, *Cihan Harbinde 3. Orduda*, 7.
12. Karatepe, *I. Dünya Savaşı'nda*, 66–67.
13. Ibid., 67–76.
14. Sağlam, *Büyük Harpte 3. Ordu'da*, 79–80.
15. Samih, *Büyük Harpte Kafkas*, 35.
16. Sağlam, *Büyük Harpte 3. Ordu'da*, 12.
17. Nâzım Şâkir, "Birinci Cihan Harbinde Erzurum ve Sağlık Organizasyonu Anıları," in Nusret Karasu-Nihat Özyardımcı, ed., *Çeşitli Yönleri ile Erzurum ve Çevresi* (Ankara: Ulusal Verem Savaş Derneği Y., 1968), 41–42.
18. Ibid., 92.

19. Server Kâmil, *Kafkas Cephe-i Harbinde Lekeli Humma* (Sivas: Matbaa-i Vilayet, 1916), 4.
20. T. İsmail Gökçe and S. Necati Üster, *Tevfik Sağlam, 1882–1963* (Istanbul: Akgün Pub., 1968), 2:92.
21. İsmail Gökçe, "Erzurum Anılarımdan Çizgiler," *Çeşitli Yönleri ile Erzurum ve Çevresi*, 50.
22. Sağlam, *Cihan Harbinde 3. Orduda*, 9.
23. Ibid., 13.
24. Ibid.
25. Ibid., 13–14.
26. Ibid., 90–92.
27. Özbay, "Tarihte Lekeli Humma," 118.
28. Sağlam, *Büyük Harpte 3. Ordu'da*, 93–97.
29. Ibid., 98–101.
30. Ibid., 125–127.
31. Becker, *I. Dünya Savaşı'nda Osmanlı*, 25.
32. von Sanders, *Türkiye'de Beş Yıl*, 57.
33. Becker, *I. Dünya Savaşı'nda Osmanlı*, 27.
34. BOA DH-KMS, from box no. 21, no. 9, in Mehmet Temel, "Birinci Dünya Savaşı," 330.
35. BOA DH İD, from box no. 165, no. 8, in Temel, "Birinci Dünya Savaşı," 33.
36. BOA DH-KMS, from box no. 31, no. 11, in Temel, "Birinci Dünya Savaşı," 330.
37. BOA DH-UMVM, from box no. 11/5, no. 10, in Temel, "Birinci Dünya Savaşı," 330.
38. Temel, "Birinci Dünya Savaşı," 331.
39. Lütfi Aksu, *Lekeli Humma* (Ankara: Ulusal M., 1943), 7.
40. Özbay, "Tarihte Lekeli Humma," 116.
41. Zühal Özaydın, "Osmanlı Hilâl-i Ahmer Cemiyeti'nin Kuruluşu ve Çalışmaları," *Türkler*, vol. 13 (Ankara: Yeni Türkiye Pub., 2002), 685.
42. American Board of Commissioners for Foreign Missions, *The One Hundred and Fifth Annual Report, Connecticut, October 26, 1915*, in Hikmet Özdemir et al., *Ermeniler: Sürgün ve Göç* (Ankara: TTK Pub., 2004), 103–104.
43. Nil Sarı and Zühal Özaydın, "I. Dünya Savaşında Osmanlı Hilâl-i Ahmer Cemiyeti," *2. Türk Tıp Tarihi Kongresi, Istanbul, 20–21 Eylül 1990* (Ankara: TTK Pub., 1999), 164.
44. Aydın Ayhan, "1914 Yılında Balıkesir'de Tifüs Salgını ve Müdafaa-yı Milliye Cemiyeti'nin İki Sağlık Beyannamesi," *Tıp Tarihi Araştırmaları* 9 (August 1999): 221–228.
45. From *Karasi Journal* of 11 January 1915 and Nu. 38, in Ayhan, "1914 Yılında Balıkesir'de Tifüs Salgını," 223–224.
46. Hilmar Kaiser, "Denying the Armenian Genocide: The German Connection," *Journal of the Society for Armenian Studies* 9 (New York, 1999): 38.
47. Sağlam, *Büyük Harpte 3. Ordu'da*, 78.
48. Gökçe and Üster, *Tevfik Sağlam, 1882–1963*, 2:79.
49. Hüsamettin Tugaç, *Bir Neslin Dramı* (Istanbul: Çağdaş Y., 1975), 27, 34.

50. Guze, *Büyük Harpte Kafkas*, 98.
51. Becker, *I. Dünya Savaşı'nda Osmanlı*, 77.

Chapter 5. Ordeal with Diseases

1. Murat Çulcu, ed., *Mehmed Fasih Bey'in Günlüğü* (Istanbul: Denizler Pub., 2002), 173–174.
2. Noyan, *Son Harplerde Salgın Hastalıklarla*, 46.
3. James, *Gallipoli*, 214.
4. Aydın Ayhan, "Çanakkale Savaşları'nda Yaralanmalar ve Hastalıklar," *Tıp Tarihi Araştırmaları* 11 (2003): 99.
5. Onul, *İnfeksiyon Hastalıkları*, 303.
6. James, *Gallipoli*, p. 221, 222.
7. C. F. Aspinall-Oglander, *Military Operations Gallipoli* (London: William Heinemann Ltd., 1932), 2:114–115, 117–118, 122, 366.
8. Ian Hamilton, *Gallipoli Dairy* (London: Edward Arnold, 1920), 1:364.
9. Osman Öndeş, "Bir Savaşın Sonrası," in Ian Hamilton, *Gelibolu Günlüğü* (Turkish edition, Istanbul: Hürriyet Y., 1972), 292.
10. Hamilton, *Gallipoli Dairy*, 1:387.
11. James, *Gallipoli*, 303.
12. Hamilton, *Gallipoli Dairy*, 2:170.
13. James, *Gallipoli*, 311.
14. Hamilton, *Gallipoli Dairy*, 2:248.
15. Ekrem Şadi Kavur, "Askerî Hekimliğin Sıhhiye Hizmetlerinde Bir Etüd," *Dirim* 48, no. 5 (May 1973): 243.
16. Hamilton, *Gallipoli Dairy*, 2:262.
17. Aspinall-Oglander, *Military Operations Gallipoli*, 2:433–434.
18. James, *Gallipoli*, 335–336.
19. *Birinci Dünya Harbi'nde Türk Harbi*, vol. 5, book 1, 272–274.
20. Ibid., vol. V, book 2, 432–433.
21. Sarı and Özaydın, "I. Dünya Savaşında," 165.
22. *Türk Silahlı Kuvvetleri Tarihi*, 9:300.
23. Aptülahat Akşin, *Atatürk'ün Dış Politika İlkeleri ve Diplomasisi* (Ankara: TTK Pub., 1991), xii.
24. *Türk Silahlı Kuvvetleri Tarihi*, 9:300.
25. ATASE Archives, A. 1-217, D. 517, F. 2-3.
26. Aspinall-Oglander, *Military Operations Gallipoli*, 2:367n1.
27. Kavur, "Askerî Hekimliğin Sıhhiye Hizmetlerinde Bir Etüd," *Dirim* 49, no. 7 (July 1973): 335.
28. Özbay, "Tarihte Lekeli Humma," 118.
29. ATASE Archives, A. 1-217, D. 517, F. 2-4.
30. Ibid.
31. *Birinci Dünya Harbi*, vol. 7, part 1, 106–109.
32. Ibid., vol. 7, part 2, 164–165.
33. Ibid., vol. 7, part 3, 74–75.

34. ATASE Archives, A. 1-217, D. 517, F. 2-5.
35. Sağlam, *Büyük Harpte 3. Ordu'da*, 106.
36. Ibid., 106–107.
37. Ibid., 107–108.
38. Ibid., 109–110.
39. Ibid., 110.
40. Ibid., 111.
41. Ibid., 102–105.
42. Ibid., 105.
43. Ibid., 65.
44. Ibid., 117.
45. Ibid., 120–121.
46. Ibid., 122–124.
47. *Birinci Dünya Harbi'nde Türk Harbi*, 6:782.
48. ATASE Archives, from no. 5/13796, box 4116, H-1, file H-1, F-1–73, in *Birinci Dünya Harbi'nde Türk Harbi*, 6:784–785.
49. Ibid., A. 1-217, D. 517, F. 2-3.
50. *Birinci Dünya Harbinde Türk Harbi, Sina-Filistin Cephesi*, vol. 4, part 1, 679–680.
51. Ibid., 680–681.
52. Seuber, *Yıldırım*, 42.
53. *Birinci Dünya Harbinde Türk Harbi*, vol. 4, part 1, 681.
54. Becker, *I. Dünya Savaşı'nda Osmanlı*, 54–55.
55. Ibid., 42.
56. Necmi Seren, "Yılların Ötesinden," *Harp Tarihi Mecmuası*, no. 211 (July 1982): 75 ff.
57. ATASE Archives, from no. 4/10832, box 3709, F. 1, 34 and no. 4/11007, box 3772, box H-7, F-1, in *Birinci Dünya Harbi'nde Türk Harbi*, vol. 4, part 2, 752.
58. Ibid.
59. *Birinci Dünya Harbi'nde Türk Harbi*, vol. 3, part 1, 800.
60. ATASE Archives, from K. 3698, D. 1/235-4, F. 1-1; F. 1-162, in Avcı, *Irak'ta Türk Ordusu*, 269.
61. ATASE Archives, A. 1-217, D. 517, F. 2-1.
62. *Birinci Dünya Harbi'nde Türk Harbi*, vol. 2, part 2, 325–326.
63. ATASE Archives, A. 1-217, D. 517, F. 2-2.
64. George Buchanan, *The Tragedy of Mesopotamia* (Edinburg: 1938), 5–7.
65. Ibid., 20–22.
66. ATASE Archives, from K. 3612, D. 42/30, F. 10, in Avcı, *Irak'ta Türk Ordusu*, 267.
67. Ismail Hakkı Süerdem, *Anılarım*, ed. Orhan Avcı (Ankara: Bilge Pub., 2004), 49.
68. ATASE Archives, from K. 3649. D. 208/140, F. 4-30, in Avcı, *Irak'ta Türk Ordusu*, 101.
69. Sir William Robertson, *Soldiers and Statesmen, 1914–1918* (London: Cassell and Company Ltd., 1926), 2:63 ff.
70. Sakaoğlu, "Bir Osmanlı Neferinin," 52.
71. Noyan, *Son Harplerde Salgın Hastalıklarla*, 68–69.
72. Ibid., 69.
73. Ibid., 74–75.
74. Ibid., 79–81.

75. Ibid., 91–92.
76. Payzın et al., *Sağlık Hizmetinde Mikrobiyoloji II*, 1020.
77. Ibid., 742.
78. ATASE Archives, box 250, *General İhsan Aksoley'in Anıları*, in *Birinci Dünya Harbi'nde Türk Harbi*, 6:824.
79. *Birinci Dünya Harbi'nde Türk Harbi*, 6:825.
80. Diamond, *Guns, Germs and Steel*, 202.
81. Bahaddin Serhan, "Savaştan da Öldürücü Bir Salgın!" *Yakın Tarihimiz* 3 (March 1983): 23–24.
82. Nikiforuk, *The Fourth Horseman*, 146.
83. F. Tezok, E. Gümrükçü, and M. Sağlam, "1971 Hong-Kong Gribinin Memleketimizdeki Özellikleri," *Mikrobiyoloji Bülteni* 6, no. 1 (January 1972): 91–92.
84. Nikiforuk, *The Fourth Horseman*, 148.
85. David Fromkin, *Barışa Son Veren Barış*, trans. Mehmet Harmancı (Istanbul: Sabah Pub., 1993), 378.
86. Ibid.
87. Serhan, "Savaştan da Öldürücü Bir Salgın!" 25.
88. ATASE Archives, from no. 5/13796, box 4116, file H, 1, F. 1-73, in *Birinci Dünya Harbi'nde Türk Harbi*, 6:791.
89. Kavur, "Askerî Hekimliğin Sıhhiye Hizmetlerinde Bir Etüd," *Dirim* 49, no. 7 (July 1973): 336.
90. Noyan, *Son Harplerde Salgın Hastalıklarla*, 86–89.
91. *Ahenk*, 1 November 1918, in Engin Berber, *Yeni Onbinlerin Gölgesinde Bir Sancak: İzmir* (Istanbul: Tarih Vakfı Yurt Pub., 1997), 100.
92. *Anadolu*, 22 November 1918, in Berber, *Yeni Onbinlerin Gölgesinde*, 101.
93. Meclis-i Âyan Zabıt Ceridesi, D. 3, İ. 5, C. 1 (Ankara, 1990), 157, in Tuncay Öğün, *Vilayât-ı Şarkiye Mültecileri, 1915–1923* (Ankara: Babil Pub., 2004), 76.
94. Nükhet Yürür Kutlay, "Refik Saydam'ın Sağlık Politikası ve Hıfzıssıhha Merkezi'nin Bu Politikadaki Yeri," *Yeni Tıp Tarihi Araştırmaları* 4 (1998): 191.
95. Ali İhsan Türkkan, ed., "İstanbul İşgal Kuvvetleri Komutanlığı Raporları (VII)," *Belgelerle Türk Tarihi Dergisi* 30 (July 1999): 58–59.
96. Selçuk, *Yüzbaşı Selahattin'in Romanı*, 1:372.
97. Becker, *I. Dünya Savaşı'nda Osmanlı*, 20.
98. Feridun Erik, "Türkiye'de Bulaşıcı Hastalıklar," *Dirim* 56, no. 9–10 (September–October 1981): 306.
99. *Vekâletin On Yıllık Mesaisi*, 41–42.
100. *The Orient*, 7/21 (April 21, 1920), in Nur Bilge Criss, *İşgal Altında Istanbul, 1918–1923*, 3rd ed. (Istanbul: İletişim Pub., 2000), 57.
101. Frank A. Ross, C. Luther Fry, and Elbridge Sibley, *The Near East and American Philanthropy*, in Criss, *İşgal Altında Istanbul*, 57.
102. "Emraz-ı Sariye Mücadelesi," no. 13 (1338–1922), in Hot, *Sıhhiye Mecmuası'na Göre*, 206.
103. Ibid., 184.
104. Ahmet Emin Yalman, *Yakın Tarihte Gördüklerim, Geçirdiklerim* (Istanbul: Yenilik Pub., 1970), 322.
105. Ekrem Kadri Unat, "Osmanlı İmparatorluğu'nun Son 40 Yılında Türkiye'nin

Tüberküloz Tarihçesi Üzerine," *Cerrahpaşa Tıp Fakültesi Dergisi* 10, no. 4 (October 1979): 277.
106. Hot, *Sıhhiye Mecmuası'na*, 107.
107. Besim Ömer, *Verem Tehlikesi, Veremle Mücadele*, in İnci Hot, Dr. Besim Ömer Paşa'nın Anne ve Çocuk Sağlığı Açısından Ülkemiz Nüfus Meselesi Hakkındaki Görüşleri (Istanbul University SBE, unpublished thesis, 1996), 45.
108. Unat, "Osmanlı İmparatorluğu'nun Son 40 Yılında," 274.
109. Erik, "Türkiye'de Bulaşıcı Hastalıklar," 306.
110. Necmi Seren, "Yılların Ötesinden," *Harp Tarihi Mecmuası*, no. 209 (May 1982): 79.
111. Hans-Lukas Kieser, "Bir Misyoner Hastahanesinin Çevresindeki Küçük Dünya: Urfa, 1897–1922," in François Georgeon-Paul Dumont, *Osmanlı İmparatorluğu'nda Yaşamak*, trans. Maide Selen (Istanbul: İletişim Pub., 2000), 278.
112. Onul, *İnfeksiyon Hastalıkları*, 408.
113. "Emraz-i Sariye Mücadelesi," *Sıhhiye Mecmuası*, no. 13 (1338–1922), in Hot, *Sıhhiye Mecmuası'na Göre*, 133.
114. Becker, *I. Dünya Savaşı'nda Osmanlı*, 19.
115. Özbay, "Tarihte Lekeli Humma," 119.
116. Becker, *I. Dünya Savaşı'nda Osmanlı*, 19.
117. Hot, *Sıhhiye Mecmuası'na Göre*, 133–134.
118. Ibid., 25.
119. Ekrem Kadri Unat, "Türkiye'de Atatürk Döneminde Bulaşıcı Hastalıklarla Savaş için Kuruluşlar ve Çalışmalar," *Türkiye'de Atatürk Döneminde Bulaşıcı Hastalıklarla Savaş Toplantısı, Cerrahpaşa Tıp Fakültesi Atatürk Haftası, 18–28 Mayıs 1981* (Istanbul, 1982), 17.
120. Hot, *Sıhhiye Mecmuası'na Göre*, 13, 17.
121. Zafer Toprak, "Istanbul'da Fuhuş ve Zührevî Hastalıklar, 1914–1933," *Tarih ve Toplum*, no. 39 (March 1987): 39–40.
122. *Meclis-i Mebusan Zabıt Ceridesi*, Term 3, Year of Session 4, 2:489.
123. Ibid.
124. Kızılay Archives, from box 265-1/1919, in Çapa, *Kızılay (Hilâl-i Ahmer Cemiyeti)*, 214–218.
125. Kızılay Archives, from box 33 (1919), in Çapa, *Kızılay (Hilâl-i Ahmer Cemiyeti)*, 218–220.
126. Halide Edip Adıvar, *Türk'ün Ateşle İmtihanı* (Istanbul: Çan Pub., 1962), 158.
127. Dr. Zeki, "Hıfzıssıha Şubesi'nin 1332 Senesi Zübde-i Mesaisi," in Hot, *Sıhhiye Mecmuası'na Göre*, 38.
128. İ. Arıkan, "25 Yıllık Sıtma Mücadele Tarihçemiz," *Dirim* 25, no. 35 (1950): 102–104.
129. Tevfik Salim, "333 Senesinde Üçüncü Ordu Mıntıkasında Yapılacak Emrâz-ı Sariye Mücadelesi Hakkında Proje," in Hot, *Sıhhiye Mecmuası'na Göre*, 40.
130. *Sağlık Hizmetlerinde 50 Yıl* (Ankara: Sağlık Bakanlığı Pub., 1973), 104–105.
131. Ibid.
132. Ayhan Yücel, "Türkiye'de Sıtma Savaşı," *Türkiye'de Atatürk Döneminde Bulaşıcı Hastalıklarla Savaş Toplantısı, Cerrahpaşa Tıp Fakültesi Atatürk Haftası, 18–28 Mayıs 1981* (Istanbul, 1981), 45–46.
133. Cevdet Timur, *Türk İstiklâl Harbi* (Ankara, 1975), 7:559.
134. Ibid., 2:286.

135. Ibid.
136. *Vekâletin 10 Yıllık Mesaisi*, Sıhhiye Mecmuası Fevkalâde Nüshası (29 October 1933), 3.
137. Meliha Özpekcan, "Türkiye Cumhuriyeti'nde Sağlık Politikası, 1923–1933," *Yeni Tıp Tarihi Araştırmaları* 7 (2001): 112, 127 ff.
138. B. Ömer (Akalın), *Nüfus Siyaseti ve Küçük Çocuklarda Vefayat*, in Zuhal Özaydın and İnci Hot, "Dr. Ömer Besim Paşa'nın Ülkemiz Nüfus Siyaseti Hakkındaki Görüşleri," *Tıp Tarihi Araştırmaları* 9 (August 1999): 216–217.
139. Onul, *Infeksiyon Hastalıkları*, p. 859.
140. Orhan Özkan, "Atatürk Döneminde Sağlık Politikası," *Atatürk Dönemi Sağlık Politikası ve Türkiye'nin Ekonomik Gelişmesi Semineri* (Ankara: AÜSBF Pub., 1982), 195.
141. Andrew Mango, *Atatürk* (London: John Murray, 1999), 274–275.
142. Talat, "Ankara'da Sıtma ve Mücadele Teşkilatı," *Sıhhiye Mecmuası* 5, no. 31–32 (1930): 1312–1313.
143. Zuhal Özaydın, "Büyük Önder Atatürk'ün Himayelerinde Yapılan I. Millî Türk Tıp Kongresi," *Tıp Tarihi Araştırmaları* 7 (June 1998): 221 ff.
144. Ibid., 225 ff.
145. Justin McCarthy, *Muslims and Minorities* (New York: New York University Press, 1983), 118–119.
146. Aydemir, *Makendonya'dan Ortaasya'ya*, 3:373. For a remarkable testimony, see M. Derviş Kuntman, *Bir Doktorun Harp ve Memleket Hatıraları* (217 Sayılı Silahlı Kuvvetler Dergisi'nin Ek Kısmı), 85th Anniversary, no. 1 (March 1966).
147. Ahmet Refik, *Kafkas Yollarında İki Komite İki Kıtal*, ed. Osman Selim Kocahanoğlu (Istanbul: Temel Pub., 1998), 214–215.
148. McCarthy, *Muslims and Minorities*, 119.
149. Ibid., 120.

Chapter 6. Unburied Corpses

1. Leon Rabinowicz, *Nüfus Meselesi*, trans. Alâettin Cemil (Ankara, 1930), 199–200.
2. Eric Hobsbawm, *The Age of Extremes: The Short Twentieth Century, 1914–1991* (London: Abacus, 1994), 23.
3. Rabinowicz, *Nüfus Meselesi*, 200.
4. *Journal de la Societe de Statistique* de Paris (December 1925), in Halûk Cillov, *Nüfus İstatistikleri ve Demografinin Genel Esasları* (Istanbul: İktisat Fakültesi Pub., 1960), 304.
5. C. R. M. F. Cruttwell, *A History of the Great War, 1914–1918* (Oxford: Clarendon Press, [1934] 1964), 630.
6. Ibid., 630.
7. Butler, *Australian Army Medical Services*, 879, taken from Table 9.
8. Hans Zinsser, *Rats, Lice and History*, in William H. McNeill, *Plagues and Peoples* (New York: Anchor Books, 1977), 194–195.
9. Baldwin, *World War I*, 156.
10. Türkkaya Ataöv, *Deaths Caused by Disease: In Relation to the Armenian Question* (Ankara: SBF Pub., 1985), 4.
11. Clement Pirquet, ed., *Volksgesundheit ik Krieg*, in McNeill, *Plagues and Peoples*, 252.

12. Zürcher, "Between Death and Desertion," 244.
13. Sağlam, *Cihan Harbinde 3. Orduda*, 10.
14. *Türk Silahlı Kuvvetleri Tarihi*, 9:578.
15. See Butler, *Australian Army Medical Services*.
16. *Statistics of the Military Effort of the British Empire During the Great War, The War Office, March 1922* (reprinted by Naval & Military Press, 1999), 356.
17. Quoted in Ataöv, *Deaths Caused by Disease*, 3.
18. Onul, *İnfeksiyon Hastalıkları*, 735.
19. McNeill, *Plagues and Peoples*, 252.
20. Ibid., 328n84.
21. Quoted in Ataöv, *Deaths Caused by Disease*, 3.
22. Onul, *İnfeksiyon Hastalıkları*, 735.
23. Keegan, *A History of Warfare*, 361.
24. Ibid., 365.
25. Quoted in Ataöv, *Deaths Caused by Disease*, 3.
26. S. Stuart Starrit, *The Life of Nansen* (London: Religions Tract Society, n.d.), 132.
27. W. E. D. Allen and Paul Muratoff, *Caucasian Battlefields* (Cambridge: Cambridge University Press, 1953), 439.
28. Ibid., 440–441.
29. Belen, *20. Yüzyılda Osmanlı*, 300–301.
30. Keegan, *A History of Warfare*, 361.
31. Aspinall-Oglander, *Military Operations Gallipoli*, 2:484.
32. John Terraine, *The Great War, 1914–1915* (London: Arrow Books Ltd., 1967), 104–105.
33. Hans Kannengiesser Pasha, *The Campaign in Gallipoli*, translated from the German (London: Hutchinson Pub., 2nd impression, 1927), 259.
34. Becker, *I. Dünya Savaşı'nda Osmanlı*, 58.
35. von Sanders, *Türkiye'de Beş Yıl*, 125.
36. Robertson, *Soldiers and Statesmen*, 136.
37. Quoted in Ataöv, *Deaths Caused by Disease*, 3.
38. Keegan, *A History of Warfare*, 365.
39. Robertson, *Soldiers and Statesmen*, 1:301.
40. R. S. Morton, *Venereal Disease*, in McNeill, *Plagues and Peoples*, 252.
41. Keegan, *A History of Warfare*, 365.
42. Quoted in Ataöv, *Deaths Caused by Disease*, 3.
43. Onul, *İnfeksiyon Hastalıkları*, 735.
44. Ibid., 355.
45. Ibid.
46. Ibid.
47. *Statistics of the Military Effort of the British Empire*, 353.
48. Quoted in Ataöv, *Deaths Caused by Disease*, 3.
49. Ibid., 355.
50. Ibid.
51. Ibid.
52. Ibid.
53. Ibid.

54. Commandant M. Larcher, *La Guerre Turque dans la Guerre Mondiale* (Paris: Etienne Chiron, Berger-Levrault, 1926), 602.
55. Hikmet Bayur, *Türk İnkılâp Tarihi*, vol. 3, part 4 (Ankara: TTK Pub., 1983), 787n99.
56. Tevfik Bıyıklıoğlu, *Çanakkale Muharebelerine Dair Konferans* (Istanbul: 1950), 50.
57. Belen, *20. Yüzyılda Osmanlı*, 271, fn.
58. Ibid.
59. Mustafa, *Cepheden Cepheye*, 136.
60. Alan Moorehead, *Gallipoli* (New York: Harper and Brothers Publishers, 1956), 361.
61. *General Maslofski'nin Umumî Harpte Kafkas Cephesi Eserinin Tenkidi*, trans. Nazmi (Ankara: Genelkurmay Pub., 1935), 47–48.
62. Larcher, *La Guerre Turque dans la Guerre Mondiale*, 602.
63. *Statistics of the Military Effort of the British Empire*, 353.
64. Ibid.
65. *Tasvir-i Efkâr*, no. 1867, in *Türk Asker Hekimliği Tarihi*, 1:316.
66. Emin, *Turkey: In the World War*, 252–253.
67. Ibid., 253.
68. Ibid.
69. Niall Ferguson, *The Pity of War* (New York: Basic Books, 1999), 295, 299.
70. Edward J. Erickson, *Ordered To Die: A History of the Ottoman Army in the First World War* (Westport, Conn.: Greenwood Press, 2001), 211.
71. Ibid., 208.
72. Kannengiesser Pasha, *The Campaign in Gallipoli*, 241.
73. Sağlam, *Büyük Harpte 3. Ordu'da*, 69–71.
74. Ibid., 69–70.
75. Ibid., 70.
76. Ibid.
77. Ibid., 70–71.
78. Ibid., 71.
79. Ibid., 69.
80. Ibid., 73–76.
81. *Birinci Dünya Harbi'nde Türk Harbi*, 2:776.
82. Sağlam, *Cihan Harbinde 3. Orduda*, 9–10; also see *Birinci Dünya Harbi'nde Türk Harbi*, 2:732.

Chapter 7. Unexpected Results

1. Panzac, *La Peste dans l'Empire Ottoman*, 44.
2. Becker, *I. Dünya Savaşı'nda Osmanlı*, 3.
3. McCarthy, *Death and Exile*, 218–219.
4. (US 867.00/1063) cited in McCarthy, *Death and Exile*, 250n194.
5. Allen and Muratoff, *Caucasian Battlefields*, 437.
6. No reference has been made here to the decision taken by the Ottoman Empire during the Great War for the deportation of some Armenians to Syria and the implementations made to that end. That subject has been mentioned only within the context of the discussions with regards to the epidemic diseases. /HÖ.

7. UK ARCHIVES, WO 157/695, September 14–21, 1915, Cairo.
8. Özdemir et al., *Ermeniler: Sürgün ve Göç*.
9. Hilmi Bayar, "Bir Ailevî Akdeniz Humması (Periyodik Hastalık)", *Dirim* 60, no. 1–2 (January–February 1985): 55.
10. UK ARCHIVES, FO 608/79; the cipher sent from Dr. H. T. Main, the American Commissioner in the Caucasus to Charles V. Vickrey (New York) on the date of 14 April 1919.
11. UK ARCHIVES, FO 248/1277.
12. BOA, Dahiliye from Cipher no. 57/337, in Bülent Bakar, Ermeni Tehciri ve Uygulaması (Marmara University TAE, Unpublished Thesis, 2003), 122–123.
13. Becker, *I. Dünya Savaşı'nda Osmanlı*, 44.
14. Mayakuşu, *Golç Paşa'nın Hatıratı*, 127.
15. *Türk Silahlı Kuvvetleri Tarihi*, 9:301.
16. Seuber, *Yıldırım*, 37.
17. Ekmeleddin İhsanoğlu, *Suriye'de Modern Sağlık Müesseseleri, Hastahaneleri ve Şam Tıp Fakültesi* (Ankara: TTK Pub., 1999), 20–21.
18. Özbay, "Tarihte Lekeli Humma," 118.
19. *Osmanlı Belgelerinde Ermeniler, 1915–1920* (Ankara: Devlet Arşivleri Pub., 1994), 108.
20. UK ARCHIVES, T 161/50, "Statistics for the year, 1918–1919," 36–38.
21. UK ARCHIVES, T 161/50, 35.
22. Ibid.
23. UK ARCHIVES, FO 248/1277.
24. Ziya Öktem, "Basilli Dizanteri Aşılarının Şimdiki Vaziyeti Hakkında," *Istanbul Tıp Fakültesi Mecmuası*, no. 16 (April 1941): 2061.
25. Abdülkadir Noyan, *İç Hastalıkları Ders Kitabı, İntan Hastalıkları* (Istanbul: Mazlum Pub., 1943), 168.
26. Becker, *I. Dünya Savaşı'nda Osmanlı*, 46.
27. Ibid., 55.
28. Kress von Kressenstein and Friedrich Freiherr, *Mit den Türken zum Suezkanal* (Berlin: Otto Schlegel, 1938), 134–135.
29. *Türk Silahlı Kuvvetleri Tarihi*, 9:302.
30. Becker, *I. Dünya Savaşı'nda Osmanlı*, 42.
31. Ibid., 62–63.
32. İhsanoğlu, *Suriye'de Modern Sağlık* Müesseseleri, 9, 17.
33. *Birinci Dünya Harbinde Türk Harbi*, 4:701.
34. Sağlam, *Büyük Harpte 3. Ordu'da*, 52.
35. Halide Edip Adıvar, *Mor Salkımlı Ev*, 5th ed. (Istanbul: Özgür Pub., 2004), 227–228.
36. McCarthy, *Death and Exile*, 222.
37. Sağlam, *Büyük Harpte 3. Ordu'da*, 38.
38. Ibid., 53.
39. Ibid., 54.
40. Ibid.
41. Ibid., 55.
42. Ibid.

43. Ibid., 56.
44. Ibid.
45. Donald Matthew, *Ortaçağ Avrupası*, trans. Mehmet Ali Kılıçbay (Istanbul: İletişim Pub., 1988), 154.
46. Albert S. Lyons and R. Joseph Petrucelli, *Çağlar Boyu Tıp*, trans. Nilgün Güdücü (Istanbul: Roche, 1997), 549.
47. *Birinci Dünya Harbinde Türk Harbi*, 3:27, 29–31.
48. Noyan, *Son Harplerde Salgın Hastalıklarla*, 71.
49. Onul, *İnfeksiyon Hastalıkları*, 858, 859.
50. Seuber, *Yıldırım*, 39.
51. Ibid.
52. Ibid., 79n141.
53. *Meclis-i Mebusan Zabıt Ceridesi*, Term 3, Year of session 1, 1:557 ff.
54. Ibid., 515–516.
55. Becker, *I. Dünya Savaşı'nda Osmanlı*, 25.
56. Ibid., 38.
57. Noyan, *Son Harplerde Salgın Hastalıklarla*, 54.
58. Ibid., 54–55.
59. Ibid., 56.
60. Ibid., 60.
61. Becker, *I. Dünya Savaşı'nda Osmanlı*, 27.
62. Noyan, *Son Harplerde Salgın Hastalıklarla*, 69.
63. Ibid., 60.
64. Ibid., 70.
65. S. Payzın et al., *Sağlık Hizmetinde Mikrobiyoloji* 2, 916.
66. Behçet Onul, "Kolera," *Sağlık Dergisi* 40, nos. 1–2 (1966): 10–12.
67. Noyan, *Son Harplerde Salgın Hastalıklarla*, 65 ff.
68. Sağlam, *Büyük Harpte 3. Ordu'da*, 64.
69. Ibid., 113.
70. Ibid., 114.
71. von Sanders, *Türkiye'de Beş Yıl*, 171–172.
72. BOA DH-KMS, from box no. 44/2, no. 3, in Temel, "Birinci Dünya Savaşı," 332.
73. Çakmak, *Büyük Harpte Şark Cephesi*, 257.
74. Sağlam, *Büyük Harpte 3. Ordu'da*, 114.
75. Ibid., 114–115.
76. Ibid., 115.
77. Becker, *I. Dünya Savaşı'nda Osmanlı*, 29.
78. Noyan, *Son Harplerde Salgın Hastalıklarla*, 85–86.
79. Sağlam, *Büyük Harpte 3. Ordu'da*, 65.
80. Ibid., 117.
81. Ibid., 117–118.
82. Noyan, *Son Harplerde Salgın Hastalıklarla*, 75–76.
83. Ibid., 76.
84. "Çekirgeye Karşı," *Tanin*, 16 February 1916, in Tuncay Öğün, *Birinci Dünya Savaşı'nda Kafkas Cephesinin İaşesi*, 110.

85. Panzac, *La Peste dans l'Empire Ottoman*, 41–42.
86. Ibid., 42.
87. Zafer Toprak, *İttihad–Terakki ve Cihan Harbi, 1914–1918* (İstanbul: Homer Pub., 2003), 98.
88. *Meclis-i Mebusan Zabıt Ceridesi*, Term 3, year of session 1, vol. 1 (İçtimai Fevkalâde), 225–239, 247–248, 388–390.
89. *Meclis-i Mebusan Zabıt Ceridesi*, Term 3, year of session 2, vol. 2, 86–89.
90. *Meclis-i Mebusan Zabıt Ceridesi*, Term 3, year of session 5, vol. 1, 56–59.
91. "Ticaret ve Ziraat Nazırıyla Mülâkat," *Tanin*, February 25 1916, in Tuncay Öğün, *Birinci Dünya Savaşı'nda Kafkas Cephesinin İaşesi*, 111.
92. "Çekirge İtlâfı", *İkdam*, from 12 February 1331, in Öğün, *Birinci Dünya Savaşı'nda Kafkas Cephesinin İaşesi*, 112.
93. Belen, *20: Yüzyılda Osmanlı Devleti*, 241.
94. Cemal Paşa, *Hatırât*, 312.
95. Ibid., 315.
96. Orhan Kılıç, "Osmanlı Devleti'nde Meydana Gelen Kıtlıklar," *Türkler* 10:718.
97. Panzac, *La Peste dans l'Empire Ottoman 1700–1850*, 42–43.
98. Öğün, *Birinci Dünya Savaşı'nda Kafkas Cephesinin İaşesi*, 296 ff.
99. Bayur, *Türk İnkılâp Tarihi*, vol. 3, part 3, 360.
100. Kurmay Albay Hulusi Baykoç, "Kafkas ve Irak Cephesinde Beşinci Kuvve-i Seferiye" (52. Tümen), *Askerî Mecmua*, no. 60 (1 June 1942): 46–47.
101. Ibid., 47–49.
102. Abdullah Saydam, "Birinci Dünya Savaşı Sırasında Istanbul Halkının Geçim Sıkıntısı," *Belgelerle Türk Tarihi Dergisi* 19 (August 1998): 66–67.
103. Toprak, *İttihad–Terakki ve Cihan Harbi, 1914–1918*, 97.
104. Ali Fuad Erden, *Birinci Cihan Harbinde Suriye Hatıraları* (Istanbul: Halk Pub., 1954), 282–283.
105. *Memoirs of Halide Edib* (New York: The Century Co., 1926), 389.
106. Erden, *Birinci Cihan Harbinde Suriye Hatıraları*, 247.
107. Cemal Paşa, *Hatırât*, 317–319.
108. Ibid.
109. Ibid.
110. Helmut Becker, *Åskulap Zwischen Reichsadler und Halbmond* (Herzogenrath: Verlag Murken-Altrogge, 1990), 316.
111. Ibid.
112. Selçuk, *Yüzbaşı Selahattin'in Romanı*, 1:342.
113. UK FO, 248/1192, report dated 5 January 1918 from John L. Caldwell to E. S. Scott.
114. UK FO, 248/1192, report dated 6 May 1915.
115. McCarthy, *Death and Exile*, 223, 230; also see McCarthy, *Muslims and Minorities*, 133–137.
116. Joseph Pomiankowsky, *Osmanlı İmparatorluğu'nun Çöküşü*, trans. Kemal Turan (Istanbul: Kayıhan Pub., 1990), 147.
117. Becker, *I. Dünya Savaşı'nda Osmanlı*, 10.
118. von Sanders, *Türkiye'de Beş Yıl*, 184–185.
119. Zürcher, "Between Death and Desertion," 244.
120. Ibid., 257.

Chapter 8. Unarmed Warriors

1. H. Braun, "Sarî Hastalıkların Devlet ve Halk İçin Ehemmiyeti," *Üniversite Konferansları I, 1933–1937* (Istanbul: University Pub., 1939), 103–108, 110.
2. Mehmet Arif, *Başımıza Gelenler* (Istanbul: Harp Akademileri Pub., 1969), 117.
3. Ekrem Kadri Unat, "Görev Kurbanı İki Mikrobiyoloğumuz," *Türk Mikrobiyoloji Cemiyeti Dergisi* 9, no. 61 (1979): 62.
4. See Chapter 3 of this study, entitled "Under the Crescent."
5. Zuhal Özaydın, Osmanlı Hilâl-i Ahmer Cemiyeti Salnamesi (Istanbul University, Unpublished thesis, 1987), 64–65 and 155.
6. Sağlam, *Cihan Harbinde 3. Orduda*, 4.
7. Sağlam, *Büyük Harpte 3. Ordu'da*, 6.
8. Ibid., 17.
9. Ibid., 6–7.
10. Ibid., 8.
11. Payzın et al., *Sağlık Hizmetinde Mikrobiyoloji* 2, 702.
12. Ayhan Yücel, "Bitlerle Bulaşan Hastalıklar," *Bit ve İnsan* (Istanbul: Cerrahpaşa Tıp Fakültesi Pub., 1993), 29.
13. Unat et al., *Unat'ın Tıp Parazitolojisi*, 175.
14. Karatepe, *I. Dünya Savaşı'nda Kafkas*, 6.
15. Ayşe Wilke, Güner Söyletir, and Mehmet Doğanay, *İnfeksiyon Hastalıkları* (Istanbul: Nobel Tıp Pub., 1996), 551.
16. Unat, "Birinci Dünya Harbinde," 255.
17. Karatepe, *I. Dünya Savaşı'nda Kafkas*, 1, 13.
18. Tevfik Salim Sağlam, "Gülhane Tarihçesinden Bir Kısım" (simplified and republished by İlter Uzel), *Tıp Tarihi Araştırmaları* 3 (1989): 90.
19. Abdülkadir Noyan, "Erzurum Hatıralarımdan," *Çeşitli Yönleri ile Erzurum ve Çevresi*, ed. Nusret Karasu-Nihat Özyardımcı (Ankara: Ulusal Verem Savaş Derneği Pub., 1968), 35.
20. Noyan, *Son Harplerde Salgın Hastalıklarla*, 16.
21. İsmail, Gökçe, and Üster, *Tevfik Sağlam, 1882–1963*, 2:67.
22. Ibid.
23. Sağlam, *Büyük Harpte 3. Ordu'da*, 78n1.
24. Abdülkadir, "Fırın ve Çadır Hamamı ile Tathirat," *Sıhhiye Mecmuası* 3, no. 7 (1915): 39–41.
25. *Sıcak Hava Cereyanıyla Tathirat Fırını* (Dersaadet: Matbaa-i Askeriye, 1916).
26. Noyan, *Son Harplerde Salgın Hastalıklarla*, 39–41.
27. Sağlam, *Cihan Harbinde 3. Orduda*, 8.
28. Ahmet Lütfü, "Lekeli Hummaya Karşı Mücadele", in Unat, "Birinci Dünya Harbinde," 261.
29. Guze, *Büyük Harpte Kafkas*, 61.
30. Lütfü, "Lekeli Hummaya Karşı Mücadele," in Karatepe, *I. Dünya Savaşı'nda Kafkas*, 46–47.
31. Aykut Kazancıgil, *Osmanlılarda Bilim ve Teknoloji* (Istanbul: Gazeteciler ve Yazarlar Vakfı Pub., 1999), 283.
32. Ibid.
33. Özbay, "Tarihte Lekeli Humma," 119.

34. Ekrem Kadri Unat, "Osmanlı İmparatorluğunda İnsanın Bulaşıcı Hastalıklarına Karşı Yapılan Koruyucu Aşılar," *Dirim* 53, no. 11–12 (November–December 1978): 369.
35. Süheyl Ünver, "Dr. Reşat Rıza'nın Hayatı ve Mikrobiyolojideki Çalışmaları Hakkında," *Mikrobiyoloji Bülteni* 20, no. 3–4 (1967): 119, 121.
36. Ziya Öktem, "Epidemik Lekeli Humma ve Aşıları," *Istanbul Tıp Fakültesi Mecmuası*, no. 13 (July 1940): 1735.
37. Becker, *I. Dünya Savaşı'nda Osmanlı*, 29.
38. Sağlam, *Cihan Harbinde 3. Orduda*, 3.
39. Reşat Rıza, Refik, et al., "Lekeli Humma Aşısı Hakkındaki Münakaşa ve Meclis-i Sıhhî Ali'de Mütehassısından Müteşekkil Komisyonun Bu Babdaki Mukarreratı," in Unat, "Birinci Dünya Harbinde," 261–262.
40. Pertev Demirhan, *Generalfeldmarschall Freiherr von der Goltz* (Gottingen: Gottinger Verlagsanstalt, 1960), 229.
41. Kâzım İsmail Gürkan, "Hamdi Suat Aknar," *Ölümünün 10: Yıldönümünde Hamdi Suat Aknar, 1873–1936* (Istanbul: Tıp Fakültesi TTE Pub., 1946), 5.
42. Sağlam, *Pratik Doktor* 16, no. 3 (1946), special edition, 4.
43. Ibid.
44. Ekrem Şadi Kavur, "Askeri Hekimliğin Sıhhiye Hizmetlerinde Bir Etüd," *Dirim* 48, no. 5 (May 1973): 243.
45. Sağlam, *Büyük Harpte 3. Ordu'da*, 88–89.
46. For examples, see *Lekeli Tifoya Ait Raporlar*, Matbaa-i Askeriye, 1335 ve Tevfik Sağlam, *Arch. Schiffs-u Trop*. 1925, Bd. 23.
47. Fethi Tevetoğlu, *Atatürk'le Samsun'a Çıkanlar* (Ankara: 1971), 141 ff.
48. Guze, *Büyük Harpte Kafkas*, 61.
49. Ülfiye Barlas, Ord. Prof. Dr. Âkil Muhtar Özden ve Dünya Tıp Literatürüne Girmiş, Buluş Kabul Edilen Çalışmaları (Istanbul University, Unpublished thesis, 1999), 32.
50. Henrique Da Rocha Lima, "Lekeli Hummaya Dair Taharriyat," trans. Ziya Nuri, *Darülfünun Tıp Fakültesi Mecmuası* 1, no. 4 (September 1916).
51. For a review of the various subjects covered in those studies, see Sait Naderi ve Gülten Dinç, "Darülfünun Tıp Fakültesi Mecmuası (1916–1933) ve Dizini," *Tıp Tarihi Araştırmaları* 12 (2004): 206 vd.
52. Kamil, *Kafkas Cephe-i Harbinde*, 55.
53. Becker, *I. Dünya Savaşı'nda Osmanlı*, 73n18.
54. Feridun Erik, "Osmanlı İmparatorluğu'nun Son Yıllarında Sağlık İşleri Yönetimi," *Dirim* 54, no 9–10 (September–October 1979): 305.
55. *Türk Silahlı Kuvvetleri Tarihi, Birinci Dünya Harbi, İdarî Faaliyetler ve Lojistik* 9:144.
56. Emin, *Turkey: In the World War*, 252.
57. Sağlam, *Büyük Harpte 3. Ordu'da*, 15–16.
58. Ibid., p. 80, and Tevfik İsmail Gökçe, "Erzurum Anılarımdan Çizgiler," *Çeşitli Yönleri ile Erzurum ve Çevresi*, ed. Nusret Karasu-Nihat Özyardımcı (Ankara, Ulusal Verem Savaş Derneği Pub., 1968), p. 52.
59. Özbay, "Tarihte Lekeli Humma," 118.
60. Quoted from Kızılay Archives in Akgün, *Hilâl-i Ahmer'den*, 1:214–215; and Osmanlı

Hilâl-i Ahmer Mecmuası, no. 3 (November 15, 1921), 61–62, in Çapa, *Kızılay (Hilâl-i Ahmer Cemiyeti)*, 120–121.
61. von Sanders, *Türkiye'de Beş Yıl*, 184; Çapa, *Kızılay (Hilâl-i Ahmer Cemiyeti)*, 120–121; and Becker, *I. Dünya Savaşı'nda Osmanlı*, 27.
62. Erik, "Türkiye'de Bulaşıcı Hastalıklar," 311.
63. Şahap Erkoç and Aykut Kazancıgil, "Osmanlı Ordusu'nda I. Dünya Savaşı'nda 3 Teşrinisani 1330–3 Nisan 1333 Tarihleri Arasında (1914–1917) Şehit olan Sağlık Subaylarının Listesi," *Tıp Tarihi Araştırmaları* 10 (June 2001): 73–88.
64. Adnan Ataç, *20. Yüzyılda Şehit Olan Türk Sağlık Subayları* (Ankara: GATA Pub., 1997).
65. For the names of the martyred medical personnel (between the years of 1914 and 1918) that were inscripted on the monument in front of Fevzi Çakmak Hospital in Erzurum, see *Çeşitli Yönleri ile Erzurum ve Çevresi*, 55–58.
66. Sağlam, *Büyük Harpte 3. Ordu'da*, 60.
67. Ibid.
68. Sağlam, *Cihan Harbinde 3. Orduda*, 8.
69. Ibid., 10.
70. Sağlam, *Büyük Harpte 3. Ordu'da*, 56–57.
71. Ibid., 57–58.
72. Adıvar, *Mor Salkımlı Ev*, 259–261, 281.
73. Ibid., 281–282.

Chapter 9. Epilogue

1. Şevki, *Osmanlı Tababeti 3*, 42.
2. Becker, *I. Dünya Savaşı'nda Osmanlı*, 25.
3. Ibid.
4. Ibid.
5. *Meclis-i Âyan Zabıt Ceridesi*, Term 3, Year of Session 4, 2:49–50.
6. Ibid., 55.
7. Köprülülü Şerif (İlden), *Sarıkamış*, ed. Sami Önal (Ankara: T. İş Bankası Pub., 2001), 35–36.
8. BOA DH İD, from box no. 164-1, no. 2; also from box no. 165, no. 16 and no. 17, in Temel, "Birinci Dünya Savaşı," 332.
9. BOA DH İD, from box no. 157, no. 5, in Temel, "Birinci Dünya Savaşı," 332.
10. Ibid.
11. *Türk Silahlı Kuvvetleri Tarihi*, 9:145.
12. Ibid., 299.
13. Sağlam, *Büyük Harpte 3. Ordu'da*, 167.
14. BOA, MV. Maz., Def. 243, no. 9, in Mehmet Temel, "Mütareke Dönemi İstanbul'unda Sosyal Yaşam ve Sorunlar," *Türkler*, 14:166.
15. Sağlam, *Büyük Harpte 3. Ordu'da*, 61.
16. Ibid.
17. Cafer Ulu, "Savaş Zamanı Osmanlı Sağlık Politikası: I. Dünya Savaşı Örneği," *Belgelerle Türk Tarihi Dergisi* 42 (July 2000): 94–95.

18. Becker, *I. Dünya Savaşı'nda Osmanlı*, 3.
19. von Sanders, *Türkiye'de Beş Yıl*, 25.
20. Noyan, *Son Harplerde Salgın Hastalıklarla*, 50.
21. ATASE Archives, from K. 3672 D. 314/37, F. 2-9, in Avcı, *Irak'ta Türk Ordusu*, 270–271.
22. Şâkir, "Birinci Cihan Harbinde Erzurum," 44.
23. Sağlam, *Büyük Harpte 3. Ordu'da*, 153.
24. Becker, *I. Dünya Savaşı'nda Osmanlı*, 16.
25. Guze, *Büyük Harpte Kafkas Cephesindeki Muharebeler*, 61.
26. Ibid., 16.
27. Becker, *I. Dünya Savaşı'nda Osmanlı*, 38.
28. Ibid., 22.
29. Panzac, *La Peste dans l'Empire Ottoman*, 45.
30. Allen and Muratoff, *Caucasian Battlefields*, 439.
31. Hot, *Sıhhiye Mecmuası'na Göre*, 126–127.
32. Onul, *İnfeksiyon Hastalıkları*, 407–410, 449.
33. Ibid., 733, 735.
34. Ibid., 823.
35. Özbay, "Tarihte Lekeli Humma," 118.
36. Ali Fuat Cebesoy, *Birüssebi-Gazze Meydan Muharebesi ve Yirminci Kolordu* (Ankara: Genelkurmay X. Şube Pub., 1938), 18.
37. Allen and Muratoff, *Caucasian Battlefields*, 436–437.
38. Pomiankowsky, *Osmanlı Imparatorlugu'nun Çöküşü*, 147. See and compare in German edition: Joseph Pomiankowsky, *Der Zusammenbruch des Ottomanischen Reiches* (Zürich: Amalthea Verlag, 1928), 165.
39. Unat, "Birinci Dünya Harbinde," 259.
40. Ibid.
41. McCarthy, *Muslims and Minorities*, 120–121.
42. *Birinci Dünya Harbi'nde Türk Harbi*, 1:195.
43. "Emrâz-i Sâriye Mücadelesi," *Sıhhiye Mecmuası*, in Unat, "Birinci Dünya Harbinde," 258.
44. Carmelite Christie and Sarah Brewer, *Typed transcript of her personal diary with entries from October 1, 1915 to December 31, 1919*, in Alan Alfred Bartholomew, *Tarsus American School, 1888–1988: The Evolution of a Missionary Institution in Turkey* (Ph.D. dissertation, Bryn Mawr College, 1989), 117n21.
45. Ibid., 118n22.
46. Başkâtipzade Ragıp Bey, *Tarih-i Hayatım*, ed. M. Bülent Varlık (Ankara: Kebikeç Pub., 1996), 57.
47. Kavur, "Askerî Hekimliğin Sıhhiye Hizmetlerinde Bir Etüd," *Dirim* 49, no. 7 (July 1973): 334.
48. Ünver, "Dr. Reşat Rıza'nın Hayatı," 118.
49. Karatepe, *I. Dünya Savaşı'nda Kafkas*, 1.
50. Yıldırım, "Tanzimat'tan Cumhuriyet'e," 5:1328.
51. Ibid., 5:1330.
52. Sağlam, *Büyük Harpte 3. Ordu'da*, 10–11.
53. Kavur, "Askerî Hekimliğin Sıhhiye Hizmetlerinde Bir Etüd," 335.

54. Sağlam, *Cihan Harbinde 3, Orduda*, 6–7.
55. Sağlam, *Büyük Harpte 3. Ordu'da*, 13.
56. Sabahattin Selek, ed., *İsmet İnönü'nün Hatıraları, Genç Subaylık Yıllarım 1884–1918* (Istanbul: Burçak Pub., 1969), 142.
57. Sağlam, *Büyük Harpte 3. Ordu'da*, 14.
58. Quoted from the message of General Hilmi Özkök, the chief of general staff, issued in commemoration of the martyrs of Sarıkamış on the ninetieth anniversary of the Sarıkamış disaster.
59. See Appendix 2: Reconstruction of Turkey, A Series of Reports, Compiled for the American Committee of Armenian and Syrian Relief, ed. William H. Hall (for private distribution only, 1918).
60. Henry Cabot Lodge, "Situation in Near East," 13 April 1920, American Congress, 66th Congress, session 2, Document no. 266 (Washington, D.C.: Government Printing Office, 1920).

BIBLIOGRAPHY

UNPUBLISHED DOCUMENTS

Turkish Military Archives, in Ankara, Turkey:
ATASE Archives, A. 1-217, D. 517, F. 2-1.
ATASE Archives, A. 1-217, D. 517, F. 2-2.
ATASE Archives, A. 1-217, D. 517, F. 2-3.
ATASE Archives, A. 1-217, D. 517, F. 2-4.
ATASE Archives, A. 1-217, D. 517, F. 2-5.
ATASE Archives, K. 1110, D. 517, F. 2-1 and 5.
ATASE Archives, K. 1110, D. 517, F. 2-1.
ATASE Archives, No. 6/13962.
ATASE Archives, No. 4/3671.
ATASE Archives, No. 5/13796.
UK Archives (formerly Public Record Office) in London:
UK ARCHIVES, FO 248/1192.
UK ARCHIVES, FO 248/1277.
UK ARCHIVES, FO 608/79.
UK ARCHIVES, T 161/50.
UK ARCHIVES, WO 157/695.
UK ARCHIVES, FO 248/1192.

PUBLISHED SOURCES

Abdülkadir. "Fırın ve Çadır Hamamı ile Tathirat," *Sıhhiye Mecmuası* 3, no. 7 (Istanbul, 1915).

Adıvar, Halide Edip. *Mor Salkımlı Ev*, 5th ed. Istanbul: Özgür Pub., 2004.

———. *Türk'ün Ateşle İmtihanı*. Istanbul: Çan Pub., 1962.

Ahmet Emin. *Turkey: In the World War*. New Haven: Yale University Press, 1930.

Ahmet Refik. *Kafkas Yollarında İki Komite İki Kıtal*. Edited by Osman Selim Kocahanoğlu. Istanbul: Temel Pub., 1998.

(Akalın), Ömer B. *Nüfus Siyaseti ve Küçük Çocuklarda Vefayat*. In Zuhal Özaydın and İnci Hot, "Dr. Ömer Besim Paşa'nın Ülkemiz Nüfus Siyaseti Hakkındaki Görüşleri," *Tıp Tarihi Araştırmaları* 9 (August 1999).

———. *Verem Tehlikesi, Veremle Mücadele*. In İnci Hot, Dr. Besim Ömer Paşa'nın Anne ve Çocuk Sağlığı Açısından Ülkemiz Nüfus Meselesi Hakkındaki Görüşleri. Istanbul University SBE, Unpublished thesis, 1996.

Akgün, Seçil Karal, and Murat Uluğtekin. *Hilâl-i Ahmer'den Kızılay'a*. 2 vols. Ankara, 2000.
Aknar, Suat. *1873-1936*. Istanbul: Tıp Fakültesi TTE Pub., 1946.
Aksu, Lütfi. *Lekeli Humma*. Ankara: Ulusal M., 1943.
Akşin, Aptülahat. *Atatürk'ün Dış Politika İlkeleri ve Diplomasisi*. Ankara: TTK Pub., 1991.
Allen, W. E. D., and Paul Muratoff. *Caucasian Battlefields: A History of the Wars on the Turco-Caucasian Border, 1828–1921*. Cambridge: Cambridge University Press, 1953.
Anderson, M[atthew] S[mith]. *The Eastern Question, 1774–1923*. London: St Martin's Press, 1966.
Anderson, M. S., ed. *The Great Power and the Near East, 1774–1923: Documents of Modern History*. London: Edward Arnold, 1970.
Arık, Feda Şâmil. "Selçuklular Zamanında Anadolu'da Veba Salgınları," *AÜDTCF Tarih Dergisi* 15, no. 26 (1990–1991).
Arıkan, İ. "25 Yıllık Sıtma Mücadele Tarihçemiz," *Dirim* 25, no. 35 (1950).
Aspinall-Oglander, C. F. *Military Operations Gallipoli*. Vol. 2. London: William Heinemann Ltd., 1932.
Ataç, Adnan. *20. Yüzyılda Şehit Olan Türk Sağlık Subayları*. Ankara: GATA Pub., 1997.
Ataöv, Türkkaya. *Deaths Caused by Disease: In Relation to the Armenian Question*. Ankara: SBF Pub., 1985.
Atatürk'ün Hatıra Defteri. Ankara: TTK Pub., 1999.
Avcı, Orhan. *Irak'ta Türk Ordusu, 1914–1918*. Ankara: Vadi Pub., 2004.
Aydemir, Şevket Süreyya. *Makendonya'dan Ortaasya'ya Enver Paşa*. Istanbul: Remzi B., 1971.
Ayhan, Aydın. "1914 Yılında Balıkesir'de Tifüs Salgını ve Müdafaa-yı Milliye Cemiyeti'nin İki Sağlık Beyannamesi," *Tıp Tarihi Araştırmaları*, 9 (August 1999).
———. "Çanakkale Savaşları'nda Yaralanmalar ve Hastalıklar," *Tıp Tarihi Araştırmaları*, 11 (2003).
Bakar, Bülent. Ermeni Tehciri ve Uygulaması. Marmara University TAE, Unpublished thesis, 2003.
Bali, Rıfat N. "Edirne Muhasarası Sırasında Tutulmuş Bir Günlük-I," *Tarih ve Toplum*, 190 (October 1999).
———. "Edirne Muhasarası Sırasında Tutulmuş Bir Günlük-II," *Tarih ve Toplum*, 191 (November 1999).
———. "Edirne Muhasarası Sırasında Tutulmuş Bir Günlük-IV," *Tarih ve Toplum*, 193 (January 2000).
Barlas, Ülfiye. Ord. Prof. Dr. Âkil Muhtar Özden ve Dünya Tıp Literatürüne Girmiş, Buluş Kabul Edilen Çalışmaları. Istanbul University, Unpublished thesis, 1999.
Bartholomew, Alan Alfred. *Tarsus American School, 1888–1988: The Evolution of a Missionary Institution in Turkey*. Ph.D. dissertation, Bryn Mawr College, 1989.
Başkâtipzade Ragıp Bey. *Tarih-i Hayatım*. Edited by M. Bülent Varlık. Ankara: Kebikeç Pub., 1996.
Bayar, Hilmi. "Bir Ailevî Akdeniz Humması (Periyodik Hastalık)," *Dirim* 60, nos. 1–2 (January–February 1985).
Baykoç, Hulusi, "Kafkas ve Irak Cephesinde Beşinci Kuvve-i Seferiye (52. Tümen)," *Askerî Mecmua*, no. 60 (1 June 1942).
Baylen, Joseph O., and Alan Conway. *Soldier-Surgeon: The Crimean War Letters of Dr. Douglas A. Reid, 1855–1856*. Knoxville: University of Tennessee Press, 1968.

Baytın, Arif. *İlk Dünya Harbinde Kafkas Cephesi*. Istanbul: Vakit Pub., 1946.
Bayur, Hikmet. *Türk İnkılâp Tarihi*, vol. 3, part 4. Ankara: TTK Pub., 1983.
Becker, Helmut. *Åskulap Zwischen Reichsadler und Halbmond*. Herzogenrath: Verlag Murken-Altrogge, 1990.
———. *I. Dünya Savaşı'nda Osmanlı Cephesinde Askerî Tababet ve Eczacılık*. Istanbul, 1983.
Belen, Fahri. *20. Yüzyılda Osmanlı Devleti*. Istanbul: Remzi Pub., 1973.
Berber, Engin. *Yeni Onbinlerin Gölgesinde Bir Sancak: İzmir*. Istanbul: Tarih Vakfı Yurt Pub., 1997.
Berke, M. Zühdi. *Tıbbî Viroloji*. Vol. 2. Ankara, 1974.
Biraben, Jean-Noël. *Les hommes et la peste en France et dans les pays europeens et Méditerranéens*, in Daniel Panzac, *La Peste dans l'Empire Ottoman 1700–1850*. Leuven: Editions Peeters, 1985.
Birinci Dünya Harbi'nde Türk Harbi, Kafkas Cephesi, 3. Ordu Harekâtı. Ankara: Genelkuurmay Pub., 1993.
Bıyıklıoğlu, Tevfik. *Çanakkale Muharebelerine Dair Konferans*. Istanbul, 1950.
Braun, H. "Sarî Hastalıkların Devlet ve Halk İçin Ehemmiyeti," in *Üniversite Konferansları I, 1933–1937*. Istanbul: University Pub., 1939.
———. *Mikrobiyoloji, Parazitoloji ve Salgınlar Bilgisi*. Translated by Vefik Vassaf. Istanbul: Yaltırık Pub., 1936.
Braun, H., and Ömer Özek. "Epidemik Lekeli Hummanın Etiyoloji ve Serolojisi," *Istanbul Tıp Fakültesi Mecmuası*, no. 4 (1943).
Buchanan, George. *The Tragedy of Mesopotamia*. Edinburg, 1938.
Butler, A. G. *Australian Army Medical Services in the War of 1914–1918*. Canberra: Australian War Memorial, 1943.
Çakmak, Fevzi. *Büyük Harpte Şark Cephesi Hareketleri*. Ankara: Genelkurmay Pub., 1936.
Çapa, Mesut. Kızılay (Hilal-I Ahmer Cemiyeti), 1914–1925. Ankara Üniversitesi TİTE, Unpublished thesis, 1989.
Cebesoy, Ali Fuad. *Birüssebi-Gazze Meydan Muharebesi ve Yirminci Kolordu*. Ankara: Genelkurmay X. Şube Pub., 1938.
Cemal Paşa. *Hatırât*. Edited by Metin Martı. Istanbul: Arma Pub., 1996. [English edition: Djemal, *Memories of a Turkish Statesman*, Hutchinsons, 1922].
Cillov, Halûk. *Nüfus İstatistikleri ve Demografinin Genel Esasları*. Istanbul: İktisat Fakültesi Pub., 1960.
Criss, Nur Bilge. *İşgal Altında Istanbul, 1918–1923*. 3rd ed. Istanbul: İletişim Pub., 2000.
Cruttwell, C. R. M. F. *A History of the Great War, 1914–1918*. Oxford: Clarendon Press, [1934] 1964.
Çulcu, Murat, ed. *Mehmed Fasih Bey'in Günlüğü*. Istanbul: Denizler Pub., 2002.
Dağlar, Oya. "Kırım Savaşı'nda Orduların Sağlık Durumu ve Bir Belge," *Tıp Tarihi Araştırmaları*, no. 12 (2004).
Da Rocha Lima, Henrique. "Lekeli Hummaya Dair Taharriyat" (trans. Ziya Nuri), *Darülfünun Tıp Fakültesi Mecmuası* 1, no. 4 (September 1916).
Demirhan, Pertev. *Generalfeldmarschall Freiherr von der Goltz*. Gottingen: Gottinger Verlagsanstalt, 1960.
Diamond, Jared. *Guns, Germs and Steel: The Fates of Human Societies*. New York: W. W. Norton, 1999.
Erden, Ali Fuad. *Birinci Cihan Harbinde Suriye Hatıraları*. Istanbul, 1954.

Erickson, Edward J. *Ordered to Die: A History of the Ottoman Army in the First World War*. Westport, Conn.: Greenwood Press, 2001.

Erik, Feridun. "Osmanlı İmparatorluğu'nun Son Yıllarında Sağlık İşleri Yönetimi," *Dirim* 54, nos. 9–10 (September–October 1979).

———. "Türkiye'de Bulaşıcı Hastalıklar," *Dirim* 56, nos. 9–10 (September–October, 1981).

Erkoç, Şahap, and Aykut Kazancıgil. "Osmanlı Ordusu'nda I. Dünya Savaşı'nda 3 Teşrinisani 1330–3 Nisan 1333 Tarihleri Arasında (1914–1917) Şehit olan Sağlık Subaylarının Listesi," *Tıp Tarihi Araştırmaları*, no. 10 (June 2001).

Erler, Mehmet Yavuz. "XIX. Yüzyıldaki Bazı Doğal Âfetler ve Osmanlı Yönetimi," *Türkler*. Vol. 13. Ankara: Yeni Türkiye Y., 2002.

Ersoy, Tolga. *Tıp, Tarih, Metafor*. 2nd ed. Ankara: Öteki Pub., 1996.

Ferguson, Niall. *The Pity of War*. New York: Basic Books, 1999.

Flinn, M. F. "Avrupa ve Akdeniz Ülkelerinde Veba" (trans. Necmiye Alpay), *Tarih ve Toplum*, no. 39 (March 1987).

Fromkin, David. *Barışa Son Veren Barış*. Trans. Mehmet Harmancı. Istanbul: Sabah Pub., 1993. [English edition: *A Peace to End All Peace*, New York: Henry Holt and Company, 1989].

General Maslofski'nin Umumî Harpte Kafkas Cephesi Eserinin Tenkidi. Trans. Nazmi. Ankara: Genelkurmay Pub., 1935.

Gökçe, T. İsmail. "Erzurum Anılarımdan Çizgiler." In Nusret Karasu and Nihat Özyardımcı, eds., *Çeşitli Yönleri ile Erzurum ve Çevresi*. Ankara: Ulusal Verem Savaş Derneği Pub., 1968.

Gökçe, T. İsmail, and S. Necati Üster. *Tevfik Sağlam, 1882–1963*. Vol. 2. Istanbul: Akgün Pub., 1968.

Goltz Paşa'nın Hatırası ve Hâl Tercümesi. Trans. E. General Pertev Demirhan. Istanbul: Askerî Pub., 1953. For German edition, see: *General Pertev Demirhan, Generalfeldmarschall Freiherr von der Goltz*. Göttingen: Göttinger Verlagsanstalt, 1960.

Görgey, Şefik. İngiliz Cerrah William Witmann'ın 19. Yüzyıl Başında Istanbul, Yafa ve Mısır'daki Gözlemleri, Uygulamaları ve Raporları. Istanbul University, SBE, Unpublished thesis, 1989.

Gürkan, Kâzım İsmail. "Hamdi Suat Aknar." In *Ölümünün 10: Yıldönümünde Hamdi Suat Aknar, 1873–1936*. Istanbul: Tıp Fakültesi TTE Pub., 1946.

Guze. "Büyük Harpte Kafkas Cephesindeki Muharebeler" (trans. Hakkı), *Askerî Mecmua*, no. 20 (January 1931).

Hafız Hakkı Paşa. *Bozgun*. Istanbul: Tercüman 1001 Temel Eser, n.d.

Halaçoğlu, Ahmet. *Balkan Harbi Sırasında Rumeli'den Türk Göçleri, 1912–1913*. Ankara: TTK Pub., 1995.

Halaçoğlu, Yusuf. *Osmanlılarda Ulaşım ve Haberleşme (Menziller)*. Ankara: PTT Pub., 2002.

Hamilton, Ian. *Gallipoli Diary*. London: Edward Arnold, 1920. 2 vols.

Hobsbawm, Eric. *The Age of Extremes: The Short Twentieth Century, 1914–1991*. London: Abacus, 1994.

Hochwaechter, Major G. v. *Türklerle Cephede*. Trans. Fahri Çeliker. Ankara: Askerî Tarih Bülteni Eki (August 1979), no. 8.

Hoehling, Adolph A. *The Great Epidemic*. Boston: Little, Brown & Co., 1961.

Hot, İnci. Dr. Besim Ömer Paşa'nın Anne ve Çocuk Sağlığı Açısından Ülkemiz Nüfus Meselesi Hakkındaki Görüşleri. İstanbul University SBE, Unpublished thesis, 1996.

———. Sıhhiye Mecmuası'na Göre Ülkemizde Bulaşıcı Hastalıklarla Mücadele, 1913–1996. Istanbul University, Unpublished thesis, 2001.

İhsanoğlu, Ekmeleddin. *Suriye'de Modern Sağlık Müesseseleri, Hastahaneleri ve Şam Tıp Fakültesi.* Ankara: TTK Pub., 1999.

İpek, Nedim. *Rumeli'den Anadolu'ya Türk Göçleri.* Ankara: TTK Pub., 1999.

İzgöer, Ahmet Zeki. "Osmanlı'nın Yıkılışı Öncesinde Hind Hilâl-i Ahmer Yardımları ve Dr. Ensari'nin Faaliyetleriyle İlgili Bazı Notlar," *Yeni Tıp Tarihi Araştırmaları* 8 (2002).

Jackson, Ralph. *Roma İmparatorluğu'nda Doktorlar ve Hastalıklar.* Trans. Şenol Mumcu. Istanbul: Homer B., 1999. For original edition, see: Ralph Jackson, *Doctors and Diseases in the Roman Empire.* 4th ed. London: British Museum Press, 1995.

James, Robert Rhodes. *Gallipoli.* London: B. T. Batsford Ltd., 1965.

Kaiser, Hilmar. "Denying the Armenian Genocide: The German Connection." *Journal of the Society for Armenian Studies* 9. New York, 1999.

Kalyan, Aziz, ed. *Kırım Savaşı.* Istanbul: Milliyet Pub., 1975.

Kâmil, Server. *Kafkas Cephe-i Harbinde Lekeli Humma.* Sivas: Matbaa-i Vilayet, 1916.

Kannengiesser Pasha, Hans. *The Campaign in Gallipoli.* Translated from the German by Major C. J. P. Ball. 2nd impression. London: Hutchinson, 1927.

Karatepe, Mustafa. I. Dünya Savaşı'nda Kafkas Cephesi'nde Tifüsle Mücadele. Istanbul University, Unpublished thesis, 1999.

Karayan, Sarkis. "An Inquiry into the Number and Causes of Turkish Human Losses During the First World War," *The Armenian Review* 35, no. 3-139 (August 1982).

Kavur, Ekrem Şadi. "Askeri Hekimliğin Sıhhiye Hizmetlerinde Bir Etüd," *Dirim* 49, no. 8 (August 1973).

———. "Askeri Hekimliğin Sıhhiye Hizmetlerinde Bir Etüd," *Dirim* 48, no. 5 (May 1973).

———. "Askerî Hekimliğin Sıhhiye Hizmetlerinde Bir Etüd," *Dirim* 48, no. 2 (February 1973).

———. "Askerî Hekimliğin Sıhhiye Hizmetlerinde Bir Etüd," *Dirim* 48, no. 3 (March 1973).

———. "Askerî Hekimliğin Sıhhiye Hizmetlerinde Bir Etüd," *Dirim* 48, no. 4 (April 1973).

———. "Askerî Hekimliğin Sıhhiye Hizmetlerinde Bir Etüd," *Dirim* 48, no. 6 (June 1973).

———. "Askerî Hekimliğin Sıhhiye Hizmetlerinde Bir Etüd," *Dirim* 49, no. 7 (July 1973).

———. "Askeri Hekimliğin Sıhhiye Hizmetlerinde Bir Etüd," *Dirim* 49, no. 8 (August 1973).

Kazancıgil, Aykut. *Osmanlılarda Bilim ve Teknoloji.* Istanbul: Gazeteciler ve Yazarlar Vakfı Pub., 1999.

Keegan, John. *A History of Warfare.* New York: Alfred A. Knopf, 1993.

Kılıç, Orhan. "Osmanlı Devleti'nde Meydana Gelen Kıtlıklar," *Türkler.* Vol. 10. Ankara: Yeni Türkiye Y., 2002.

Kieser, Hans-Lukas. "Bir Misyoner Hastahanesinin Çevresindeki Küçük Dünya: Urfa, 1897–1922." In François Georgeon-Paul Dumont, *Osmanlı İmparatorluğu'nda Yaşamak.* Trans. Maide Selen. Istanbul: İletişim Pub., 2000.

Koca, Salim. "Türklerin Göçleri ve Yayılmaları." *Türkler.* Vol. I. Ankara: Yeni Türkiye Pub., 2002.

Köprülülü Şerif. *Sarıkamış.* Edited by Sami Önal. Ankara: T. İş Bankası Pub., 2001.

Kuntman, M. Derviş. *Bir Doktorun Harp ve Memleket Hatıraları.* 217 Sayılı Silahlı Kuvvetler Dergisi'nin Ek Kısmı, 85th Anniversary, no. 1 (March 1966).
Kutlay, Nükhet Yürür. "Refik Saydam'ın Sağlık Politikası ve Hıfzıssıhha Merkezi'nin Bu Politikadaki Yeri," *Yeni Tıp Tarihi Araştırmaları* 4 (1998).
Lamouche, Kolonel. *Türkiye Tarihi.* Trans. Galip Söylemezoğlu. Istanbul: Kanaat K., 1943. 2 vols.
Landry, Adolphe. *Traite de Demographie.* Paris: Payot, 1949.
Larcher, Commandant M. *La Guerre Turque dans la Guerre Mondiale.* Paris, 1926.
Lodge, Henry Cabot. "Situation in Near East." 13 April 1920. *American Congress, 66th Congress,* session 2, doc. no. 266. Washington, D.C.: Government Printing Office, 1920.
Lyons, Albert S., and R. Joseph Petrucelli. *Çağlar Boyu Tıp.* Trans. Nilgün Güdücü. Istanbul: Roche, 1997. [English edition: *Medicine: An Illusrated History*/Par le Dr. Albert S. Lyons et le Dr. R. Joseph Petrucelli].
Mango, Andrew. *Atatürk.* London: John Murray, 1999.
Mansel, Arif Müfid. *Ege ve Yunan Tarihi.* 6th ed. Ankara: TTK Pub., 1995.
Matthew, Donald. *Ortaçağ Avrupası.* Trans. Mehmet Ali Kılıçbay. Istanbul: İletişim Pub., 1988.
Mayakuşu, Salih. *Golç Paşa'nın Hatıratı.* Istanbul: Askerî Pub., 1932. 'den: Edited by Faruk Yılmaz. *İmparatorluk Döneminde Türk-Alman İlişkileri.* Ankara: Berikan Pub., 2004.
McCarthy, Justin. *Death and Exile: The Ethnic Cleansing of Ottoman Muslims, 1821–1922.* Princeton, N.J.: The Darwin Press, 1996.
———. *Muslims and Minorities.* New York: New York University Press, 1983.
McMurray, Jonathan S. *Distant Ties: Germany, the Ottoman Empire, and the Construction of the Baghdad Railway.* Westport, Conn.: Praeger, 2001.
McNeill, William H. *Plagues and Peoples.* New York: Anchor Books, 1977.
———. *A World History.* New York: Oxford University Press, 1967.
Meclis-i Âyan Zabıt Ceridesi. Term 3, year of session 4, vol. 2.
Meclis-i Mebusan Zabıt Ceridesi. Term 3, year of session 1, vol. 1.
Meclis-i Mebusan Zabıt Ceridesi. Term 3, year of session 1, vol. 1 (İçtimai Fevkalâde).
Meclis-i Mebusan Zabıt Ceridesi. Term 3, year of session 2, vol. 2.
Meclis-i Mebusan Zabıt Ceridesi. Term 3, year of session 4, vol. 2.
Meclis-i Mebusan Zabıt Ceridesi. Term 3, year of session 5, vol. 1.
Mehmet Arif. *Başımıza Gelenler.* Istanbul: Harp Akademileri Pub., 1969.
Memoirs of Halide Edib. New York: The Century Co., 1926.
Moorehead, Alan. *Gallipoli.* New York: Harper and Brothers Publishers, 1956.
Müderrisoğlu, Alptekin. *Sarıkamış Dramı.* Vol. 2. Istanbul: Kastaş, 1988.
Mühlmann, Carl. *Das Deutche-Türkische Waffenbündis İm Weltkriege.* In Veli Yılmaz, *1 nci Dünya Harbi'nde Türk-Alman İttifakı ve Askerî Yardımlar.* Istanbul: Cem Pub., 1993.
Mustafa, Münim. *Cepheden Cepheye.* 2nd ed. Istanbul: Arma Pub., 1998.
Mutusis, Tostantin. "Mikrop Harbi," *Istanbul Tıp Fakültesi Mecmuası,* no. 3 (1952).
Naderi, Sait ve Dinç, Gülten. "Darülfünun Tıp Fakültesi Mecmuası (1916–1933) ve Dizini, *Tıp Tarihi Araştırmaları* 12 (2004).
Nazilmof, A. *Bulgar Süvari Tümeninin Harekâtı.* Ankara: Genelkurmay Pub., 1935.
Nikiforuk, Andrew. *The Fourth Horseman: A Short History of Epidemics, Plagues and Other Scourges.* London: Fourth Estate, 1991.
Noyan, Abdülkadir. "Erzurum Hatıralarımdan." In *Çeşitli Yönleri ile Erzurum ve Çevresi,*

edited by Nusret Karasu-Nihat Özyardımcı. Ankara: Ulusal Verem Savaş Derneği Pub., 1968.

———. *İç Hastalıkları Ders Kitabı, İntan Hastalıkları*. Istanbul: Mazlum Pub., 1943.

———. "İntani ve Salgın Hastalıklara Karşı Tıbbın Eski ve Yeni Durumu," *Istanbul Tıp Fakültesi Mecmuası*, no. 4 (1947).

———. "Sıtma Üstüne Konferans," *Istanbul Tıp Fakültesi Mecmuası*, no. 3 (1947).

———. *Son Harplerde Salgın Hastalıklarla Savaşlarım*. Ankara: Tıp Fakültesi Y., 1956.

Öğün, Tuncay. *Vilayât-ı Şarkiye Mültecileri, 1915–1923*. Ankara: Babil Pub., 2004.

Öktem, Ziya. "Basilli Dizanteri Aşılarının Şimdiki Vaziyeti Hakkında," *Istanbul Tıp Fakültesi Mecmuası*, no. 16 (April 1941).

———. "Epidemik Lekeli Humma ve Aşıları," *Istanbul Tıp Fakültesi Mecmuası*, no. 13 (July 1940).

Öndeş, Osman. "Bir Savaşın Sonrası." In Ian Hamilton, *Gelibolu Günlüğü*. Turkish edition: Istanbul: Hürriyet Y., 1972.

Onul, Behçet. "Kolera," *Sağlık Dergisi* 40, nos. 1–2 (1966).

Onul, Behiç. *Infeksiyon Hastalıkları*. 5th ed. Ankara: Tıp Fakültesi Pub., 1974.

Operatör Cemil Paşa. *Canlı Tarihler*. Vol. 8. Istanbul: Türkiye Pub., 1945.

Osmanlı Belgelerinde Ermeniler, 1915–1920. Ankara: Devlet Arşivleri Pub., 1994.

Özaydın, Zuhal. "Büyük Önder Atatürk'ün Himayelerinde Yapılan I. Millî Türk Tıp Kongresi," *Tıp Tarihi Araştırmaları* 7 (June 1998).

———. Osmanlı Hilâl-i Ahmer Cemiyeti Salnamesi. Istanbul University, Unpublished thesis, 1987).

———. "Osmanlı Hilâl-i Ahmer Cemiyeti'nin Kuruluşu ve Çalışmaları." In *Türkler* Vol. 13. Ankara: Yeni Türkiye Pub., 2002.

Özaydın, Zuhal, and İnci Hot. "Dr. Ömer Besim Paşa'nın Ülkemiz Nüfus Siyaseti Hakkındaki Görüşleri," *Tıp Tarihi Araştırmaları* 9 (August 1999).

Özbay, Kemal. "Tarihte Lekeli Humma-Tifüs ve Ordularımızda Tahribatı," *Dirim* 54, nos. 3–4 (March–April 1979).

———. *Türk Asker Hekimliği Tarihi ve Asker Hastahaneleri*. Vol. 1. Istanbul: Yörük B., 1976.

Özdemir, Ahmet. "Milli Mücadele'de Üserâ Taburları," *Atatürk Yolu* 5 (May 1990).

Özdemir, Hikmet, et al. *Ermeniler: Sürgün ve Göç*. Ankara: TTK Pub., 2004.

Özkan, Orhan. "Atatürk Döneminde Sağlık Politikası." In *Atatürk Dönemi Sağlık Politikası ve Türkiye'nin Ekonomik Gelişmesi Semineri*. Ankara: AÜSBF Pub., 1982.

Özpekcan, Meliha. "Türkiye Cumhuriyeti'nde Sağlık Politikası, 1923–1933," *Yeni Tıp Tarihi Araştırmaları* 7 (2001).

Panzac, Daniel. *La Peste dans l'Empire Ottoman 1700–1850*. Leuven: Editions Peeters, 1985.

Payzın, S., K. Özsan, N. Aksoycan, H. Ekmen, and M. Akman. *Sağlık Hizmetinde Mikrobiyoloji 2, Özel Mikrobiyoloji*. Ankara: Tıp Fakültesi Pub., 1968.

Pomiankowsky, Joseph. *Der Zusammenbruch des Ottomanischen Reiches*. (Zürich: Wien, Amalthea Verlag, 1928.

———. *Osmanlı İmparatorluğu'nun Çöküşü*. Trans. Kemal Turan. Istanbul: Kayıhan Pub., 1990.

Rabinowicz, Leon. *Nüfus Meselesi*. Trans. Alâettin Cemil. Ankara, 1930.

Reconstruction of Turkey, A Series of Reports, Compiled for the American Committee of Armenian and Syrian Relief. Edited by William H. Hall. For private distribution only, 1918.

Robertson, Sir William. *Soldiers and Statesmen, 1914–1918*. Vols. 1–2. London: Cassell and Company Ltd., 1926.

Ryan, Charles S. *Under the Red Crescent: Adventures of an English Surgeon with the Turkish Army at Plevna and Erzurum, 1877–1878*. London: John Murray, 1897.

Sağlam, Tevfik. *Büyük Harpte 3. Ordu'da Sıhhî Hizmet*. Istanbul: Askerî M., 1941.

———. *Cihan Harbinde 3. Ordu'da Sıhhî Hizmete Ait Küçük Bir Hulâsa*. Istanbul, Askerî Tıbbiye Pub., 1940.

———. "Gülhane Tarihçesinden Bir Kısım." Simplified and republished by İlter Uzel. In *Tıp Tarihi Araştırmaları*. Vol. 3. Istanbul, 1989.

Sağlam, Tevfik. *Pratik Doktor*. Year 16, no. 3 (1946).

Sağlık Hizmetlerinde 50 Yıl. Ankara: Sağlık Bakanlığı Pub., 1973.

Sakaoğlu, Necdet. "Bir Osmanlı Neferinin I. Dünya Savaşı Anıları," *Tarih ve Toplum* 11 (November 1984).

Şâkir, Nazım. "Birinci Cihan Harbinde Erzurum ve Sağlık Organizasyonu Anıları." In *Çeşitli Yönleri ile Erzurum ve Çevresi*, edited by Nusret Karasu-Nihat Özyardımcı. Ankara: Ulusal Verem Savaş Derneği Pub., 1968.

Salim, Tevfik. *Lekeli Tifo*. Istanbul: Kader M., 1929.

Samih, Aziz. *Büyük Harpte Kafkas Cephesi Hatıraları*. Ankara: Büyük Erkânıharbiye Y., 1934.

Sarı, Nil-Özaydın, Zühal. "I. Dünya Savaşında Osmanlı Hilâl-i Ahmer Cemiyeti," In *2. Türk Tıp Tarihi Kongresi, Istanbul, 20–21 Eylül 1990*. Ankara, TTK Pub., 1999.

Saydam, Abdullah. "Birinci Dünya Savaşı Sırasında Istanbul Halkının Geçim Sıkıntısı," *Belgelerle Türk Tarihi Dergisi* 19 (August 1998).

Selçuk, İlhan. *Yüzbaşı Selahattin'in Romanı*. Istanbul: Remzi Pub., 1975.

Selek, Sabahattin, ed. *İsmet İnönü'nün Hatıraları, Genç Subaylık Yıllarım 1884–1918*. Istanbul: Burçak Pub., 1969.

Seren, Necmi. "Yılların Ötesinden," *Harp Tarihi Mecmuası*, no. 209 (May 1982).

———. "Yılların Ötesinden," *Harp Tarihi Mecmuası*, no. 210 (June 1982).

———. "Yılların Ötesinden," *Harp Tarihi Mecmuası*, no. 211 (July 1982).

Serhan, Bahaddin. "Savaştan da Öldürücü Bir Salgın!" *Yakın Tarihimiz* 3 (March 1983).

Seuber. *Yıldırım*. Trans. Kaymakam Nihat. Istanbul: Askerî M., 1932.

Şevki, Osman. "Kırım Muharebesi," *Askerî Tıbbiye Mecmuası* 1, no. 4 (March 1919).

———. *Osmanlı Tababeti, Türk Tarihinin Ana Hatları Eserinin Müsveddeleri*. Serial 2, no. 16. Istanbul: Akşam Pub., n.d.

———. *Osmanlı Tababeti 3, Türk Tarihinin Ana Hatları Eserinin Müsveddeleri*. Serial 3, no. 12. Istanbul: Akşam Pub., n.d.

Seyhülislam Cemaleddin Efendi. *Siyasî Hatıralarım*. Trans. Ziyaeddin Engin. Istanbul: Tercüman 1001 Temel Eser, 1978.

Shaw, Stanford J. *Idea to Realization: My Study of Ottoman History*. Ankara: Türkiye Bilimler Akademisi Pub., 2003.

Sıcak Hava Cereyanıyla Tathirat Fırını. Dersaadet: Matbaa-i Askeriye, 1916.

Şimşir, Bilâl N. *Rumeli'den Türk Göçleri, Belgeler*. Vol. I. Ankara: TTK Pub., 1989.

Somel, Akşin. "Türk Ordusu ile Filistin'de," *Toplumsal Tarih*, no. 66 (June 1989).

Starrit, S. Stuart. *The Life of Nansen*. London: The Religions Tract Society, n.d.

Statistics of the Military Effort of the British Empire during the Great War, the War Office, March 1922. Reprinted by the Naval & Military Press, 1999.

Süerdem, İsmail Hakkı. *Anılarım*. Edited by Orhan Avcı. Ankara: Bilge Pub., 2004.
Sunata, İ. Hakkı. *Gelibolu'dan Kafkaslar'a*. Istanbul: T. İş Bankası Pub., 2003.
Suphi, Hamdullah. "Boğa Dağları," *Türk Yurdu* 7(14), no. 156 (1918). Ankara: Tutibay Pub., 2000.
Talat. "Ankara'da Sıtma ve Mücadele Teşkilatı," *Sıhhiye Mecmuası* 5, nos. 31–32 (1930).
Temel, Mehmet. "Birinci Dünya Savaşı ve Mütareke Yıllarında Türkiye'deki Bulaşıcı ve Zührevi Hastalıklara Karşı Alınan Önlemler," *Çağdaş Türkiye Tarihi Araştırmaları Dergisi* 3, no. 8 (1998).
———. "Mütareke Dönemi Istanbul'unda Sosyal Yaşam ve Sorunlar," *Türkler*. Vol. 14. Ankara: Yeni Türkiye Y., 2002.
Terraine, John. *The Great War, 1914–1915*. London: Arrow Books Ltd., 1967.
Terzioğlu, Arslan. "Kırım Harbi Esnasında Osmanlı Hastahaneleri ve Dünya Hastahaneciliğine Etkileri," *Toplumsal Tarih* 85 (January 1991).
Tevetoğlu, Fethi. *Atatürk'le Samsun'a Çıkanlar*. Ankara, 1971.
Tezok, F., E. Gümrükçü, and M. Sağlam. "1971 Hong-Kong Gribinin Memleketimizdeki Özellikleri," *Mikrobiyoloji Bülteni* 6, no. 1 (January 1972).
Timur, Cevdet. *Türk İstiklâl Harbi*. Vol. 7. Ankara, 1975.
Toprak, Zafer. "Istanbul'da Fuhuş ve Zührevî Hastalıklar, 1914–1933," *Tarih ve Toplum* 39 (March 1987).
———. *İttihad–Terakki ve Cihan Harbi, 1914–1918*. İstanbul: Homer Pub., 2003.
Topuzlu, Cemil. *İstibdat-Meşrutiyet-Cumhuriyet Devirlerinde 80 Yıllık Hatıralarım*. 2nd ed. Edited by Hüsrev Hatemi-Aykut Kazancıgil. Istanbul: Cerrahpaşa Tıp Fakültesi Pub., 1982.
Trotsky, Leon. *Balkan Savaşları*. Trans. Tansel Güney. Istanbul: Arba Pub., 1995.
Tugaç, Hüsamettin. *Bir Neslin Dramı*. Istanbul: Çağdaş Y., 1975.
Türkan, Ali İhsan, ed. "Istanbul İşgal Kuvvetleri Komutanlığı Raporları (7)," *Belgelerle Türk Tarihi Dergisi* 30 (July 1999).
Turkish Military History Council. *Birinci Dünya Harbi'nde Türk Harbi, İran-Irak Cephesi*. Ankara: Genelkurmay Pub., 1979.
Türkmen, Zekeriya. "Balkan Savaşlarında Hilâl-i Ahmer Cemiyetinin Osmanlı Ordusuna Yönelik Sağlık Hizmetleri," *Belleten* 68, no. 252 (August 2004).
Türk Silahlı Kuvvetleri Tarihi, Birinci Dünya Harbi, İdari Faaliyetler ve Lojistik. Vol. 9. Ankara: Genelkurmay Pub., 1985.
Ulu, Cafer. "Savaş Zamanı Osmanlı Sağlık Politikası: I. Dünya Savaşı Örneği," *Belgelerle Türk Tarihi Dergisi* 42 (July 2000).
Unat, Ekrem Kadri, "Birinci Dünya Harbinde Türk Ordusu'nda Tifüs Savaşı," *Cerrahpaşa Tıp Fakültesi Dergisi* 20, no. 2 (April 1989).
———. "Görev Kurbanı İki Mikrobiyoloğumuz," *Türk Mikrobiyoloji Cemiyeti Dergisi* 9, no. 61 (1979).
———. "Kış ve Bulaşıcı Hastalıklar," *Dirim* 55, nos. 7–8 (July–August 1980).
———. "Osmanlı İmparatorluğu'nda 1910–1913 Yıllarındaki Kolera Salgınları ve Bunlarla İlgili Olaylar," *Yeni Tıp Tarihi Araştırmaları* 1 (1995).
———. "Osmanlı İmparatorluğunda İnsanın Bulaşıcı Hastalıklarına Karşı Yapılan Koruyucu Aşılar," *Dirim* 53, nos. 11–12 (November–December 1978).
———. "Osmanlı İmparatorluğu'nun Son 40 Yılında Türkiye'nin Tüberküloz Tarihçesi Üzerine," *Cerrahpaşa Tıp Fakültesi Dergisi* 10, no. 4 (October 1979).

———. "Türkiye'de Atatürk Döneminde Bulaşıcı Hastalıklarla Savaş için Kuruluşlar ve Çalışmalar." In *Türkiye'de Atatürk Döneminde Bulaşıcı Hastalıklarla Savaş Toplantısı, Cerrahpaşa Tıp Fakültesi Atatürk Haftası, 18–28 Mayıs 1981*. Istanbul, 1982.

———. "Türkiye Cumhuriyeti'nde Bulaşıcı Hastalıklarla Savaş," *Cerrahpaşa Tıp Fakültesi Dergisi* 12 (Sp. Issue, 1981).

Unat, E. K., A. Yücel, K. Altaş, and M. Saması. *Unat'ın Tıp Parazitolojisi*. 5th ed. Cerrahpaşa: Tıp Fakültesi Vafkı Pub., 1995.

Ünver, Süheyl. "Dr. Reşat Rıza'nın Hayatı ve Mikrobiyolojideki Çalışmaları Hakkında," *Mikrobiyoloji Bülteni* 20, no. 3–4 (1967).

*Vekâletin 10 Yıllık Mesaisi*I. Sıhhiye Mecmuası Fevkalâde Nüshası, October 29, 1933.

Villalta, Jorge Blanco. *Atatürk*. Trans. William Campbell. Ankara: TTK Pub., 1991.

von Kressenstein, Kress, and Friedrich Freiherr. *Mit den Türken zum Suezkanal*. Berlin: Borhut-Verlag, 1938.

von Sanders, Liman. *Türkiye'de Beş Yıl*. Trans. M. Şevki Yazman. Istanbul: Burçak Pub., 1969. [English edition: Liman von Sanders, *Five Years in Turkey*. U.S. Naval Institute, 1927].

Wilke, Ayşe, Güner Söyletir, and Mehmet Doğanay. *İnfeksiyon Hastalıkları*. Istanbul: Nobel Tıp Pub., 1996.

Witmann, William. *Travels in Turkey, Asia Minor, Syria and Across the Desert into Egypt during the Years 1799, 1800 and 1801 in Company with the Turkish Army, and the British Military Mission* (London, 1803).

Yalman, Ahmet Emin. *Yakın Tarihte Gördüklerim, Geçirdiklerim*. Istanbul: Yenilik Pub., 1970.

Yıldırım, Nuran. "Tanzimat'tan Cumhuriyet'e Koruyucu Sağlık Uygulamaları." In *Tanzimat'tan Cumhuriyet'e Türkiye Ansiklopedisi*. Vol. 5. Istanbul: İletişim Y., 1985.

Yılmaz, Faruk. *İmparatorluk Döneminde Türk–Alman İlişkileri*. Ankara: Berikan Pub., 2004.

Yılmaz, Veli. *1 nci Dünya Harbi'nde Türk–Alman İttifakı ve Askerî Yardımlar*. Istanbul: Cem Pub., 1993.

Yücel, Ayhan. "Bitlerle Bulaşan Hastalıklar." In *Bit ve İnsan*. Cerrahpaşa: Tıp Fakültesi Pub., 1993.

———. "Türkiye'de Sıtma Savaşı." In *Türkiye'de Atatürk Döneminde Bulaşıcı Hastalıklarla Savaş Toplantısı, Cerrahpaşa Tıp Fakültesi Atatürk Haftası, 18–28 Mayıs 1981*. Istanbul, 1981.

Zürcher, Erik J. "Between Death and Desertion: The Experience of the Ottoman Soldier in World War I," *Turcica* 28 (1996).

———. "The Ottoman Conscription System in Theory and Practice." In *Arming the State: Military Conscription in the Middle East and Central Asia, 1775–1925*. Edited by Eric J. Zürcher. London: I. B. Taurus, 1999.

Index

Abdülhamid (sultan), 136
Abdülkadir Bey, 48
Abdülkadir Noyan (doctor), 30, 36, 49, 68, 147, 149, 169, 172, 174, 191
acute bronchitis, 95
Adana, 30, 31, 33, 102, 143, 147, 200
Adnan Adıvar (doctor), 188
Adolf Friedrich (Grand Duke of Mecklenburg), 48
Ağvanis Hospital, 45
Ahmet Emin, 96, 122, 123, 178
Ahmet Fikri, 171
Ahmet Lütfi (doctor), 172
Ahmet Şadi, 207
Akbaş, 74
Akçakale, 31
Akdere, 74
Akil Muhtar (doctor), 177
Alakilise, 47
Albania, 19
Al-Budayri, 194
Aleppo, 30, 31, 37, 83, 84, 85, 86, 89, 137, 138, 139, 140, 141, 149, 156, 194, 198
Ali Fuad, 159
Ali Osman, 42
Ali Selim, 207
Allenby, Edmund (general), 37
Altunian (doctor), 141
Alucra, 144
Amasya, 65, 100, 145, 151
American Missionary Board, 64
American Zionists, 161
Anafartalar, 74, 75, 207
Anatolia, 2, 6, 8, 11, 14, 20, 26, 28, 29, 30, 31, 32, 63, 64, 65, 67, 75, 78, 94, 98, 99, 100, 101, 102, 105, 115, 120, 124, 125, 128, 135, 136, 137, 140, 141, 142, 143, 147, 148, 149, 150, 154, 158, 159, 162, 163, 177, 184, 189, 190, 192, 198, 199, 202, 203
Ankara, 9, 98, 100, 101, 102, 123, 139, 145, 148, 151, 189, 190, 193, 194, 205
Antranik, 184
Anzac, 69, 70, 71, 73, 115
Ardahan, 181
Arıburnu, 114
Arif Bey, 51
Army Station Hospital, in Kut, 90
Asaf Derviş Pasha (doctor), 102
Asir, 124
Atlantic Ocean, 10, 92
Attila, 106
Australian Army Medical Services, 5, 13, 110, 112
Australian Army, 5, 13, 108, 110, 112
Austria-Hungary, 20, 108, 110
Austrian Army, 118
Austrians, 76, 118
Austro-Hungarian Army, 110
Austro-Hungarian Casualties, 110
Avni Pasha, 59
Aya Tura Abbey and Orphanage, 142, 161, 183, 184, 185
Ayastefanos, 189
Aydın, 64, 93, 151, 156
Aziz Samih, 59, 134

Baalbek, 86
Baghdad, 30, 31, 36, 37, 48, 88, 90, 91, 149, 150, 152, 174, 191, 192
Baku, 79, 136

Baldwin, Hanson, 109
Balıkesir, 64, 65, 66, 101
Balıkesir Society of National Defence, 64
Balkan, 3, 6, 8, 16, 18, 19, 20, 23, 24, 25, 35, 47, 66, 96, 100, 135, 139, 165, 166, 169, 186, 199
Balkan War, 3, 6, 8, 16, 18, 19, 20, 23, 24, 25, 35, 47, 66, 100, 135, 139, 165, 166, 169, 199
Baltic, 91
Baratov (general), 113
Basra, 88, 146
Batman Bridge, 50
Battle of Sarıkamış, 201
Batum, 152, 181
Bayburt, 36, 41, 62, 65, 79, 99, 142, 151, 167, 168, 175, 181, 198
Beirut, 86, 152, 159, 160, 161, 184
Belemedik, 148
Belgian, 107, 119
Besim Ömer (doctor), 96, 177
Bingöl, 113, 125
Biraben, J. N., 4
Birdwood (general), 71
Birseba, 140
Bitlis, 50, 62, 64, 135, 139, 163, 167, 168, 197
Black Sea, 19, 78, 95, 100, 124, 130, 143, 151
Bliss (doctor), 185
Boer War, 5, 6
Börnstein (doctor), 194
Boston, 91
British Army, 5, 72, 75, 87, 88, 114, 115, 116, 139; and Command in Egypt, 136
British casualties, 114
British Command, 12, 71, 75. *See also* British Army
British Navy, 30
bronchopneumonia, 95
Bucharest, 77
Bulanık, 62
Bulgaria, 6, 22, 111
Bulgarian Army, 19, 22, 169
Burdur, 156
Bursa, 101, 139
Butler, A. G., 5, 13, 108, 109, 110, 111, 112, 117

Çamlıhan, 148
Çan, 64
Canik, 100, 151, 190
Çapakçur Front, 87
casualties, 5, 13, 37, 52, 116, 117, 119, 124
Catos, 22
Caucasian Front, 208
Cavit, 144
Çekmece, 101
Cemal (captain), 59
Cemal Pasha, 31, 138, 139, 141, 142, 159, 160
Cemaleddin Efendi, 19, 25
Cemil Pasha, 25
Cemile, 139
Çengelköy, 12
Central Hospital of Erzincan, 80
Central Military Hospital in Baghdad, 149
Central Military Hospital in Damascus, 141
Central Powers, 7
Çeşme, 155
Champagne, 6, 112
Charing Cross Hospital, 20
China, 1, 91, 168
cholera, 16, 21, 23, 57, 148, 177; epidemic, 19
Christians, 136, 162
Christie, Mrs., 199
Cilicia, 139
Çilingir, 94
Colley (doctor), 54
Conkbayırı, 75
Çorlu, 4, 19
Council of Medical Affairs, 18
Crimean War, 5, 11, 12, 13, 14

Damascus, 83, 86, 140, 142, 161, 162, 194
Dardanelles Strait, 73
Davutpaşa, 27
deaths, in Baghdad, 153
Denizli, 101, 156
Der, 86
Derbisiye, 150
Dersim, 113
Deveboynu, 37, 45
Dimetoca, 23, 24
diphtheria, 95, 103

INDEX

disease, 5, 13, 19, 38, 95, 97, 103, 123, 137, 177
Diyarbakır, 32, 44, 45, 62, 99, 143, 156, 167, 168, 176, 208
Dobruja, 76, 77
dysentery, 55, 57, 71, 123, 148

East Anatolia, 36, 66, 138, 205
Eceabat, 73
Edirne, 13, 15, 23, 24, 135, 207
Egypt, 20, 166
Egyptian Front, 116
Ekrem Kadri, 12, 18
Ekrem Şadi, 6, 25, 200
El-Arish, 11
Elazığ, 22, 62, 143, 164, 167, 168
Eloğlu, 33
Emin Çölaşan, 205
England, 20, 108, 111. *See also* Great Britain
Entente Powers, 114, 120, 161
Enver Pasha, 8, 50, 59, 63, 161, 179, 210, 211, 215
Erickson, Edward J., 123
erysipelas, 82, 95, 97
Erzincan, 31, 43, 53, 54, 58, 61, 62, 65, 80, 99, 104, 130, 142, 167, 168, 173, 174, 181, 189, 192, 193, 198
Erzurum, 10, 14, 22, 23, 29, 31, 35, 37, 38, 40, 41, 42, 43, 45, 47, 51, 53, 54, 55, 58, 59, 60, 61, 62, 63, 64, 65, 66, 79, 80, 100, 102, 103, 113, 130, 134, 135, 136, 142, 143, 149, 151, 163, 166, 167, 168, 172, 174, 175, 178, 179, 180, 189, 190, 192, 193, 197, 199, 202
Eskişehir, 101
Euphrates River, 104, 146
Eyüp Cemetery, 15

Fahri Belen, 113, 120
Falkland Islands, 107
Farm of Jasmiyah, 139
Fatsa, 151, 152
Ferguson, Niall, 123
Fevzi Çakmak, 51, 52, 143
Finike, 101
First Expeditionary Force, 30
First National Medical Congress, 102
Flinn, M. W., 2

4th Army, 30, 36, 86, 127, 129, 138, 141, 142, 156, 157, 159, 160, 172, 183, 197, 198
France, 10, 12, 91, 92, 93, 107, 108, 109, 111, 113, 118, 198
French Army, 12, 112
French casualties, 112
French Front, 116
French Navy, 112
French-Prussian War, 5

Galicia, 76
Galician Front, 77
Galip (doctor), 198
Gallipoli, 13, 68, 69, 70, 73, 74, 75, 76, 107, 114, 120, 121, 122, 124, 125, 128, 131, 194, 207
"Gallipoli Gallop," 69
Gallipoli Peninsula, 68, 76
Garian, 166
Gazi Ahmet Muhtar Pasha, 51
Gelibolu, 24
General Directorate of Health, 189
Genius Epidemicus, 149
George Washington, 107
German casualties, 116
German Consulate, 38
German Embassy, 15
Germans, 34, 54, 118, 141, 149, 173, 206
Germany, 4, 20, 54, 92, 93, 108, 111, 116, 141, 173, 174, 176, 198, 199, 210
Geron, A., 23
Giresun, 42, 99, 151, 152
Gleich, 48
Godley (general), 71
Goltz (field marshall), 48, 49, 86, 138, 174
Grand National Assembly, 98, 205
Great Britain, 92, 115, 116
Great War, 6, 28, 31, 35, 37, 47, 48, 49, 55, 56, 63, 64, 65, 66, 67, 68, 80, 81, 91, 92, 93, 96, 98, 102, 106, 107, 109, 110, 114, 115, 116, 117, 119, 120, 122, 124, 128, 135, 137, 139, 142, 147, 163, 169, 174, 175, 177, 178, 186, 189, 190, 193, 194, 196, 198, 199, 200, 202, 203, 205, 207. *See also* World War I
Greece, 2, 92, 111
Greek Army, 104

Guhr, 44, 63
Gusse, 41
Gülek Pass, 29, 208
Gülhane Military Hospital, 172, 174
Gülhane Military Medical Academy, 61
Gülhane Park, 24
Gülnihal, 75
Gümüşhane, 130, 198
Gümüşsuyu Cemetery, 15

Hadımköy, 17, 20
Haerle (doctor), 48
Hafız Hakkı, 28, 47, 48, 65
Hakkari, 65
Halep, 156
Halide Edip, 32, 100, 142, 159, 183
Halil Bey, 49
Hama, 86, 139
Hamadan, 139
Hamdi Suat (doctor), 173, 174
Hamdi Village, 36
Hamdullah Suphi, 31, 32, 142
Hamilton, Ian (general), 71
Hamit Osman (doctor), 102
Harput, 44, 64, 100, 136
Hasan İzzet Pasha, 47, 211
Hasan Zühtü Nazif, 166
Hasanbeyli, 208
Hasankale, 37, 38, 40, 42, 50, 53, 59, 60, 61, 62, 167, 172, 175
Havran, 156
Havza, 145
Haydarpaşa, 12, 15, 28, 30
Heybeliada, 188
Hilmi Özkök (general), 202
Hınıs, 62
Hijaz Front, 159
Hikmet Bayur, 120
Hobsbawm, Eric, 106
Holland, 92, 93
Homs, 91
Hopa, 95
Hoy, 79
Hüdavendigar, 64
Humus, 86, 156
Hun, 106

hunger, 24, 86, 99, 104, 109, 162, 194
Hüsamettin Cindoruk, 205
Hüseyin (doctor), 172

İ. Hakkı, 29, 33
İbrahim (major), 179
İbrahim Tali (doctor), 176, 178
İhsan Aksoley, 91
Ilıca, 43, 59, 62, 192
Indian, 20, 39, 88, 89, 90, 92
Indian Muslims, 20
İnebolu, 99
infant deaths, 102
infectious diseases, 23, 26
influenza, 55, 57, 95
İskenderun, 30
Islahiye, 29
Ispartakule, 17
İspiye, 152
Italy, 92, 93, 108, 111, 118, 119
İzmir, 22, 91, 95, 96, 104, 139, 151, 156, 207

Jabal Lubnan (Mount Lebanon), 160
Jaffa, 11, 161
Jak Efendi, 214
James, Robert Rhodes, 69, 73
Japan, 91, 92, 111
Jewish School, 149, 191
Jews, 95, 102, 137, 178, 180

Kale-i Sultaniye, 64
Kan, 43, 59, 62
Kandıra, 170, 171
Kanlısırt, 75
Karacaahmet Cemetery, 15
Karahisar, 144, 189
Karakilise, 181
Karaman, 156
Karapınar, 29, 32, 33
Karasu, 113
Karesi, 155
Kartal, 22, 24, 189
Kasımpaşa, 12, 97
Kasır, 191
Kavak, 12, 145
Kayseri, 100, 151, 190, 200

Kelkit, 41, 113, 168
Kemal Özbay, 12
Kerevizdere, 75
Kerte, 75
Keteb-ul Halil, 83
Kiesling, 186
Kiğı, 45
Kilitbahir, 73
King of Spain, 160, 161
Kisling, 48
Konya, 24, 29, 61, 64, 137, 142, 194
Korean War, 92
Korna, 146
Koyulhisar, 47
Kressenstein, Kress von, 141
Kumkale, 73
Kurds, 103, 184, 210
Kuruçay, 100
Kütahya, 155

laboratory, 193
Lamouche (colonel), 48
Lapseki, 63
Larcher (commandant), 119, 120, 121
Lebanon, 142, 159, 160, 161, 184
Lenin, Vladimir, 7, 114
Liebert (doctor), 164
Lower Mesopotamia, 146
Lütfi (doctor, captain), 142
Lütfi Aksu (doctor), 64

malaria, 84, 95, 102, 123, 147, 148, 177, 190, 200
Malazgirt, 62
malnutrition, 95, 131
Malta, 96
Maltepe, 189
Mamahatun, 136, 181
Mamure, 29, 208
Manisa, 155, 207
Maraş, 33, 143
Mardin, 44, 64, 101
Maronite, 160
Marseilles, 158
massacres, 104
Maude (general), 49

Mayer (doctor), 58
Mazhar Osman, 181
McCarthy, Justin, 135, 142, 198
measles, 97, 103
Meclis-i Ayan, 187
Medina, 82, 159
Mediterranean Expeditionary Force, 71
Mediterranean Fleet, 97
Mehmet Arif, 166
Mehmet Emin (doctor), 180
Mendep, 82, 83
meningitis, 97
Menteşe, 156
Merzifon, 145, 151, 183
Mesopotamian Front, 116
Mesudiye Recovery Center, 47
Middle East, 11, 107, 124, 186
Military Hospital in İzmit, 170
Ministry of War, 63, 155, 169, 183, 191
missing, 112, 116, 117, 118
Mişki, 62
Mobile Hospital, 75, 77
Moltke, 186
Mondros Armistice, 91, 119, 183
Montenegro, 111
Mosul, 30, 31, 34, 36, 37, 88, 89, 90, 91, 93, 147, 149, 150, 153, 154, 156, 157, 162, 191, 192
Müdürke, 45
Mühlens, P. (German hygiene expert), 4
Münim Mustafa, 30, 120
Murat-Çay, 136
Muratoff, Allen and Paul, 136
Muş, 62, 66, 113, 136, 167, 168, 197
Musa Kazım (doctor), 172
Mustafa (doctor), 23, 172
Mustafa Kemal Pasha, 102
Mustafa Şakir (doctor), 180

Nail (captain), 214
Nasiriyah, 146
Nazım Pasha, 21
Nazım Şakir (doctor), 192
Nazlımov, 19
Near East, 91
Nebi Han, 40

Nestorians, 103
Neşet Ömer, 138, 198
New York, 91
Niğde, 58, 66, 189, 190
Nightingale, Florence, 13
Nihat (lieutenant colonel), 120
Nikau, 44
Nothnagel (doctor), 165
North America, 92
Norway, 92
Nusaybin, 89, 90, 93, 154, 192
Nute, William L., 200

Oberndörfer (doctor), 49
Ognot, 113
Ordu, 144, 151, 152, 169
orphanage, 183
Osman Şevki (doctor), 11, 14, 122, 186
Osmaniye, 30
Ottoman Armenians, 125, 137
Ottoman Army, 6, 9, 11, 12, 14, 19, 20, 22, 28, 29, 30, 40, 43, 44, 58, 63, 64, 66, 74, 75, 77, 88, 89, 91, 93, 109, 110, 119, 120, 121, 122, 123, 124, 128, 132, 143, 166, 169, 173, 179, 182, 189, 192, 199, 200
Ottoman Empire, 4, 8, 9, 10, 19, 26, 29, 31, 47, 100, 105, 109, 119, 130, 142, 157, 160, 165, 177, 188, 190, 194, 195, 199, 202
Ottoman-German Treaty of Alliance, 7
Ottoman-Greek War, 166
Ottoman Ministry of Internal Affairs, 63
Ottoman-Russian War, 11, 14, 166
Ovtse Polje, 22
Ömer Besim Pasha, 101

Palestinian Jew, 36
Panzac, Daniel, 4, 10, 135, 154
Paraguin (major), 40
paratyphoid, 57
Paris, 107, 166
Pasinler Plain, 53, 211
Philippopolis, 4
plague, 10, 95, 97
Plevna, 14
pneumonia, 95
Polatlı, 98

Pomiankowsky, Joseph, 163, 197
Portugal, 92, 111
Pozantı, 30, 37, 87, 89, 147, 148, 149
prisoners, 116, 119
Prussia, 2, 3, 114
Pürk, 145

Radovishte, 22
Ragıp Bey, 200
Rahmi Bey, 151
Rami, 27
Recai (doctor), 61
Recovery House in Çorum, 144
Red Army, 7
Red Crescent (hospital), 61, 77
Red Crescent (Indian), 20
Red Crescent (mark), 10, 14, 21, 64, 77
Red Crescent (Ottoman), 99, 166, 174, 180, 185, 198
Red Crescent Society, 64
Red Cross, 20, 54, 55, 99, 166, 181, 182, 185, 193
Refik Saydam (doctor), 102, 174
Reşat Rıza (doctor), 23, 26, 172, 175
Restorf (major), 48
Rıza Nur, 122
Robeck (general), 71
Robertson, Sir William, 115
Rodenwalt (doctor), 151
Romania, 6, 20, 76, 111, 158, 159
Rousseau, Jean Jacques, 165
Rousso, Carl, 12
Rumelia, 75, 78, 154
Russian Army, 13, 14, 39, 51, 87, 103, 113, 137
Russian casualties, 113
Russian Caucasus Army, 50
Russian-Japanese War, 5
Ryan, Charles S., 10

Sadık Sabri (colonel), 35
Sağlam (doctor), 61, 169
Saint Sophia Mosque, 15
Şakir (doctor), 61
Salonika Front, 116
Samara, 66, 67
Samargha, 146

INDEX

Samsun, 65, 93, 102, 143, 145, 151, 152
Sanders, Liman von, 34, 39, 44, 63, 114, 191
Sandrock, 49
Sarıkamış, 8, 28, 40, 42, 50, 51, 52, 53, 54, 55, 62, 63, 66, 167, 179, 188, 200, 201, 202
Sarkis Karayan, 7
Scandinavian, 106
Schilling (doctor), 44
2nd Army, 44, 87, 125, 126, 129, 158, 180, 189, 207, 211
Seddülbahir, 73, 176
Şekip Habip (doctor), 169
Selimiye Barracks, 13, 27
Selmanpak Battle, 191
Serbia, 6, 67, 111, 112
Serbian Army, 109
Seres River, 77
Server Kâmil (doctor), 61
Serviburnu, 170, 175
Seuber, 31, 32, 85
Seyhan, 101
Siberia, 91, 92, 196
Sille, 24, 64
Silvan, 50
Sinai, 86, 140, 159
Sirkeci, 24
Sivas, 63, 65, 66, 100, 144, 151, 175, 177, 182, 189, 190, 192, 193
6th Army, 30, 40, 47, 49, 78, 86, 88, 89, 90, 125, 127, 129, 147, 149, 152, 153, 154, 157, 191
smallpox, 11, 95, 97, 103, 148
Soğanlık, 189
Sohumkale, 152
South America, 92
Southeast Asia, 92
Söke, 102
Spain, 92, 93, 106, 160
spotted fever, 172
St. George Hospital, 12
Stanford Shaw, 7
Stavuk, 43
Stip, 22
Sublime Porte, 7, 15
Süfyan (doctor), 61
Sultaniye, 64

Suşehri, 45, 47, 145, 182, 200
Suvla Bay, 114
Süleyman Numan (doctor), 53, 168
Sweden, 92, 93
Switzerland, 92, 106, 160
syphilis, 101, 102, 123
Şebinkarahisar, 66
Şemseddin, 59
Şemsettin Bey, 99

Tacettin (doctor), 180
Taiz, 82
Talas Hospital, 182, 183
Tarsus American School, 200
Tarsus, 150, 200
Tbilisi, 79, 141, 152
Tehama, 83
Telleübyas, 37
Tercan, 43, 192
tetanus, 81, 95
Tevfik Sağlam, 43, 55, 58, 65, 110, 131, 142, 151, 174, 175, 176, 178, 192, 201
3rd Army, 6, 16, 28, 35, 36, 38, 39, 40, 41, 42, 47, 50, 52, 53, 54, 55, 56, 58, 59, 60, 61, 62, 63, 65, 79, 80, 81, 100, 126, 129, 130, 131, 132, 142, 144, 152, 153, 166, 169, 175, 176, 177, 178, 180, 181, 182, 183, 189, 190, 200, 201
Thrace, 18, 19, 76, 199
Tigris River, 31, 34, 89, 146, 150, 191
Tikrit, 149
Tokat Hospital, 172
Tokat, 65, 100, 151, 172
Toprakkale, 30
Trabzon, 22, 42, 53, 62, 65, 79, 94, 99, 142, 143, 144, 145, 151, 167, 181, 189, 190, 193, 197
trachoma, 94, 98
Tripoli, 91, 166
Trotsky, Leon, 22
Tselonika, 18
tuberculosis, 95, 97
Turkey, 7, 8, 9, 78, 91, 92, 93, 98, 101, 103, 108, 111, 119, 120, 123, 125, 133, 163, 168, 172
Turkish General Staff, 86, 121, 198

Turkish Military Archives, 75, 82, 83, 87, 120
Turks, 7, 22, 33, 49, 51, 68, 71, 92, 94, 95, 103, 104, 114, 129, 130, 178, 184, 186, 187, 194, 198, 200
Tuzla, 22, 26
typhoid, 55, 57, 70, 95, 97, 103, 148, 189, 196

Ulukışla, 29, 32, 54, 65, 130, 178, 208
United States, 3, 91, 92, 98, 107
Ünye, 151, 152
Urfa, 97, 156
Üsküdar, 207

Van, 62, 64, 65, 66, 103, 135, 142, 143, 163, 167, 181
Varna, 13
Vasfi Cindoruk, 205
Vehib Pasha, 144, 197
Velibaba, 35
Vietnam War, 92
Viranşehir, 30, 35
Virchow, Rudolf, 3

War of Liberation, 98, 101, 176
Weber Pasha, 71
Western Europe, 91, 92
White Army, 7
Wilson, Woodrow, 160
Witmann, William, 11

World War I, 1, 5, 6, 7, 8, 9, 20, 26, 29, 91, 94, 95, 96, 97, 99, 100, 101, 106, 108, 109, 110, 117, 123, 133, 135, 154, 155, 157, 165, 168, 174, 190, 198, 203. *See also* Great War
wounded, 13, 69, 112, 116, 117, 118, 119

Yakacık, 22, 97, 189, 205
Yalova, 189
Yassıviran, 16
Yassıviran Hospital, 169
Yemen, 82, 124, 207
Yeniköy, 192
Yerevan, 137
Yeşilköy Hospital, 23
Yeşilköy, 20, 21, 22, 23, 175
Young Turks, 163
Yozgat, 145
Yusuf Ziya, 14

Zahle, 86
Zemlin, 77
Zencidere Hospital, 182, 183
Zeytun, 66
Ziemann, Hans, 177
Zığındere, 75
Ziya Pasha, 24, 25
Zlosisti (doctor), 54
Zor, 156
Zouara, 91
Zürcher, Eric Jan, 8, 110